NO ORDINARY JUDGMENT

Frontispiece At the unveiling of Edward Koiki Mabo's tombstone, Mer, 18 September 1995 (courtesy Film Australia National Interest Program, photographer Trevor Graham)

NONIE SHARP

NO ORDINARY JUDGMENT
Mabo, The Murray Islanders' Land Case

ABORIGINAL STUDIES PRESS

Canberra 1996

FIRST PUBLISHED IN 1996 BY

Aboriginal Studies Press
for the Australian Institute of Aboriginal and Torres Strait Islander Studies,
GPO Box 553, Canberra ACT 2601

The views expressed in this publication are those of the author and not necessarily those of the Australian Institute of Aboriginal and Torres Strait Islander Studies.

The publisher has made every effort to contact copyright owners for permission to use material produced in this book. If your material has been used inadvertently without permission please contact the publisher immediately.

© NONIE SHARP 1996

Apart from any fair dealing for the purpose of private study, research, criticism or review, as permitted under the Copyright Act, no part of this publication may be reproduced by any process whatsoever without the written permission of the publisher.

NATIONAL LIBRARY OF AUSTRALIA CATALOGUING-IN-PUBLICATION DATA:

Sharp, Nonie.
No ordinary judgment: Mabo, the Murray Islanders' land case.

Bibliography.
Includes index.
ISBN 0 85575 287 4.

1. Torres Strait Islanders — Queensland — Murray Islands — Legal status, laws, etc. 2. Torres Strait Islanders — Queensland — Murray Islands — Land tenure. 3. Land tenure — Law and legislation — Queensland — Murray Islands. I. Title.

346.9430432

3000 03 96

COVER DESIGN by John Waller, based on a photograph of the Murray Islands,
courtesy Peter Lik
Unless otherwise indicated photographs and illustrations were taken or produced by the author.

DESIGNED AND PRODUCED BY Aboriginal Studies Press
PRINTED IN AUSTRALIA BY Southwood Press, Marrickville NSW

For my mother, who nurtured the seed of hope

CONTENTS

Foreword ix
Chronologies xi
Abbreviations xvii
Preface xix

PART I INTERESTS OF A KIND UNKNOWN TO ENGLISH LAW
Chapter 1 Bearers of Cultural Change 3
Chapter 2 Of Silences and Secrets 19
Chapter 3 Rights of a Kind Unknown to English Law 45

PART II MERIAM PERSPECTIVES
Chapter 4 My Father Gave Me all the Rights and Every Responsibility 63
Chapter 5 If You Want To Be a Real Murray Islander You Follow Malo's Law 87

PART III EUROPEAN PERSPECTIVES
Chapter 6 Hearsay or Traditional Evidence? 103
Chapter 7 Assimilation or Basic Continuity? 115

PART IV NO ORDINARY CASE
Chapter 8 A Trial of Truth: Outcomes 149
Chapter 9 Two Categories of Land Law: The High Court 171

PART V NATIVE TITLE IN AUSTRALIA
Chapter 10 The Sea: Within the Compass of Native Title 189
Chapter 11 Native Title in the Reshaping of Australian Identity 207

Notes to Chapters 233
Glossaries 259
    Common law terms 259
    Meriam language words 261
References Cited 265
Index 285

FOREWORD

In *No Ordinary Judgment*, Nonie Sharp documents the ten-year history of the *Murray Island Land case*, which overturned the concept of *terra nullius* in Australia. Nonie discusses the case itself and the different 'players' in the case, the resultant native title legislation and the impact and implications of this legislation on both the Meriam people of the Murray Islands and Aborigines in the broader Australian community.

Nonie has been working in the Torres Strait since 1978 and has contributed to the *Murray Island Land case* from its early stages. Apart from perusing local court documents, collecting oral evidence and participating in community meetings, she also considered the Murray Island claim in light of Justice Blackburn's findings rejecting the Yolngu claim to land in Yirrkala and related homelands in east Arnhem Land. The analysis of these findings was crucial to the presentation of the first statement of claim to land in the Murray Islands in 1982.

The summary issued with the final judgment of the High Court (*Mabo [No 2]*) says that the Murray Islanders have the exclusive right to title and use of the land against the whole world, except for a small number of leases. The outcome for the Meriam people, which Nonie is describing, makes clear that they now have those rights restored to them for islands claimed by them. The rights described in the judgment are substantially unchanged from those which existed in pre-settlement times — the limits imposed are relatively minor. What they have is pretty much what the High Court said they would have.

The *Mabo* judgment seems to have served the Torres Strait Islanders reasonably well. It has established clearly their sovereignty in the conduct of their own affairs, and has provided an acceptable basis for title, tenure, use and inheritance of land and sea. They have a structure of government, a form of bottom-up federalism which preserves substantial autonomy for the various island councils while establishing an overall Council for the debate and decision of issues of common concern. They are in a strong position to demand a UN-supervised Act of Self-determination, ensuring the continuation of these gains into the future, or to negotiate a form of association with Australia acceptable to, and consistent with, their own vision. It is a pattern which Aborigines in Australia are coming to realise they are likely to be denied.

By contrast, Aborigines in Australia are having thrust upon them an interpretation of native title utterly alien to the principles which underlay their traditional practices and their contemporary conduct, where they have been free to continue them. The essential component of Aboriginal title to land was its inalienability though this incorporated relatively easy access for others to its use and its resources. Native title as embodied in Commonwealth legislation can be more accurately described as an instrument to validate past alienation and to ensure progressive extinguishment. The currently favoured interpretation that practically any lease extinguishes Aboriginal title is, I believe, unacceptable. Both the High Court's and the Federal Court's judgments make clear that native title is extinguished only to the extent of any incompatibility between its continuance and the terms of any lease, and that such incompatibility cannot be assumed or lightly inferred — that is, that it must be demonstrated beyond reasonable doubt. Yet the trend of political opinion seems to foreshadow legislation or judicial action to embody this interpretation, which would deny Aboriginal rights to a large proportion of the economically usable land in northern Australia.

If this is the outcome, not merely will Aborigines be denied the right to claim large areas of land and its related resources upon which their chosen way of life depends, but the moral link between the land and the culture which gives meaning to that way will be broken. Assimilation especially into the international economic system will become increasingly the only option: the dream of autonomy within a multicultural Australia will be ended.

Perhaps the slow processes of the judicial system are incapable of achieving the compromises which alone can provide, in reasonable time, the certainty which governments, corporations and Aboriginal groups and their organisations need to plan and to act in order to achieve or to reconcile their often conflicting purposes. The processes of negotiation which followed the *Mabo* decision have demonstrated a willingness and capacity in Aboriginal organisations and the Commonwealth government to negotiate acceptable outcomes. Perhaps the time has come for limited, experimental agreements in which the parties search for common ground. The recent interest expressed in regional agreements between the Commonwealth and groups of Aboriginal organisations may provide an opportunity for such experiments.

H C Coombs, 1994

CHRONOLOGY I: August 1981 – 3 June 1992

The *Mabo* case

1981
14 August
At a public meeting in the Torres Strait at Tamwoy Town, Thursday Island, Flo Kennedy calls for a court case.
29 August
Three Torres Strait Islanders (two from Murray Island), meet with two representatives of the Aboriginal Treaty Committee at James Cook University, Townsville, and Nonie Sharp, to discuss a legal case.
September
Counsel for intending Meriam plaintiffs chosen.

1982
January/February
Murray Island court document on sale of land at Zeub, Mer, by Meriam landowner to the Queensland government in 1913, made available to counsel for the plaintiffs.
20 May
Writ or statement of claim lodged by five Murray Island plaintiffs in the High Court of Australia: *Eddie Mabo and Others v the State of Queensland and the Commonwealth of Australia*, B12 of 1982.
16 August
Affidavit (sworn statement) of PJ Killoran lodged for the first defendant, the state of Queensland.
13 September
Amended statement of claim drafted by the plaintiffs.
22 October
Affidavit of Dr Jeremy Beckett for the plaintiffs obtained.

1984
May
Torres Strait Islanders Act 1971–79 (Qld) repealed. Community Services (Torres Strait) Act 1984 assented to.
15 May
High Court orders that plaintiffs may amend their statement of claim.

1985
29 March
Queensland responded to plaintiffs' particulars.
2 April
Queensland Coast Islands Declaratory Act 1985 (the 1985 Act) assented to (Queensland's attempt to short-circuit the case by extinguishing Meriam title retrospectively).
19 April
Supplementary response of Queensland to plaintiffs' particulars.
24 April
Aborigines and Torres Strait Islanders (Land Holding) Act (Qld) 1985 assented to.
24 May
Amended defence of Queensland.
19 June
Plaintiffs' demurrer (legal challenge) to Queensland's amended defence (now based on the 1985 Act).

1986
27 January
Murray Islanders at Mer expressed their wish to give evidence in support of the plaintiffs.
9 February
Resolution stating their wish to give evidence passed at a meeting of Murray Islanders in Townsville.
27 February
Chief Justice Gibbs ordered that issues of fact raised in the case be remitted to the Supreme Court of Queensland.
4 April
Plaintiffs' reply to Queensland's amended defence.
13 October
Justice Moynihan began to hear the evidence ('the facts') in the Supreme Court of Queensland, Brisbane.
17 November
Supreme Court of Queensland adjourned to 23 February 1987.

1987

13 February
Case referred back to the High Court to settle questions of law (Justice Deane).

23 February
Hearing resumed in the Supreme Court of Queensland before Justice Moynihan.

4 March
Affidavit of the plaintiffs.

3 April
Agreement before Justice Toohey in the High Court that the Murray Islanders would surrender their case if the demurrer judgment (*Mabo [No 1]*) went against them.

October
Before the High Court. Postponed to February 1988.

1988

15 March
The Full Bench of the High Court considered the plaintiffs' demurrer to Queensland's defence based on the 1985 Act.

18 March
The court reserved its decision.

8 December
High Court issued the reasons for judgment in plaintiffs' demurrer, *Mabo and Another v the State of Queensland and Another* (1988) or *Mabo (No 1)*, finding the 1985 Act invalid.

1989

22 February
Proceedings before Justice Moynihan in the Supreme Court of Queensland on arrangements for hearing issues of fact.

2 May
Adjourned hearing of evidence before Justice Moynihan in the Supreme Court of Queensland, Brisbane.

3 May
Ruling by Justice Toohey in the High Court that the Supreme Court of Queensland may make orders to add parties or to amend the statement of claim.

22 May
The Supreme Court of Queensland visited Mer where Justice Moynihan inspected land boundaries at the village of Las, adjoining fish traps and other lands claimed.

23–26 May
The Supreme Court of Queensland met at Umar, Mer, and later Thursday Island, to hear Islanders' evidence.

5 June – 6 September
Evidence heard in Brisbane before Justice Moynihan.

21 June
Amended defence of Queensland delivered.

26 June
Statement of claim amended.

7 July
Justice Moynihan dismissed plaintiffs' claim against the Commonwealth after claims to offshore reefs and seas were abandoned.

1990

16 November
Determination of Issues of Fact by the Supreme Court of Queensland of the Remitter from the High Court of Australia (3 vols). Case moves back to the High Court for finalisation.

1991

28–31 May
High Court hearing of ultimate legal issues.

12 June
Torres Strait Island Land Act 1991 (Qld) assented to. Repeal of Queensland Coast Islands Declaratory Act 1985 (the 1985 Act).

1992

3 June
High Court issued the reasons for judgment in *Mabo v the State of Queensland* or *Mabo (No 2)*, recognising native title in Australian common law.

CHRONOLOGY II: 3 June 1992 – 3 June 1995

Native Title legislation in Australia

1992
3 JUNE
Mabo (No 2).
SEPTEMBER
Commonwealth government began policy development process. Interdepartmental Committee (IDC) started consultations.
22 NOVEMBER
Australian Human Rights Medal awarded jointly to Meriam plaintiffs and barrister Barbara Hocking.

1993
27 APRIL
Aboriginal delegates from ATSIC, Aboriginal land councils and legal services met with prime minister and Cabinet subcommittee and delivered a peace plan.
3 JUNE
Commonwealth discussion paper on proposed Commonwealth legislation on native title released. Land councils reacted angrily to document as reducing Aboriginal special relationship to land to a land management question.
JUNE
Prime minister met state premiers at Council for Australian Governments (COAG) meeting and encountered substantial resistance to discussion paper.
JULY
Claim to land by Wik Mungkan Aboriginal people, raised questions of fiduciary duty of governments to indigenous people, continuing Aboriginal rights to land covered by pastoral leases, and whether native title extends to the sea.
27 JULY
Federal Cabinet proposed native title holders be given a right of negotiation with those wishing to develop natural resources, subject to tribunal rulings in accord with federal or state governments' determination of 'the national interest'.
5 AUGUST
Meeting of 400–500 Aboriginal and Torres Strait Islander delegates at Eva Valley, Northern Territory, formulated the Eva Valley Statement.
19 AUGUST
Cabinet decision on Wik claim foreshadowed validation of all existing titles granted since 1788.
2 SEPTEMBER
Commonwealth released its outline for proposed legislation on native title.
26 SEPTEMBER
Eva Valley II meeting decided not to take national negotiations further, but allowed individual organisations to take up issues with the government.
LATE SEPTEMBER – EARLY OCTOBER
Aboriginal representatives signalled the suspension of the Racial Discrimination Act 1975 (Cwth) (RDA) as a central issue and proposed a 'special measure' approach which would allow validation of titles without suspension of the RDA.
5 OCTOBER
ATSIC and land councils form the Coalition of Aboriginal Organisations (CAO) which met with the prime minister (later known as A-Team).
6–7 OCTOBER
Prime minister met the CAO on five occasions. At 9 pm on 7 October, he released a statement saying negotiations had almost reached agreement.
8 OCTOBER
('Black Friday') In response to the slow process of negotiations, the representatives of the CAO gave a press conference indicating they feared that they would be 'sold out'.

14–15 October
CAO members met again with the prime minister. A 19-point agreement was reached, which included the undertaking that the RDA would not be suspended. Prime minister agreed to take the issue of coexistence of native title and pastoral leases to Cabinet.

18 October
Cabinet endorsed the agreement reached by the prime minister and the CAO, subject to small changes.

19 October
('Ruby Tuesday') CAO announced the making of a genuine start towards a process of reconciliation.

16 November
Native Title Bill introduced into the House of Representatives.

24 November
Green senators and Aboriginal Alliance, (later known as B-Team), newly formed by the Aboriginal Provisional Government and the NSW Land Council, announced they would not support the Bill without an amendment providing that Aboriginal people cannot be evicted from pastoral leases.

25 November
Bill passed by House of Representatives.

November
Western Australian parliament passed the Land (Titles and Traditional Usage) Act 1993 (WA), extinguishing native title without compensation and empowering the minister to grant title to and interests in land similar to rights to traditional usage and to extinguish or suspend these rights at his discretion.

3 December
Kimberley Land Council lodged a challenge to the Land (Titles and Traditional Usage) Act 1993 (WA) on behalf of four Aboriginal people.

9 December
Senate committee reported on federal Bill and recommended minor changes. Greens announced they would not support the Bill without further amendment.

15 December (Wednesday)
Greens and Democrats, together with A and B Teams, met Gareth Evans, the leader of the government in the Senate.

16 December (Thursday)
Native Title Bill introduced into the Senate. Government amendments circulated. Second reading speeches completed.

17–18 December (Friday–Saturday)
Committee stage continued. Government mining and pastoral industry amendments defeated.

19 December (Sunday)
National Farmers' Federation director, Rick Farley, condemned the Opposition for failing to support industry amendments and withdrew support for legislation.

20 December (Monday)
Committee stage continued. Democrats negotiated further amendments to allow renewal of pastoral leases and to ensure no eviction of Aboriginal residents could flow from validation. Prime minister said parliament would sit until Christmas if necessary.

21 December (Tuesday)
Committee stage continued. Government introduced motion to guillotine debate in anticipation of Green support. Remaining amendments agreed on passed. At 3 pm Greens announced they would support the legislation. At 11.58 pm the Bill was passed (Native Title Act 1993).

1994
1 January
National Native Title Tribunal, set up under Native Title Act 1993, ready to hear claims.

1995
16 March
High Court delivered decision rejecting a challenge by the state of Western Australia to the Native Title Act 1993.

29 March
Land Fund and Indigenous Land Corporation (ATSIC Amendment) Act 1995 (Cwth) assented to.

3 June
Ceremony in Townsville unveiling the tombstone of the late Eddie Mabo on the third anniversary of the High Court decision recognising native title at the Murray Islands.

ABBREVIATIONS, TERMS AND NAMES

ATSIC	Aboriginal and Torres Strait Islander Commission
CJ	Chief Justice, as in Gibbs CJ
counsel	legal representative/s
DAIA	Department of Aboriginal and Island Affairs; Department of Aboriginal and Islanders Advancement, Brisbane, Qld
DCS	Department of Community Services, Qld (previously DAIA)
DLR	*Dominion Law Reports* (Canada)
DNA	Department of Native Affairs, Brisbane, Qld
DOGIT	Deed(s) of Grant in Trust, Brisbane, Qld
HCA	High Court of Australia
ICC	Island Coordinating Council
J	Justice, as in Brennan J
JJ	Justices, as in Brennan and Deanne JJ
LHA	Aboriginal and Torres Strait Islander (Land Holding) Act 1985
LMS	London Missionary Society
QSA	Queensland State Archives
RAAF	Royal Australian Air Force
RDA	Racial Discrimination Act 1975 (Commonwealth)
SCQ	Supreme Court of Queensland
T	High Court of Australia, Transcript of Proceedings
'the Act'	Aboriginals Protection and Restriction of the Sale of Opium Act, Torres Strait Islanders Act
'the 1985 Act'	Queensland Coast Islands Declaratory Act 1985
'the Commonwealth'	the Commonwealth of Australia, the second defendant
'the defendant'	the state of Queensland, 'Queensland'
'the plaintiffs'	the five (later three) Meriam or Murray Islander claimants to land, the Murray Islanders
TQ	Supreme Court of Queensland, Transcript of Proceedings
UN	United Nations

the Meriam/Meriam people, Meriam speakers (also Miriam, Haddon 1904–35) or Murray Islanders

Murray Islands or Mer Islands

Mer Islands Council or Murray Island Council

the *Murray Island Land* case, or the *Mabo* case, *Mabo*.

Edward Koiki Mabo (pronounced Maabo), the first of five original plaintiffs in the Murray Islanders' case, known as Eddie Mabo in European Australian circles and as Koiki Mabo by Meriam people, other Torres Strait Islanders and close friends. Throughout this book, the name Eddie Mabo is used, except where Meriam people are speaking of him.

PREFACE

This book is about a land case brought by members of a seafaring and gardening community who occupy three small islands in the Torres Strait at the northern end of the Great Barrier Reef. These three islands were named Murray's Islands by the captain of the *Pandora* in 1791. In Meriam Mir, the language of the inhabitants, the three islands are known as Mer, Dauar and Waier.

The distinctive approach here contrasts and compares Meriam and European Australian perspectives on land and culture as they presented themselves in spoken word and written document in a long legal battle. The courtroom became the meeting point of two seemingly 'natural', but nevertheless different, conceptions of rights to land and sea. It did so under conditions where the principles, definitions and rules of Anglo-Australian law were used to determine the property rights of the Meriam people. As this book attempts to show, Anglo-Australian law was unable to offer a suitable medium through which to express Meriam people's relationships to land. At the root of this 'badness of fit' lie Meriam interrelationships with land and sea which can not be compared with the idea of land as an economic item tradeable on the commodity market.

The judiciary were aware of the possible incompatibility of the rules of two parallel laws, and proceedings were set in train for a hearing of factual evidence from many Meriam witnesses before Justice Moynihan in the Supreme Court of Queensland. Great effort was made to ensure that all Meriam witnesses could be heard and members of the court made an expedition to Mer and Thursday Island to hear aged or sick Murray Islanders; where necessary the court sat in the open air beside the homes of witnesses. Nevertheless, this long hearing of Meriam claims to traditional title to certain lands, reefs and sea areas and the existence of a system of Meriam land law, was beset by distortion and trivialisation. The overall effect of this was often to diminish Meriam meanings and certain matters of profound meaning to the Meriam were bypassed. Even as the case moved into its tenth year, the High Court faced the question unresolved by the findings of this long inquiry into the facts concerning Meriam interests in land: what is the nature of those rights to land?

Relationships carrying the full weight of the cultural ensemble of the Meriam — the realm of their 'natural inheritance' — were those most often lost on the court. 'I am born into the ownership of this land', said plaintiff Reverend Dave Passi. 'It is against our traditional law that we sell the land . . . it is trespassing against Malo's [our traditional god's] law.' Reverend Passi was speaking of a sacred endowment which attaches him to land through an indissoluble interrelationship which English speakers call inalienable; it knots together the spiritual and the material relationship between himself and the land and between himself and the generations who came 'first' with those who come 'after'.

The Meriam witnesses varied in age, in knowledge and in what they were asked about in court. The custodians of Meriam cultural tradition gave a sense of their fidelity to certain cultural principles which they themselves feel bound to follow and which they see as a guide to their children. What they see as the Meriam 'cultural way' has an underlying continuity with their pre-colonial past; it is a contemporary expression of a resilient and dynamic culture subjected to enforced change. Most witnesses identified the set of principles they follow as Malo's Law, an indigenous law which combines the religious and the secular. At its centre is what one Meriam leader called the 'Malo Law story', a hero myth which joined together the eight totemic clans of the Meriam, establishing a sacred centre on the eastern side of Mer and a hereditary 'priesthood'.

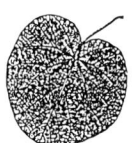

This book does not attempt to give cut-and-dried solutions to the dilemmas created by differences in cross-cultural meaning systems, but to explore these differences through a court drama. It seeks to clarify and correct misunderstandings within this cultural realm: some of the facts I present were not put to the court; some were understood incompletely by European Australian expert witnesses; others are corrections and reinterpretations of the conventional wisdom about the Meriam people, some of which go back to the work of A C Haddon and the anthropological expedition from Cambridge University to the Torres Strait in 1898. These include the belief that totems disappeared with the arrival of the Meriam gods Malo-Bomai, and in turn, that the beliefs and meanings associated with the latter and their laws were extinguished by Christianity. The cultural reality of the Meriam given expression in court is by no means agreed upon by its contemporary interpreters.

Between 1978 and 1984, I had completed the first stage of work focused on the interrelationship of processes of cultural continuity and change in the Torres Strait Islands with special reference to the Meriam. That study took place within a context of a renascent culture, when the seeds of a renewal, barely visible in 1978, were sending up lively shoots in the 1980s. My conclusions, published in *Stars of Tagai: The Torres Strait Islanders* in 1993, owe a major debt to previous work, especially Haddon's six-volume *Reports of the Cambridge Expedition to Torres Straits* (1904–35). At the same time, it makes an explicit break with the widely accepted image of fading and fragmenting cultures in the Torres Strait Islands. It was the lively image of themselves, which I had observed, that the Meriam who appeared as witnesses projected forcefully, often eloquently in court. In placing these facts within the context of the reshaping of thought about Australian national identity in the post-*terra nullius* era, I attempt to show that the prospects for a re-formed Australia carry a debt to the *positive* side of some basic principles of Meriam society being upheld by most Murray Islanders. Paradoxically it is those principles, often lost in court and in real danger of being lost to Meriam culture, which strike a chord with many people in the wider Australian culture.

I am not alone in examining a land case in Australia from the standpoint of contrasting cultural perspectives. In a major study of the case brought by Yolgnu Aboriginal clans of Yirrkala on the Gove Peninsula (*Milirrpum v Nabalco Pty Ltd and the Commonwealth of Australia* [1971]), Nancy Williams draws quite different conclusions to those of Justice Blackburn who heard the case in the Supreme Court of the Northern Territory. In her book, *The Yolgnu and Their Land: A System of Land Tenure and the Fight for its Recognition*, published in 1986, she concludes that the Yolgnu people's interests in land are proprietary and that their claim to continuous occupancy of certain lands was correct. Her experience of courtroom misunderstandings and her historical study of European concepts of property are distilled in this seminal study, which has a link with this book.

Nevertheless, *No Ordinary Judgment* has a rather different overall focus. Unlike that brought by the Yolgnu, the Meriam people's case secured court recognition of native title. This has led to public debate on questions fundamental to cross-cultural relations, to economic and social development and to the question of cultural identity in Australia. It has led also to national and some state legislation on native title.

This book is intended for any woman or man able to put aside the time to explore and contemplate the series of dramatic events which have begun to change the face of Australia. It has five parts. The first four focus on the beginnings, the progress and the outcomes of the case itself over a period of some 11 years; the fifth, on the period of recognition of native title in Australia, explores the implications of the High Court judgment for the reshaping of Australian national identity, and its expression in changes in public consciousness over the period since June 1992. Because of the cross-cultural nature of this exploration, the book does not follow a strictly chronological form and I suggest that you use the chronologies provided at the front of the book for some of the details.

The title of Part One, 'Interests of a Kind Unknown to English Law', is taken from the words of Lord Denning in the case of *Adeyinka Oyekan v Musendiku Adele* (1957) (Privy Council), and cited by three judges of the High Court in their final decision in the *Murray Island Land* case. The 'one guiding principle' followed by the Privy Council in that case was full respect for the rights of property of the inhabitants 'even if those interests are of a kind unknown to English law'. The Murray Islanders' case provided an opportunity for indigenous rights in land to become at least partly known in Australia. This theme carries through the whole book, which documents the way the proceedings both clarified and also obscured the nature of Meriam interests in land, and of native or traditional title in general.

Parts Two and Three explore the court contest over contrasting customs and laws, the validity of the spoken versus the written word in bequeathing land, the continuity of principles and changes in outward forms in the process of colonisation, and the identification of meeting points and common ground between two moral discourses. Part Four returns to the question of the limitation in European Australians' perceptions of a second 'category' of law — that is, indigenous law — and the related issue of the significance of the historic 3 June 1992 judgment in reclaiming the integrity of the common law.

Since 1978 I have developed close relations with members of the Meriam community both at the Mer Islands and among émigré Meriam people on the mainland. 'It's better if we make you our sister; then all the family will know what to call you', Etta Passi said when I arrived at Mer Island. In many other parts of the Torres Strait Islands and at Injinoo Aboriginal community at Cape York,

I am shown the respect due to a senior community person, being addressed often as Aunty. The possibilities of a case were considered in association with Flo Kennedy, Eddie Koiki Mabo, Dave Passi, Sam Passi and other Meriam. I took part in the beginnings of the case, being a participant in an informal meeting of six people in August 1981 when plans for the case were made. My own contribution concerned the special difficulty which a court might find in sustaining the arguments advanced by Mr Justice Blackburn in 1971 for rejecting the Yolgnu plaintiffs' claims in relation to claims which might be brought by Meriam landowners. An eminent constitutional lawyer's estimate, obtained in Melbourne early in 1981, confirmed this view.

I assisted with the early stages of research for the case, especially at the Murray Islands, where I perused local court documents, collected oral evidence and participated in community meetings on land in 1982 and 1986 at Mer and in Townsville. I attended nine days of the first hearing of evidence in the Supreme Court of Queensland, and I prepared written evidence for the plaintiffs' (the Murray Islanders) legal counsel. In June 1992, my successful application to the Australian Institute of Aboriginal and Torres Strait Islander Studies (AIATSIS) for a full-time study grant to carry out the work upon which this book is based was accompanied by written support from the chairman of the Mer Islands Community Council; in 1993 I was asked by the council to assist in documenting Meriam customary marine tenure.

I wish to thank AIATSIS for its financial support for this project over the period from 1 May 1993 to 30 April 1994. Personal thanks are extended to Jacquie Lambert for her personal interest and encouragement. I am most grateful for the many helpful suggestions of the referee and those of the director and senior editor of Aboriginal Studies Press; the staff offered their usual care, consideration and technical expertise. I was also assisted by a grant from the Australian Research Council for travel and other expenses associated with two visits to Townsville, Cairns, the Mer Islands, Thursday Island, Cape York Peninsula and Darwin, in February, May–June and July 1993. Travel funds from the Research Committee, School of Social Sciences, La Trobe University, assisted me in these research visits; I would like to thank this committee especially for its support in earlier years, which allowed me to carry out research upon which this project builds.

I thank Trevor Graham, director of the documentary film *Land Bilong Islanders*, Yarra Bank Films Pty Ltd, for photographs which appear in this book. I thank cartoonist Bruce Petty for the use of his cartoons on the challenge to the doctrine of *terra nullius*, national reconciliation and on hearsay and traditional evidence. Russel Baader and Lindsay Howe at La Trobe University prepared the plates for the book with skill and patience. My Chronology II carries a debt to Kathy Whimp's chronology published in *Arena Magazine* 9, 1994, 17. Map 3, drawn by Andrew Passi for the Mer Islands Council in 1993, is re-published here from Mulrennan and Hanssen 1994, with the permission of the publisher. I thank Barbara Hocking for her gift of many of the pleadings; Bryan Keon-Cohen for lending me the transcripts of the remitter court hearings; Greg McIntyre for his advice during the writing of this book. This study impels me to commend the lawyers who fought the case and to note their determination, persistence, self-sacrifice, and at times, brilliant insights.

Beth Robertson of the School of Sociology and Anthropology, La Trobe University, not only typed most of the drafts of the book; she took a close personal interest in it; I thank her for her patience, her competence and her goodness of heart. Noelle Vallance encouraged and helped me with her professional knowledge and good offices. Elaine Young, Therese Lennox, Merle Parker assisted with word processing. Judy Carr gave her time and indispensable office skills. I thank the School of Sociology and Anthropology as a whole for its support, effort and imagination. I would like to thank the Australian National University North Australian Research Unit, in Darwin, for giving me material support during my stay there as a visiting research fellow in July 1993; special thanks go to librarians Sally Roberts and Colleen Pyne, who provided me with essential research documents promptly and miraculously. At different stages Jenny Sharp, Richard Hinkson and Geoff Sharp helped with newspaper items from May 1992 until April 1994. Parts of the book were written in the serene atmosphere of the Pajinka Wilderness Lodge; I thank all the staff there for their kindness and concern.

My special debt is to the Meriam people of the Mer Islands and Townsville communities. I thank the Mer Islands Community Council and senior Meriam people at Mer, Thursday Island and Townsville, for their generous support; Meriam family members, Dolly Nasslander, Reverend Dave Passi and Etta Passi, gave me emotional and intellectual support; and members of the community who entrusted me with this task sustained me by giving voice to that trust at unexpected times and places. I hope my presentation justifies their patience, their interest and their confidence. I thank Flo Kennedy who first made a public call for this case; Nugget Coombs and Judith Wright for their strength throughout the years it was being fought; Fiona Mackie for her intellectual and enduring moral support.

My gratitude goes again to Geoff whose inspiration, judgment and patient concern with the central moral issues of the case and this book have helped me to probe some of the deeper issues. For many years the group of people associated with *Arena* have been concerned with cultural identity and the rights of the indigenous peoples of Australia and its neighbourhood. *Arena* has provided the main public forum for articles I have written as the case proceeded and came to a climax.

Nonie Sharp

I

INTERESTS OF A KIND UNKNOWN TO ENGLISH LAW

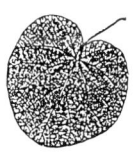

1 BEARERS OF CULTURAL CHANGE

BREAKS IN A SILENCE

Some 30 years ago, the Gurindji Aboriginal people employed at Wave Hill station in the Northern Territory, went on strike for better pay, walked off the station and set up camp on a part of their land at Wattie Creek. And 'now we want the land back', leader Hobbles Danayarri stated on their behalf.[1] In voicing the wish to establish an independent cattle enterprise on a portion of their land, Gurindji people were expressing a desire to pursue their own economic, social and cultural development. This sentiment was given a more general expression when Australia relinquished the doctrine of *terra nullius* and 'joined the world'[2] on 3 June 1992; our wish, said Social Justice Commissioner Mick Dodson (Human Rights and Equal Opportunity Commission), is 'to regain control over our own lives'.[3]

At the time of the Gurindji strike and the land claim of the Yolngu people of the Gove Peninsula against bauxite mining company Nabalco Pty Ltd, which followed soon after, few non-Aboriginal Australians were able to listen to Gurindji or Yolngu voices.[4] Australia remained *terra nullius*, a land belonging to no one, a land whose indigenous people were taken to be so primitive in their social organisation that it was, socially speaking, unoccupied. There were, however, figures within Australian public life who could see beyond this legal fiction of Australia as empty, waste and desert. One of these people was anthropologist W E H Stanner. He spoke and wrote of how 'living Aborigines' could demonstrate 'beyond cavil' in an appropriate court the patent fact of their unbroken titles to parcels of land into the times of their ancestors.

In a prophetic statement he foretold of a time when this fact, buried within 'the great Australian silence', would find 'a suitable set of conditions to come to the surface and be very consequential indeed'.[5] That moment of consequence seemed to have arrived on 3 June 1992 when the High Court announced its decision in the case which has come to be known simply as *Mabo*. The group which demonstrated an unbroken line of title before a court were not Aboriginal people. They were a group of Meriam people: the Murray Islanders of the Torres Strait.

When the High Court decided to discard the legal fiction of Australia as *terra nullius* altogether, rather than limit its decision to the Mer or Murray Islands, it was making a statement about justice: the injustice as well as the illegality of English law in Australia over 200 years. In finding the resources to reclaim the integrity of the common law, to dissociate themselves and the law from complicity in events which wrought 'unutterable shame' upon the Australian nation, the judges were speaking to the question of a 'moral claim to nationhood'.[6] The Meriam became the bearers of this major break in the social and moral discourse: the Meriam people differ 'in culturally significant ways . . . from the Aboriginal peoples of Australia', Justice Toohey noted, but for the purposes of determining indigenous interests in land throughout Australia as a whole, '[t]he relevant principles are the same'.[7] The break in the silence was profound indeed.

THE BEARERS OF CULTURAL CHANGE IN AUSTRALIA

News of the High Court decision cut through the air at the Murray Islands on an early June day when the southeast trade winds blow up from the south. Calling out to each other and whistling loudly, Meriam people joined one another on the road linking the villages which stretch along the sandbeaches.

There was joy in the air, the joy of knowing that the High Court of Australia had recognised Meriam rights to the Murray Islands: 'the Meriam people are entitled as against the whole world to possession, occupation, use and enjoyment of the island of Mer' except for certain leased lands.[8] There was sadness too, the sadness of knowing that Edward Koiki Mabo, the first plaintiff, had not lived to celebrate the victory. Over ten years until his death on 21 January 1992, some four months before the judgment, his inspiration, his steadfastness and his courage had taken him through many arduous and often painful experiences. With his wife Bonita (Neta) he had faced them patiently, cheerfully and with hope.

When the Meriam people burst into the roadway next to their homes, they knew they had won their case. They could hardly have known then that theirs was a victory for all indigenous peoples, with major consequences for the ultimate reality of Australian identity. In recognising Meriam rights to land, the High Court reversed the legal position on which Australia as a political entity was founded. The voting was six to one. Recognition of 'common law native title' placed Australia alongside other former British colonies.

An expanded doctrine of *terra nullius* assumed that the Meriam people, together with all other indigenous people in Australia, were primitive and uncivilised, without recognisable land laws or social organisation and hence lower in the scale of humanity than the European settlers and their descendants. The judgment strikes at the foundation upon which their inferior status rested. The Murray Islanders, Justices Deane and Gaudron concluded, undoubtedly possess 'a local native system under which established familial or individual rights of occupation and use were of a kind which far exceed the minimum requirements necessary to found a presumptive common law native title'. Moreover, after annexation of the islands in 1879, Meriam title was 'recognized and protected by the law of Queensland' (454).

When the High Court affirmed the Meriam people's possession of most of the islands of Mer 'as against the whole world', the court had the choice of two legal principles. As Justice Brennan explained, it could 'inquire whether the Meriam people are higher "in the scale of social organisation" than the Australian Aborigines'; or it could overrule the whole idea of *terra nullius* altogether (421). It took the second course.

In making a decisive break with the assumption of the exclusive operation of one law, which formed the everyday common sense of the majority of Australian citizenry, the High Court justices were completing a process that had been pursued in court for ten years. In their first decision on 8 December 1988, known in legal circles as *Mabo (No 1)*, a majority of the High Court allowed for the possibility that traditional Meriam legal rights to land, still to be ascertained at this stage, may exist. This decision declared the Queensland Coast Islands Declaratory Act 1985, which extinguished any Meriam rights to land that may have existed prior to and been restored since annexation of the Torres Strait Islands in 1879,[9] as inconsistent with the federal Racial Discrimination Act (RDA) 1975, which inscribed equality before the law in legal statute. On 3 June 1992, in *Mabo (No 2)*, the High Court identified a second category of legal rights as 'native' or 'traditional' title, which Justice Brennan described as 'interests and rights of indigenous inhabitants in land, whether communal, group or individual, possessed under the traditional laws acknowledged and the traditional customs observed by the indigenous inhabitants' (429).

The Meriam had exceedingly good credentials as potential bearers of a change that transformed interests in land which had been invisible to non-indigenous Australia for some 200 years into visible title: their plots of land have marked boundaries and the entire island of Mer is like a mosaic of garden plots and residential land, the latter being sub-divided into eight clan territories with residential allotments set out in clusters of villages stretched out along the sandbeaches.

The chapters of this book will unfold in some detail how the Murray Islanders managed to demonstrate to an Anglo-Australian court the existence of a system of customary land tenure which has continued from the period before annexation of the Murray Islands in 1879. Their success has its origins in the specific character of their colonial history (which itself relates to their geographic position and size); in points of apparent and real similarity between Meriam and English land tenure systems; and in the period of history in which the Meriam plaintiffs brought their case.

WHO ARE THE MERIAM PEOPLE?

A people with a reputation as intrepid seafarers and fighters, the Meriam continue to engage in fishing and seafaring. They are a Melanesian people, who, like their northern neighbours in the island of New Guinea (Papua New Guinea and Irian Jaya), live a sedentary existence as cultivators of the soil. Their cultivating activities extend to privately owned crayfish houses outside the reef flats that fringe the islands, which their owners make ingeniously out of coral.

Every inch of the three isles of Mer is owned by Meriam landowners and the boundaries of the plots of land extend across the sandbeaches to the edges of the fringing reefs. There is no concept of vacant or unowned land, although community projects, including an airstrip and community hall, have been constructed in recent times with the permission of the customary landowners.[10]

Stone fish traps were constructed by the brothers, Kos and Abob, in mythical time. The feats of stonemasonry embodied in the fish traps, which extend for some 4 kilometres, are a source of wonderment today among the Meriam: were their forebears people of vast physical strength? Did their magical chants, or *zogo mir*, give them more-than-human powers?

The eight clans of the Meriam, known to them as *nosik*, which they refer to in English as tribes, occupy clan territories facing and extending across the sandbeaches. Allotments of land, foreshore and reef flats are owned by the eldest son *on behalf of* the lineage or family, and these properties are grouped together as villages within the spatial setting of their clan territories. The size of landholding units varies. The landholders, or *lu kem le* in Meriam language, may hold land on behalf of their immediate families, as in the case of plaintiffs Eddie Mabo or James Rice; Passi land is held undivided by the eldest male on behalf of the Passi sub-clan, which includes the second as well as the first generation.[11] In either case, the eldest brother holds rights on behalf of the group who are joint owners or *ged kem le*. Coextensive with this right is a responsibility to the joint owners, in particular to younger brothers and unmarried sisters, to allocate land and resources.[12]

This layered or 'nested system' of ownership of residential land, foreshore and reef is something like the subdivisions which make up an onion: the divisions and subdivisions overlay one another.[13] Traditionally, fish traps within clan territories were subdivided further by leafy bamboo poles: ownership of a corner of a fish trap by the eldest male of a family or lineage is 'anchored' within a clan division.

Residential or clan territories are composed of clusters of villages beside the sandbeaches. Plots of garden and orchard or plantation land, owned by either men or women and often given to a woman by her father as a wedding present, make up a patchwork of allotments, sometimes as small as 900 square feet (around 100 square metres). All allotments have boundaries whose exact location is constantly contested by landowners. The most ancient of these are mounds composed of rotted vegetable matter and shell, known to the Meriam as *daip*. Others are imaginary lines joining boundary markers (*nener*), some of which are natural topographical features, others being marked by stones, shells, or, in recent times, concrete markers. 'They are crooked boundaries', as plaintiff James Rice explained in court, not like the straight boundaries of farms and suburban allotments of Australian people.[14]

Rights to land and its bequeathing are given and protected by the law of the Meriam known as Malo's Law, a set of religiously sanctioned rules which Meriam people feel bound to observe. Stemming from the myth of the Meriam culture heroes Malo-Bomai (Malo and his maternal uncle, Bomai), a myth of land tenure and inheritance, interclan unity and Meriam identity, reciprocity with certain neighbours and with departed ancestors, Malo's Law has the authority and force of a religious commandment.

Young children are inducted into the system of land ownership and use, learning (to a greater or lesser degree today) how to cultivate and how to follow the laws against trespass: Malo *tag mauki mauki, Teter mauki mauki*, Malo keeps his hands and feet off other people's land. Malo keeps to his own place. Follow in the footsteps of your father. These words were heard almost every day in the court which heard evidence from 33 Murray Islanders.

Meriam uniqueness as a people is grounded in a system of land ownership described by the plaintiffs' legal counsel as an 'Oral Register of Title'.[15] There is a growing written tradition, which the case itself stimulated further.[16] Malo's Laws had been written down in Meriam language by a leading Meriam figure, Marou Mimi, on 23 January 1962.[17] The Meriam's writing skills go back to about 1873 when missionaries of the London Missionary Society established the Papuan Institute at Mer. In 1898, Pasi (Passi), the grandfather of two of the original five plaintiffs, Sam Passi and Reverend Dave Passi, requested an exercise book from the linguist Sidney Ray, of the Cambridge anthropological expedition, in which he, Pasi, wrote 59 pages on Meriam myths, custom and classificatory systems in English and in Meriam language.[18]

During some 150 years of sustained intrusion by missionaries, marine entrepreneurs and government officials, authorised by Acts of the Queensland parliament and more recently by federal laws, the Meriam have managed to carry on their traditional adoption practices and other customs in ways which accommodated Queensland and Commonwealth laws on land tenure and inheritance, written wills, and eligibility for social welfare services.[19] It was on the issue of acculturation versus cultural continuity that a major part of the fact-finding hearings was centred. Evidence was given on traditional title to land and the existence of a system of Meriam law and custom. Contemporary Meriam culture is ongoing and developing, not frozen in tradition, the plaintiffs argued; yet there is an essential continuity in the system of land tenure, in other institutions and beliefs. That continuity is itself qualified by the emigration of more than half the population of the Murray Islands to Thursday Island and the mainland, an exodus that began in the late 1950s. Meriam people wished to be free of the 'closed box' of Protection and work and learn about 'white culture' in an atmosphere free of 'the Act', as Islanders called the Torres Strait Islanders Act.[20]

In the legal proceedings, questions of fact or evidence on events were separated from questions of law. A major inquiry was made into 'issues of fact' by Justice Moynihan in the Supreme Court of Queensland. In hearings of the evidence there was much judicial comment, some of it critical, on the way Meriam witnesses drew selectively on Meriam cultural traditions. The context of that reflexive selectivity of cultural principle, it will be argued, was a process of renewal among Meriam people, which began very quietly in the 1970s and rose to prominence in the 1980s. Custodians of Meriam cultural tradition tell their young to go out and learn in order to come back and sow new seeds of knowledge among their people. A major forerunner of this revival was Marou

Mimi, born in 1886, a conserver of tradition and a strong fighter for the right of Meriam people to self-determination.

Two rather different exemplars of this revival are Eddie Mabo and Reverend Dave Passi, each of whom made creative syntheses, each of whom was a prime mover and plaintiff in this case, which was itself an expression of this cultural renewal. Through comparison and contrast, custodians of cultural traditions may bring the principles and truths of the past into the process of the reconstitution of the present, in order that the culture may have a future. Some of these syntheses were dismissed by Justice Moynihan as 'idiosyncratic'.[21] Yet whatever the discontinuity of outward form, the displacement of Malo-Bomai rites by Christian ceremonial and professed belief, senior Meriam people retain a fidelity to certain basic cultural principles.[22]

The essence of Meriam life was and continues to be the creation and re-creation of symmetry or balance through exchanges: within a face-to-face community the exchange of people, things, symbolic meanings, of what I lack and you, my neighbour have. Balance and symmetry between groups and persons always holds within itself the tension of opposition or division; the Meriam are intensely competitive among themselves as well as cooperative. The quest of the culture is to find ways of bridging those divisions. The result is a social life regulated by a competition and a cooperation between equals. In pre-colonial Meriam society, heads of clans and families played important mediating roles; through the religious order known as Malo-Bomai, persons with special spiritual–magical power or *zogo* extended the mediation of the familiar and unknown, the visible and the invisible. In a society with no courts or constables, the reciprocities of giving and returning formed the bedrock of everyday life or 'civil' society. Meriam witnesses argued that the local court, established by the Queensland administration, was a new vehicle for the exercise of their traditional law; the state of Queensland's argument was that the court system constituted a decisive break with the past.

The Meriam people's link to land is two-sided: they both own land *and* belong to it, a dual relation of right and responsibility. This double-sided tie to place, where place begins from land handed down through patrilineal inheritance, includes simultaneously the wind or season to which celestial alignment or 'quarter' that land belongs. In this way, the Meriam are positioned or located within natural cycles, which create the milieu of rights and obligations to land. The pattern of the movement of these cycles provides the metaphoric language of fundamental truths upon which the moral order rests: stars follow their own path across the sky. This, one of the laws of Malo, has several layers of meaning which, above all, define identity: it is a law of property rights in the sense that everyone belongs to their own place, it is a statement about the immorality of trespass, and at the same time it is a statement of land inheritance from fathers to sons (where the key word is 'follow'). In the hearing of the evidence, the court often failed to understand this metaphorical language, the carrier of several different and *non-exclusive* meanings, which was often used by Meriam witnesses. But the words of Malo's Law do not say that 'land is handed down to the eldest son', said the senior Queensland counsel with some irritation in her cross-examination of a witness.[23] In a literal sense nor do they.

It was the religious–mythical ensemble of meanings which provided the Meriam with a preparedness to see the Cross as a symbol: out of the old knowledge of Malo-Bomai and those parts of Christian teaching which resembled and extended old beliefs, they made their own syntheses in ways which fulfilled bequeathed certainties about the mysteries of life and death and rebirth. In Reverend Dave Passi's perspective, the Meriam were chosen by God as the bearers of the change which the judgment brought about in Australia. The case tapped into the 'natural inheritance' of the Meriam: those Meriam who fused the deeper levels of their culture with Christian universalism were most able to give expression to a cultural pride — not always accessible to the court — of certain fundamental truths about themselves as a people.[24]

Plaintiff and priest, Reverend Dave Passi, had been developing an explanatory framework to which he had begun to give public expression in the mid-1970s. 'It came to me strongly' on 'July First 1976', the anniversary of the coming of Christianity to the Torres Strait: in the light of Christian universalism he evaluated 'the greatness of Malo', a greatness revealed in the failure of the missionaries' efforts to extinguish the teaching and *zogo* of Malo. Through comparison and contrast he saw Malo as the god who prepared the Meriam for a bigger truth.[25]

In this moment of pride in what his culture had to offer he was following the most creative of the laws of Malo, the law that makes for change. 'Malo plants everywhere . . .', has a strong resonance with the positive side of the Christian message, 'As ye sow, so also shall ye reap'. This was the special interpretive contribution to the meanings of Malo's Law made by his eldest brother, Sam Passi. Sam Passi's tomb now lies on land to which title was claimed at the village of Zomared on the island of Mer, for which he was the landholder on behalf of the family. 'It's important for the benefit of this island

and your people that whatever you do outside, don't forget to bring that idea back to Murray', he told a youthful Eddie Mabo as he set off in search of the knowledge that 'white culture' had to offer. Out of the rich kernel of the Law came a new exchange. This is how I like to think of Eddie Mabo's contribution to the case that came to bear his name. As we shall see, his experience of the case was a bitter-sweet experience; nor did he live to hear the heroic music of the ultimate finding nor to partake of the events which became the foreground of a post-*Mabo* landscape, a time when his name became a household word.

COMMON SENSES AND SHADOWED TRUTHS

Meriam and European perspectives on the case as it developed are contrasted here. Taking the primary source material for the ten years of the case — 1,000 pages of pleadings, and some 4,000 pages of the transcripts of evidence given by witnesses, supplemented by reflections on the case by some Meriam witnesses, the transcripts of legal argument and High Court judgments — the book unfolds the stages of a compelling drama, unique, intense and confrontational. The case itself is both revelatory and obscuring: in the context of an adversarial legal combat, it brought forth previously hidden truths. As an interface between cultures in which Meriam culture was 'on trial', it also continued, exaggerated, and re-formed previously held misrepresentations and misperceptions, which carried into the Determination of Issues of Fact about the Meriam, past and present, and thence, to a degree, into the final High Court judgment. The result of the hearing of evidence in the Supreme Court of Queensland at the request of the High Court was sufficient for the majority in the High Court to reach a verdict recognising the Meriam people's right to the Murray Islands. The facts pertaining to the Meriam were, however, so minimalist that many 'live coals' of misrepresentation of the Meriam and the nature of their differences from Aboriginal societies remain, a matter considered in Chapter 8.[26]

In major respects the case is a microcosm of the history of contact, a condensed version of the period of the conquest, the state of Queensland producing much the same arguments which were used to justify the long-term subordination of the Meriam. Both as local Protector and later as director of the Department of Aboriginal and Island Affairs, the key witness for the defence, Patrick J Killoran, was a figure of singular influence in the Torres Strait Islands since 1947.

For the purposes of conquest and colonisation, the Meriam and the rest of the Torres Strait Islanders were lumped together with Aboriginal people. This case pulled them apart again in the Determination of Issues of Fact in the Supreme Court of Queensland, which identified them as a very different people to the Yolngu clans of Yirrkala in northeast Arnhem Land, who had brought the case known as *Milirrpum v Nabalco Pty Ltd and the Commonwealth of Australia* (1971).[27] The High Court decision put all the indigenous people back together again, but within a totally new framework that rejected *terra nullius* altogether.

Despite the unfortunate and erroneous decision in the *Milirrpum* case, a series of paradoxical events have come to link the Yolngu and the Meriam cases. The Yolngu's claim to 'communal native title' was rejected by Justice Blackburn as outside the common law, yet the High Court ruled in favour of the collective right of the Meriam to native title at the Murray Islands. Moreover, the Meriam plaintiffs' claims to particular allotments of land were reformulated as a claim to collective rights of the Meriam against the whole world: the High Court was given no instruction to make a ruling on rights to particular allotments of land on the basis of the Determination of Issues of Fact by Justice Moynihan in the Supreme Court of Queensland. Again, Justice Blackburn's definition of law as a 'system of rules of conduct which is felt as obligatory by the members of a definable group of people', one argued for by the Meriam plaintiffs,[28] was not accepted by Justice Moynihan. He drew the conclusion, disputed strongly by the Meriam, that they were ruled more by custom than law.[29] To this the Meriam answer that, while outsiders may wish to define the set of principles they follow as 'custom' or 'precepts' or 'framework',[30] within their cultural terms it is indubitably and palpably law. And finally, six of the seven judges of the High Court ruled that evidence of a system of Meriam land tenure was a sufficient basis on which to recognise the general compatibility of principles of Meriam and Aboriginal land tenure and so reject the doctrine of *terra nullius* for Australia as a whole.

In this context *No Ordinary Judgment* illustrates on the one hand the way in which the decision of the High Court broke the 'chain of authority' which goes back to principles enumerated by William Blackstone in his *Commentaries on the Laws of England* in 1765, which rationalised the right of the more industrious peoples to supplant 'primitive peoples' without 'civilised' laws, property, or a tradition of cultivation of the soil. In the final section, this book also demonstrates how a significant strand of debate which that rupture set in train became the carrier of reified social Darwinist assumptions about evolutionary stages, with hunters and gatherers continuing to be given an exceedingly 'bad press'.[31] The particular form that denigration has taken is through an invidious and ill-informed contrast between the sedentary Meriam horticulturalists with well-defined plots of land, and Aboriginal 'nomads' who 'roamed' over large tracts of the continent and whose current 'rights' were seen to be confined to 'ceremonial sites' and 'walkabout land' for 'traditional' hunting and gathering purposes.[32]

No Ordinary Judgment attempts to bring to light previously shadowed truths about the Meriam. These truths relate to the Meriam people themselves, and the uniqueness of their culture and their law. Their 'land tenure system . . . refers to the invisible social and cultural bonds that exist in the spaces between humans and material objects and which regulate their interrelationships'.[33] These invisible bonds which make up Meriam society associate people in direct person-to-person relations: speaking to another person face to face is a first priority. For example, the Meriam see 'the proper way' to hand on land to one's children as through the voice: 'All my lands I now pass on to you my eldest son'. 'When I am ready to die I will say, "My land, you take over my land". This is the last word when I am ready to die.' This is 'a Malo Law'. As a justice of the peace, the speaker, Meriam landowner, Henry Kabere, is a writer of wills for others, but his will is 'going to pass from my mouth, not from writing', because those words are the law of Malo.[34] Spoken words come first because they are the medium of the face to face. In passing on the words, a pledge 'is sealed'.[35] They are like a covenant, an act of honesty and faithfulness, something akin to the ancient meaning of troth. At this level, this case offers a window on a people with their own intricate social organisation, on what constitutes their 'common sense'. In other words, there are a set of rules which the Meriam have internalised as natural to their existence and which each generation bequeaths to the next; this is the moral order, a set of obligations and constraints.

In a discursive way, the book also explores some general principles regulating Aboriginal and Islander societies and their relationships to land. Stanner concluded that all Aboriginal peoples 'had a conception of land as property' in which 'the relation of ownership between persons and land could be *dual* at one and the same time': a spiritual relation (*in animum*) and a material relation (*in rem*). Thus in Aboriginal understanding 'human corporeal life was indivisibly in pair with spiritual life', a person's indissoluble spiritual connection with place is manifest externally 'in land as an outward and visible sign'.[36]

Here it is suggested that this duality is a representation of the reciprocal social relationships to land and to others (ancestors, living family, future descendants, which are manifest as rights to land ('ownership') and responsibilities/obligations to land ('belonging to'), and that these are inseparable; 'owning' and 'belonging to' are two sides of the one coin. Islanders explained this very simply in court: to own land is a right which is accompanied by an equivalent responsibility to share it with those on whose behalf one acts as landholder. These statements are the essence of a reciprocal system of social *inter*relationships in which land is an outward and visible sign of the invisible bonds which 'inhabit' the apparent 'spaces' between people themselves and between them and their habitat. Hence the inalienability of land in this interrelationship. In European perspectives 'owning' is possessing — I alone own it, this object — and this is seen as a economic–utilitarian and real property right; 'belonging to' is seen as spiritual and non-proprietary.[37]

This position draws upon my own work in the Murray Islands and Torres Strait since 1978, as well as on the work of others. Inasmuch as central issues of Meriam culture, of historical fact and interpretation, became the subject of controversy in the Murray Islanders' case, this book continues and in many ways crystallises a position concerning Meriam existence and culture within a context of debate among scholars of the area.

For a very long time my interest has been in the representation of those areas of difference which form the ground of what we take to be human in different social contexts, the province of the cultural. In Western societies the cultural is increasingly woven out of abstract or extended relations. Yet for all the changes wrought by the newcomers, what it is to be human in Meriam society is formed mainly in face-to-face relations and within oral tradition; that is why the vast majority of the evidence given by the Meriam in court was based upon what 'My father said . . .', or 'My grandfather showed me all his lands and boundaries and said . . .'.

The starting point here is the relevance for the Murray Islanders' claims of two contrasting systems of law: English law on the one hand, Malo's Law on the other. It presupposes a different framework to that which concentrates upon the elaboration of the common law as *the* law. It considers the interplay between two contrasting cultural perspectives on interests in land. It does so under conditions where property rights created by the Crown in Australia have been taken to be *the* property rights — at least until the High Court judgment on 8 December 1988 in *Mabo (No 1)*.[38]

NATIVE TITLE IN THE RESHAPING OF NATIONAL IDENTITY

Generally speaking, Aboriginal and Islander people have taken some heart from the High Court judgment, although it is recognised that a very small proportion of indigenous people will be able to claim native title successfully: a modest, belated, but welcome recognition.[39] Aboriginal and Islander people have become aware of the new cultural and political necessity for the dominant culture to take their opinions into account. As Mick Dodson noted when the federal government was developing native title legislation, 'indigenous people played an active role in negotiating an outcome'.[40]

Practically speaking however, the High Court judgment gave only the Meriam direct acknowledgment of their native title. Other Torres Strait Islanders and all Aboriginal people must prove its continuing existence. For these groups, the recognition of native title — forms of land tenure held according to local law and custom — means firstly that all rights to land extinguished by inconsistent grants from the Crown cannot be claimed. Moreover, native title can be recognised only among those who can demonstrate unbroken and active links to the land claimed since settlement, and this includes only a very small proportion of Aboriginal people.[41] As from 1 January 1994, the Commonwealth Native Title Act 1993 provides a mechanism for consideration of claims to native title within the terms laid down by the High Court.

The justices had asked themselves whether the absence of native title in the common law is an essential doctrine of our legal system. It has been argued that answers given by the majority and by the minority hinge upon opposed readings of the intended morality of British colonialism and the moral attributes of the Australian nation.[42] The consequence of this historic break is a new set of questions about national identity, which most European Australian people had taken for granted within the silence of common sense. Are we a nation with one dominant cultural centre in which Aboriginal and Islander people are pushed back into a new *terra nullius*? A unity between the majority, mainly European Australians and diverse Aboriginal and Torres Strait Islander cultural units? A sea-bound territory with coastal surrounds freely accessible to all? Or does native title extend to traditional foreshore, reef and sea areas?

Because the very questions themselves signal a rupture in the assumptions seemingly 'natural' to most Australians, critics of the recognition of native title recoil with a reaction akin to horror. The decision is a break in a legal system which 'has long since become the natural inheritance of the entire population', Colin Howard, legal scholar and barrister, wrote critically of the judgment.[43] So pervasive is a naturalised notion of English land law as *the* law, so deeply has this conviction permeated common sense, that it becomes a feat of some magnitude to admit the existence of, to comprehend within its own terms, and to place on the same footing, a type of land law which remains embedded in genealogy and is consequently not 'free' to be traded.

Fortunately there are signs of an awakening sensibility. Going with this break in 'the natural inheritance' of those born of the conquerers is an acceptance of the integrity of cultural difference and with it the tenet that the peoples who were dispossessed 'are their moral equals'.[44] A process set in train by the High Court has begun to stir a half-articulate awareness that the 'unknown' Aboriginal and Islander relationships to land may even be of a deeper kind than the narrow conception of ownership of land as a thing to be mastered or traded, the conception embodied in English law.[45] A more searching view has gained some ground: critics even refer to 'barbaric economic rationalists', for whom religious beliefs and spiritual attachments run a very long second in the national interest to the balance of payments.[46] However, morally spirited recoil needs to be accompanied by the capacity to listen to voices calling for practical alternatives to the idea that land is simply real estate.

The change in perspective which the judgment brought with it has also stirred the fears of developers, mining company spokespeople and state premiers. Moves have been made to satisfy the demand for a return to the certainty of *terra nullius* so that, as before, they can go ahead as though Aboriginal people do not exist. Close on the heels of mining industry spokesmen, Labor premier of Queensland, Wayne Goss, voiced the hope that, as cultivators, the Meriam could be considered an exception, people with 'an effective system of title' composed of 'individual lots of land handed down from generation to generation', a quite different state of affairs 'from the nomadic situation which existed on the mainland'.[47]

Over the several years since the decision, conservative commentators have shown themselves wistfully or stridently hopeful that the clock might be turned back to exclude all but the Meriam from native title rights. Thus, for example, conservative commentator John Hyde argued that as cultivators the

Meriam had special rights, so dragging into the public realm unsubstantiated judgments on 'more' and 'less' civilised, the area which the High Court had decided to leave alone.[48] The high swells that followed in the wake of the case were enlarged by some media. As director of the Cape York Land Council, Noel Pearson, has observed, a mirror 'game' was played big and deliberately to ensure 'that, in those few cases where rights survive, they [the opponents of native title] could create the necessary furore to ensure those few rights are neutralised'.[49]

Old assumptions about 'primitive' and non-adaptive Aboriginal societies found new forms of expression. These centred on the idea that what is claimed as native title is automatically lost to Australia for economic development. This view arises from the belief that indigenous societies are exclusively subsistence and stationary, so that native tenure may be 'equated' with 'traditional' or 'subsistence' uses, which are sharply divided from modern, that is, profit-creating ones.

This assumption is readily refuted not only by the Meriam, who moved quickly from 'the first stage' of securing their native title to a new stage of engaging in commercial fishing in the second half of 1992.[50] It is also refuted by the commercial activities of Aboriginal communities in diverse parts of Australia: by the activities of the Kimberley communities, by the Jawoyn's successful work in the area of cultural tourism, by the Yolngu of Arnhem Land and by communities of Cape York Peninsula in tourism and management of vast areas of land.[51]

International developments on the rights of indigenous peoples have provided a developing context for the thinking of Aboriginal and Islander people. Twenty years ago, the Supreme Court of Canada in the case of *Calder v Attorney-General of British Columbia* (1973), ruled that the Nishga nation held proprietary interest in lands claimed.[52] The *Calder* case was followed by others, notably *Hamlet of Baker Lake v Ministry of Indian Affairs and Northern Development* (1978), a case brought successfully by 112 Inuit plaintiffs.[53] Over the past 12 years, Aboriginal and Islander people have worked together with indigenous people from other countries, considering and formulating rights which Mick Dodson described recently as 'inherent, inalienable, indivisible and non-negotiable' and 'the minimal condition for our integrity and survival as distinct peoples'.[54] Through this experience they have become adamant that land rights and self-determination are inseparable. They have brought firm and mature insights into the ravages of the past and the conditions for change in the 'post-*Mabo*' era. The executive director of the Kimberley Land Council, Peter Yu, summed up these conditions in August 1993: 'Australia has arrived at a time in its history when the structural relationship between Aboriginal and non-Aboriginal must change. And it is Aboriginal people themselves who will force this change'.55

A characteristic of drama is that it creates ruptures in the fabric of meaning systems in such a way that one can glimpse the other side — a side that did not appear to be there before — so offering the beginnings of new ways of seeing. This did not happen of itself in this case. It gave only pin-holes through which to peer. Consideration of multiple perspectives is a form of cross-cultural reflection: the hope is that through this process new ways of seeing — and acting — may be created.

Terra Litigious by Bruce Petty, from the *Age*, 13 June 1993 (courtesy Bruce Petty)

2 | OF SILENCES AND SECRETS

CULTURAL PERSPECTIVES

The long relationship between the two cultures is saturated in silences. The Meriam were well endowed to create a silence of secrecy, for it was the natural inheritance of their cultural way. The European culture was well endowed to create a silence of superiority, resting upon assumptions which go deeply into social evolutionary perspectives: feudal rights in land, law as the command of the sovereign, are integral with the more general presumption that the Western social form is the model towards which all other societies are developing.

Between 1982 and 1992, the two cultures continued a relationship which had spanned generations in a unique adversarial confrontation: customary owners were making a claim to land deemed under English law to be part of the 'waste lands of the Crown', by an act of annexation in 1879. This created the silences of direct if polite combat: the two cultures met at a new frontier, a frontier of words in an English institution, regulated by the rules of the dominant society.

THE MERIAM SILENCE

The Meriam observance of silence on arriving at another person's place was recalled during the hearing of evidence. At the end of the 1950s, Meriam leader, Marou Mimi, had explained the meaning of Meriam secrecy enshrined in Malo's Law to a young anthropologist: Keep to your own path, do not go on to other people's land. The Meriam were very quiet and Murray Island was a very quiet place. If you approached another person's place as a friend, you did so in a very quiet way by giving a special hand signal. And this the anthropologist Jeremy Beckett, now an expert witness, recalled for the court (Transcript Queensland 2233).

This silence of secrecy is the essence of Meriam cultural ways: Malo walks on tiptoe, silent and careful, Meriam plaintiff, Reverend Dave Passi, explained. This is a metaphorical way of saying what every Meriam person knows: if people keep to their own path, their own land, mind their own business, social life will continue. The secrecy of attending to one's own business is fundamental to the culture. It is its motif; it is the shared common sense of the Meriam. That is why plaintiff James Rice says that the heart of Malo's Laws (and he listed 24 laws for the court) is 'Hands off'. 'Everyone knows that', he said. That is why 'I don't see anybody break the law. They go on their own property' (TQ1615).

As Meriam witness Mary Noah said, in referring to Meriam cultural adoption practices, 'that cultural way not to tell', is part of a culture locked together by secrets and silences (TQ2177). So when a child is adopted by a family, a custom basic to the perpetuation of Meriam social life, the child is not told. In pre-colonial Meriam society, where marriages were arranged, children may never have known who their natural parents were. The Queensland government made it necessary to tell the child, and today a teenage person is told who his or her natural parents are. The strictest secrecy is still maintained until then: 'When you adopt a child, that secret had to be kept' (TQ2161). Even talking about adoption occasioned deep emotion: 'we are a very, very emotional people'.[1] It has the power of a sacred rite in which a person is transformed or re-created into a new position in the society. Like other rites, adoption practice is established by social rules, and after it occurs there is no return.

It is 'natural' for the Meriam to keep secrets when social life and 'the cultural way', as they call it, require it. In the period in which they became subject to the laws of Queensland, the rules of Protection, which began to encompass them after 1904, made severe inroads into the conduct of their social life and custom. Secrecy became the means to ensure their social survival. Over a period they responded with the common sense of a culture of secrecy: they went on following rules they felt to be obligatory, which many witnesses identified as Malo's Law; where the demands of the external power infringed the 'free space' in which they might follow 'the cultural way', they refused to cooperate.

Thus on one dramatic occasion in January 1936, when the Chief Protector of Aboriginals moved to close up those 'free spaces' altogether by increasing government powers, their silence of secrecy caught the Protector unawares. Networks across the Torres Strait, invisible to authorities and born out of the necessities of social survival, were carried by cultural practices 'natural' to the Meriam and to all Torres Strait Islanders. They made a pact refusing to work the 'Company boats' owned by the clans and controlled by the Protector, and demanded control of the affairs of the Island, the boats and the finances.[2]

PLOTS OF LAND

Out of the silence, on 20 May 1982, there came a claim on behalf of five Murray Islanders in the High Court of Australia to land owned by them at the three islands of Mer, Dauar and Waier, known as the Murray Islands, Torres Strait. These five plaintiffs were members of the Meriam people who since 'time immemorial' have lived continuously in settled communities and cultivated land in those islands according to Meriam law and custom. The plaintiffs, said their statement of claim, together and separately, 'bring this action' against the state of Queensland and the Commonwealth of Australia 'on their own behalf, and on behalf of the members of their respective family groups'.[3]

According to the plaintiffs, the Meriam had been recognised by the British Crown '[i]n or about 1879' as 'the rulers, owners, possessors and occupiers' of the Murray Islands (page 8). Moreover, the plaintiffs — Edward Koiki Mabo, Sam Passi, Reverend Dave Passi, James Rice, Celuia Salee — were themselves 'owners by custom, holders of traditional native title, and holders of usufructuary rights with respect to their respective lands' (page 22).

These five Meriam people were bringing claims to lands on behalf of three family groups, those of Mabo, Passi and Rice. Not one of them was speaking or acting on behalf of *more* than his or her family group; but each knew that the principles of land ownership were the same throughout the island — each male head of family had land passed on to him by his father, each claimed to follow the law against trespass. In their terms, the law against trespass was inseparable from the *direct* handing down of land as a secret gift. So people must 'hands off' because father and mother 'pass it over by words to me' (TQ1533). In the Meriam tradition, you can't walk over another person's land because the private act of handing down from you-to-me seals a trust. The idea of outside, 'independent' and unrelated witnesses to this exclusively you-and-me relationship is anathema to the Meriam; it cuts across the grain of their lives. As we shall see, from the perspective of an English court, Meriam custom likewise cuts across 'the grain' of its rules.

'Hands off' is automatic for the Meriam, therefore trespass does not usually occur. Generally speaking it is not an issue because all Meriam are brought up with it. So if each person is following the same custom or law — each to his own — then that adds up to a pattern being repeated across the whole island. There is a direct connection in plaintiff James Rice's mind between people following their own path, and how he as an individual and landowner on behalf of his family group brought this action for *all* Meriam people. He sees his claim as one instance of a general pattern for the Meriam people as a whole: 'I can picture the whole of Murray Island speaking about the same thing as I do here' (TQ1574). The connection between himself as a landholder keeping to his secret ways, and his action as a test case of a general system and pattern of ownership which he 'knows' exists (as does every Murray Islander), is set firmly in his mind: 'Well, if he got the right and they got the right too . . . that's why this case here [is] for Miriam people' (TQ1662). He confirms the acting out of a set of principles which all Meriam felt bound to follow.

BEGINNINGS

Behind the scenes, organisation had been quietly taking place. It was mid-August 1981. We sat at Flo Kennedy's flat on Thursday Island pondering how to find a third fare. We knew we'd make the journey together to attend a conference in Townsville on rights to land, even though we did not know how this would happen. Dave said, 'I have to go. It's very important.' We remained without speaking. The next day, Dave returned to Flo's place: 'I'm coming. Got the ticket.' We could feel something very important was going to happen, and each of us was looking for signs.

Each of us remembers the trip down: early morning in Cairns, an air of suppressed excitement. A glorious ride along the coast and through the black mountain range that gives Tully its outstanding rainfall. Time to ponder coming events.

The conference titled Land Rights and the Future of Race Relations was arranged nicely, the place was convenient for Aboriginal and Islander people from Queensland communities. The program was relaxed but tightly scheduled. We had little time to reflect upon the name, James Cook University, or to consider certain events of the coming days which might challenge the law of Captain James Cook. A tightly sprung coil of meaning behind a name was under threat.

We found time for an impromptu meeting of Islanders with two representatives of the Aboriginal Treaty Committee, whose Townsville committee had organised the conference with the James Cook University Students Union. Flo Kennedy reflects on how the case began.

> Details of Meeting held at Tamwoy Town, 14 August 1981. Chaired by George [Mye]. Doug Bon was present. Flo Kennedy on 'outside' [aisle] seat, Nonie, then Father Passi. George said during the meeting: 'I see we have Nonie Sharp here with us, perhaps she would like to talk to us, tell us something about the Court Case in the Northern Territory'. When Nonie got to Blackburn's verdict Flo's hand shot up and at the same time she stood up and said: 'They can't give us a verdict like that as no "more virile and industrious nation ever came in and worked our land" and we have never left our islands'.
>
> 'We can take the Governments to court. Let's take them to courts.'
>
> A couple or few days later we were at Townsville to a Land Rights meeting at the James Cook University. The Treaty [Committee] was being wound up then. We met Dr Coombs. Nonie invited . . . Before we started I went outside and invited Phillip to observe the meeting we were going to have: Dr Coombs, Garth [Nettheim], Koiki, Dave, Nonie, Phillip Mills (observer) and Flo.[4]

The meeting was a brief one, but its significance turned out to be far reaching. Those present were agreed that the time was ripe for a new test case on land rights, and that, for reasons given by the Murray Islanders at the conference, the latter would have a very strong case to put to a court.

The three Torres Strait Islanders foreshadowed the core of the Murray Islanders' case. Flo Kennedy restated what she had said at the meeting on Thursday Island several days before: Islanders 'have never left their islands', and it would be difficult to find 'a more industrious people than us'. The Islanders are claiming 'our lands and with them we want all our natural resources' including the fish in the Torres Strait.[5]

Eddie Mabo explained how he had come to inherit land at Mer, how his knowledge of his people and their culture 'did not come from books written by academics'. 'My textbooks', he explained, 'were my parents'. He explained how 'individual or family holdings' existed within clan areas, how the first white men who visited the Murray Islands found a 'people as village dwellers who lived in permanent houses and in well-kept villages', who 'were expert gardeners and hunters'. He gave details of the clan system, the system of land inheritance, and the way in which the laws relating to land were maintained through the sacred order of Malo-Bomai.[6]

Reverend Dave Passi explained in a hushed voice the meaning and significance of the law of Malo-Bomai, through which people came to respect the land.

> I remember when I was a little boy going with my father who had a garden in one of his relations' place. We had to tiptoe where he tiptoed. That means he didn't disturb weeds and other things, and I followed him tiptoeing till we got to the garden. Until today where there are . . . garden roads, if there is a big branch lying across . . . a Murray Islander would not cut it. It is a taboo to us because we were brought up that way, and that was the law that governed our society, and we have great respect for the land as well.

He went on to provide the context for a land claim by Murray Islanders, explaining how Meriam and other Torres Strait Islanders took the ownership of their land for granted, and how their sense of security was suddenly shattered by the news in 1981 that the Queensland government planned to repeal the Torres Strait Islanders Act 1971–79, to degazette the reserves on the islands which had been created by the legislature in 1912, and to concede only 50-year leases to Islanders.[7]

Long before the 1981 conference at James Cook University, a process of questioning was in train. For several years, Eddie Mabo had advanced a proposal for the transfer of the Torres Strait Islands to the Commonwealth.[8] In response to the Queensland government's proposal for 50-year leases, Reverend Passi had asked cogently, 'How can we lease what is already ours?'. Many Islander leaders, such as the chairman of Kubin Council, Wees Nawia, whom we had farewelled forever a few days before; Crossfield Ahmat, chairman of Badu Council; Tabipa Mau, chairman of Dauan Council, and many others, had been working for the rights of the traditional landowners.[9] As early as August

1937, the first inter-island councillors' conference had reaffirmed fundamental traditional rights to land according to Island custom.[10]

In 1981, a question began to stir in a number of people's minds: given the facts of the projected claim, would the Australian judiciary develop the understanding and the courage to overturn the *terra nullius* doctrine that had been upheld, in effect, by Justice Blackburn in the *Milirrpum* case? Would Murray Islanders be able to establish that their rules relating to land tenure and inheritance can be accommodated within the common law as a local legal system and set of customs, so clearing the way for the recognition of legal pluralism in Australia?

The non-Islanders present at the impromptu meeting at which the idea of a case crystallised, brought with them not only articulate ideas on the urgency of a new land case, but also a strength born of a developed moral sense as public intellectuals. Its most organised expression was in the Aboriginal Treaty Committee, and when we explained to Nugget Coombs why we thought a meeting with the Murray Islanders would be useful, his first words were, 'Yes, we have been looking for a test case'. The committee's representatives at the conference were speaking in very plain language: the 'deprived and unrecognised state' of Aborigines and Torres Strait Islanders were among Judith Wright's strong words. Outlining the situation in the Kimberleys where local people were 'being driven from their homelands . . . by the Ashton diamond venture', she addressed Aboriginal people: 'until you have a watertight and satisfactory treaty at Commonwealth level' your 'deprived and unrecognized state will continue'. 'Accept nothing . . . from the Commonwealth government', she warned. Don't be pushed around by a weak Commonwealth government, she continued, 'however traitorous it may be to your people, you have your rights under British law'.[11] A strong commitment had developed to seek 'by judicial process to invalidate the principles on which the Blackburn judgment in the Gove case was based', as Nugget Coombs wrote later.[12]

The six participants in the impromptu meeting readily agreed that the arguments given by Mr Justice Blackburn in rejecting the Yolngu plaintiffs' case in *Milirrpum* might be very difficult to sustain in relation to any claims brought by Meriam landowners.

Justice Blackburn had recognised a system of law among the Yolngu clans. However, he had dismissed the case on the grounds that the common law does not recognise communal title, and that as members of a migratory people, the plaintiffs could not prove that they were descendants of the 'clan owners' present in 1788 on the land claimed by the plaintiffs. Among the sedentary village horticulturalists of the Murray Islands, land is boundaried in a visibly marked way and potential plaintiffs claimed that they could trace their lineages back to those who were owners and occupiers of the respective plots of land at the time of annexation in 1879.

Today a number of people nurse the belief that he or she 'began' the case.[13] Islanders' perspectives contrast sharply with those of most Europeans in seeing the wellsprings of the case as religious rather than secular. For them the question of origins becomes one of first-order importance. Hence Flo Kennedy's call for the case in 1981 was inspired in her by divine power through her sacred 'people-line'.[14] Reverend Dave Passi believes that God chose his people and himself as plaintiffs, together with Flo Kennedy and the non-Islander people who helped them begin and carry through the case. He did so, believes Passi, because the Meriam had a good argument to put to a court, and Passi links this 'good argument' with the Meriam gods Malo-Bomai, whom God sent to the Murray Islands 'to prepare people for Christianity' and bring the Meriam people Malo's Law.

Two practising lawyers spoke at the conference: Gregory McIntyre, who became the instructing solicitor for the Meriam plaintiffs, and Barbara Hocking, a Melbourne barrister who was briefed to give an opinion and to consult several senior Melbourne barristers experienced in customary land

Flo Kennedy at the grave of her grandfather, Sam Savage, Mauar–Rennel Island

cases.[15] In September 1981, Ron Castan QC was briefed to appear; in November 1981, barrister Bryan Keon-Cohen was introduced into the case. In that month counsel concluded that the most accurate statement of the land ownership system at the Murray Islands was 'nameholders on behalf of respective individuals and family groups'; *not* communal ownership by clan groups.[16]

Barbara Hocking enjoined everyone who knew about the proposed proceedings to complete secrecy: Queensland authorities must not get to hear of the claim before a writ was issued. The Islanders had no difficulty following this instruction. Some of us interpreted the caution quite rigidly. Preparatory research began and intending plaintiffs were contacted quietly. It was good to have one plaintiff from 'each side' of the islands: the Meriam side (Eddie Mabo from Piadram clan on the eastern side of Mer, with his aunty, Celuia Salee, who lived at Mer) and the Dauar side (Sam Passi, the nameholder for Passi land at Dauar, the area of the southwest clans, with Reverend Dave Passi, a younger brother deeply committed to a land case). Both Sam Passi and Eddie Mabo believed themselves to be descendants of the *Zogo le* or 'high priests' of the sacred order of Malo-Bomai. A fifth plaintiff was added: James Rice, who was chairman of the Murray Island Council at the time, and who claimed lands at both Dauar and Mer.

During a visit to the Murray Islands in February 1982, I went through the records of cases heard by the Murray Island Native Court set up by Queensland in the 1890s, known as the Court Book, with the permission of the Murray Island Council. The pages of the Court Book were rather worn by salt air and tropical heat, and although some sections remained stitched together, others were completely loose. They were records of many land disputes, disputes over boundaries, disputes between families, clans and neighbours. I was looking for government recognition of Meriam ownership of plots of land. Suddenly this one appeared: September 1913, Case no 55: sale of land at the village of Zeub in the Komet clan territorial division for a courthouse and gaol. I had been told quite definitely by George Passi, then council chairman, that I might view these documents only in the council offices. Some pages were cracking at the corners, like pieces of parchment. These were rare and 'ancient' documents. I made pencil notes and sketched the plots of land, their dimensions, the names of their owners: three sales, two at £1-10-0 each, one at £3.0.0, with the well-known signature of Jack Bruce, government schoolteacher at Mer for more than 30 years. From 1911, the schoolteacher had been empowered under the Aboriginal Protection Act 1904 as government superintendent on each island.

I was urged to find a way of bringing the actual documents back to Melbourne; notes were not sufficient. Here was a dilemma. This was still the preparation time for the Murray Islanders' claim, and from August 1981 we all remained sworn to secrecy. I spoke with a senior Meriam landowner, Henry Kabere, who became a major witness for the plaintiffs; it was his grandmother who had owned that land at Zeub. The decision rested with the chairman, George Passi, brother of Sam and Dave Passi, who were already plaintiffs-to-be.

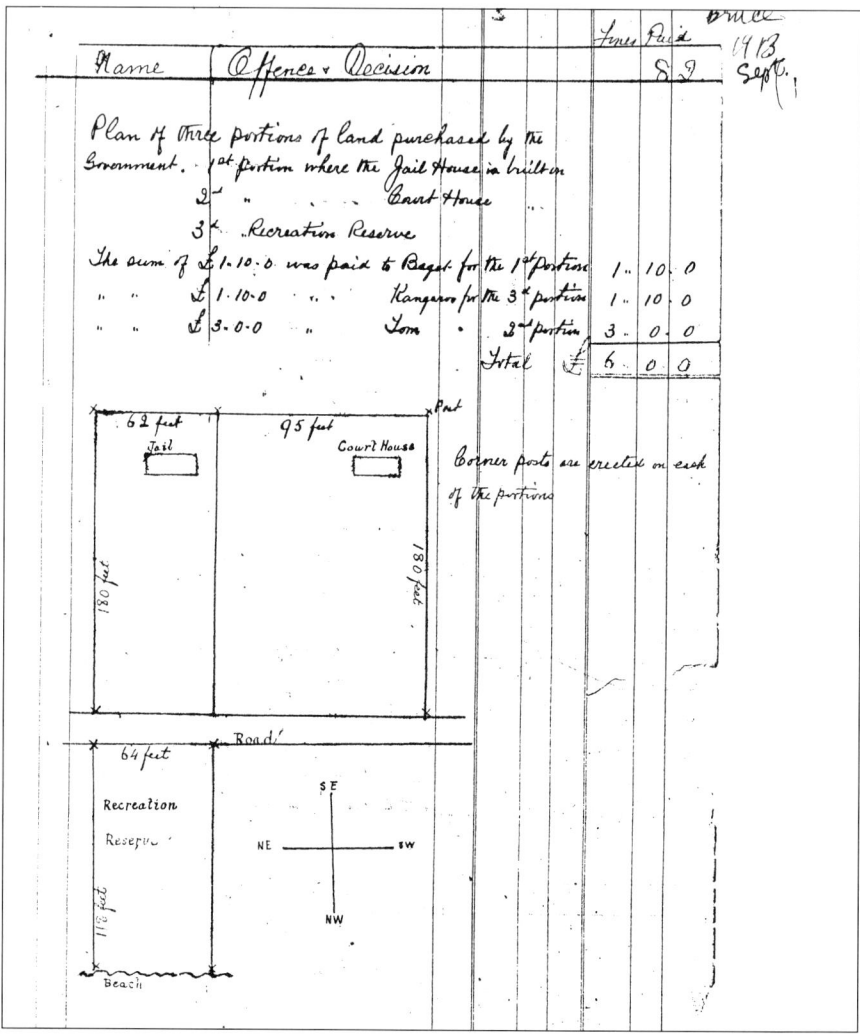

Record of purchase of land at Zeub village, Mer, 1913 (Murray Island Court Book). The signature of Jack Bruce is partially visible (top right)

George had worked for the Department of Aboriginal and Islanders Advancement, a state government department, and was regarded on the island as a man with both a strong attachment to Meriam culture and at the same time 'pro-Queensland'. Dave Passi was the Anglican parish priest on neighbouring Darnley Island; Eddie Mabo lived in Townsville. It was Saturday, there was a wedding celebration and that evening the chairman was sitting on a verandah at the village of Gigred. 'The documents belong to the council; they can't be taken away.' I elaborated on how it would help Meriam people and the conservation of their culture . . . and finally, 'Yes'. The next day I returned to the pages, gently placed them in an envelope, and hid them. There could be a phone call.

On Thursday Island the four documents were hidden safely after Flo Kennedy and I had talked over the story. Flo understood the necessity of bringing a case in a Kole or white man's court: 'It is a terrible thing for us to have to go to this kind of court to prove what we have always known: that these islands are our homes, not something to be bought or sold. But we have no choice.'

Soon after my return to Melbourne, counsel requested the whole Court Book as a matter of urgency. They were delighted with the records of sale of lands at the village of Zeub by the traditional owners to the government during the post-annexation period. They saw the entire court records as '[a]n exciting discovery': a body of Meriam jurisprudence consisting of decisions of a court 'set up under Queensland government legislation . . . based on the traditional land tenure system' and highly relevant to the case.[17] There was no time to lose. Through the good offices of Reverend Dave Passi and Flo Kennedy, the Court Book was soon on its way to the Cairns office of Greg McIntyre; the contents were quickly deposited in a deed box in a bank by McIntyre's assistant, Denise McAllister.

Flo became a go-between liaising with the lawyers and the Meriam people. Greg McIntyre saw the importance of this. She combined political experience with the cultural and spiritual vision that was needed to get the important things done: to find and keep suitable plaintiffs, to ensure that Meriam plaintiffs and witnesses and their counsel were talking to each other, not past one another, and to use her good offices to help things to flow smoothly under conditions where those who were to argue the case were some 3,000 kilometres away from the Murray Islands. Those good offices were called upon soon after the writ was issued. In June 1982, Flo accompanied the four legal counsel — instructing solicitor Greg McIntyre, Ron Castan QC, and barristers

Barbara Hocking and Bryan Keon-Cohen — to the Murray Islands to meet with the plaintiffs, including Eddie Mabo, who flew there from Townsville, and to inspect plots of land, boundaries, reef flat areas and fish traps.

Flo Kennedy's own knowledge of Meriam tradition is considerable; this came to her partly from her father; not himself a Murray Islander, though he had a special place there. He was a man highly respected for his spiritual powers, which were acclaimed throughout the Torres Strait, for his choreographic and song-making skills, and for his inspiration as a composer of hymns. Both the Meriam and the lawyers had their own legal protocols, their own priorities, and Flo anticipated and overcame various potential difficulties and misunderstandings: 'You see that tall man with the dark hair and that lady. Well, they're the assistant barristers. Now that smaller man in the stripey singlet, well, in Meriam language, he's the *Au le*, the senior man; the man to whom you show the greatest respect. He's called the QC, that's Queen's Counsel.' As was to become evident in the courtroom, Ron Castan was a gifted advocate with an outstanding knowledge of the common law. He took on the key role in shaping the legal argument. He also displayed qualities esteemed in Meriam society: practical imagination, empathy, wisdom, clarity of thought.

Each member of the legal team played an essential role in a division of functions that had scarcely emerged at this stage. Barbara Hocking carried out research in the preparation of the pleadings as the case proceeded. Questioning of the witnesses, which began over a period of ten days in October 1986 and recommenced at the island of Mer in May 1989, was conducted by barrister Bryan Keon-Cohen and barrister and solicitor, Greg McIntyre.

COUNTERPLOTS: THE SILENCE OF SUPERIORITY

Although the initial response to the lodgement of the Murray Islanders' claim was one of total silence, the years following 1982 saw an evolving drama, with plots, subplots and counterplot. In response to the issuing of a summons by Queensland to strike out the plaintiffs' claim, on 16 August 1982, P J Killoran, permanent head of the Queensland Department of Aboriginal and Islanders Advancement, issued an affidavit, or sworn statement, for the first defendant (Queensland), together with 25 annexures marked 'A' to 'Y'. It challenged the extent to which the Meriam had continuously and to the exclusion of all others used and enjoyed the islands referred to. It cited two instances of intrusion and implied a third one. The first referred to the London Missionary Society taking up residence at Mer, leasing land from the owners, establishing the 'Papuan Industrial School and Teachers' Seminary' there and, by their presence, altering 'the former modes of life on the Murray Islands'.[18] Specifically, it claimed that the rapid conversion of Murray Islanders to Christianity signified their rejection of their old beliefs and practices. A second intrusion was made by South Sea Islanders, who engaged in fishing in the area and many of whom took up residence for a time on the Murray Islands. The third concerned the arrival of the Queensland government administration and its influence on the Murray Islanders. On 1 October 1885, the government resident reported the 'taming' of the Islanders: 'Dangerous and savage as the people of these Islands were, they are now perfectly harmless and friendly'.[19]

The Murray Islanders' amended statement of claim, issued on 13 September 1982, took up some of the questions raised in P J Killoran's affidavit. A brief hearing was held before Justice Deane in the High Court in October 1982, when it was agreed that the plaintiffs (the Murray Islanders) would draw up a statement of facts. Once the facts were agreed upon, the legal issues could be determined by the High Court. Preparation of their statement of facts was completed by the plaintiffs after many months of work, following which intermittent negotiations were held with Queensland in an effort to reach an agreement on the facts. For much of the following year, the two defendants — the state of Queensland and the Commonwealth of Australia — were silent. As foreshadowed in the affidavit issued on their behalf in August 1982, Queensland argued that a 'considerable time and effort' would be required to prepare for and resolve issues of fact.

As Greg McIntyre wrote of this phase of the case: 'When it became apparent that no agreement could readily be reached with Queensland, the plaintiffs took the matter back to the Court for directions'. On 27 November 1984, Chief Justice Gibbs 'heard the application in Chambers and remarked on the importance of the case'.[20] He ordered that the plaintiffs' statement of facts (which comprised four volumes of information) become particulars and further particulars of an amended statement of claim. The plaintiffs were to deliver this amended statement of claim on or before 19 December 1984, and Queensland and the Commonwealth were to deliver their respective defences to it by 5 February 1985.

The Chief Justice had now to decide between two courses. In one course, the questions of law would be determined by the Full Bench of the High

Court. In an alternative course, the issues of the matters in dispute, not the province of the High Court, would first be remitted to a lower court — the Federal Court or the Supreme Court of Queensland — for resolution. He was to decide on a remitter court.

The actions of the state of Queensland in the phase which followed, accord with its own submission that the issues of fact were 'ultimately irrelevant'.[21]

STRIKING BACK

In the three years after the Meriam had issued their writ, the precise contours of the case and its substance were being shaped, often in private. On Good Friday eve, 2 April 1985, the Queensland government quietly took the offensive. The Queensland Coast Islands Declaratory Act 1985 (the 1985 Act) was passed without debate and almost unnoted. It sought to extinguish retrospectively any rights to land at the Murray Islands which may have survived annexation in 1879, so leaving the Meriam with no arguments to put to a court and thus ending the case. It became law, taking the Meriam and their counsel unawares. Flo Kennedy got wind of it and informed the Murray Islanders' counsel. In response, on 19 June 1985, the Murray Islanders challenged the validity of this legislation (and consequently Queensland's amended defence) in a legal document known as a demurrer; it claimed that the Queensland parliament lacked the power to extinguish their proprietary rights to land retrospectively.

The intention of the Act was to remove 'any doubt that may exist as to the application to the islands of certain legislation upon their becoming part of Queensland'. In moving its second reading on 2 April 1985, Mr W Gunn, the deputy premier of Queensland, made explicit its integral connection with the Murray Islanders' case. The intention of the Bill, he explained, was to forestall 'interminable argument' and 'remove the necessity for limitless research being undertaken'. He summed up nicely Queensland's response to the plaintiffs' claim. When the Queensland Coast Islands Act of 1879 was passed, declaring the islands of the Torres Strait annexed as part of the colony of Queensland, the islands became subject to the laws of Queensland:

> This position was accepted until a small group of Murray Islanders commenced an action in the High Court Australia on 20 May 1982 against the State of Queensland and the

> Commonwealth of Australia to challenge the annexation to Queensland in 1879 of three of the Torres Strait islands. The islands are Murray, Dowar and Waier in the Western [sic] Group of Torres Strait Islands.[22]

In a quiet display of cultural arrogance the Queensland government reduced the Meriam claim to property rights to the activities of a small group of 'troublemakers'. In 1936, when the Torres Strait Islanders went on strike against Protection, Deputy Chief Protector C O'Leary had sought to isolate 'the malcontents' and 'troublemakers'. He had done this silently, with confidential reports to the Chief Protector of Aboriginals.[23] In 1985 the 'small group' was to be silenced through Act of parliament.

The 1985 Act carried forward the subjective certainty of the coloniser that Meriam culture no longer existed in any real sense: in this view they were an acculturated people. With this went the certitude that Queensland would win the case. As Queensland's main witness, P J Killoran, who had been a powerful presence in the whole gamut of Islander affairs since 1947, testified in court, he genuinely believed that one might find no more than a wistful nostalgia among the Meriam for the ways of their forebears. Thus he could reasonably believe there was no substance to the Murray Islanders' claims.

In the history of colonisation, one face of power has typically been upheld by the gun; the other is that soft form of power which can exclude consideration of other cultures by defining the property rights of Western colonising countries as *the* property rights, and written records of ownership and inheritance as the only legitimate ones. The Murray Islanders' legal action exposed in several ways the soft face of power which rules by legitimation. The main defendant, Queensland, held to the basic assumptions of *terra nullius*. This presumption was manifest in three propositions: that the Murray Islanders were primitive people without any proprietary rights in land recognisable in British law; that the only valid evidence is the written or 'objective', which puts a system of rights to succession in oral form outside the scope of the law; and that with the coming of missionaries, pearlers and government officials, Islanders made an essential break with their traditional culture and were assimilated into the dominant culture.

There may well be no indigenous group in Australia which can demonstrate more clearly than the Meriam the cultural assuredness of the coloniser that there was no invasion, only a 'civilising influence' which the Meriam were duty-bound to internalise. Yet because the Meriam remained in occupation of their lands they could follow custom and build their 'domain' in those spaces which indirect rule left vacant.[24]

Self-evident certitudes notwithstanding, the Queensland government was taking the Murray Islanders' action very seriously and the substance of the 1985 Act was to become the centre of Queensland's pleadings, comprising a defence to the plaintiffs' statement of claim. In March 1988, in a hearing by the Full Bench of the High Court on the Murray Islanders' legal challenge to the 1985 Act, Justice Deane reflected upon the manner of its enactment. If one assumed a proprietary interest, he said, 'the Queensland Parliament, by those twenty lines with no debate intended to simply abolish all those rights of ownership, and that is what we read in this Act'.[25] Although the 1985 Act was incorporated into an amended Queensland defence, in the first half of 1985 Queensland issued a series of legal documents as ordered by Chief Justice Gibbs the previous December.

PLOTS THICKEN

On 15 May 1984, the Torres Strait Islanders Act 1971–79 had been repealed, an event foreshadowed publicly by the Queensland government in 1980. Simultaneous with its repeal had been the enactment of the Community Services (Torres Strait) Act 1984. In 13 island communities, trust areas then replaced the island reserves which had existed in Queensland law for 73 years, since 1912, and in government practice for more than a century. A 'trust area' is land granted in trust or reserved and set apart for Islanders by the Governor-in-Council, under provisions of law relating to Crown lands. The Murray Island community, however, had refused to accept a Deed of Grant in Trust (DOGIT) under the new Act. The significance of this Act may be understood in the context of the two interrelated Acts passed by the Queensland legislature in the following year: the 1985 Act (previously discussed), and the Aborigines and Torres Strait Islanders (Land Holding) Act 1985.

As we have seen, the 1985 Act sought to strike out any traditional rights which might have existed when the Meriam claim was made in 1982, or in 1985 when the legislation was passed. On 24 April, three weeks after passing the 1985 Act, the Queensland parliament passed the Aborigines and Torres Strait Islanders (Land Holding) Act 1985. Under this Act, complementary both to the Community Services Act, and also to the 1985 Act, island councils may surrender pieces of land of less than one hectare to the

Queensland government, which may then make them available as perpetual leases to 'qualified persons'. Fixed-term leases of more than one hectare may be taken out by such persons with the approval of the Governor-in-Council. A 'qualified person' is a member of a community who is deemed by the island council to be a resident of the community in which the trust area is vested.[26]

These three interrelated pieces of legislation together served as the means of 'disposing' of Torres Strait lands, which are taken to be 'waste lands of the Crown for the purposes of sections 30 and 40 of the Constitution Act' (the 1985 Act s3[a]). When the islands became part of Queensland following their annexation in 1879, and subject to laws in force there, they 'were vested in the Crown in right of Queensland freed from all other rights, interests and claims of any kind whatsoever' (s3[a]). Acts of 'disposal' of island land could be validly made where 'disposal' is taken to mean 'an exercise of power conferred by Crown lands legislation whether by way of alienation, sale, leasing, letting, licensing, reservation and setting apart, grant in trust or in any other way whatsoever' (s3[a]). These Deeds of Grant in Trust, were simply an alternative way of disposing of 'waste lands' of the Crown. They differed from the old reserve system, where land could not be removed from the reserve for lease to individuals and had to be retained as one whole.[27]

In 1986 and 1987, in the course of the court hearings, important new elements were introduced into the case. Although the 1984 and 1985 Acts passed by Queensland to end the case were later to become the subject of legal argument before the High Court, events began to take a new turn at this stage: for different reasons both parties were to address themselves to the facts.

Before hearing arguments on the substance of the plaintiffs' June 1985 demurrer to Queensland's defence, on 27 February 1986, Chief Justice Gibbs referred the case to a remitter court, the Supreme Court of Queensland, where Justice Moynihan was asked to hear evidence and make a determination on the facts raised by the Murray Islanders and responded to by Queensland and the Commonwealth.[28]

OUTSIDE THE COURT: AN INVISIBLE BATTLE

Originally, the plaintiffs had argued that their demurrer be heard before the High Court 'since the resolution of the legal issues so raised might obviate the necessity for a lengthy complex and expensive hearing of factual issues'.[29] By February 1986, though, both the plaintiffs and the state of Queensland wanted the remittal procedure, but for different reasons. Queensland was not prepared to have questions of law determined on facts it could not agree with, and so was keen to have the facts determined on admissible evidence before any question of law was determined. Queensland's counsel also believed this course the most likely to succeed quickly. The reversal in the plaintiffs' approach came about during 1985, when they made clear to counsel their wish to give evidence in the plea. As witnesses may not give evidence to the High Court, it then became plain that their evidence would be heard in the Supreme Court of Queensland.

On 27 January and 9 February 1986 respectively, the Meriam people's preference to give evidence was expressed in resolutions passed at meetings of Murray Islanders at Mer and in Townsville. These supported the land claim and reaffirmed Murray Islanders' ownership of lands which they had 'farmed continuously from times long before written history and which were handed down to us by our ancestors'.[30] The Islanders explained their perception of the reasons for their land claim: the existence of proprietary rights in land and the presence of boundary markers between allotments of land; and the continuation of an indigenous system of law, known as Malo's Law, which upholds both a system of land ownership and the practice of a style of cultivation.

In emphasising their uninterrupted inheritance of visibly boundaried land, the Meriam issued an invitation to the judges to visit the Murray Islands and see the boundaries, some ancient, for themselves. They also expressed confidence in their ability to trace their genealogical ties to the land allotments that they were claiming to times before annexation or sustained intrusion (known as chains of title in English law).

There were, too, other practical and legal considerations which impelled the plaintiffs' counsel to press for an early hearing of the facts. But the wish of the Meriam to take part in the hearings was palpably evident at this stage. In July 1986, counsel obtained written proofs of evidence from the plaintiffs and from those Meriam people chosen to appear as witnesses.

For its part, Queensland sought the hearing and determination of the issues of fact before the hearing on the legal issues by the Full Bench of the High Court. In the subsequent proceedings before Justice Moynihan in the Supreme Court of Queensland, the defendant argued first that there was no substantive case to answer on the facts, and second, and related to this, that a rule against hearsay would preclude consideration of oral testimony by Murray Islander witnesses.

Early in 1986, before the hearing of evidence by Judge Moynihan in Brisbane from 13 October to 17 November, Queensland released and made available to the court, and to the Murray Islanders' counsel, a set of documents as part of its response to the Islanders' pleadings. Piled one upon the other they stood more than 2 metres high. Important though is not their height, but the content of at least one of these documents: it concerned transactions relating to the sale of land by Murray Islander owners in (or about) 1967 for the building of a kindergarten — a document of such interest to the plaintiffs that they subsequently incorporated it into their pleadings.

Most Islanders believed that given the opportunity to recall relevant facts about land tenure, inheritance, and how they came to know these facts, they would be judged fairly. In their eyes, the truth of their ownership would then become evident to the judge.

Many Meriam wished to give evidence. The reasons for this are inextricably woven within taken-for-granted assumptions which the plaintiff James Rice explained: 'In our thinking we can do everything fair and square' (TQ1682). The logic of the system is one in which the clan groups exist on the same level, rather than in a tiered system: the see-saws of everyday life oscillate between being on a par and 'getting ahead of someone'. There are always matters in dispute, and these may be latent; so the opportunity to demonstrate one's case is grasped eagerly. The court became a vehicle for pressing and contesting some claims. Meriam landowner Marwer Depoma, for example, gave evidence as a witness for the defence in his disputation with Eddie Mabo over land boundaries at the village of Sebeg in Komet clan territory.

In the openings days of the court hearing in October 1986, it became apparent to Eddie Mabo and to counsel that the process of giving evidence to the court on what he believed to be his rights to land, how they had become known to him, their grounding in a system of Meriam law and custom and their relation to Meriam social organisation and system of meanings, would not be a straightforward one at all. Plaintiff James Rice and three witnesses who remained for more than a week outside the court waiting to be called, eventually learned about the tactics of the defence, which they saw as consistent with their experience of Queensland as their ruler and policeman. They could hardly be aware of what most non-Islander citizens of Queensland were also unaware: the armoury of technicalities born of a system alien to their own which Queensland had at its disposal to defeat their action. Nevertheless, they were surprised and shocked to be told that the evidence they intended to give on the oral transmission of title was arguably inadmissible according to historically established rules of the court. Moreover, while they knew the defence's key witness, P J Killoran, personally, they were not prepared for the degree to which Queensland sought to drive them into contradicting what they had said in their initial statements, which could lead to their discrediting as witnesses.

They could hardly have been aware that Queensland had the full-time services of an anthropologist and a senior archivist. Nor were they acquainted with a legal procedure which involved pursuit of errors of detail, personal weaknesses, and inconsistencies pertaining to evidence and to actions, and which sought to question the witnesses' credibility and point to apparent discontinuities in the observance of customary land law. It also became evident during the hearing of evidence that, through birth to death records of each individual and personal familiarity, Queensland was in a position to know certain facts about witnesses which could be used to disadvantage them.

Above all, the theme that underlay Queensland's case — that the Meriam did not exist today as a people with a recognisable system of law — simply did not make sense to Meriam people. That argument was as inconceivable to them as the ideas that their lands did not belong to them. Historian Henry Reynolds records Eddie Mabo's astonishment and horror when he learnt in the late 1970s that, in Queensland law, Mer was regarded as Crown land since 1879.[31] Like the Yolngu Aborigines of Arnhem Land, who had been 'more or less free to have virtually complete enjoyment of their land rights as they understood them' until about 1969, when plans for a bauxite mine at Gove Peninsula were made,[32] the Meriam had had the Murray Islands more or less to themselves. Again, like the Yolngu 'the possibility of their being ousted was unthinkable'.[33] They were not bringing their case to the tribunal of the Crown in a state of mind in which failure was conceivable. The chairman of the Murray Island Council, Ron Day, made this clear both firmly and courteously before the cameras with Justice Moynihan alongside him outside the court at Mer in 1989: the Murray Islanders owned the land from which they grew, something that no judge, no lawyer, no politician — not even the Crown could take away.[34]

The Meriam had begun to make their terms clear to themselves seven years before, in 1982, at a meeting on 29 January in St James Parish Hall, at the village of Beur, Mer, when they unanimously reaffirmed their wish for inalienable freehold tenure.[35] A few years after the case began, they had also expressed a unanimous preference for their case to be heard in the High Court in Canberra; in a show of hands at a meeting on Mer in January 1986, they expressed their wish for a hearing in Canberra, *not* in Brisbane. That emphasis I took to relate to their association of any proceedings in Brisbane with their experience of 'the Act' and their supervision by 'the Department'. The Meriam have a long history of preference for dealing with the Commonwealth; perhaps their expressed wish has a resonance with that of the Yolngu's action, which one informed observer perceived as 'probably best considered not solely as a resort to the law as it is' but also 'as an appeal to the Crown's sovereign justice'.[36] Half a century before this action, the Murray Islanders, along with the rest of the Torres Strait Islanders, in calling for an end to the total supervision by the Chief Protector of Aboriginals, had sought the substitution of Commonwealth for state control.[37]

Given their historical experience, they were not altogether surprised to be questioned in an adversarial and often hostile way. As I shall illustrate from the cross-examination, this did not appear to affect the answers witnesses gave; it did, however, make it difficult, even impossible, for them to explain the complexities of many important issues, to resolve apparent contradictions into which the adversarial style and the 'if this, then that' type of logic sometimes forced them.

Their long experience of the Queensland government and its variously named Aboriginal and Islander department notwithstanding, the Meriam idea of a court was 'to make things fair and square', an expression used by one witness to describe the role of the island court, which had come to complement and to displace in part the endless negotiations and displays of physical strength of pre-colonial times that were used by the Meriam to re-create a balance between groups and persons. From this perspective there is a similarity to the Yolngu's perception of the court in the case of *Milirrpum*. As Williams concludes, the Yolngu 'perceived the court situation less in adversary terms than as a setting where their role was to assist the court to learn about their ownership of land'; the hearing was 'an opportunity "to explain" '; they believed 'explanation would result in understanding'.[38] At the same time, like the Yolngu, the Meriam were also suspicious of a mode of questioning which attempted 'to elicit from them inconsistent or contradictory responses'; a court procedure where people tried to 'explain only enough to "win" ' is totally alien to their consensus style of dispute resolution.[39]

The Meriam will use 'psychological' techniques to outwit their opponents and these techniques may fall within European definitions of magic: these involve a dialogic relationship between the giver and receiver in which the strength and potency of one's gods are pitted against an adversary. James Rice recounted to me in August 1989 how he had brought all the strength of his *lubabat* or totem, a large 'warrior' fish, to bear on his confrontation in cross-examination with Queensland counsel.

INSIDE THE COURT: FACE TO FACE

Senior counsel, Ron Castan, opened the case for the Murray Islanders in the Supreme Court of Queensland, Brisbane, on Wednesday 5 October 1986 at 10.29 am (see TQ19ff). Two events material to the possibility of the plaintiffs pursuing their action, which had occurred outside the court, were reported within the first minutes of the hearing. One concerned the intention of Sam Passi and Reverend Dave Passi to withdraw from the case; the other a reported attempt to persuade another plaintiff to withdraw. Celuia Mapo Salee, the second plaintiff, had died, leaving four plaintiffs. If the alleged endeavour to encourage the fifth plaintiff to withdraw were to succeed, one plaintiff — Eddie Mabo — would have been left to carry the argument. A note of dramatic intrigue had appeared on the scene, albeit in the low-key way characteristic of English law.

In the light of these events, two amendments were made to the statement of claim. As Eddie Mabo's paternal aunt and 'the oldest living member' of Mabo's family group (TQ22), Celuia Salee had entered the case as the caretaker of Eddie Mabo's property. Given this context of her participation in the case, which of course included the fact of her residence at Mer and Eddie Mabo's absence, counsel incorporated claims in respect of her portions of land into his claims.

Sam Passi and Reverend Dave Passi, the second and third plaintiffs, had expressed their intention of withdrawing from the proceedings. Instructions to this effect had been received from the solicitors now acting for them; the latter had also 'filed a notice of discontinuance in the High Court' (TQ24). This event had been foreshadowed a month before by a statement signed by Sam Passi, the nameholder for the Passi family group, on 22 September 1986. Regardless of the younger brother's personal wishes and intentions, the conduct of matters pertaining to Passi landholdings rested in the hands of the eldest living male, as landholder on behalf of the Passi family. At this stage the matter appeared to be final. The second event notified to the court was a reported effort by the defendant to dissuade plaintiff James Rice from proceeding with his action. In bringing this matter to the attention of Justice Moynihan, senior counsel Ron Castan referred to 'elements in the way in which that approach came about' or 'the air of a possibility' of contempt of court. The 'endeavour to suborn a plaintiff' is a grave matter indeed and senior counsel mentioned certain 'independent steps' which were being taken: the briefing of counsel from the Brisbane Bar 'to advise and review those matters' (TQ24).

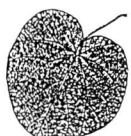

In the first 14 days of the hearing of Eddie Mabo's evidence in the Supreme Court of Queensland, 289 objections were made by Queensland to the reception of oral testimony. During this period Justice Moynihan deferred the rulings on the question of the admissibility of oral evidence.

The question moved to that of hearsay not as hearsay but as 'traditional evidence' (or as a category of hearsay evidence admissible as an exception to the general rule against admitting hearsay evidence). At a hearing before Justice Deane in the High Court on 13 February 1987, the Murray Islanders submitted that a rule of evidence existed in the common law which permits the admission of traditional evidence in cases where a particular kind of title is contended for, that is, one passed on by way of oral transmission. In these circumstances, they contended, 'much of what is objected to as hearsay is not, in truth, hearsay, at all. It is evidence of, what one would term, 'oral events'.[40]

The continuity of title of a particular kind was being contended for by the plaintiffs. The difficulty which had emerged in the course of hearing the evidence or facts is that 'the one thing that cannot happen is for a judge determining issues of fact to determine a question of admissibility in a way which, in effect, assumes the non-existence of the basic right that is claimed'.[41] In other words, the judge must avoid making a decision on issues of fact which might imply a decision on the questions of law yet to be made by the High Court.

In reply, Justice Deane was meticulous in attempting to avoid pre-empting in any way the purposes of the hearing by Justice Moynihan, while at the same time making clear that any determination of questions of admissibility must take into consideration the need to avoid effective exclusion of questions of law yet to come before the High Court.[42] He declined to rule on this matter and directed that it would be appropriate for Justice Moynihan to consider the admissibility of hearsay evidence on the basis of the several exceptions to the rule against admission.

When the hearing resumed before Justice Moynihan on 23 February 1987, Queensland agreed that traditional evidence is not required to 'fall within established exceptions' to hearsay. The admissibility of traditional evidence was a question of law — a matter for the High Court. As counsel for the Islanders put it, 'the dilemma referred to by His Honour cannot be satisfactorily resolved until questions of law raised on the pleadings, and in particular, by the demurrer have been determined by the High Court'.[43]

One of the justifications for the Murray Islanders' counsel agreeing to the move to the Supreme Court of Queensland (known in legal language as the remitter court), was, in McIntyre's words, 'the Islanders wish to have the right to give evidence' (they couldn't do this in the High Court). After the first days of the Eddie Mabo's evidence-in-chief, it had become apparent to the Murray Islanders' counsel that, given the strategy being used by Queensland (and the judge's incapacity to rule against the constant objections), the continuation of the hearing of evidence might not offer Islanders 'the chance to present their case and so add to the strength of their community'.[44]

Moreover, the feeling was also growing among counsel for the Murray Islanders that the frequent interruption of witnesses, their subjection to behaviour which they may construe as ridicule, had become a fixed feature of the hearing. There was no certainty that the Murray Islanders would win their case, and the process they would be 'put through' would be unpleasant and probably belittling. A view had developed by at least one member of counsel that, while Mabo could handle the interruptions which sought to cast doubts on his credibility as a witness, other 'more traditional' Islanders living on Murray Island may not be equipped or confident to do so.[45]

On this basis and another consideration, the case was referred back to the High Court. The additional consideration, not unconnected with the course that events had begun to take in the Supreme Court of Queensland, concerned funds. On 27 March 1987, Greg McIntyre, instructing solicitor for the plaintiffs, was informed by officers of the Office of Legal Aid Administration, Attorney-General's Department, Canberra, that moneys being provided to the plaintiffs had been exhausted and that they would be recommending to the Attorney-General that no further funds be made available to them. A recommendation from the legal aid officers to the Attorney-General was foreshadowed, approving a grant in aid to the plaintiffs to fund proceedings in the High Court on questions of law. This related to logistical problems encountered in hearing the facts. This had originally been intended to take four weeks, but a further 11 weeks had been set aside in the first half of 1987. Justice Moynihan stated that this was probably not long enough to complete the hearing, and that there was unlikely to be court time available in the second half of 1987. Although each may have had different reasons, the state of Queensland, the plaintiffs, and Justice Moynihan were all in favour of determination of questions of law at this stage by the High Court.

The Attorney-General's Department had noted that a continued hearing of the facts with 27 Islander witnesses and six expert witnesses would incur a financial burden of an estimated further $200,000 if Queensland's continued objections to oral evidence were to be pursued at the previous rate.[46]

Following a hearing before Justice Toohey in the High Court on 3 April 1987, it was agreed that, should the Queensland Coast Islands Declaratory Act 1985 (the 1985 Act) be upheld by the Full Bench of the High Court as 'operative and having effect in relation to the alleged rights claimed by the plaintiffs in relation to land areas the subject of this action', the Murray Islanders undertook not to 'pursue any further proceedings' in pursuit of their claims.[47]

The hearing of the High Court was first set down six months ahead for mid-October 1987. Not long before that date it was postponed until mid-February 1988 and the hearing began eventually on 15 March 1988.

3 RIGHTS OF A KIND UNKNOWN TO ENGLISH LAW

TWO CATEGORIES OF LEGAL RIGHTS?

On Tuesday 15 March 1988, the Full Bench of the High Court began hearing arguments made by the Murray Islanders' senior counsel, Ron Castan, concerning the power of the state of Queensland to extinguish rights to land claimed by the Murray Islanders. The question of law which the High Court had been asked to decide was whether Queensland had the power to extinguish retrospectively customary rights in land which may have existed and been revived at the Murray Islands. Specifically, the court focused on the Murray Islanders' legal challenge (or demurrer) to the 1985 Act.

Section 3 of the 1985 Act contained provisions 'freeing' the islands from any pre-existing rights. Seeking to remove 'any doubt' about the effects of annexation of the islands to Queensland in 1879, it stated that the islands were vested in the Crown and therefore 'freed from all other rights, interests and claims of any kind whatsoever' thence becoming 'waste lands of the Crown in Queensland', subject to the laws of Queensland 'including Crown lands legislation' passed at any time and therefore able to 'be dealt with as Crown lands'.[1]

The overall result of the plaintiffs proceeding by way of demurrer was that the High Court was obliged to consider the legal consequences of the 1985 Act on the basis that the facts were as set out in the plaintiffs' statement of claim. The Murray Islanders' legal challenge assumed the existence of the rights and interests they were claiming. This posed a major problem for some members of the court. In Chief Justice Mason's view, this assumption 'unaccompanied [as it was] by a precise definition or description of the rights and interests' claimed, presented 'a formidable obstacle to the resolution of the issues' debated by the court.[2] Justices Brennan, Toohey and Gaudron, on the other hand, were agreed that for the purposes of the hearing, the traditional legal rights claimed by the Murray Islanders remained 'in existence unless they have been validly extinguished by the 1985 Act'.[3]

In a fundamental sense, the question of law before the High Court was quite new for Australia. As senior counsel for the Murray Islanders, Ron Castan, pointed out to the court, the 1985 Act was novel in the sense that 'there are no cases dealing with the equivalent of a 1985 Act' (Transcript (T)146). The very hypothesis that rights to land may exist at the Murray Islands made a break with legal tradition in Australia, for it introduced the notion of acknowledging and respecting rights to land which are of a kind unknown to English–Australian law. The High Court justices were placed at the cutting edge of legal pluralism, and, as we shall see, it was on the equivalence or otherwise of these presumed and unknown legal rights to land to those of English law that the court divided very sharply.

From the perspective of the Meriam people, the question before the court was whether they had the same right as other Australian citizens to follow their own interests in land and to have these respected even though the rights they claimed were different to those existing under English law.

TRESPASSING ON FACTS OF HISTORY?

Through their legal counsel, the Murray Islanders challenged forcefully the provisions of the 1985 Act on four grounds.[4] The overall thrust of their argument was that even if the 1985 Act was effective in extinguishing any rights that may have existed in 1879, they could point to a wide range of evidence that Queensland had since then dealt with them in ways which recognised the rights being claimed by Mabo, Passi and Rice. Paragraph 13 of the plaintiffs' statement of claim stated that since the proclamation of British sovereignty over the islands, the rights of the plaintiffs 'have been recognised and continued' by the Crown and by Queensland.

The first of the broad areas in which the Murray Islanders argued was that the 1985 Act was inconsistent with provisions of the Commonwealth Racial Discrimination Act (RDA) 1975, a contention which came to be pivotal to the High Court's decision. The second concerned the denial of fundamental rights to property in land protected in English law since the signing of the Magna Carta in 1354: 'That no man of what Estate or Condition that he be shall be put out of Land or Tenement without being brought in Answer by due Process of the Law'. The third area of argument was that, in the 1985 Act, Queensland went beyond its constitutional powers in seeking to effect a change in sovereignty. The constitution of the colony provides that the lands are vested in the Crown, 'subject to rights of occupants preserved by Imperial legislation'. Only the British parliament can take away such rights and Britain had bought land from the Murray Islanders and legislated as if the latter had proprietary rights. Here counsel relied on the judgment of Justice Hall in the *Calder* case (1973) (Canada), which stated that

> original native title . . . must be presumed to exist unless the contrary is established by the context or the circumstances . . . It being a legal title it could not therefore be extinguished except by surrender to the Crown or by competent legislative authority, and then only by specific legislation . . . Any inhabitant of the territory can make good in the municipal courts established by the new sovereign only such rights as that sovereign has . . . recognised. *In inquiring, however, what rights are recognised . . . the courts will assume that the British Crown intends that the rights of property of the inhabitants are to be fully respected . . . even though those interests are of a kind unknown to English law.*[5]

The fourth argument was that the 1985 Act was not effective in extinguishing the rights claimed. In 1982 when the Murray Islanders brought the claim, and at the time when the 1985 Act was passed, it was argued, there was demonstrable evidence that the rights existed. Even if the 1985 Act took effect in 1879, vesting the islands in the Crown in right of Queensland and freeing them from other rights and interests, 'there has been a subsequent revival of, creation of, restoration of customary rights and interests' Ron Castan argued cogently in the High Court on 16 March 1988 (T141). Assuming the effectiveness of the 1985 Act in extinguishing the interests of persons in 1879, it 'does not operate to bar the plaintiffs' claims'; the rights claimed to exist today are not those of *persons* whose interests were operating before 1879. In other words, the legislation is addressed to persons living in 1879, not 'to the present plaintiffs'. It is 'the body of law', a system 'pre-existing annexation', the plaintiffs submitted, that continues (T141). As McIntyre summed up the argument later: 'The way we described it to the Court is as a resumption of the right to land. If it was extinguished in 1879 by operation of the 1985 Act, then it was revived and continued to be reinforced by the Queensland Government.'[6]

Plaintiffs' counsel presented two kinds of evidence that the Queensland government had dealt with Murray Islanders in ways consistent with recognition of rights to land claimed by the plaintiffs. The first was that the Queensland government set up courts in Murray Island in which land disputes between Meriam landowners were resolved in accordance with local laws and customs. 'Over 400 Murray Island Court decisions and transactions', the plaintiffs argued, 'recognise the restoration of claimed traditional native interests in land, as customary rights of the Common laws from annexation until the issue of the writ'.[7] Moreover, officers of the Queensland government charged with the administration of island affairs sat on such courts of appeal at Murray Island, appending their signatures on behalf of the government to court judgments on land cases which dealt with traditional rights to land.

The second kind of evidence of post-annexation recognition of indigenous interests in land was that the Queensland government bought land from time to time from Meriam traditional landowners. The purchase of three portions of land by the government at the village of Zeub, Mer, for a gaolhouse, courthouse and recreation reserve in September 1913 for the sum of £6.0.0 is a case in point.[8] The signature of Jack Bruce, the government representative on the island, upon the transaction for the sale of land from the three traditional owners, was claimed by the plaintiffs as an act of recognition by the Crown of customary rights to land in the post-annexation period. Counsel for the plaintiffs explained to the court the existence of this record of sale of land in 1913, the year after Murray Island had been declared a reserve by Act of parliament.

Following the finding of this record at Mer in February 1982, the plaintiffs' counsel had visited Mer and themselves made the 'exciting discovery' of 'a body of jurisprudence' of the Murray Islanders in the form of 400 judgments 'based on the traditional land tenure system'.[9] Together known as the Murray Island Court Book, the judgments were part of a set of the written records of the Murray Island Native Court established by the Queensland government. Counsel had these bound into a book which they presented to the High Court as part of their evidence of the post-1879 recognition by the government of proprietary rights in land among the Meriam. The Court Book contained cases where Pat Killoran, C O'Leary (who preceded him as Director of the Department of Aboriginal and Islanders Advancement), and earlier again, a series of government teacher-superintendents at Mer, had witnessed those decisions and sat on courts of appeal there, approving under their respective signatures those decisions which dealt with traditional rights in land according to Meriam customary law.

Counsel drew the High Court's attention to 'the legislative framework' in which the Murray Island court had 'been constituted' and the basis upon which it had made the decisions recorded in the Court Book and developed the body of Meriam jurisprudence (T140). Acts of 'legislative recognition' which go back to statutes of 1886, were presented in a series of items by counsel seeking to show that the Murray Island 'court has, in fact been deciding and resolving issues on the island upon the basis that the persons before it were owners according to tradition' (T140).

The evidence presented creates 'a picture', it was contended, 'of a constant recognition of the customary rights' of the Meriam since 1879, in two main ways: first by legal structure, by the establishment of a series of statutory instruments; and second, 'by the actual operation of the dispute resolving mechanism' — the court. Evidence of the long-term operation of that 'mechanism' was presented to the court by the plaintiffs as a Court Book containing a 'body of jurisprudence' belonging to the Meriam community 'recorded in writing and available to be observed' (T140).

The legislative history called upon by the plaintiffs is substantial, dating from 1897 through to 1980. The Acts passed provided for the creation of a local court at Mer 'to determine matters in accordance with custom' (T114). These events, consequent on Queensland legislation over a long period, 'cannot go away' or be forgotten; in a later era, 'Parliament can declare laws but Parliament cannot change what has occurred. And what has occurred here includes legislative history' (T114). An interchange between the Murray Islanders' counsel and Justice Brennan helps to clarify this argument that no legislation can erase historical events:

Mr Castan:	The problem with it is that there are facts of . . . 'executive history' or 'executive conduct' that have occurred in the intervening 106 years. Legislation cannot make these facts go away . . .
Justice Brennan:	But does not that really bring you to the point of saying that this Act, in its form, goes beyond what is legislative power? Legislative power does not extend to saying that black is white and it certainly does not extend to saying it retrospectively. But if the declaratory form is used by legislature it can be used to declare what the law is or shall be or, perhaps, what the law was, but that this Act goes beyond saying what the law is or shall be or, perhaps, even what the law was and trespasses upon facts of history. Is that your proposition?
Mr Castan:	Yes, it is, Your Honour . . . [The 1985 Act] is an attempt to do what no Parliament can do. Parliament

> can declare laws but Parliament cannot change what has occurred. And what has occurred here includes legislative history . . .
>
> No sweep of the legislative pen, we would respectfully submit, by the passage of this kind of legislation can extinguish the fact of that prior legislation. It can cause it to cease to operate but it cannot cause it to vanish or to go off the statute books and it cannot cause the fact of the purchasers [*sic*] to go away [T113–14].

An aspect of legislative history with far-reaching consequences for the Murray Islanders' claim is the Torres Strait Islanders Act 1939, the first Act to legislate for the Torres Strait Islanders as a separate people. Section 18(1) delegated 'the functions of local government of the reserve' to the Murray Island council, elected by the community every three years, which was charged under the Act 'with the good rule and government of the reserve in accordance with *island customs and practices*' (emphasis added). Furthermore, the council 'shall have power to make by-laws for such good rule and government and to cause all such by-laws to be observed and carried out' (s18[1]). These by-laws pertain to a range of matters including 'subdivision of land and use and occupation of land' (s18[3]).

The 1939 Act gave the Murray Island council the power to constitute the island court by a majority of council members (s20). Court records, it stated, shall be entered in a 'court book', a book in the custody of council, the particulars entered in it being prescribed by the by-laws.

These provisions of the 1939 Act, which formalised indirect rule in the Torres Strait Islands as a whole, legitimated certain provisions with respect to courts which had their origins in the delegation of powers in 1886 to a headman or *mamus* and his assistants, to settle disputes on customary land boundaries, on trespass on others' land or theft of fruit. The provisions were also carried through legislation subsequent to the 1939 Act, at least in their basic form, and they were supplemented by by-laws in later Acts. The main difference in subsequent Acts is some dilution of indirect rule. Thus for example, the 1965 Act replaced the words 'delegated to it' (1939, 18[1]) by 'and may exercise'.

The additions relevant here relate to community by-laws to the Torres Strait Islanders Act 1971, which provided for a survey of land (no 33), 'Register of Allotments' (no 34), the transmission of land on the death or permanent departure of a holder 'in accordance with native custom' (no 35), and the leaving and making of wills (no 38), which gave to the court the power to 'distribute the land and property of a deceased Islander by native custom' of registered holders of land. This power also included the right to hear and determine disputes by the Island court, the proceedings being required to 'be recorded in the Court Book' (no 38).[10] This was the period in which the customary law of the Meriam and other Torres Strait Islanders was being codified in written form. Thus we shall see in the following chapters, in the Supreme Court of Queensland, James Rice refers to his intention of making a will according to 'traditional ways' (TQ1532). Highly significant is the manner in which the enactment of English law — written wills, land survey, the registration of allotments — are all required by Queensland statutory law to be carried out in accordance with Murray Island custom.

If the 1886 regulations mentioned above gave a minimum expression to the operation of local rules and customs, it was only the 1939 Act which gave full expression to an indirect rule in accordance with island customs and practices. This included the court's role in relation to the occupation, use and demarcation of land boundaries. The Court Book showed numbers of cases of decisions on land disputes before 1939, and it recorded the sale of land to the Crown in 1913 under the signature of the government representative upon the island.

In the period between 1904 and 1939, notwithstanding the uninterrupted operation of the court and the formalisation of direct government powers over the island in 1912, the powers of the government teacher in relation to the council had increased, culminating in 1934 in the Aboriginal Protection Amendment Act, under which those powers became virtually total.

The inter-island strike of 1936 reversed all that in a 'New Law'. In 1982 the Meriam plaintiffs were aided very materially by the direct actions of the Meriam in the 1936–37 period. Without the gains of that strike, the Meriam case for the recognition of customary law would have lost much of its strength, for the delegation of powers to council and court according to island customs and practices, expressed in statutory form in the 1939 Act, was a direct result of the strike. The Meriam leader Marou Mimi was a leader of that strike.[11]

Thus, whatever the freeing of 'other rights' that might have occurred under annexation in 1879, 'the system of law' at the Murray Islands, counsel submitted, 'is not touched by the annexation or the 1985 Act'.[12] The common law was introduced, yes, but 'otherwise the [Meriam] system of law continued' (T144). That system meant 'the interests of the native owners [existed] as a burden upon the title of the Crown', that 'burden' 'being the ownership by native interests capable of extinguishment' (T145), counsel submitted, following the terminology used in the *Calder* case and the case of *Guerin v the Queen*.[13]

At times the court experienced difficulty in grasping the complexities of the argument. This difficulty is illustrated by the following interchange between Justice Dawson and Ron Castan upon the same argument as that which he had sought to clarify for Justice Brennan a little earlier: that the Meriam rights had been revived when the writ was issued in 1982 and at the time the legislation was passed.

Justice Dawson:	It is a curious conception, Mr Castan. You are really resurrecting these rights retrospectively, are you not?
Mr Castan:	No, we are not resurrecting them retrospectively.
Justice Dawson:	You see, the Act is retrospect[ive] in its declaration and it eliminates them and you do not deny that it eliminates those rights.
Mr Castan:	For the purposes of this argument, yes, Your Honour.
Justice Dawson:	Yes. Now, somehow they have got to be resurrected again.
Mr Castan:	That is not the analysis, with respect, Your Honour. All that one draws from that is that in 1985 this was not effective. The net result of that is to say this did not work . . .

Mr Castan then referred again to the 'whole range of statutory instruments' established under Acts of parliament. The interchange continued.

Justice Dawson:	Well, that is what you must be saying, the Act is entirely ineffective?
Mr Castan:	It is ineffective in this context.
Justice Dawson:	Had no operation at all?

Mr Castan:	It had operation, that is not the position, Your Honour, with respect. It had operation in relation to the rights of persons in 1879 . . .
Justice Dawson:	So at that point momentarily they are extinguished but they are immediately revived in the same way.
Mr Castan:	No, we do not necessarily seek to say they immediately revive, and that is why we have drawn attention to the pattern of the whole legislative framework over a period of time. We say they are revived in 1982 when this writ was issued and revived certainly in 1985 when this legislation was passed. The position, with respect, is that it does not deny an effect on the legislation, but it says it is totally ineffectual in terms of this action and that is why we say it is demurrable.
Justice Dawson:	But, you see, that it is to deny the situation. You do not have the benefit of legislation for that part of the argument. These did not revive at all; they were always there . . .

'Retrospective legislation' cannot annul previous legislation unless it specifically sets out to do so, Mr Castan replied. That would mean stating that all decisions of the Murray Island court, 'every transfer recorded in accordance with the court book', are 'all set at nought' (T147–48).

THE MEANINGS OF EQUALITY BEFORE THE LAW

In a closely divided judgment of four to three, the High Court ruled on 8 December 1988 that the Murray Islanders were precluded from enjoying their traditional legal rights while other Australians were left unaffected by the 1985 Act (*Mabo [No 1]*). Certain provisions of the Commonwealth Racial Discrimination Act 1975, which guarantees equality before the law, were decisive in upholding the Murray Islanders' challenge to the 1985 Act. Following article 17 of the United Nations Declaration on Human Rights, section 10 of the RDA identifies and upholds the right to own and inherit property, and not to be deprived of that property arbitrarily.

The court was making a hypothetical recognition of Meriam property rights, and these were taken to be a second category of property rights which were presumed to be on a par with Anglo–Australian rights in land. In a country still bound by the legal fiction of Australia as *terra nullius*, this decision was a milestone in the development of law in Australia.

The division between the majority and the minority view hinged upon the issue of whether the court's decision was contingent upon, or separable from, the precise character of the rights claimed by the plaintiffs. The majority — Justices Brennan, Toohey and Gaudron in a joint judgment and Justice Deane in a separate decision — felt themselves able to separate their decision on the legality of the 1985 Act from the issues of fact yet to be determined in the Supreme Court of Queensland. The minority — Chief Justice Mason and Justices Wilson and Dawson — concluded that the arguments being put by the contestants were inextricably bound up with whether the rights asserted existed at the time of the 1985 Act, with whether those rights really are rights to own and inherit, and if so, whether those rights are *equivalent* to those enjoyed by other Australians under English common law. In this view the 1985 Act was not in breach of section 10 of the RDA because the plaintiffs had not demonstrated that the rights they were claiming constitute property rights equivalent to those enjoyed by other persons in Queensland.

Thus the core difference between the majority and the minority judgments lies in the power of the imagination to entertain the possibility that rights of a kind claimed by the plaintiffs could be 'matched' with those intrinsic to Anglo–Australian law. The majority expressed an entirely new position, which recognises the right to own and inherit in ways qualitatively different from those recognised in Australia before. Because the contrasting arguments are of great consequence in the development of legal thinking in Australia, which culminated in June 1992 with the High Court's recognition of native title (considered in Chapter 9), I shall give a brief account of the respective arguments and conclusions, to some extent in the justices' own words.

Justices Brennan, Toohey and Gaudron stated that the intention of the 1985 Act, 'is to extinguish the rights which the plaintiffs claim in their traditional homeland', an effect they described as 'Draconian' (Mabo [No 1], 213). For the purposes of making a decision on the 1985 Act they were being asked to assume that 'two categories of legal rights' are recognised by Queensland law 'in and over the Murray Islands: traditional rights and rights granted in pursuance of Crown lands legislation' (218). Their opinion was that the 1985 Act precludes the Meriam people from enjoying some or all 'of their legal rights in and over the Murray Islands' (218). Non-Murray Islanders, on the other hand, are left 'unaffected in enjoyment of their legal rights in and over the Murray Islands' (218), presumably as a result of their role as beneficiaries of that Crown lands legislation which nullified any traditional Meriam property rights by declaring those islands 'waste lands of the Crown'.

The interpretation made by Justices Brennan, Toohey and Gaudron of the proviso accepted by the court at the outset (that it should not comment on the existence or survival of the rights at issue), is one which accords the assumed traditional rights 'the status of recognised legal rights under Queensland law' (218). In other words, for the purposes of the legal argument, those traditional rights, unknown and as yet unsubstantiated as they were at this stage (in 1988) until the evidence was heard, sifted and the facts determined (in 1990), were taken to be property rights *broadly equivalent* to the rights deriving from English law enjoyed by other Australian citizens.

In contrast, each of the three minority judgments placed a proviso upon the agreement made which amounted to saying the task set at this stage was impossible. Each raised the question of the need to ascertain the equivalence or otherwise of the rights alleged by the plaintiffs with those conferred by English law. Are the factual circumstances comparable?, Justice Wilson asked. Do the rights asserted constitute rights to property within the meaning of the Racial Discrimination Act?, Chief Justice Mason queried. To attempt to resolve the legal issues raised in the Murray Islanders' challenge at this point, Chief Justice Mason concluded, 'would require the Court to make assumptions on matters of fact instead of allowing issues of fact to be determined in the ordinary way' (196).

In his judgment, which sought to overrule the demurrer, Chief Justice Mason argued that the purpose of section 10 of the RDA is 'to bring about equality before the law', and of section 9 'to prohibit racial discrimination' (198). In order to bring section 10 into operation, the Chief Justice argued, the Murray Islanders must show that the 1985 Act produces inequality before the law. They would have to demonstrate that the rights and interests they assert constitute rights to property and inheritance within the meaning of Article 5, paragraph (d), of the International Convention on the Elimination of All Forms of Racial Discrimination, on which section 10 of the RDA is based. They would also need to show that these rights 'are equivalent to rights and interests pursued by persons of another race' (199).

Justice Wilson's central argument focused on the uniqueness of Murray Island law, but less on its equality or otherwise with the law enjoyed by other Australians. In being more formally logical, one might say that his judgment is also more legalistic. Since 'the plaintiffs were alone in the enjoyment of traditional rights', as their statement of claim discloses, the 1985 Act does not deprive them of rights enjoyed by persons of any other race. Hence, far from producing an inequality between them and other citizens, the practical effect of depriving them of their traditional rights 'is to remove a source of inequality' (206) and put them on a par with other Queenslanders.

As an expression of formal logic this argument has a certain cogency. Behind that formality lies the assumption that there is only one law — English law. That assumption rules out completely a second category of law which the Murray Islanders were seeking to demonstrate.

Justice Dawson's main line of reasoning was similar to that of Chief Justice Mason: each centred upon the need to determine the equivalence or otherwise of the rights claimed by the Murray Islanders. Justice Dawson said that if Meriam rights are different to those enjoyed by other persons in Queensland, then to deprive them 'of those rights would not necessarily be to deprive them of rights enjoyed by persons of another race' and therefore would not contravene section 10 of the RDA. He foreshadowed the possibility of an argument that the land rights claimed represent 'rights of ownership equivalent to the rights of ownership enjoyed by others, albeit in a different form' (243). However, the foundation of such an argument rests upon 'a conclusion upon evidence concerning the nature and extent of the rights alleged by the plaintiffs' (243).

The hypothesis in all three minority judgments is that the cultural difference to which the Meriam plaintiffs gave expression carries an intrinsic cultural inferiority, that their 'law' may be inferior to the 'real' law of Anglo-Australian tradition. Hence the task set them — that of assuming the existence of the traditional Meriam rights claimed — is an impossible one. For unless the factual circumstances of the Murray Islanders are equivalent to those of other Australians, the assumption of formal legal equality of the two sets of rights may have the effect of entrenching inequality to a disadvantaged group. Thus to uphold the plaintiffs' stated claim to the right to exercise their land law is to discriminate against them. This may be to suggest that the Murray Islander claimants do not know what is best for them, that unbeknownst to themselves, their insistence on the right to their cultural difference may be a form of self-deprivation.

Such an interpretation may be borne out by the continuity between the arguments pursued by the minority here (in *Mabo [No 1]*) and those made by Justice Dawson in his minority judgment in June 1992 (*Mabo [No 2]*). In the latter judgment, the difference is one of interpretation of the Meriam rights identified by Justice Moynihan in November 1990 in the Supreme Court of Queensland. There is more than a suggestion that because the rights found among the Murray Islanders do not fit the categories of English law they cannot be counted as rights at all. This position retains a recognisable continuity with the position inherent within the doctrine of *terra nullius* — that the Meriam are too primitive to have rights to land comparable with those of English law.

In summing up the reasons for the procedure of establishing at this stage of the case whether or not rights claimed by the Murray Islanders were extinguished by the 1985 Act, Chief Justice Mason noted that its 'suggested advantage' is that, should Queensland's case that the Act is valid be proven, there would be no need to continue the complex, time-consuming and financially draining hearings of fact begun in the Supreme Court of Queensland. Yet the advantage of this course 'of resolving the demurrer is illusory', the Chief Justice continued, because '. . . if the plaintiffs ultimately are to succeed in the action, at some stage they must establish the existence and nature of those rights and interests' (196).

However, there is an implicit irony in all three minority decisions proposing that the equivalence or otherwise of the rights claimed by the plaintiffs with common law rights be tested by hearing the evidence. For, as noted in Chapter 2, should the demurrer have been overruled, there would have been no opportunity to hear the evidence, as the agreement made was that, should the High Court uphold the 1985 Act in respect to the rights claimed, the Murray Islanders would refrain from pursuing their claim. The case would have ended at this point. Given the decision of the majority, the proceedings moved back to a hearing of evidence in the Supreme Court of Queensland.

FORESHADOWING NATIVE TITLE

In its narrow interpretation, 'equality before the law' denies the right to cultural difference in legal rights, for its implicit premise is homogeneity: attainment of legal equality presupposes the relinquishment of rights differing qualitatively from those recognised by the Crown. The alternative view places emphasis upon the human right to own and inherit, where rights to property 'are of a kind unknown to English law'. As we have seen, this was the position taken by Justice Hall in the *Calder* case (1973) in the Supreme Court of Canada and, given the majority judgment of 8 December 1988, a view also being followed by the High Court.

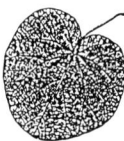

The following two parts — Meriam Perspectives and European Perspectives — present contrasting perceptions of the same events. These events were the proceedings of the Supreme Court of Queensland in the hearing of the evidence or 'facts' before Justice Moynihan. As I have indicated at the end of Chapter 2, these hearings actually began in October 1986, and were then postponed on 17 November until May 1989. Because those early days of the hearing, held before the High Court proceedings in 1988 just discussed, are integral to the later hearing, they are considered together (see Chronology I).

The main actors enter, exit and reenter the court performance. In this interlocked dialogue, the focus was on Meriam law and custom: was there a system of Meriam law and had it survived?

English law distinguishes two mutually exclusive categories of rights: public rights (the 'communal rights' claimed by the Yolngu in the *Milirrpum* case) and private rights (the 'individual rights' claimed in this case). Through a presentation of evidence given by Meriam witnesses, the next chapter (which opens Part Two, Meriam Perspectives) seeks to demonstrate that the statement 'I am the owner' has a different meaning in Meriam law and culture to that given it by English law. That difference is a central peg on which hangs a complex of differences misunderstood by the presiding judge in the Supreme Court of Queensland. Part Three, European Perspectives, opens with a consideration of cultural contrasts on the meaning of law and evidence.

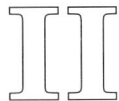

MERIAM PERSPECTIVES

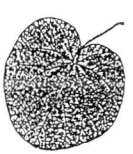

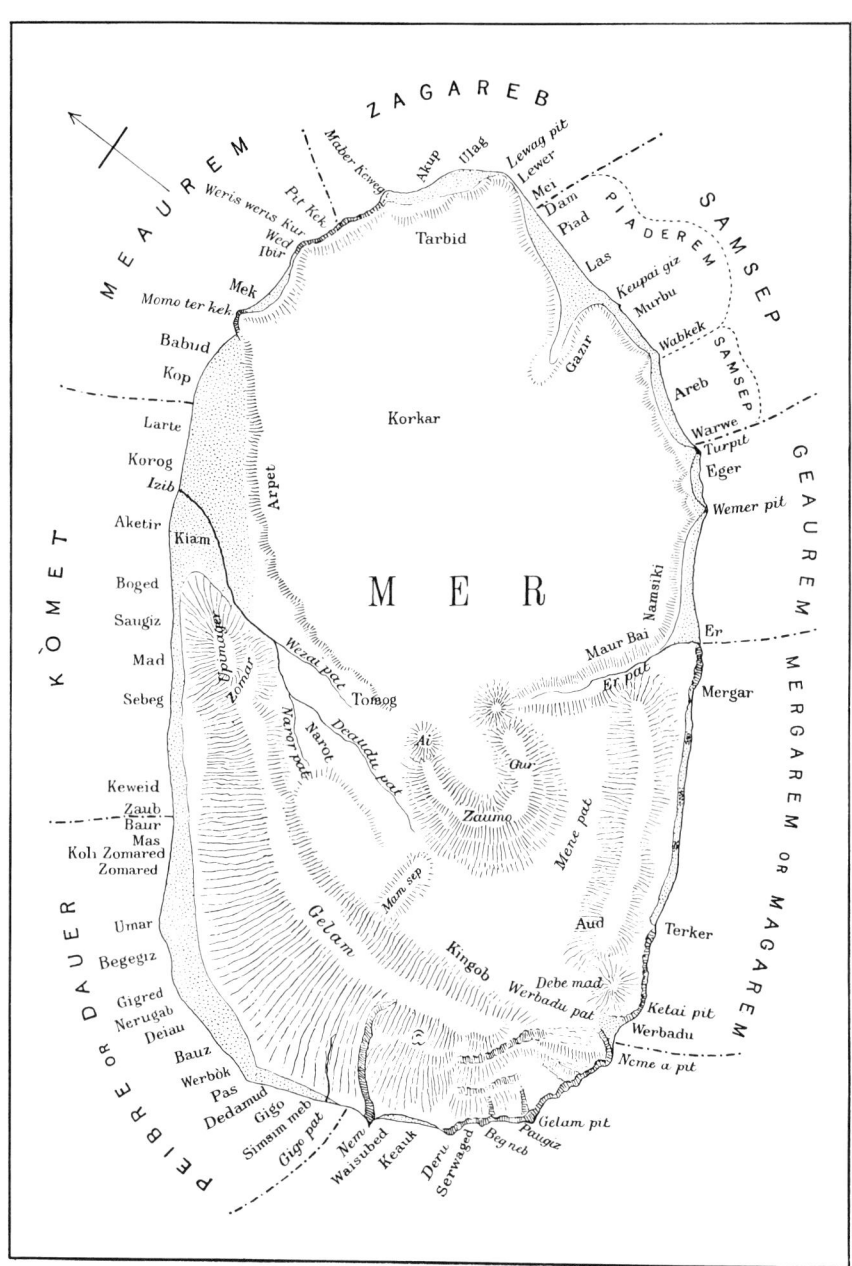

Map 2 Sketch map of the island of Mer (from Haddon 1908)

4. MY FATHER GAVE ME ALL THE RIGHTS AND EVERY RESPONSIBILITY

THE MERIAM IN COURT

THE FIRST PLAINTIFF: EDWARD KOIKI MABO

Brisbane, October 1986. The first plaintiff sat in the Supreme Court of Queensland, hands clasped. He was explaining to the court in very good English how he came to know that part of Malo's Law which says, 'Keep off other people's land, *Teter mauki mauki* . . . Malo keeps his hands to himself, *Tag mauki mauki*, He does not touch the property of others'. He believed himself to be a descendant of the *Zogo le*, the sacred people of Malo. His name was Edward Koiki Mabo and he was born at Mer on 29 June 1936. He had lived away from the Murray Islands since he was a young adult, at first voluntarily and later as an exile, being prevented from visiting Mer until 1977.[1] He was politically radical and a staunch upholder of the Malo tradition.

His Piadram clan have been noted gardeners from times predating Malo. Ancient Piadram tradition is distilled in the myth of the Muiar, a gardening people with a code of behaviour respecting the land and the rights of other landowners, which was incorporated into the religious order of the Meriam known as Malo-Bomai. A sacred and fundamental principle of behaviour for the Meriam people, the code was known as Malo ra Gelar, Malo's Law.[2]

In his evidence-in-chief, Mabo explained to the court how, as a growing boy, he came to internalise and respect it as a way of life. He also showed how, at the same time as he was absorbing the Meriam social values of respecting others' land, he was also reinforcing what he had been told about his own land and its boundaries. He explained how his grandfather had taken him to the village of Las and shown him his land boundaries and his fish traps (TQ191, 196). He recalled two events which illustrated for him how Malo's Law is woven into the fabric of social life. The first concerns the rule his mother had taught him that, if he trespassed on another person's land, something bad would befall him. Mabo related how he took a short cut through someone else's land without asking permission. While he was there he identified a *maid le*, that is a person who practises hostile magic: 'I ran for my life . . . and came to my mum' (TQ247), who hardly needed to re-emphasise that he stay away from other people's land in future. In the second example, the plaintiff related an event he witnessed as a boy when his father rebuked another Meriam for pulling up wild yam (*ketai*) and leaving the holes open rather than covering them in (TQ240). These are learning experiences; they are also vivid illustrations of how the young Mabo personally witnessed the potency of Malo's Law in the eyes of his family.

He told the court how his grandfather explained to him in Meriam Mir how a particular 'post was the boundary marker of what we call in our language *nener elikup*' (TQ200); of other kinds of boundary markers such as 'a clump of stones' with a stone in the middle larger than the rest, 'which represents the boundary marker and that can be aligned with another stone marker further on, about 200 yards . . . inland' (TQ208); of how, '*meriba ged*' or 'our land', came to be handed down through five generations to his father (TQ214); of the various conversations about land with his grandfather before his death in 1948 (TQ224); of how his grandfather told him, 'If your father will get old you will take his land like he did when I got old' (TQ225); that a special place called Muiar 'was a peaceful place for the *zogo le* [priests of Malo] to be buried' (TQ226); of the myth of Malo (TQ231–33); and of the Muiar or law-makers, who defined the land boundaries and whose own behaviour foreshadowed Malo's Law against trespassers on other people's properties (TQ233).

Eddie Mabo explained how his grandfather had told him that, after the missionaries arrived, the men continued to participate in Malo initiation ceremonies in secret because the missionaries threatened to kill them if they caught them doing this. The last such ceremony, which his grandfather had attended, took place about 1922.[3] Mabo recalled his grandfather saying that the boys were taught 'the laws and principles of Malo' (TQ249) and the 'correct use of land plus the method of cultivation' (TQ249). When Mabo himself was nine or ten years old he was taken with other boys and first taught 'play dances', myths such as that of Gelam, who formed the isle of Mer in the shape of a dugong, and the history of Malo (TQ250). When he was about 15 years old, the dances became more serious because they 'had the *zogo* [sacred, religious] flavour' (TQ252), and they learnt many dances and songs about the sacred ceremonies of Malo and Bomai (TQ252). He recalled one session in which he was among the boys of the older of two groups, spending four weeks receiving instructions on the laws of Malo and how they should be applied, about behaviour towards other males and towards women, how to tend gardens, the right season to plant, the signs to watch (TQ251).

Given the long time he had spent away from the Murray Islands, some people may have been surprised to find Mabo explaining Meriam custom and demonstrating how he had come to know it; in the course of giving his evidence he also revealed his socialisation in Meriam Mir, the language of the Meriam. Who was Edward Koiki Mabo?

I first met Eddie Mabo at the office of the Black Community School in Townsville in December 1980. This was a time of cultural revival among the Meriam. It was also the time when the Queensland government had announced plans to repeal the Torres Strait Islanders Act and to abolish the 'reserves'. I found our ideas on politics and culture meshed and, whatever may have been his perception, he readily agreed to record his life story as part of a project to create a picture of Torres Strait Island culture through a mosaic of life stories given in 'the active voice', something new for the Torres Strait Islands at that time.[4]

His core idea was to establish a school at Mer which combined the best of both Meriam and European Australian cultural traditions. The idea had

The late Edward Koiki Mabo with Bonita Mabo, Brisbane, 1986

its origins in his early socialisation in the Meriam way and in the awareness he gained through his schoolteacher at Mer, Robert Miles, from whom he learned the 'cultural value' that Kole or white culture had to offer. As a young man he 'went south' in search of that knowledge. His idea for a school independent of the Department of Aboriginal and Islanders Advancement, which at that time ran a special school system for people under 'the Act', was suddenly given a chance for practical realisation in Townsville in the early 1970s. At a meeting of trainee teachers he requested the help of those present in this project. It was proper, he said, that 'we have our own school because we're culturally different'. Opinion divided sharply and this occasion marked Eddie Mabo's moment of truth:

> I got up and did my dance.
> Everyone stood on their feet and I walked out . . .

'I really thumped the floor . . .', he told me, laughing softly. In Meriam dancing, the foot comes down firmly, making a strong encounter with the earth.

Three weeks later, the Black Community School opened in Townsville with eight students and two white teachers.[5] Through his practical experience of cultural comparison and contrast, Eddie Mabo reflexively developed his vision of establishing a school at Mer in the tradition of the *Zogo le*, or priests of Malo-Bomai — 'an *Aets*' school' as he described it to me then.[6] His father, Benny Mabo, had instructed him in the tradition of his Piadram clan and Meriam culture in the face-to-face life of the daily round and ceremonial occasion. His mother, Maiga Mabo, acquainted him with the traditions she wrote down, and she stood out in his memory as a distinctive woman: 'Amongst all the baskets and mats . . . [the women wove] I could pick out my mother's ones. They were so different', he said to me, his voice suddenly growing softer.[7] He sought out the *Reports of the Cambridge Anthropological Expedition to Torres Straits,* he looked to Kole choral societies and the arts for inspiration, he was drawn to 'the Oxford system of English', and he found friends who gave 'moral support' to his ideas and helped to increase his self-confidence.[8]

Out of the paradoxes of a complex life, he knotted together his experiences of two cultures into an articulate and courageous vision of the future of the Meriam people which, in the manner of the Meriam, he sought to translate into practice. True to his commitment to a form of change which combined the written with the oral, he did not shrink from a contradiction implicit in the idea of an '*Aets* school', recording and implementing a living Meriam oral culture. He believed one might retain its core by writing it down, even though 'there are some things that . . . can only be expressed by people [orally]'. In his vision, the school at Mer would 'link back' to the authority of the *Zogo le* through their descendants, of which he was one: 'we're going to work back to the way we control our education by the *Aets* of Mer'.[9] In preparation for this event, with seven children still growing up, he became a trainee teacher at James Cook University.

In the years between 1980 and Eddie Mabo's death in January 1992, I had no reason to question his belief that he was truly the adopted son of Benny and Maiga Mabo. He used to say to me how he carried the tradition of the *Zogo le* from both sides of his family: through his adopted father, Benny Mabo and through Benny's sister, Paipe, who died soon after giving birth to Eddie. I admired his sincerity, his honesty, his belief in the integrity of Meriam culture, his vision. I did not interpret his genealogical claim to authority among the Meriam in the literal way he probably interpreted it. To a greater or lesser degree the authority of the *Zogo le*, or *Aets,* as he called them, had been effaced by the actions of missionaries and government authorities; his own authority had been marginalised by his partly unintended long absence from Mer. Were the Meriam to come to take his cultural authority seriously, as I saw it, he would have to seek their confidence in the process of face to face living over a period.

As events during the court case were to verify, in a very literal way, Eddie Mabo took himself to be one of those on whom rested the mantle of Malo-Bomai and their hereditary priests. The 65-page statement of evidence prepared for the court on the basis of his instructions to his lawyers strongly assumes that.[10]

Eddie Mabo believed passionately that he should restore the standing of the *Zogo le* of Malo. He aired his view of the 'divine right' of the *Aets* at a land conference in Townsville in 1981. The *Aet*, he said, 'is much the same as you have King of England who was the defender of your Christian faith . . . the upholder of our laws, the defender of *Malo-Bomai* cult and the *Au zogo zogo le*, the central figure of all the sacred people'.[11]

Eddie searched for knowledge about his own culture. In what may seem to be a paradoxical way, in seeking to know the best of Kole culture, he developed his own Meriam identity. Jeremy Beckett depicts him as 'a particularly attentive child' with an inquiring mind, a person seeking after diverse avenues of knowledge: 'In the long run, I suspect, what he had heard as a child, what he heard in Townsville, and what he read in books at the university, became a single web of traditional knowledge'.[12] He treasured that knowledge as a man who believed himself to be a carrier and a custodian of Meriam cultural tradition. That conviction, interwoven with his passionate belief in the moral and historical rightness of *Mabo and Others*, as he (always) referred to the case, did not falter to the end of his life.

THE MERIAM WITNESSES

On Friday 17 October 1986, during the opening of the Murray Islanders' case, senior counsel informed the court that more than 20 Meriam witnesses were ready to give evidence in support of claims being made by the plaintiffs: the court had a copy of Eddie Mabo's statement and Justice Moynihan noted that 'other witnesses are to say more of the same' (TQ62). All of them were ready to identify lands handed down to them, all of them were claiming to live according to a set of principles which leading Meriam identified as Malo's Law. The oral evidence to be presented was outlined to the court by senior counsel:

> The witnesses will describe their earliest childhood experiences, especially those relating to land and planting: how their grandfathers and fathers, or their grandmothers or mothers showed the way planting occurred and what happened; about the clearing of the land for planting; about boundaries; about where they came from and their lines of succession.

Outside the Supreme Court of Queensland, 1986: (from left) Ron Castan QC, witness Robert Pitt, Greg McIntyre

These were their 'traditional rights' to plots of land which had been handed down to them; they were ready to recount the way in which they had come to know the boundaries of the various plots of land they took to be theirs.

Through the accumulation of successive evidence, it was argued, the existence of an overall system of rights to land, inheritance, occupation, use and enjoyment would become apparent to the court:

> The witnesses will recount how they came to know Malo's Law, its content and what it required them to do, their obligations particularly in relation to land. They will recount how they wish to deal with land which they see as belonging to them; the means by which they claim to own certain lands, how they came to know about them and how they came to be the owners.[13]

These two categories — chains of title and the existence of a system of law — may be seen to overlap: evidence from a wide range of witnesses, each about his or her claims to interest in land, may create an overall picture or mosaic of rights in land (TQ142; cf TQ149).

Counsel's perspective was consistent with the idea which plaintiff James Rice explained later to the court: if each plaintiff has 'the right', then because all other landowners could bring the same rights to the court, he can say that he is bringing this case 'for all Meriam people' (TQ1662).

This idea fits Meriam land tenure and its regulation in a special sense because, as we have seen, rights in land presuppose secrecy: the operation of the system rests upon Meriam people's utmost respect for it. Each owner must keep to his or her own land and his own business, and 'each to his own' adds up to a pattern being repeated across the island. Each person may speak for himself and no one else; if each person follows the same custom or law then this provides overall stability. Thus witnesses spoke for themselves and their families; they commented on neighbours' lands which border theirs. Beyond this point they refused to go. This formed an important theme in the hearing of evidence from Meriam witnesses. Like refraining from calling an in-law by name, keeping out of other people's business is part of the taken-for-granted rules of the Meriam. They refer to this as 'traditional ways' or 'good manners'. Manifesting itself in the secretive mode, it performs a key function in a society without a corporate political authority. For even though the Malo-Bomai sacred order is believed to have been a hereditary government by some Meriam people, including Eddie Mabo, the *Zogo le* were not chiefs or rulers, they were exemplars for others to follow.[14]

The witnesses were not named, but details of each person were given in the order in which they were to be called. James Rice and four Meriam witnesses were waiting outside the Supreme Court in Brisbane. Eddie Mabo's evidence-in-chief was interrupted in order that the court might hear one witness, Robert Pitt, because he was in his eighties. At that point all the court's available time had been used up until February 1987. Plans to hear many of the witnesses at Mer Island and possibly in Townsville, where many Murray Islanders have lived since the 1960s, were deferred. The slowness of hearing Eddie Mabo's evidence-in-chief was due largely to the numerous objections raised by Queensland to oral evidence of the kind, 'My grandfather said to me when I was six years old . . .'. Because the speakers had died and were therefore not available to give evidence in the court, that kind of evidence was taken to be hearsay, that is, recounting someone else's impressions.

Overall, some 80% of the evidence given by Meriam witnesses was oral evidence of the kind which had been objected to as hearsay.[15] This body of evidence, which forms the main substance of this and the following chapter, was admitted into evidence by the judge.[16] Important here are the shared assumptions and the variations between witnesses in their conception of land tenure and the modes of its transmission. Special attention is given here to the way in which witnesses indicated how they handled the requirements of a written culture; since the creation of new statutes in 1965 especially, the Meriam and other indigenous people in Queensland have been required to produce written agreements.

Witnesses answered questions according to law and custom which they took to be the 'proper Meriam way'. It was only in detailed examination that variations in and divergences from Meriam custom emerged: this is the important area of discrepancy between Meriam law and custom and the requirements of the external situation.

Of the 30 Meriam witnesses (23 finally appearing for the plaintiffs, and seven for the defendant), all but two were over 50 years old. Four of these witnesses live in Townsville. Four spoke in their mother-tongue, Meriam Mir; one answered some questions directly, others through an interpreter; the rest spoke in English, their third language. The grammar and some of the idiom of the latter were often strongly influenced by the shared language of the Torres Strait, Torres Strait Creole.[17] There were plenty of expressions which the court may not have understood. An example of this is provided by the following comment by witness Marwer Depoma, who was disputing the boundaries of one allotment of land claimed by Eddie Mabo. 'He never talk to me . . .' He should 'face me and talk each other whatsoever [talk things through]' (TQ1210).

At times the witnesses were baffled by the double negatives and the many syllabled words often used by counsel. Mr Depoma, a strong-spirited dramatic figure, an outstanding humourist among a people for whom the joke and the pun are woven tightly into the fabric of daily interchange, shed his usually genial demeanour and spoke in a very loud voice. In the following interchange during cross-examination by senior defence counsel for Queensland, Justice Moynihan was having difficulty understanding a lot of Mr Depoma's words and Mr Depoma was having difficulty understanding senior counsel. Mr Depoma managed to display his good manners to the court.

Q. Can you try and speak very clearly about 1986?
A. Yes, ma'am.

Q. Did Eddie Mabo communicate with you?
A. What [is] communicate [TQ1210]?

The witnesses were forthright, most of their evidence was internally consistent, and they were courteous, even in the face of adverse questioning. The plaintiffs' evidence in court was consistent with what they had told me outside the court in the period before they gave evidence, and before the case began. Many of the witnesses did not get the opportunity to give a full account of their claims to various allotments, nor the opportunity to tell the court their beliefs about the existence of a Meriam system of law. Where they did, the thrust of their evidence was towards gaining the court's understanding of their system of interests in land and their rights to particular allotments. Stanner has written of how the Yolngu, in the preparations for the *Milirrpum* case, believed that if they showed the court the holy emblems of the clan 'the court will then "understand" '. Although they had been warned they could not conceive matters otherwise.[18] I think the Meriam plaintiffs and their witnesses had a similar orientation, although they were both wary of a Kole court and certain that a negative outcome could make no difference to their right to their lands.[19] In their eyes, the task was to acquaint the court with Meriam cultural principles; thus it was only in (hostile) cross-examination that they even referred to exceptions to or modifications of their rules (usually made under pressure of external requirements).

Seven of the Murray Islander witnesses for the plaintiffs were able to use the opportunity to 'display' Meriam culture, to explain their own syntheses, to try 'to get their message across', a phrase often used by Sam Passi in private conversation. Meriam people like to explain things about themselves to those who wish to hear; and in this court situation they excelled themselves in putting *their case* on the customs and law which had been instilled into them in childhood and were therefore self-evident to them. Some witnesses' evidence ran to 200 pages of transcript; that of others was quite short, some ten or 20 pages. Senior Meriam people are often didactic. It is very important to them that outsiders 'get things straight', and they go to great lengths to ensure this happens, often ending an 'untangling' session with their version of 'That's clear now isn't it?'. And if they sense you don't understand they say things over again. One senior landowner, Christian pastor Gobedar (Goby) Noah, who has lived in Townsville for more than 20 years, told the court how to pronounce the Meriam word for boundary marker, *nener*: you roll your tongue at the end of the 'r' to make the pronunciation in the Meriam language (TQ2119).

Rarely did Meriam witnesses show irritation or frustration with the tedium of the proceedings or the repetition of questions by legal counsels. At one time Gobedar Noah added an edge to his courteousness: 'I said that before, a couple of times' (TQ2159). Queensland counsel had been pressing the question of Malo's Law as 'sayings' or just 'good manners', not law, and therefore Noah went over the same ground that he had traversed in great detail with the Murray Islanders' counsel.

From time to time, moments of tedium were relieved by Justice Moynihan's display of good humour. After prolonged examination of a Meriam witness on how his forebears handled village squabbles, there was a sharp interchange between the legal counsels: 'We have our little haggles [too]', Justice Moynihan quipped (TQ1824–25). This case 'has a will of its own', he also noted, of the unanticipated prolongations of the proceedings (TQ1915).

Eddie Mabo's claims to 36 plots of land were the subject of dispute by other Meriam; of the nine Meriam witnesses called by Queensland, five were called specifically to dispute his claims. No Meriam people challenged the claims made by Reverend Dave Passi or James Rice.

Some Meriam witnesses who appeared for Queensland also disputed the boundaries of particular plots of land claimed by Eddie Mabo. In doing so, they were reaffirming the existence of a Meriam land tenure system and what they saw as their places in it. In different circumstances, Queensland witness Marwer Depoma, an elderly Meriam man, would have made an excellent witness for the plaintiffs. As it was, in the context of a fierce boundary dispute with Eddie Mabo over land adjoining his own at the village of Sebeg in Komet clan territory, he could hardly have let the occasion pass without using the Kole court as an arena in which to press his claim. He did so most vigorously and the vigour with which he confronted the inspection party who arrived at the site of the disputed boundary may itself be taken as graphic confirmation of the existence and strength of a system of ownership rights in land which Mr Depoma took to be his 'natural inheritance':

> I told you people, 'Go other side', but you come in . . . That's why I been yell out. I get up and take [tighten?] my belt. I whoop whoop for you people . . . 'No, this is wrong boundary' [TQ1209].

Two other defence witnesses, whose evidence challenged the claim made by the plaintiffs and many of their witnesses that the Meriam people continued to follow Malo's Law, indicated by their statements that the same principles continued, even though they now followed them in the name of Christianity. Other Meriam must ask permission to use my land, 'That's the right way', said a senior Meriam witness for the defence, who lived at Thursday Island (TQ1364).[20] The witness said that it was not the law of Malo any more, that was only in the early days. 'It's the same thing', he added, effectively verifying the plaintiffs' claim (TQ1365).

The only Meriam witness called by Queensland who challenged more or less comprehensively most of the evidence recorded in Eddie Mabo's 65-page statement was George Passi, brother of Sam and Reverend Dave Passi. He contested Mabo's claim that the Malo-Bomai institution was a traditional government with a mediating role in land disputes (TQ2505). He also challenged all the plaintiffs' statements, including that of his eldest brother, Sam, that Malo's Law was used by the Murray Island Council and Murray Island Court in his lifetime to settle land disputes.[21] Malo's laws 'are sayings', not laws, he said (TQ2507).[22] Malo's teaching sets out basic principles of proper conduct, especially in relation to trespass, but only in the late 1930s did he first hear the words of Malo's Law spoken. This occasion, when Meriam leader, Marou Mimi, placed a restriction on the use of land in Komet clan territory, was written in 'indelible ink' on the minds of many Meriam people and recalled vividly by those who witnessed it.[23]

Notwithstanding his claim to the disappearance of Malo as a guiding light, George Passi told the court that the 'basic principles of proper conduct', especially those relating to trespass, remain (TQ2508): each individual owner makes his own decision on land use and management. Presumably these various owners follow the same set of rules which each has 'absorbed' at his mother's knee. This position does not contradict the claims made by other

Meriam people in any basic way; and it was around the continuity of basic principles rather than outward signs that the plaintiffs had built their argument.

In an overall sense, the Meriam witnesses provided confirmatory evidence on the following four aspects of Meriam life: first, the oral form of Meriam culture remains primary; second, ownership of land is not an individual property right in the mode of English law, but a form of joint ownership, even though the size of the owning group varies; third, land tenure and inheritance are validated in myth and this is reflected in rules which are formulated in the metaphorical language of myth; and fourth, rights in land are part of an inalienable system.

By and large, the 'raw materials' of evidence for the existence of a system of law were available to the court, but these were not recognised by Justice Moynihan. Several interrelated reasons may be given for this. First, evidence was not always presented in a form which the judge could understand, and this was not primarily a problem of language. For example, the mythical–religious idiom of many fundamental truths for the Meriam is one of metaphor and analogy, and hence not readily accessible to the literal mind. Second, the cultural basis of the claims being made was incompletely understood by non-Meriam witnesses. Some matters were so deeply cultural that they were not open to question; they were the fabric of Meriam life and taken by the Meriam to be their 'natural inheritance'. Finally, as a consequence of the difference in cultural genre, certain questions, some central to Meriam culture, were judged as irrelevant and simply not asked of Meriam witnesses. Thus for example, the connection between the Meriam myth of Malo-Bomai and the Meriam law of the land, known as Malo's Law, was seen as irrelevant by Justice Moynihan (see Chapter 8), yet this myth lays the foundation of Meriam land tenure and practice.

SPOKEN WORDS COME FIRST

In pondering whether to admit evidence of oral transmission of title in 1986, Justice Moynihan could scarcely have known that he was treading on ground sacred to the Meriam. When James Rice said people must 'hands off' his land, because it was passed over to him by his father's words, he was associating what lawyers and courts call his chain of title with a system of law. In court that intersection was received as a 'throwaway' remark. He was speaking about what he called the 'traditional way'; how passing over land is regulated by 'our laws' (Malo *tag mauki mauki* and *Teter mauki mauki*) (TQ1533). There is a moral sanction against trespass which derives ultimately from the authority of the *words* of the one who has come first — the forebear — to those who come 'behind'.

Other witnesses confirmed this sacred endowment: 'I know what's happening there [about my own lands] because I have been told by my grandmother and my dad concerning the lands' (TQ2720). This speaker, Gobedar Noah, who was brought up by his grandmother, was also explaining here why a Meriam can only identify his or her *own* lands: 'with the word from the authority he can be sure because Stars follow their own course'. Everything and everyone has a proper place. Other witnesses simply took for granted that this is the Meriam way. Even where a person may have written a will, the voice continues alongside it. Witness Kakim Tapim recalled how his mother-in-law 'stated' her will, which read that she followed 'the statement and the voice of my husband' in the handing of 'all my properties and belongings . . . including garden properties' (TQ1084). When her uncle (who had written a will) was sick and 'ready to die', witness Etta Passi told the court, he called 'my father and said, "I adopted you from my sister because you are my blood. It's your blood from me to claim all my lands" ' (TQ1069).

Witness Henry Kabere at Mer, 1995

Words carry the greatest authority: Meriam witness Henry Kabere, who is also a justice of the peace, opts for the will passing from his mouth, when he is 'ready to die', to his son. His last word will be: 'My land, you take over my land'. 'This is "a Malo law",' he explained (TQ1717). He is handing down a right and a responsibility to another person in a face to face interaction.

The certainty of the words from the right person is absolute. 'In Meriam ways, white man say verbally, if it is passed on by words it is sealed', witness Gobedar Noah reflects on the transmission of a right by a solemn and sacred vow. Uppermost in his mind is the changing context of Meriam oral tradition and very strong 'outside' pressures to conform and to assimilate to Kole, that is, white men's ways. 'The Kole way and our way are different. When assimilation comes in, it presses us into the white man's society. When we say "the land belongs to my son", Kole say, "We won't believe you, you must have a written document". So we have to find ways in conducting adoptions and wills that suit us as well as Kole.' [24]

This is, of course, part of the ongoing process of enforced acculturation. Some welfare-minded officials see it simply as part of the process of achieving parity and equality for all Australians in respect to welfare payments. Cultural adoptions do not fit the bureaucratic categories which require registrations of adoptions. This is part of the same process which first found statutory form in the Torres Strait Islanders Act of 1965 which required written wills.

Most of the 24 witnesses had already reached adulthood before these new requirements were placed upon Islanders. Thus they themselves were inducted into the land-owning system and were taught its rules from the mouths of their grandparents and parents, although Sam Passi's uncle and Reverend Dave Passi's father, Charles Passi, wrote a will passing all his land to Sam as landholder (*lu kem le*). Sam, who was born in 1912, had himself written a will, as had some other witnesses of his age or older. Several witnesses said they were considering writing a will and at least one mentioned a will to an eldest son.

James Rice's evidence on his intention to write a will displays an important facet of the contradictions which beset the Meriam. The following example and many others were not understood by the court. It concerns a *choice* of principles under conditions of a long process of Meriam accommodation to enforced acculturation. In cross-examination he said he would write a will and also verbally pass the land to his daughter or to his son; it could be 'a little son' (TQ1539). The explanation for this may be found in the answer to another question not asked in court. Who will look after it better on behalf of the family? In a period when children have grown up or spent a great deal of their lives outside Mer, some of them retain their culture, others do not. Is this a move towards individual ownership? Certainly not, James Rice affirmed: 'She [the daughter] would be *lu kem le* or caretaker for all the family'.[25] The decision addresses the primordial question of how to conserve culture under conditions of partial cultural dissolution, a matter to which we now turn.

ON BEHALF OF . . .

In his critical examination of the *Milirrpum* case, Indian writer Upendra Baxi pointed out that legal statements such as having a right 'are rolled-up ways of saying a number of things': in English law the statement 'X has a right', automatically means Y has a duty; it also rests on the assumption that there is a legal system.[26] These propositions also hold true for the Meriam. Many witnesses also made it clear that, for the Meriam, 'X has a right' also means that X has a duty or responsibility: 'My dad told me . . . If I am gone, you have every

Witness Etta Passi at Mer, 1993

right and all the responsibility' for my land as my eldest son (TQ2108). The two, said explicitly by this witness, Gobedar Noah, are assumed or taken for granted by other Meriam. Whether they are referred to explicitly or not, the two sides are present: 'every right and all the responsibility' is a way of saying that the right X has to this land is *not* an individual right in the sense that I alone own this to the exclusion of *all* others, but that I own these allotments of land on behalf of my family or clan grouping. The Meriam call this *lu kem le* or nameholder on behalf of the group who are *joint owners* of the land or *ged kem le*, in Meriam language. When the same witness says, 'What belongs to me is mine, I own it' (TQ2146), he means I own it, my family or patrilineage owns it, not some other man or family. These are statements made in *two quite different contexts* and must not be confused.

During the hearings they were confused, becoming one of the factors that led some analysts of the case to conclude that the plaintiffs were claiming some sort of 'peculiar individual rights'.[27] When Meriam people said in court, 'I own this. This is my land', their statements were not equivalent to 'I alone own this' of the English property system. Ownership confers a right to exclude. At the same time, in the Meriam situation, a right automatically confers a responsibility to make provision for the 'proper' people to use portions of it, and those 'proper' people are the *gem kem le*, the joint owners. Meriam witnesses affirmed in court that the land passes from the father to the eldest brother, who shares or passes on some of it to the youngest brother (TQ1194).[28] This is an empowering relationship in which the exercise of rights is held in check by the associated duty.

The 'proper' people include those who will come after, and Meriam thinking is saturated with the taken-for-granted tenets of what will happen 'later on in life', by which they mean 'in new generations'. In the context of a frequent selfish disregard of a radical decline in the world's energy resources, I find this concern for future generations poignant and strong. In many cases, choice of a written will simply continues the ancient principle in a new form: 'I'm thinking of writing a will to . . . He [will] hold the land for all the family' (TQ2448).[29] It is a subject about which they worry. It is this same concern with 'later on in life' that forms the imperative of their adoption system — a way of creating heirs — the custom which has taken on the secrecy and sanctity of an enduring Meriam rite, a highly charged subject emotionally for all Meriam people.[30]

McIntyre notes that a 'heavy emphasis upon the rights of one individual Islander as against another' may have been based 'upon a misconception inherent in the manner in which the case proceeded' and on which the

Determination of Issues of Fact in the Supreme Court of Queensland was based.[31]

In order to avoid misconception it is necessary to understand four features of the contemporary Meriam landholding system, not all of which were accessible to the court. First, the Murray Islanders' original claims were brought by themselves and on behalf of family groups; they were not communal or community rights in the sense of rights held in common by a group or collective. Thus 'the doctrine of communal native title', the name given by Justice Blackburn to the rights claimed by the plaintiffs in *Milirrpum* — 'communal occupation of land by the aboriginal inhabitants of a territory acquired by the Crown' — is inappropriate to the Meriam situation.[32] As we shall see in Chapter 7, it was made plain during the court hearings of evidence that there is no concept of public land owned by the community in Meriam society, and even where plots of village land have been made available for community use by landholders, those plots are still bequeathed in the same way as all other plots of residential land.

Within this first feature lies a second: when a landholder or, as we have said, *lu kem le* acting 'on behalf of', said 'I own it; I can tell whomsoever I please to get off my land', the words are likely to be taken by the 'I alone' mind to mean individually owned. Third, the changes in Meriam society brought about by compulsory statute and regulation (for example, written wills), or by social processes which have led to emigration, may create a pressing need to make choices (for example, to decide which child will best preserve the Meriam custom of acting 'on behalf of'), as we have seen with James Rice. Finally, the variations in the size of the units of ownership of portions of land, foreshore and reefs left the way open for Justice Moynihan to interpret the differences within the terms of the rules of his own culture. The Passi family system, where undivided properties were vested in the landholder, that is, the eldest son, from one generation to another, looked like group or joint ownership to the court; in James Rice's role as landholder to properties that he might allocate to one or other child, he appeared to speak to the court the language of individual entitlement.

In reflecting back in 1992 and 1993 on these events of the hearing, Meriam people lay explicit emphasis on how to preserve Meriam culture and resist assimilation in the process of accommodating irresistible demands from 'the outside'. They still cling to the idea formulated clearly by Reverend Dave Passi, which culture change has eroded to varying degrees, that each group must have a nameholder whose function is to maintain 'a centre for the clan [family], to hold unity within' (TQ1892).

Witness Gobedar Noah explained to the court the Meriam people's priorities under conditions not chosen by themselves. He had explained how he had every right and all the responsibility for lands handed down from his father. In cross-examination, counsel sought to pressure him into agreeing that his rights to land and its transmission were no different to those pertaining to Australian landowners, that is, the exclusive rights pertaining to the category of possessive individual ownership.

Q.   You own it?
A.   I own it as willed by my father.

Q.   If you wished, could you in your will give part of the lands to your son and part to your daughter and part to your brother's children, if you wish?
A.   If it is my wish.

Q.   In other words, you can really do what you choose with the lands, is that correct?
A.   That's right, because of my responsibility [TQ2159].

The key statements here are 'as willed by my father' and 'because of my responsibility'. He said that this is a sacred right and that he must 'dispose' of the land, or more accurately, give the land to the child who will treat it in accordance with Meriam custom. This is a weighty responsibility, a matter for deep consideration, even anguish.

By the words, 'really do what you choose', Queensland was seeking to put foreign words into the witness's mouth; an attempt was being made to gain his agreement with the idea that the old system had dissolved and the land is now more like a thing to be disposed of according to wish or whim, rather than a trust held by those who come first on behalf of those who will come 'later'.

In re-examination by counsel for the Murray Islanders, the witness explained that the eldest son was the next in succession and there had 'to be agreement in the family even though I am the head of the family'. He is the caretaker on their behalf as joint owners: 'I learnt this from dad. I follow it' (TQ2167).

In clarifying for me in December 1993 what he had said in court, Gobedar Noah re-emphasised how 'the son has every right'; and if the daughter claims because there is no son it goes back into the male line eventually.³³ Perhaps the message here is that what people affirm as the custom handed down to them and what they themselves do in practice are not necessarily equivalent. In circumstances of cultural transition, the Meriam are often faced with a practical choice between two principles: handing it to a son who may accept a right but not a responsibility; or handing to a daughter who may accept the responsibilities of a customary caretaker. Those owners who wish to preserve Meriam culture will certainly make the latter choice; not to change the system but to create a new 'loop' in it in order to preserve it. The principle of *lu kem le* or nameholder with 'every right and all the responsibility' remains the first-order one for the conservation of culture.

'Every right' goes with 'all the responsibility': it is the essence of a reciprocal system of land ownership, of inheritance, and of use. To own is a right which, of course, the plaintiffs claimed. Covalent with, and inseparable from, that right is the *obligation* to share its resources with those who also hold some right in it. Together they form a system of a two-way relationship of rights and responsibilities. The indetachability of the two is reflected in language: thus for example, Gobedar Noah explained how he could order a person 'to get out of my land, no doubt at all' because of his 'responsibility' in respect of that land (TQ2146–47).³⁴ In the dominant stream of European thought, one side, 'the land belongs to me', is termed economic, and the other side, 'I belong to the land' is termed spiritual. Meriam 'rights' or interests in land encapsulate the idea of both 'owning' and 'belonging to'. The strength of one's right to have and one's responsibility to share it with *ged kem le*, or joint owners, is inherent in the naming process. Simultaneously, the latter implies an obligation to the land itself — to look after it, to sow and make it bountiful. Nancy Williams has shown how, among the Yolngu, this obligation to respond to the land is attendant upon and given its moral force and compulsion by the naming process through succession.³⁵

CONTINUITIES AND CHANGES: PLAINTIFF JAMES RICE

James Rice began his evidence in the Supreme Court in Brisbane on 7 June 1989, after the *Mabo (No 1)* judgment made it possible for the hearing of evidence to continue. Nearly three years before, he had expected to give his evidence; the unexpected prolongation of Eddie Mabo's examination-in-chief, created by some 300 objections made by Queensland, had left no time for the hearing of James Rice's evidence in 1986.

He explained to the court how he 'created' banana gardens at Mene Pat and Deimi (TQ1518–20), his 'grandma's wedding present' (TQ1530), which had been handed down to him. Sitting on his garden land at Deimi, he explained the real significance of the naming process with an élan not elicited in court:

> This area, this land is ours. Our ancestors were living here. There were no white people here . . . I know my boundaries; I know my areas. I can name them where the ancestors been naming all these places. These are not any white people's names . . . I say Bazmet — this is my ancestor's name. And this land belongs to my ancestors.[36]

In 1986 he had explained to me, in the context of land given to his grandmother as a wedding present, how he came to have 19 names; he had written them on a card with accompanying sketches, beginning with his great grandfather.[37]

Plaintiff James Rice at his garden land at Deimi, Mer, 1989 (courtesy Trevor Graham)

James Rice was born at Mer on 1 October 1929, the son of Loko, son of Jimmy Rice. Grandfather Rice was born at Aepkess, Dauar, a descendant of one of the original Daureb people. Aepkess people belong to the southwest wind. As a subclan of Giar Daureb clan or *nosik*, Aepkess lineages have *dabor* or mackerel as their main totem or *lubabat*. *Dabor* are great warrior fish with sharp teeth, and as James Rice said again and again, the strength of his *lubabat* was with him in court when he was confronted by cross-examination which he found demeaning, insulting and prying. He also told his father's strong story, of the years at Murray Islands when the Protector and his representative upon the island had the right both to prohibit the Meriam from visiting their relatives and neighbours at Darnley and other islands, and to deport them to Palm Island, off the city of Townsville, if they contravened the Protection Act. Loko Rice was one of these 'troublemakers' singled out for deportation from their homelands in 1930.[38] It was the inter-island strike in 1936 against Protection as a whole, and in support of home rule, which averted the implementation of that decision.

Loko Rice showed James the land and sea boundaries at Dauar: 'This is our boundaries, this is our land. This is our reef' (TQ1528). James recalled how as a school boy he used to go with his parents up to their garden at Mer and then cross over by boat to Dauar 'and garden out there' (TQ1528). His father and grandfather used to tell him and his brothers 'regularly' about the family plantation at Bazmet. Plantations or *sau*, as the Meriam call them, are located in thick bush; on the outer rim coconut trees are planted, inside there are bananas and varieties of yam. James Rice calls them the 'Murray Islanders' banks' because they offer food for a 'rainy day'.

He is a living example of a man of 'traditional ways'; he also embodies a culture in transition. His evidence reaffirms the sanctity of the patriline up until his generation. Thus when his father, Loko Rice, died, his land at Bazmet (which came from Sue, his mother, who had received it as a wedding present from her father), was passed by him to his second wife, Balo, who made a will in 1971 or 1972, through which the land passed to James when she died (TQ1500, TQ1530–31). This was recorded in the chain of title to lands claimed by this plaintiff, the rest of which came 'straight down' the male line.

The way that Bazmet land was passed down combines the oral and the written, the latter being actually required by changes to the Torres Strait Islanders Act 1971, which added a whole bundle of written requirements according to 'traditional ways', a phrase which James Rice picked up on himself in his evidence (TQ1532).[39] James related that Loko used to say to his wife Balo that if he died 'just take care of it for me [James]' (TQ1515); in due course, Balo asked Henry Kabere, council chairman, to write out a will leaving the land to James. James stated his own intention of making a will (TQ1532), although he too said he will also tell them: according to traditional ways 'this land was passing over by words' (TQ1533).

In contrast to the Passi family, where the eldest son is the landholder automatically, James Rice regarded it as a matter for his decision who will receive the lands, who will be the controller (TQ1532). Yet later he noted how custom says it should be the eldest son; but he was divided between two principles: the custom of the eldest son and who will 'look after the whole area' 'on behalf of all the family' (TQ1538). With sons absent, the *lu kem le* has to choose and this he will do in due course when his time comes.

A PLACE IN THE WORLD

Ownership of land gives a Meriam a place in the world in the sense that the attributes of earth, wind, sea, and celestial bodies are integral to Meriam existence and thought. These are separated in Western thought and in Western conceptions of ownership — people own land only. Among the Meriam, ownership of land extends to the foreshore and reef. It carries a relationship which situates a Meriam person in relation to natural cycles, and his or her relationship to others is inseparable from this milieu. This may be difficult for a Western mind to grasp, and in the hearing of the evidence various aspects of this interrelationship were often distracting, even at times working against a sympathetic hearing, and at others, contributing positively to Justice Moynihan's belief in the existence of a state of affairs both inchoate and pragmatic. Location is primary for the Meriam; every person (including an unborn infant) must have a *ged* or homeland. In social life these homelands are situated along the sandbeaches fronting the sea and the horizons. Yet location is not conceived narrowly on one dimension: a relationship to *place* creates a *simultaneous* relationship or ownership of portions of foreshore, reefs, cays and outer seas, including fishing grounds, the wind which blows in that particular quarter, particular stars in their rising or waning phases. Given Meriam clanship and kinship structures, relationship to place is integral to social relationships with other groups.[40]

The anthropologists from Cambridge became aware of the multi-dimensional meaning of location for Meriam people at the end of their visit to Mer in 1898: 'Just as we were on the point of leaving Mer we discovered that there was a personal or family ownership in certain stars . . . There was also a distinct idea of proprietorship in local legends, for a man never liked to tell the story belonging to another man's place', and Haddon wrote a little about the 'ownership' of stars and winds.[41] He displays insight into the relationship of villages to larger territorial areas, which he saw as comparable with the relationship between species and genus.[42] This parallels his description of ownership of stars and constellations.

In the course of the hearing Meriam witnesses were not asked about their ownership of stars or winds; their claims extended to foreshore, lagoons and fish traps, and reef areas, but not to stars. James Rice mentioned the instruction of the mythical hero Tagai, also a constellation belonging to the clan at Giar Pit, Dauar Island, as the twenty-fourth law of Malo; 'twenty-three and one for Dauar' (TQ1643). Each of the plaintiffs and many Meriam witnesses elaborated on off-shore claims, which were not always understood by Justice Moynihan: 'I claim the waters at Neh Lagoon and everything . . .', Dave Passi stated. 'I'm not sure what a claim to the waters means', Justice Moynihan replied (TQ2006). Still less did he comprehend the concept introduced to the court by Queensland witness, Margaret Lawrie, of Meriam ownership of stars, winds (TQ2613) and tracts of sea, a concept of ownership integral with a very different society to his own (D57).

This very different set of cultural concepts is also integral to a life in which geographical location automatically entails a positioning within the totality of natural cycles: elsewhere I have referred to this as a 'cosmic positioning'.[43] Within the cultural genre of the Meriam these rights suggest a 'cosmic responsibility'. This may be one reason why, in the world context of resource depletion and acute environmental crisis, it was 'natural' for Reverend Dave Passi, when he first talked with me in July 1980, to lay special emphasis on that part of Malo's Law which says *Eburlem es maolem*, Let the fruit you don't need drop and rot on the ground.[44]

5   IF YOU WANT TO BE A REAL MURRAY ISLANDER YOU FOLLOW MALO'S LAW

THE LAW OF THE MERIAM PEOPLE, MALO RA GELAR

Malo's Law is integral with the cultural ensemble of the Meriam. It exists within the heart of the Malo-Bomai myth, it is encapsulated within the sacred chants or *ikok* of Malo, which were sung at the three-yearly Malo rites. In the language of Malo, Malo *wali aritarit, sem aritarit*, means Malo plants everywhere, under *wali* and *sem*, a hibiscus tree referred to by one witness as the 'tree of peace'. *Aritarit*, to sow, derives from the Malo language, 'a language of devotion', whose meanings were not known to most of the Meriam, only to the *Zogo le*.[1] For the purposes of particular acts of everyday life, or for the purposes of a legal argument, Malo's Law may be separated from the myth. But when James Rice said in court that other myths were for particular clans or sub-groups, but Malo was for everyone, he meant this was so because it showed a way for the eight clans to live together according to certain rules. That is, it denotes a moral order for the Meriam to abide by. Marou Mimi began to return the myth and the Law to the centre of Meriam life in the late 1950s, referring to the myth as the 'Malo Law Story' in his diary entry of Friday 16 January 1959.[2] It has four aspects: in the name of Malo it gives sacred authority to rights in land; through Malo it enjoins the Meriam to cultivate and conserve the land; it is normative in assigning rights and obligations instructing the Meriam how to behave towards others and the land; and it unifies the diverse groups of the Meriam. Like any system of law, it distinguishes between what is right and wrong.

    The various versions and numbers of separate laws or clauses of Malo's Law given by different witnesses share the same core. Most versions begin with *Tag . . .* and *Teter mauki mauki*. Marou Mimi had written down 13 laws of Malo.[3] In James Rice's list of 24 separate laws, one is for the island of Dauar: 'Stars follow their own course', a law like that of the cultural hero, Tagai (TQ1643). 'One cannot take the path that is Usiam's [the Pleiades], or the path that is Seg's [Orion]'; these two form part of the vast constellation of the mythical hero, Tagai.

Sam Passi's list of seven laws, written by him for the court in Meriam Mir and in English on 5 July 1986, begins uniquely with 'Malo *wali aritarit, sem aritarit*, Malo plants everywhere even under the trees'. No soil is left vacant, according to the first law, which enjoins people to cultivate everywhere, under *wali* and *sem*; *sem*, says plaintiff James Rice means 'Leaf makes peace'. Speaking of the laws to the court in Meriam Mir, Sam Passi said, 'Certainly I follow them' and the law he had applied in the Murray Island Court had 'nothing to do with English law'. He recalled his grandfather and Marou Mimi and other old men telling him to 'stand firm on Malo Law' (TQ1109, 1110). He said the laws applied 'as good as Christianity'; in cross-examination he said that as a Christian he did not worship Malo. He then continued without further questioning, 'If you want to be a real Murray Islander you follow Malo's Law' (TQ1115), perhaps the most famous statement of the whole proceedings.

Most of the Meriam witnesses called by the plaintiffs said they followed Malo's Law, although some of them were not given the opportunity to speak about law. In doing so many of them associated Malo's Law with Christianity because they 'go together', because they are 'as good as one another', because Christian law is 'Alongside with Malo' (TQ1055); uncle told me 'Malo's Law, Christian Law. Follow the Ten Commandments . . . One is . . .

The late Mr Sam Passi and Mrs Passi in the foreground at the Supreme Court hearing, Mer, 1989 (courtesy Trevor Graham)

Don't trespass on the other man's land' (TQ1193). They sometimes followed their affirmation on Malo's Law with such words as, 'I have told my eldest son all my lands will go to him' (TQ1146). In long-established custom, residential land is passed down to the eldest son, who shares it or passes on some of it to the youngest, but not to the sisters; this is according to traditional law, Malo (TQ1194).[4] One witness said his father told him Malo's Law when he was 18 years old (TQ1177); another when he was ten or 11 (TQ1177).

Some people gave their experience of how transgressions of Malo's Law were punished by fines. Henry Kabere, a former chairman of the Island Community Council and now a justice of the peace with a long experience of presiding over court cases, recalled how he took a person from another clan to court for entering his area and breaking off a branch: 'She break [Malo's] law' (TQ1725).

At least two Meriam witnesses mentioned spontaneously how Malo's Law was applied by the chairman in the Murray Island Court. Gobedar Noah explained how his grandad 'always have the same law plus the white man's law . . . in a case he always informed the people by saying that law, Malo's Law, to the people' (TQ2133). He also explained to me later his vivid memory of Marou Mimi placing a *gelar* or taboo at Deo village in Peibre clan territory when he, Noah, was a small boy, before the Second World War. This latter recollection accords with that given to me in 1983 by a senior Meriam man, the late Mr Lui Bon, who appeared as a witness for Queensland.[5]

The idea that the Meriam applied Malo's Law in the local court was objected to by Queensland on two grounds: that Malo's Law disappeared at the same time as the Malo religion was extinguished by the conversion of the Meriam to Christianity; and that the court was an institution established by Queensland, and there was no continuity between its functioning and any law-enforcing procedures which had existed in the past (itself a matter of controversy).

Meriam witness, Henry Kabere, recalled his grandmother telling him how 'a system' of law was still used at Mer in the time of Mr Bruce, who had lived at Mer from 1890 to 1923: 'the same Malo law' (TQ1695), 'about not to enter your feet in another man's land' and how land disputes were settled 'in Malo law' (TQ1696). He went on to confirm his interpretation of by-laws based upon the Torres Strait Islanders Act 1939 and subsequent Acts, which required that actions of the council 'be in accordance with native custom', meaning they had to be in accordance with Malo's Law (TQ1704). He mentioned how he and George Passi 'applied Malo law' in court (TQ1783).

George Passi, Sam and Dave Passi's brother, was the only Meriam witness who might be classed as an 'expert' in the court's terms. He had a Bachelor of Arts and received a Master of Social Planning and Development from the University of Queensland in 1986. In 1979 he had been chairman of the Murray Island Council, and he was employed by the Department of Aboriginal and Islanders Advancement, renamed the Department of Community Services in 1984, and by the same department in previous years.

In opening their argument, senior counsel for Queensland summarised the evidence to be given by George Passi (TQ2502–10). He claimed that in pre-missionary times and before a *mamus* or head man was appointed by the Queensland government, 'Disputes were settled largely on the principle might is right with the strongest person winning' (TQ2505); the punitive duties of the assistants of the *Zogo le* or priests of Malo, known as the *Tami le*, had nothing to do with land disputes (TQ2505).

He first heard the statements of Malo's Law against trespassing as a child in the 1930s, when a taboo was placed on Komet land by Marou Mimi: 'It was such an unknown concept that it created great interest'; but, he continued in a somewhat contradictory manner, 'it was not of particular interest to me and [was] not talked about in my presence until Margaret Lawrie arrived in 1967' (TQ2508). In that year she began collecting myths and legends and she acknowledged a large debt to George Passi along with others like Marou Mimi, who helped her with Malo ra Gelar and the Malo-Bomai myth. He said he did not use Malo's Law in disputes heard by the local court, and had never heard any reference to it by other Meriam in relation to its proceedings (TQ2507). He referred to Malo's laws as 'sayings' not laws (TQ2507),[6] a term which had become fashionable in the proceedings where counsel was debarred by Justice Moynihan from using the word 'law' in asking questions of the Meriam: ' "Under what law do people use the lands?" ' Justice Moynihan said, 'predetermines the whole question' (TQ1086). Later, he suggested that 'criteria' be used to avoid the word 'law'; not a word with which most Meriam witnesses would feel comfortable. In the meantime, Queensland counsel used the word 'sayings' to Meriam witnesses (TQ2159). When a witness for the plaintiffs was asked in re-examination whether 'Malo "sayings" were simply good manners or more than that?', an attempt by counsel to get beyond 'sayings' without using the illicit word 'law', the witness replied in a forthright manner, 'It is [can be] compared to the white man's law in Queensland' (TQ2167). In 1993 when I naively asked this witness, Gobedar Noah, to choose the nearest English word, he translated Malo ra Gelar as Malo's Law, the same translation given to Margaret Lawrie by Marou Mimi (and presumably George Passi) in 1967.[7]

A RELIGIOUS LAW: PLAINTIFF REVEREND DAVE PASSI

Whether Malo's Law simply corresponds more or less with the Ten Commandments and has therefore become the Meriam version of the latter, or whether it is more specific and unique to the Meriam, it is nevertheless a religious law or commandment. This comes from the myth of Malo-Bomai. 'Law concerns what is right and wrong', witness Gobedar Noah reflected on Meriam law: 'Malo ra Gelar begins with God (*Agud*) who gives the customary laws to the people'.[8]

Reverend Dave Passi explained to the court his deep attachment to Malo's Law in more or less the same words as those he used to me on Thursday Island in 1980 and in Townsville in 1981, when the initiatives for the case began to find shape.[9] 'Who told you Malo's Law?' he was asked by his counsel. 'I was brought up with it. It is the general knowledge in Murray Island' (TQ1893).

In response to the 'either-or' way in which Queensland had posed the question of Meriam tradition, which was put as a choice between the Malo tradition and Christianity, Reverend Passi continued to develop a position which he had begun to explain publicly since 1976. He dug to the roots of Meriam tradition in its process of change and renewal, seeing in that tradition the hand of Malo; and seeing Malo as 'the same God the missionaries brought to the Torres Strait. God was working in the Torres Strait long before the Coming of the Light. It was God, we believe, who sent Malo to Murray Island.'[10] He said this at the beginning of his written proof of evidence and Queensland's counsel responded by describing it as 'a theological notion' reading 'a little more like a sermon' than a statement prepared for a court, and not 'acceptable as evidence'.[11]

Reverend Passi's personal story illustrates how a strength from the past helped him to resist assimilation and establish his identity in the tradition of Malo. When the missionaries came to Mer they forbade the Islanders to worship their 'heathen' gods; they destroyed the 'idols' of Malo-Bomai and burned the sacred house known as *pelak* at a very sacred place at the village of Las. The 'Coming of the Light' supposedly obliterated the 'old Darkness'. Dave

Passi's grandfather, one of the *Zogo le,* who was converted to Christianity as a young man soon after the missionaries arrived, recounted to Dave how he proposed to take his special knowledge of hostile magic, part of the Malo tradition, with him to the grave.

The period in which he acted as dean of Rockhampton Anglican Cathedral provided Dave Passi with a context in which he could reflectively compare and contrast Malo-Bomai with Christianity. This was the 1970s, a time of cultural revival among many formerly colonised peoples. Out of this comparison he arrived at an overall understanding of the two traditions. He saw Christianity as the fulfilment of the ancient promise of Malo, giving him and his people a place on which to stand: 'The truth is not easy to cross out'. The greatness of Malo, he says, was that he was not destroyed by the missionaries, because 'Jesus Christ is where Malo was pointing'.[12] In a sermon in Cairns on 1 July 1976, he preached this personal philosophy of continuity-in-change. In 1980, he recounted to me how he had compared the two cultural traditions in the light of Christian universalism. Through this comparative process he had been able to crystallise how his own and Murray Island identity were something to offer as an example to others. Appreciating the two-sidedness of both cultures (one takes heads and practises sorcery, the other kills with bombs and missiles as opposed to the life-enhancing laws professed by both of their religions), he differentiated between those who came and stole his land and the Christian message which came out of the thieves' culture. On 6 September 1989, he elaborated this in a sermon delivered at St James Church, Mer. In the name of the universality of Malo, Reverend Passi turned his face towards the world beyond the Murray Islands. In offering a firm message to Australia and the whole non-Meriam world on the meaning of the law of his land, he was affirming Meriam identity: 'Malo says to you as he says to me, and as he says to the rest of the world, *Tag mauki mauki, Teter mauki mauki* . . . Your hands and your feet must not take you to steal what is other people's'.[13]

Dave Passi does not ignore the continuation of a two-sidedness in the Murray Island tradition, but in the positive side he sees a future. Through his attachment to the most powerful theme of his tradition — diversities in unity brought about through reciprocal exchange — he was fortified against oncoming difficulties. He was able to overcome practical problems to attend the conference in Townsville in 1981 where the move for a land case originated and so become a plaintiff with a message emerging from the Malo tradition. Like others, he is aware that we are living at a time when conscious choice about what we will conserve lies at the forefront of social awareness.

The myth of Malo-Bomai tells of how the god Bomai, Malo's maternal uncle and the more sacred of the Meriam people's two culture heroes, made a long sea journey, appearing in many forms along the way, and appearing finally in the shape of an octopus at a village on the island of Mer, where the people recognised him as a god. The sacred octopus symbolised the unity of the eight clans of the Murray Islands. Malo-Bomai gave them the magical-spiritual power known as *zogo,* both to turn enemies into friends and to avenge their enemies.14

THE LANGUAGE OF MYTH

None of Reverend Passi's syntheses or revelations impressed Justice Moynihan, and although he regarded him as an honest witness, he did not see Dave Passi's evidence as shedding any special light on the existence of a system of traditional law among the Meriam. In fact he made use of only one side of Reverend Passi's beliefs about the justice dispensed by the pre-Christian Meriam. He asked the witness what his ancestors would have done if they had found intruders in the lagoon he was claiming. Passi replied, 'Our understanding of the law was the club, the gabba gabba was the justice' (TQ2007). Nor did Justice Moynihan see any relevance in Passi's association of the myth of Malo-Bomai with Malo's Law. Much earlier in the hearings, when an opportunity to explore this association presented itself through another witness, Marou Mimi's son, he considered it irrelevant and turned to other matters. The witness had just presented the court with a document written by his father (who was born on 13 November 1886) consisting of entries in his diary on 13 laws of Malo, on the 'Malo Law Story' or myth of Malo-Bomai, and some detailed descriptions of how a Meriam person should garden.

Old Marou's title for the myth — the Malo Law Story — is highly significant: for the myth of Malo-Bomai is a narrative of cultural heroes through whom the Meriam as a people received a charter on the way life should be on the three isles. Its 'anthropological importance' is unquestioned, said Justice Moynihan. 'But at the moment it's of absolutely marginal relevance at best, isn't it?' (TQ1163).

Had the witness announced the impending presentation of sacred objects to the court, those allowed to stay would have shaped themselves into solemn and reverent positions, as perhaps they did for Justice Blackburn when the Yolngu revealed some of their sacred objects as 'title deeds' to their lands in the Supreme Court of the Northern Territory in 1970.[15] Meriam history ruled out this possibility. In 1898 Meriam sacred objects came to form a highly significant part of one of 'the most complete and fully documented' collection of artefacts 'of any made among native peoples in any part of the world'. Through Dr Haddon's efforts they were housed at Cambridge University where they remain to this day.[16] The Meriam retained the myth and the Law; the judge took no interest in the myth and he was unprepared to recognise Malo's Law or its principles as law.

In the absence of these objects lay the realities of the colonial history of the Meriam; these provided both a chief basis of Queensland's case and, as events were soon to show, a serendipitous consequence. Because the spiritual–religious centre to the Meriam's land ownership was apparently invisible to the judge, and because their allotments were small, readily identifiable and seemingly individually owned, their relationship to land was, in contrast to Yolngu Aborigines, secular–utilitarian and hence conceived by him as ownership.

The witness, Gaul Marou, was in the process of giving the court the sacred text which held the answer to the question which emerged repeatedly during the trial: why were all the Meriam behaving so resolutely and so 'automatically' with respect to certain principles of land use and land transmission? 'Well', witness Douglas Bon said, 'it is sort of built in us' (TQ2398), it is our common sense. Justice Moynihan did not determine the answer to his question.

The piling up of references by Meriam witnesses to Malo's Law as a living system did not impress Justice Moynihan: 'it does not become a rule of law because any number of witnesses call it a rule of law' (TQ1811). He also displayed a certain irritability in his interchange with the Murray Islanders' counsel, Bryan Keon-Cohen, on the latter's apparent presumption about the existence of Meriam law.

His Honour:	We have heard rules or expressions of modes of conduct to which the label 'Malo Law' has been attached but I suspect we are in the area of whether or not that begs the question. It sounds — there are people more cynical than I would say it sounds more like a system of anarchy rather than a system of law that disputes are resolved by having a brawl or avoiding a brawl.
Mr Keon-Cohen:	The submission will be it is less anarchy, more law.

His Honour: I am not surprised because that is the only submission you can make [TQ1807–08].

Certain basic questions remained unanswered to the judge's satisfaction. These related to the absence of a law-enforcing agent for the whole society in chiefless Meriam society and, even if there had been a law, the conflicting evidence on its relinquishment or continuity with the coming of Christianity and English law, about which mainstream European perspectives appeared to have a lot to say to the judge.

Before turning to these perspectives, a major aspect of the inbuilt ways of thinking and acting among the Meriam is that they take these cultural ways for granted, so constituting their common sense. Importantly, that common sense has its own genre, one in which 'ordinary' plain statements like *Teter mauki mauki* doesn't *only* mean keep out, or keep to your own land; or *Malo wali aritarit* doesn't only mean plant gardens everywhere. They are also metaphorical statements, holding the possibility of burgeoning layers of meaning; like the onion of layered ownership or locality levels, they are foliated.

As I have illustrated, keeping to one's own place was extended by many witnesses to mean I may speak about my own land, but not about that of others. Some witnesses explained this as a reason for not giving evidence about others' lands; direct knowledge (the most real to a Meriam person) has clearly defined limits: 'I am a Komet tribe people. Komet man . . . My place only there' said Marwer Depoma (TQ1211).

Sam Passi defined his position clearly in respect of Eddie Mabo's land claims, so pre-empting further questions. Having given his opinion that Eddie was adopted by Benny Mabo, he immediately followed this by saying I have nothing more to say about that family because of 'our rule', the 'Malo rule' (TQ1137), which says one must not trespass on other people's family business. This behaviour was intrinsic to the secrecy and the separateness of Malo custom; it was the Meriam way of keeping the peace. Malo as exemplar turned it into what Margaret Lawrie termed 'a sacred and fundamental principle of behaviour'.[17]

Keeping to your own path also means following in the footsteps of your father. 'Where my father put his foot I had to put mine', Reverend Passi explained to me in 1980 and 1981. He was talking of a garden at a place called Mek, to which his father took him as a small boy. But following in the footprints is not only a law of the land; it is also a metaphor relating to land inheritance and continuity of custom.[18] One Meriam witness, Dalton Cowley, a schoolteacher in his thirties, was thinking exactly this way. Beginning in a low voice, he explained how he used to be 'the garden boy' of his father: 'I would follow him behind' (TQ1317). In cross-examination he repeated what he had said in his examination-in-chief: that land was passed down his father's side to the eldest son (TQ1332, cf TQ1324). The witness's thought processes and symbolic meanings escaped Queensland counsel, Mrs White, who had asked him to write down that law of Malo which says the land is handed down to the eldest son. He wrote down in Meriam language the words that were beginning to engrave themselves on the minds of members of the court — *Tag mauki mauki, Teter mauki mauki*. Counsel responded by saying that what he had translated did not say that 'land is handed down to the eldest son'. 'Yeah, but everybody in Murray Island knows that the eldest son always inherits the land' (TQ1333).

Justice Moynihan did his best to explain the 'cross-purposes' of the witness and Mrs White: oral tradition works through key phrases or mnemonics as aids to memory, not 'in terms of literal translation at all'. Like 'a key card in a filing cabinet' it reminds you 'about all the other things that are further down' (TQ1333).

It is metaphor, not for the literal mind: the injunctions keep to your own path and follow in the footsteps (*teter mek*) carry layers of meaning. When this witness was first asked about talking to his father about Malo's Law he answered with an anecdote: 'Whenever we used to do gardening, he would walk ahead. I would follow him behind. Wherever he walks, I walk behind him' (TQ1317). That is a statement about rights to land, about keeping to one's own property. It is also a statement about succession to land, to inheritance from father (ahead) and son (behind). To grasp these non-exclusive layers of meaning is a process of discernment and this means a suspension of disbelief. Mrs White made plain her frustration and her incapacities: 'not even by the most [highly developed] conceptualization of those phrases can one discern . . . [the meaning he is giving to those words]' (TQ1333).[19]

The metaphorical texture of thought, or the analogic mode, was illustrated sharply in the cross-examination of Eddie Mabo's next door neighbour at Las, Jack Wailu, a close associate and mate of the first plaintiff. He was 52 years old at the time of the hearing. A softly spoken person whose gentle, sincere nature might not be obvious to the unobservant, he was determined to affirm his belief in the Malo tradition as a code to live by today. His unruffled manner in a situation defined by Queensland as sharply adversarial was the outward sign of an inner resilience of belief and experience. Looking back on the sharp cross-questioning, he told me in 1993 that he 'expected it to be like that'.[20]

Cross-examination was directed towards the principal laws of Malo and Bomai that he had presented in his written statement. He translated them in a way in which the role of particular natural 'objects' — flora and fauna — provided the texture of Meriam thought: *bezar*, the 'lonely' fish that hides under rocks and slithers through narrow passages, quiet, secretive, keeping to the narrow path, became a metaphor for Meriam people keeping to their own ways, secretive, not interfering. *Sem* must just be let grow, for it is the tree of peace, 'Don't cut it out' (TQ1247). The behaviour of fish that you observe as you swim in the lagoon offers an analogy for 'proper' human behaviour: they don't mix up with each other, they keep separate, as the clans must. The most important or 'principal law' of Malo, that the eight clans should live 'in a proper way' — the moral order of things — is given in the metaphor of an octopus floating on the water: Malo takes the form of the octopus, the 'eight-in-one', symbolising the clans who suppress their arguments in Malo's name. In this way Malo is life-giving (TQ1248). Like other witnesses, Jack Wailu is comfortable with the idea that Malo's Law is based on exemplification and the use of simile: 'Malo is like the Muiar [ancestral figures of the Piadram clan] . . . Treat another man's fruit as the Muiar would have done.'

GATHERING MEANING AND ENHANCING LIFE

As we have seen, when Meriam witness, Sam Passi, wrote down his list of seven laws of Malo, which he appended to his written proof of evidence requested by the court, it began with Malo *wali aritarit*, Malo plants everywhere. Several years before, in conversations we recorded sitting beside his home at Zomared village, Mer, and at the Anglican dean's residence at Thursday Island (the home at that time of Dave, his brother), he talked about its various meanings: the law and the expression of being of a great gardening lineage. This he associated closely with 'the ways' (a favourite Meriam phrase) of 'that class of people' to which he belongs — the *Zogo le* or priests of Malo. He meant that the *Zogo le* were great gardeners, that this activity had Malo's deepest blessing, and that they provided the example for other Meriam to follow. The Malo dances are accompanied by five sacred chants, and the fifth one is for the sacred emblem, or symbol of Malo, a star-headed stone club (five of them in all), known by the Meriam as *seuriseuri*. Sam told me that the words of that fifth chant or *ikok* are Malo *wali aritarit, sem aritarit*, and he went on to sing it to me softly.

Yet he had just begun to excavate the meanings for me. Malo *wali aritarit* may also mean that whenever you go out from Murray Island and sow the seeds of your own ideas (from Malo) in other ground, always bring back the new ideas that spring up from that planting to Murray Island. Sowing and harvesting had now moved into the realm of knowledge, without losing its earthly (or earthy) meaning. Malo has mediated a new level of discourse for which the original meaning provides the metaphor. Sam alone had put this law at the head of his list, written in Meriam Mir and in English. He had the creative powers of a 'speculative philosopher' in Paul Radin's sense: a man of special knowledge and creativity in the tradition of his forebears.[21] Sadly, by the time the Supreme Court met at Mer in May 1989, Sam had become an old man with a fading memory. In any case, given the definitions and categories evolved by English courts, even in his 'top nick' days, this man of special knowledge and powers, who was born in 1912 in the era of Protection, was ineligible to hold the title of 'expert witness'. Unlike his younger brother, George, born in 1929, he had no opportunity even to hold the certificate of, 'Government teacher', and certainly not that of university graduate. What he had had to say a few years before would have enriched the deliberations of the court. However, given the lack of interest in Marou Mimi's 'Malo Law Story' — Marou being the man who came to have much the same standing as Sam Passi's grandfather — perhaps the message Sam had received from them, 'Stand firm on Malo Law', would not have got through to the court. He did manage to say that the law he applied as chairman of the council had 'nothing to do with English law', that Malo's laws apply as well as Christianity, which he espoused; they are living laws, a guide to his life — and those of all 'real' Murray Islanders.

When Sam Passi puts Malo *wali aritarit* at the head of Malo's Law he is invoking the religious: Malo is the god of the Meriam and he is sowing. An exemplar or model, he is also engaging in practical 'economic' activity: his example illustrates the indissoluble tie between the other-worldly and the this-worldly.

God stands at the head of Meriam law; it is a religious law which leads people back into this world in practical activity, which enhances life. Sam was a champion gardener. His younger brother, Reverend Dave Passi, follows that same tradition: when they work, I work, he says of his parishioners; when they don't work I still work, he continues humorously. In the Malo tradition, his priesthood leads him back into the material world as exemplar and participant.[22]

Malo's Law is not given the sanction of immemorial time by the Meriam, but the myth of the Muiar, which belongs to the strong gardening clan known as Piadram, encapsulates and prefigures Malo's Law in its named form.

The Muiar and Piadram people were forerunners and exemplars of Malo. When Malo came, these 'foreshadowed' laws became the property of all the Meriam. That is why Meriam people say that while other myths belong to particular people (nameholders on behalf of lineages or clans), the Malo myth (and Malo's commandments or Law) belongs to all Murray Islanders. Because the *Zogo le* symbolise a 'tribal unity' of the clans, the *Zogo le* and their descendants hold the right to tell the myth.

When Meriam people such as Sam Passi, Kaba Noah, James Rice, Henry Kabere, George Kudub, Reverend Dave Passi, Gobedar Noah, Mary Noah, Jack Wailu, Eddie Mabo, Douglas Bon and others explained in court the positive aspects of Malo's Law as a way of living together, they were grappling with the problem of Meriam identity, or Meriam uniqueness, as Reverend Passi would say — that which lies at the centre of their distinctiveness as a people.

When Matthew Flinders anchored near the Murray Islands in 1802, he counted the men in the canoes he saw there, and from this figure he estimated the population at 700.[23] The total area of Mer and Dauar (Waier being mainly rocky outcrop) is only some 6 square kilometres. Visually, much of the landscape was a patchwork of garden plots providing staple food for a highly concentrated population. Malo gave the Meriam a sacred law and himself as the model or exemplar for them to follow. It is no accident that Sam Passi, a descendant of the *Zogo le*, gives the first principle of Malo's Law as Malo *wali aritarit, sem aritarit*, Malo plants here and there, enhancing life by sowing and conserving the land. 'I belong to that class of people', he said, great gardeners: practising an 'economy' in the name of the god who bore the most sacred symbol of unity — eight clans in one body.

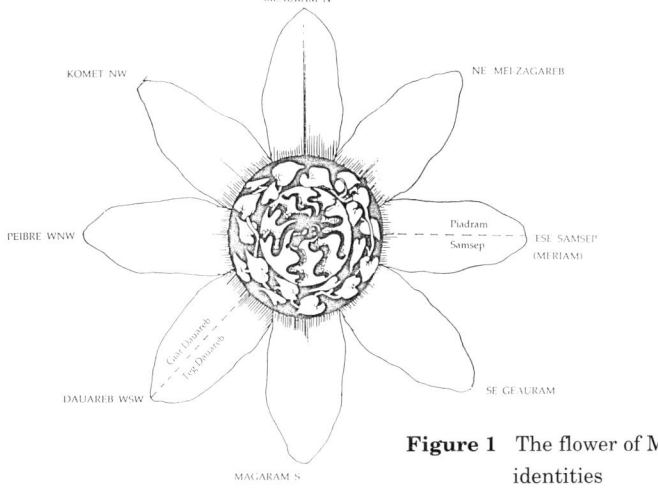

Figure 1 The flower of Meriam identities

'Real' Murray Islanders follow Malo's Law: this is a distilled statement about the quality of the Meriam cultural tradition, the quality of Meriam life and law. When contemporary Meriam people like Reverend Passi identify what they see 'as desirable "traditional Meriam" values',[24] they are drawing upon the 'be kind to others' (*omar lam*) tradition. They are also aware of the other side of Meriam tradition, the '*gabba gabba* justice', which says to the wrongdoer, 'your jaws for Malo's necklace'. To Reverend Passi, for example, this is the kernel of truth which foreshadowed 'the Light', the coming of Christianity. He admits and reflects upon 'the more unpleasant aspects of the culture', to use the words of Justice Moynihan.[25] Yet, as a guardian of Meriam culture, he is seeking a path to the future. What kind of people will the Meriam be in the infinite tomorrows? The Meriam had created their own 'Meriam domain' by the end of the 1930s (a decade of confrontation born of excessive domination, which forced them to grow or go under), within which they conducted their social relations within the tenets of continuing custom, so presenting a public face of 'a unitary personality that was hospitable yet fiercely jealous of its autonomy'.[26] Marou Mimi, who, as we have seen, kept a diary and later wrote down Malo's Law, was an active leader and architect of this process, which reached clash point and gave rise to an exciting chapter in the making of the modern Meriam: the demand for complete autonomy in 1936 and 1937.

Thus Reverend Passi began his written statement for the court with 'God sent Malo'. Malo was sent in response to the 'political situation'; and Passi's listing of the genealogy of Koit Number One, Malo's first *Zogo le* or high priest, is not a historical statement. The following difference with the defence counsel illustrates the rather different worlds which Father Passi and Mrs White inhabit.

Using genealogical information supplied by Dave Passi, Mrs White calculated that, if each generation of male progenitors was 25 years old at the time of the birth of the eldest son, then Koit Number One would have been born about 1760 and 'sent to Dauar' (as emissary) by Malo, and one 'might fix Malo's arrival at approximately 1780' (TQ2038). This is a literal reading of Reverend Passi's statement and not the meaning he intended. Within his own terms, Passi is demonstrably logically consistent. He went on to explain 'that Koit's transfer to Dauar' arose not out of Malo's arrival, 'but out of the political situation'. There is no point in fixing a point in linear time: he is referring to Koit being chosen by Malo, as well as his human representatives, the *Zogo le*; he was sent in the same sense as he, Father Passi, was 'sent' by God to Darnley Island (TQ2039).

III

EUROPEAN PERSPECTIVES

6 HEARSAY OR TRADITIONAL EVIDENCE?

PERSPECTIVES OLD AND NEW

All legal cases rely on precedents. For 20 years in Australia the *Milirrpum* case provided a benchmark of legal argument, government inquiries and legislation.[1] Both the misunderstandings inherent in Justice Blackburn's 1971 judgment of the case and his clarifications are closely woven into the thinking of participants in the Meriam case.

In her analysis of the *Milirrpum* case, Williams asks whether 'perceptual barriers' prevented the court from recognising proprietary rights to land among the Yolngu. She answers that question through a searching analysis of the 'ideas underlying English institutions of property' and 'how they worked to compromise recognition of the Yolngu system'.[2] By following Justice Blackburn's reasoning for his decision on each of the issues in the statement of claim, she explores the reasons why some 'evidence was understood by the court and some was not'.[3] The judge recognised the existence of 'a subtle and highly elaborate system' of law, but in his view this system 'did not provide for any proprietary interest'.[4] This finding, Williams concludes, was founded upon the faulty equation of Yolngu land use with ownership and possession, an association which anthropologist W E H Stanner had predicted would occur, with melancholy consequences for the Yolngu clans.[5]

Two areas of comparison and contrast are highly relevant to the European perspectives considered here. The first concerns individual versus communal rights. The Yolngu claims to land, argued within the category of 'communal native title', had the legal status of public rights; the Meriam plaintiffs' claims to 'individual' allotments fitted into the legal category of 'private' rights. The second area concerns the definition of law. Justice Blackburn rejected the Commonwealth's argument that law is exclusively 'the command of the sovereign', made a distinction 'between rules of morality and legal rules',[6] and went on to draw his now well-known and important conclusion that a system of law existed among the Yolgnu. He defined this as a 'system of rules of conduct which is felt as obligatory by the members of a definable group of people'.[7] Baxi notes with approval Justice Blackburn's 'conscientiousness and perceptiveness' in rejecting a conception of law as the command of the sovereign: his observations enshrine 'a luminous understanding of the nature of law which no lawman can afford to overlook'.[8]

As we shall see in Chapter 8, in concluding that the Meriam were ruled more by custom than by law, Justice Moynihan does 'overlook' Justice Blackburn's definition, which the Murray Islanders' senior counsel drew on in his final summing up.

Ron Castan argued cogently that whatever the impact of Christianity on the former religious life and belief systems of the Meriam people, they feel certain 'rules of conduct' to be obligatory (TQ3467). Ultimately, he continued, it does not matter whether one calls this set of rules 'Malo's laws' or 'a set of principles'; the main issue is the fact of continuity (TQ3474).

This chapter examines these two positions on rights to land and definitions of law in the context of arguments developed by the Murray Islanders' counsel on the admissibility of oral evidence as an exception to rules against hearsay. Chapter 7 considers the evidence given by European expert witnesses on the continuity of certain principles underlying a system of rules of conduct.

The first conclusion I am drawing is that the obligatory choice between the two categories of rights available within the English legal system led necessarily to a severe misrepresentation and distortion of the Meriam mode of ownership of land, which militates against an understanding of its culturally specific character. Second, in the context of the argument pursued, the assumption by Justice Moynihan about the absence of a system of law implies a rejection of any ultimate moral authority among the Meriam: it 'creates' a people ruled by the 'habit of custom'.

These two misrepresentations worked together to compromise recognition of the authenticity and the integrity of a Meriam system of rights and responsibilities. They provided the elements of an illusory picture of a people with individual rights to land shadowing those of English law, whose relationship to land held no spiritual component, and who lacked a religiously based legitimation of ownership. The effect was to reduce their life to the pragmatic pursuit of utilitarian goals within the terms of competition for scarce resources and a quest for 'social harmony'.[9]

ORAL TESTIMONY AS HEARSAY

Oral tradition, and therefore oral evidence, are at the core of Meriam culture: the bequeathing of land 'from the mouth' is of first-order priority. Islander witnesses demonstrated that the rights and duties of Meriam owners differ from those held under Anglo-Australian law, as does the manner in which knowledge of inheritance rights is transmitted from generation to generation. Such cultural differences are embedded within each system of law and these are manifest as rules which respective social and cultural systems take for granted. In circumstances where the Anglo-Australian legal system has assumed a dominant position, legal practice may not admit as valid the rules which have evolved within the Murray Island system. This point is nicely illustrated in relation to the admissibility of oral testimony.

The legal context for the admissibility of oral testimony is one of rules of evidence which exclude what the common law refers to as 'hearsay' — recounting what are somebody else's impressions — a rule well established in England by the end of the seventeenth century. The introduction of the rule excluding hearsay from the English legal system is itself symptomatic of the transition from a social organisation founded upon the local rural community, where the face-to-face relations of the parish held sway, to one dominated by the impersonal relations which accompanied the division of labour, increased population densities and the rise of the object relations of commodity systems. In the small community '[A] witness swears to what he hath heard and seen ... generally ... to what hath fallen under his senses'.[10] Changes in the patterns of social life brought with them a new form of 'objectivity', where the risk of distorting the facts in retelling another's impressions and the need to have the prime source available gave rise to a rule against hearsay. A system developed in which rules of evidence, characteristically those concerned with presentation of oral testimony, became formalised, exceptions to the 'hearsay rule' becoming increasingly elaborate. In Queensland, the relevant Act setting out rules of evidence is very narrow in its admission of exceptions to the rule against hearsay.[11]

Queensland employed the hearsay rule to challenge oral evidence, in an attempt to leave the plaintiffs without admissible evidence to support their case. The question arose as to whether repetition of statements made to witnesses by deceased persons was hearsay or, as the plaintiffs claimed, traditional evidence based upon a set of principles different to those of Anglo-Australian law.

This was the legal context in which Eddie Mabo was first called upon to give his evidence on Friday 17 October 1986, the fourth day of the first phase of hearing. Counsel, Bryan Keon-Cohen began to take him through his evidence. 'Mr Mabo . . . will be a fairly lengthy witness on any view', Ron Castan had predicted accurately (TQ33).[12]

Referring to the oral evidence about to be canvassed, Justice Moynihan observed, 'We are told . . . that other witnesses are to say more of the same' (TQ62). The early stages of the hearing of the facts from these witnesses were conducted within the interplay between witnesses seeking to say 'more of the same' and the defendant's moves either to prevent them from doing so or to render their evidence ineffective.

Eddie Mabo proceeded to describe the boundaries and details of land he was claiming, to explain his personal history in relation to the Murray Islands — matters of a relatively uncontroversial character (TQ132). Immanent, although buried beneath this description of largely physical details, the timing of events in Mabo's life, and other questions not objectionable, lay the question of the admissibility of oral evidence. A 'major evidentiary matter' was looming (TQ132).

Mabo had prepared a written statement of 65 pages, containing the basic part of his evidence supporting claims to 'portions of lands, seas and fish-traps as set out in the statement of facts' (TQ133). His counsel had marked out some minor passages which they no longer wished 'to assert as admissible' (TQ134).[13]

As Eddie Mabo's statement of proof was tendered, Queensland's strategy, which had been contained by the plaintiffs' counsel's careful selection of non-controversial material in their opening, began to break into full view. Mr Byrne, senior defence counsel began.

Mr Byrne: I object to the reception of the whole of the document . . . I do have it in mind to object specifically to the overwhelming majority of the things that are said in Mr Mabo's statement [TQ134].

This objection was intended to be total: Mr Mabo's written statement 'will be largely unintelligible if my objections are sustained', Byrne announced (TQ133).

At this stage, the signs were that if the defence's intentions were matched by the weight of argument, Eddie Mabo would be left without a leg to stand on. If intended objections 'to particular passages' were sustained by the court, Mabo's proof of evidence would not then 'serve any useful purpose in the trial' (TQ134).

Justice Moynihan had the problem of 'finding facts for someone else'; in this case, the High Court. It was a 'curious gloss' of not determining all the issues of 'mixed questions of fact and law' (TQ133), but of the facts in isolation, a task which, as he was to report four years later, was unsatisfying as well as difficult.

For the moment, the question for Justice Moynihan was to decide how to handle the veritable torrent of objections that Queensland was foreshadowing in a way which allowed proceedings to go ahead with efficiency and decorum. To this end, he proposed to admit Mabo's proof of evidence (and those of other witnesses yet to appear), marking it as an exhibit subject to all proper objections the defence might make (TQ133). In other words, he received the evidence and set aside the question of its admissibility for later consideration.

At this juncture Queensland raised no objection to debating the question of substance regarding admissibility (TQ132), that is, the principle of whether oral testimony be rejected by the court as hearsay or accepted as traditional evidence.

Arguing for the preferred course of objection to the document as a whole (on the above grounds that the parts of the statement remaining if all objections were sustained would be unintelligible), Queensland's senior counsel identified three classes of substantial objections: first, that much of the document was hearsay; second, that some of it was irrelevant to issues arising in the proceedings; and third, that some of it was (or purported to be) evidence on oath as to an issue to be decided by the court and was therefore objectionable in form (TQ135). Queensland detailed a series of assertions made by Mabo. These included events which occurred before the plaintiff's lifetime to which he testified 'by reference to things of which he can only have become aware through hearsay' (TQ135): ' "Miriam people are descended from Melanesian people"; "The eight tribes stem from the law of Malo and Bomai. This is generally known in the community"; "Traditionally Murray Islanders traded with aboriginals [sic] in the south, Papuans to the north"; "This system [of traditional government] prevails with me, as the modern Aiet".'[14] All these, and others mentioned by Queensland (TQ136–37) are assertions 'about what things once were' (TQ137) and could be based only upon hearsay.

Statements that some trading and exchanges occurred with neighbours in the past or that Malo-Bomai is the source of the eight clans, raised not only the question of admissibility, Justice Moynihan observed, assisting the debate, but also whether Mabo's claim that they are generally known is true (TQ136). Other statements, such as those referring to 'inheritance laws', or 'traditional law', were, Queensland argued, the subject of the debate (TQ137).

PRIVATE VERSUS PUBLIC RIGHTS

At this stage, given Queensland's identification of the type of statement to which it was intended to object, it was agreed that senior counsel should outline 'the relevant general principles', 'how they should apply and make the appropriate submissions' (TQ138). Ron Castan then outlined the context in which the rules of evidence would be applied. The plaintiffs were making claims to specified allotments of land, not to a system of clan or collective ownership as argued in some African cases, or in the Yolgnu case heard by Justice Blackburn. They were classified in Australian law as individual or private rights. However, it was put to the court that 'an element of their system of rather unique individual ownership' also recognises the collective, overall context in which that ownership exists (TQ142). In the process of clarification of the Meriam system as presented to the court, Castan elaborated the relationship between landowners and an overall system. While the plaintiffs were both entitled to and could 'show a successive chain of title in relation to the particular land they own', because each plot of land was owned according to the same 'traditional principles', the plaintiffs were also entitled to argue that the whole island was and is occupied by the Meriam community 'according to its traditional principles' (TQ143). In the sense that any landowner's rights are dependent upon and embedded in a system of rights of tenure, counsel's formulation corresponds with that explained to the court by James Rice, who saw his claim as one instance of an overall system composed of an identical pattern of claims: 'I can picture the whole of Murray Island speaking about the same thing as I do here' (TQ1574). The sense was that if he could prove his right to an allotment, so too could all other Meriam landowners (TQ1662).

Replying to Justice Moynihan, Castan distinguished the rights being claimed from those claimed in the Yolgnu case: 'it is a much more precise, a much more active kind of system in relation to particular items of land, as well as in relation to particular individuals' (TQ142). The advantage to the plaintiffs of their 'novel' or 'unusual' claim (TQ141), was that disputes over inheritance rights and boundaries of particular allotments recorded in the Murray Island Court Book over more than 90 years, and witnessed by the government representative on the island, could be communicated meaningfully to an Anglo-Australian court. Its practical disadvantage was that common law rules relating to hearsay exist within a framework which associates community or collective rights with public rights and individual rights with private rights. The difficulty is that exceptions to hearsay rules are more difficult to establish or prove in the case of private than public rights because of the way the rules of evidence are framed. Consideration of this matter came to absorb a great deal of the time of the court.

Counsel sought to bridge this gap, congealed within legal procedure, by the suggestion that, because the community in question is not 'a great metropolis', but a small and close-knit one, there is no vast array of private rights which are 'secret from each other' (TQ162). Thus, in practice, the title is inherently public: 'who owns which land and who trespasses on which land' is public knowledge (TQ162). As Justice Moynihan summed up the plaintiffs' argument: 'before you can have a private right there has got to be a system which recognises such rights and such a system is a system of appropriate general rights' (TQ162).

The Murray Islanders' argument was directed towards establishing that the chains of title claimed were part of a traditional system which continued after the proclamation of British sovereignty. Within this system, any given individual can say, 'I am the owner of this particular piece' of land (TQ143). Hypothetically then, Justice Moynihan observed, a court might conclude that a system of 'individual land ownership' existed, even though plaintiff X had not established his entitlement. In being hypothetical, Justice Moynihan was also being prophetic, albeit unintentionally, at least in regard to Eddie Mabo's claims.

As it transpired, the selection of the court category of 'individual' rather than 'communal' rights to land may have helped Justice Moynihan to find ownership rights among the Meriam. However, as we have seen in Chapter 4, irrespective of the variation between the Passi family's 'joint' ownership and James Rice's 'individual' ownership, there exists a common basic principle: *on behalf of* is embedded in a system of rights and responsibilities or obligations. At this level, the Meriam and the Yolgnu share basic common ground, which also distinguishes both their systems from the 'I alone' system of individual 'economic man': 'In Yolgnu society . . . to control land is not to enjoy it exclusively but rather to exercise the right, which is at the same time an obligation, to allocate rights in its resources to others'.[15]

One may agree with the Murray Islanders' counsel that the Meriam system being argued for 'is much more precise . . . a more active kind of system in relation to particular items of land' and 'to particular individuals' than the communal native title claimed by the Yolgnu plaintiffs. However, a distinction needs to be made between the categories in which the respective cases were argued, and the fact that *neither* category fitted the form of land ownership which exists in Yolngu or in Meriam societies.

The practical burden placed upon the plaintiffs was that common law exceptions to hearsay rules exist within a framework which assumes public not private rights. In other words, they had to argue how exceptions to the rules of hearsay might be applied to the claims to so-called private rights. Ron Castan explained to the court how paragraph 12 of the Meriam plaintiffs' statement of claim had been framed deliberately in terms of three bases of right: the rights of the Meriam people to lands, seas, seabeds and reefs as set out in paragraph five, according to their local custom ('ownership by custom'); original native ownership ('traditional native title'); and actual possession, use and enjoyment ('usufructuary rights').

Critical to this argument was that the claim was unusual or rare, and that its framing took into account that such rights were unfamiliar to English law, except where similar situations existed in some colonies or ex-colonies (such as Nigeria) (TQ141). Citing the case of *Amodu Tijani v Secretary of Southern Nigeria* (1921),[16] often considered the classic reference on the question of oral testimony, Ron Castan drew attention to jurisprudence concerning usufructuary rights as a burden on, or qualification of, the sovereign's title or the framing of claims in terms of custom (TQ141).

Five exceptions to the hearsay rule were considered in turn by Castan. These concerned pedigree or genealogy, custom, reputation (what ought to be), declarations by deceased persons in the course of duty, and traditional evidence, which is sometimes seen as encompassing the first four (TQ143). Of course, he was not arguing these exceptions in a legal vacuum; the context of his task is provided by recent case law.

The admissibility of 'traditional evidence' is closely bound up with European perspectives on the character of communities where written 'memorials' are absent, peripheral or, as in the example of the Meriam, important but secondary to the culture. Thus, in a case known as *Administration of Papua New Guinea v Daera Guba* (1973–74), Chief Justice Barwick defined traditional evidence as evidence of a witness who himself claims to be 'the repository of the folk lore of a primitive community', or to have been told facts by forefathers with special standing and knowledge.[17] Justice Blackburn referred to traditional evidence as 'a special field of law of evidence, not part of the common law as it is understood in Australia'.[18] Notwithstanding his use of a 'traditional evidence exception' argument to allow evidence relating to clan claims to be admitted, he went on to argue that traditional evidence was applicable only after or if native title was recognised. Given the absence of recognition of native title in Australia, a situation in contrast to Papua New Guinea, West African states and New Zealand, traditional evidence was inapplicable. This was the position until 3 June 1992 when the High Court ruled that native title exists at law, presumably bringing with it the necessary adjunct that courts hearing the facts are bound to recognise its *bona fides*.

Senior counsel went on to explain the central relevance of the second area, custom, to Meriam oral tradition. Ron Castan summed up that system as an 'Oral Register of Title' (TQ148), a system of land ownership and succession 'founded upon oral communication', those communications themselves being 'a critical component of the existence of the system' (TQ149). He referred the court to a Nigerian case heard by the Privy Council in 1931 concerning 'native custom'. Relevant passages indicated that it is necessary to show recognition in the 'native community' that gives a custom its validity. Certain things said in a certain way are themselves 'evidence of a custom' and this can be separated from the fact of whether or not its content is taken as evidence (TQ148). There are other relevant questions: being in a position to know whether a custom is well known, observing it being exercised, and observing other members of the community recognising or participating in its exercise (TQ151–52).

These three components of evidence for the existence of a custom led to an interchange which revealed both the strength and the deficiency of an approach which relies on people's observations as evidence of a custom. Its strength is that putting together what a large number of witnesses say may create a pictorial mosaic of rights. A deficiency pointed out by Justice Moynihan is that, at least in Eddie Mabo's statement, the source of the evidence is not stated, a matter counsel offered to amplify. Given 'the absence of the source or the foundation' of the conclusion reached or a statement made, counsel concluded that this would have to be led orally from the witnesses (TQ153).

AN ORAL REGISTER OF TITLE

The following example illustrates the way in which the hearsay rule was used. Eddie Mabo was explaining his first recollections of how, when he was seven or eight years old, he was taken by his grandfather to his land at Las, Mer, and shown its boundary markers.

Mr Byrne [Senior Counsel for Queensland]:	I object to the evidence, Your Honour. There are two distinct aspects of it: the first is the assertion that the gentleman to whom reference is being made is Mr Mabo's grandfather. I object to that on the basis that it is hearsay, and as to the conversation which is about to be related, I object to that on the grounds that so far as one can tell from what has been indicated by the material intended to be adduced from Mr Mabo, the evidence must also be hearsay [TQ191–92; typographical errors corrected].

The central point of cultural difference was explained to the court by plaintiffs' counsel, who sought to create a picture of the structure and fabric of Murray Island culture. Counsel posed the question in broad terms: whether a system of land inheritance exists at Murray Island which is handed down as an 'Oral Register of Title' and whether this will be recognised in Australian domestic law (TQ148).

Specifically, counsel sought to explain that customary right and the existence of a custom may be revealed by statements of now deceased persons (or others who cannot appear in court for cross-examination) which are not in this context hearsay, but traditional evidence, that is evidence based upon a set of principles differing from those of English law. So, in the example where Mabo's grandfather told the witness the details of his land, 'the fact that it was said by the grandfather is, itself, evidence of the existence of a custom . . . part of the custom is the fact of telling small children what their interests are and what their lines of succession are, where the boundaries are, how they have come to be within the family' (TQ192). In other words, counsel was seeking to show that oral testimony was expressive of a different set of customs and a different meaning system. When the court had in due course 'heard a great deal of such evidence', there would be grounds for concluding that the 'system of succession' and its method of 'oral recording of title and ownership' were complementary parts or aspects of one overall system (TQ193).

Justice Moynihan handled the objections on the basis of hearsay by receiving the evidence, in each case reserving 'the question of whether it is admissible as to the truth of matters stated' (TQ193–94). Referring to Mabo's statement about his grandfather, Justice Moynihan stated that for the time being he would reserve the question as to whether oral evidence from parties mentioned by the witness, but unavailable for cross-examination, would be admitted 'partly because we are not going to finish this year anyway and partly because I am not, to be frank, confident of the shape of the case enough yet to be confident that I ought to rule definitively one way or another on that point, on that objection' (TQ194).

An interchange ensued in which counsel for Queensland reiterated the view, expressed several days earlier, 'that there may be some potential for prejudice so far as we are concerned' (TQ194). Counsel expressed apprehension that, should the rulings be delayed beyond the conclusion of Eddie Mabo's evidence-in-chief, Queensland would confront the prospect of prejudice (that is, the potential that their case would be damaged irretrievably). Justice Moynihan replied that he had intended at the conclusion of the evidence-in-chief to 'see where we stood with these reserve questions and then form a concluded view as to whether or not there should be argument' and a ruling (TQ194).

The plaintiffs were asking the judge to 'reserve the questions of admissibility whenever they arose' (TQ194) until the conclusion of the Queensland hearings, a procedure followed by Justice Blackburn in the Supreme Court of the Northern Territory in *Milirrpum*'s case.[19]

Justice Moynihan saw the problem at issue as being how far he could enter from one system of law into the other to determine matters of evidence. He 'accepted that it would be undesirable to rule on evidence in a way that might shut out the reception of material which might ultimately be held to be admissible'. He 'also accepted that there were elements of unfairness to the first defendant in not providing an objecting party with a decision upon an objection, so that cross-examination and rebutting evidence could be tailored accordingly'.[20]

On the one hand, the practical problems of dealing with issues of fact on the basis of alternative legal arguments given '[t]he great number of grounds of objection', seemed 'to render virtually impossible, the course of making alternative findings'.[21] As Justice Moynihan stated: 'The extent, multiplicity and complexity of the issues to be determined make it at least likely that the framing of alternatives would involve so many permutations and combinations as to make that course unjustifiable if not impossible . . . Such considerations make it desirable . . . if not necessary, that consideration be given to determining issues of admissibility before facts are found.'[22]

In other words, the making of alternative findings in relation to the facts to be ascertained had become impracticable. The hearing of some 300 objections to Mabo's evidence-in-chief, each of which might be justified by say five legal arguments, would create an impossible task for a court. Many other witnesses were yet to be called.

On the other hand, the whole question of admissibility was integrally tied to the question of oral testimony and traditional evidence. The plaintiffs had 'contended that it was not possible to deny the reception of evidence objected to by Queensland as to do so would presume that the substantive legal rights contended for by the plaintiffs did not exist, prior to the High Court having the opportunity to determine their existence as a matter of law'.[23]

Referring to the weight that should be given to traditional evidence, Justice Moynihan reflected upon the impasse created: 'That is the nicety of my dilemma. We are talking about two parallel systems of law and their effect on each other.' 'Ultimate questions revolve around how far I enter from one into the other in order to determine matters of evidence', Justice Moynihan continued. 'That's the question I cannot decide.' [24]

'Only Hearsay?' by Bruce Petty (from the *Age*, 9 December 1995, courtesy Bruce Petty)

7 ASSIMILATION OR BASIC CONTINUITY?

THE GREAT NORTHERN EXPEDITION TO MER

After the *Mabo (No 1)* judgment, the Supreme Court of Queensland resumed hearing the issues of fact in 1989. Meriam life moved in a crescendo in May of that year when the Supreme Court met for the first time at the island of Mer, in the new public hall at the village of Umar. Behind the judge's bench, like an island vista seen through glass, stood a mural of Mer painted by a local Meriam artist, Sigar Passi. The hall was decorated in Murray Island style. The bench was covered with cloths carrying local motifs, vases of cerise and white bougainvillea decorated the tables, pandanus mats lay on the floor. The message on the fascia boards bearing the Meriam words *Gelar meta ged sikeramem*, 'Protect the law of home and land', could have been taken as a warning. 'The great northern expedition', as the participants in the court proceedings affectionately called it (TQ1908), was underway.

All Murray Islanders were involved either directly in the court and its activities, or in providing the hospitality for which they are noted: food and green coconuts with straws for the visitors, and traditional dancing, including the shark dance, which symbolises the strength of the Murray Islanders as a blue-water seafaring people. In 1986 they had issued an invitation for the court to visit Mer; now the court had arrived.

Justice Moynihan and legal counsels were preparing to hear those Islander witnesses who had difficulty in making the journey to Brisbane. The court also sat at Thursday Island and, later in 1989, hearings were continued in Brisbane. Members of the court also came to the Mer Islands to inspect plots of land claimed by the plaintiffs and other sites of significance (known as 'a view' in legal terms) including reefs, fish traps and cays surrounding the three islands, which provided the visual base of much subsequent court reference.

The twenty-fifth day of the hearing of the evidence began at 9.28 am on 23 May 1989. The court's customary proclamation concerning witnesses was made in English and in Meriam Mir.

This was a historic occasion. As Justice Moynihan noted in opening the hearing, the Supreme Court had not sat as far east or as far north before. Before graciously thanking the Meriam for their hospitality to himself and the court participants and in making relevant facilities available, Justice Moynihan emphasised the role of the sitting at Mer as a two-way process: his understanding of the evidence to be evinced concerning the Meriam claims, and the Meriam community's participation 'in the process of justice' embedded in the proceedings (TQ1038). With matching graciousness the barrister for the Murray Islanders, Bryan Keon-Cohen, who was about to undertake a questioning marathon with the assistance of instructing solicitor, Gregory McIntyre, of the 13 Meriam witnesses and two interpreters called by the plaintiffs, and two Islander witnesses called by Queensland at Mer and at Thursday Island,[1] explained counsel's intention to call those Islander witnesses at these home area sittings who, for reasons of age or ill health, were unable to give evidence in Brisbane when the Supreme Court of Queensland resumed there on 5 June.

At this stage of the hearing, Queensland's technical objections to oral testimony were not pursued. They appeared 'to recede from centre stage' Justice Moynihan reported later.[2] The Murray Islanders' senior counsel had argued for a course in which a good deal of evidence from the heads of many families and community leaders would create a picture of Murray Island culture, revealing

The Supreme Court of Queensland sits at Mer, May 1989 (courtesy Trevor Graham)

Outside the court, Mer, May 1989: (front left) Justice Moynihan with community council chairman, Ron Day; (front right) Wilfred Tapau and Jack Wailu (courtesy Trevor Graham)

The late Eddie Mabo (left) with Murray Islanders, Mer, 1989. Witness, the late Gaul Marou, second from right (courtesy Trevor Graham)

Women preparing a welcome to members of the court, Mer, 1989. Foreground, Bai Day (courtesy Trevor Graham)

The late Mr Kaba Noah with 'Wasikor', the sacred drum of Malo, Mer, 1989 (courtesy Trevor Graham)

An open-air feast for legal counsel, Mer, 1989. Fourth from left, interpreter Del Passi (courtesy Trevor Graham)

The shark dancers of Mer, Townsville, 3 June 1995

the way in which a 'system of succession' and 'oral recording of title and ownership' are complementary to one another (TQ193). The impending mass of oral testimony may have deterred Queensland from pursuing this line of challenge; to persist would have meant impeding completely the work of the court. An abrupt change of tactics was made by Queensland. The focus of the court now shifted from the question of admissibility to new questions. Was there a system of Meriam land tenure and inheritance regulated by specified laws? And if so is there a continuity in the general principles of land tenure in the period since the annexation of the Torres Strait Islands in 1879?

A DEVELOPING PLOT: SOME NEW ALLEGATIONS

The Murray Islanders submitted that a traditional land tenure system exists today at the Murray Islands which 'is continuous with the system that previously existed before these islands were annexed'. They rejected the idea 'that the system as it existed prior to contact has continued in its pristine state, untouched by the effects of European contact until the present time'.[3] In the period between May and September 1989, the court heard the plaintiffs, and

Witness Mrs Gunnear Blanco fishing at Zomared village, Mer, 1995

Witness Jack Wailu at the village of Las, Mer, 1989 (courtesy Trevor Graham)

Norita Wailu harvesting yam at Las, Mer, 1989 (courtesy Trevor Graham)

Witness George Kudub at the unveiling of Eddie Mabo's tombstone, 3 June 1995, with Celuia Mabo

Witnesses Gobedar and Mary Noah, Townsville, 3 June 1995

Murray Islander witnesses were called. Eddie Mabo completed his evidence, James Rice gave his, Celuia Salee had died, and Sam Passi and Reverend Dave Passi had withdrawn from the case in 1986. Reverend Passi re-entered the case as a plaintiff, and Sam Passi appeared as a witness for the plaintiffs.[4] Expert witnesses were called. The Islanders who gave evidence for Queensland did not contest the existence of a continuing land tenure system at the Murray Islands.

On 15 June 1989, the thirty-seventh day of the hearings, counsel opened the evidence of plaintiff Reverend Dave Passi in Brisbane. On the same day, the court was notified of new pleadings by the defendant, which raised four allegations against Eddie Mabo challenging his adoption and some of his land claims. Twenty-three claims contrary to those of Mabo were being made by other Meriam. New allegations were made as evidence of the modification of the traditional life of the Meriam and the forfeiture of any interests in land that may have existed: these concerned the leasing of land to outsiders;[5] the existence of non-Islander fisheries at the Murray Islands;[6] and government-sponsored activities regarding the removal of South Sea Islanders from the Murray Islands in 1885.[7]

The manner in which the new pleadings were tabled raised 'a real question of surprise, and, perhaps, significant prejudice to the plaintiffs'

Witness the late Mr Meb Salee outside his home at Deo village, Mer, with legal counsel Bryan Keon-Cohen (right) and Greg McIntyre, May 1989 (courtesy Trevor Graham)

(TQ1908), counsel noted: 'the first inkling' of a countermove against them had become visible earlier, in the cross-examination of Mabo in Brisbane at the beginning of June; however, as counsel went on to say, an unexplained line of questioning in the cross-examination of witnesses at Murray Island in May 'did intrigue us' (TQ1910). The situation was a serious one for the Murray Islanders; in their counsel's view, these allegations should have been put before them prior to their opening their evidence in October 1986 and counsel foreshadowed a possible need to raise new questions with the Meriam witnesses heard at Murray Island in May 1989 (TQ1908).

Murray Islander plaintiffs with barrister Bryan Keon-Cohen outside the Supreme Court of Queensland, Brisbane, 1989: (from left) Reverend Dave Passi, the late Eddie Mabo, Bryan Keon-Cohen, James Rice (courtesy Trevor Graham)

Given the general context of the High Court's ruling on 8 December 1988 that the Queensland Coast Islands Declaratory Act 1985 was in breach of the Commonwealth Racial Discrimination Act 1975 (which we considered in Chapter 3), it was not unexpected that Queensland would make a new move to win the case. The plaintiffs had some intimation of such a move; nevertheless, Queensland had moved quietly, taking them by surprise.

The rules of examination require a relationship with the individual being questioned that is free of influence of the ideas and presuppositions of counsel both outside and inside the court. Counsel's role is to elicit responses containing the witness's understanding of relevant events, his or her beliefs and interpretation: to follow the witness's thought patterns, an often difficult task in a cross-cultural context where it has not been possible to create that bond of mutual awareness essential to dialogue. In a period when the court proceedings had moved into a state of very serious argument backed up by new allegations, this problem made it difficult for barrister Bryan Keon-Cohen, who conducted some 80% of the examination and cross-examination of Meriam witnesses, to formulate questions which were not perceived by opposing counsel as leading the witness, and which were also meaningful to Murray Islander witnesses. There is a very fine line between what is and is not a leading question (that is, a question to which only one answer can be given). The following interchange exemplifies those where the defendant objected that counsel was leading the witness, in this case the late Mapa Kudub. It may also suggest an end of Justice Moynihan's patience on this question:

Mr Keon-Cohen:	Did he say anything about if people want to fish there they need permission?
Witness:	No.
Mrs White:	That's a leading question of this witness.
His Honour:	There come times in this case actually where I wonder that we don't dispense with the witness and just let Mr Keon-Cohen give the evidence [TQ2073].

Ironically, the question seems not to have been a leading question, judging by the witnesses' negative answer. Counsel for the plaintiffs would have been hoping for a positive answer to support the plaintiffs' case.[8]

SOME VARIATIONS IN PERSPECTIVE: THE EXPERT WITNESSES

The state of Queensland called six non-Meriam witnesses with specialist knowledge or practical experience relevant to the hearing of evidence, four of whom were state public servants.[9] The Murray Islanders called one anthropologist and a marine biologist.[10] All of these specialists were classified by the court as 'expert witnesses', although the expertise of Queensland's main expert witness P J Killoran, a former Protector and director of the Department of Aboriginal and Islanders Advancement, was challenged by the plaintiffs (TQ3030).

At a general level there is a contrast between the dominant European perspective and that of the Meriam. There is also a contrast between the perspectives of the expert witnesses called by Queensland and those called by the plaintiffs. The three main expert witnesses (two of whom were called by Queensland) each displayed varying insights into Meriam land ownership and culture. The case had already developed its own peculiarities and uniqueness. During the hearing of witnesses, major and minor paradoxes appeared. On the one hand, as we have seen, the Meriam witnesses all held the same basic view of land ownership and the principles of its inheritance, regardless of whether they appeared for the plaintiffs or whether they were called by Queensland to dispute boundaries or other claims by Eddie Mabo. On the other hand, certain strands of evidence given by expert witnesses called by Queensland supported the Murray Islanders' claim. For example, genealogist Colin G Sheehan gave evidence clarifying, supplementing and to some extent correcting genealogies published in volume VI of the *Reports of the Cambridge Anthropological Expedition to Torres Straits*. In cross-examination he noted the primacy of the oral in written genealogies. Thus, for example, he pointed out that the register of births kept by a schoolteacher at Mer, Jack Bruce, claiming that Benny Mabo's father was born in 1870, was drawn from information given to him orally by the Meriam and was not necessarily any more accurate than oral information given today (TQ2556). Mr Sheehan himself had had to correct some of his own charts from oral evidence, including some given by Eddie Mabo (TQ2558).[11]

The state of Queensland called upon the full-time services of Dr Ruth Kerr, a senior archivist and historian, in preparation of a case in reply to the plaintiffs' claim. She also gave evidence in the Supreme Court of Queensland. In 1986, 40 volumes of Crown documents which Dr Kerr had catalogued were released by the defence. From her reflection upon the case as 'a trial of the truth', it is clear that she saw her role as documenting the system; her task was 'to provide the truth and to be objective'. In this context, the volume containing records of the sale of land by Meriam customary owners to the Queensland government at the village of Umar about 1967 for the building of a kindergarten, a fact which the Murray Islanders regarded as favouring their claims, was part of a contribution to this 'trial of the truth'.[12]

Her attitude of intended impartiality is implicit in that of some other expert witnesses. As we shall see, Queensland witness, Margaret Lawrie's presentation of the facts, as she saw them, to the court conveyed an imperative: her desire to know the truth about Meriam people's pride in their ownership of specified territories, and the strength of their conviction that this meant the right to exclude others as well as to share with kinfolk. Her evidence suggests that even though some of her presuppositions and initial lack of knowledge of the Meriam may have compromised her ability to 'cross over' and appreciate the authenticity of Meriam culture, her own family farming background may have sensitised her to the Meriam's 'Golden Rule against trespass';[13] her sensibilities also mesh with the spiritual unity between the Meriam and their land. In the Meriam idiom of friendly interchange, perhaps they decided 'to teach her some things'.

Whatever the intentions of the expert witnesses, their evidence provides lively illustration of the proposition that the truth is not culturally neutral; nor are 'the facts' or 'the truth' simply 'out there' to be provided by the objective social scientist, historian or practitioner.

In the case of *Milirrpum*, 'certain ideas underlying English institutions of property . . . worked to compromise recognition of the Yolngu system'.[14] Cultural bias also permeated the hearing of the evidence in the Murray Islanders' case although, given the way in which the High Court ruled on the collective rights of the Meriam, misunderstandings of the Meriam people's relationship to land and the way in which cultural continuities were often masked by radical changes in outward forms were shadowed by the ultimate outcome of the case.

The following account and analysis of the evidence given by the two main expert witnesses for the defendant and by one witness for the plaintiffs provide vivid illustration of cross-cultural misperception on the one hand and significant inter-cultural understanding on the other. Placed beside one another, they may assist in the understanding of two issues: the principles and practice of land tenure and inheritance, and the identification of an authority which, implicitly or explicitly, legitimated those principles.

A POLITICS OF IGNORANCE

Patrick J Killoran began work with the Meriam and other Torres Strait Islanders in 1947, remaining in close association with them until his retirement as director of the Department of Aboriginal and Islanders Advancement in 1985. His expertise came 'from his own experience' over nearly 40 years (TQ3031). He had risen through the ranks from organiser of departmental savings bank services at Thursday Island in April 1947 to acting Protector a year later. After 1963 he moved to Brisbane as director of the Department of Aboriginal and Island Affairs.

Taking the example of Mr Killoran's use of four categories of adoption practices among the Meriam, plaintiffs' counsel raised the question of his 'precise ambit of expertise' (TQ3030). In accepting the witness's claim to expert knowledge, Justice Moynihan referred to a case which distinguished 'two equally cogent foundations' of knowledge, experience versus academic learning, represented respectively by the truck driver and the physicist (TQ3031): the question is, Justice Moynihan noted, whether 'Mr Killoran's opinion is sustained by an experience which he's had which you and I can't share' and whether he can give us insights into those experiences (TQ3030).

Killoran himself provided details of many of those experiences together with their context as he perceived it. He visited Murray Island once or twice a year; after an airstrip was built there in 1980 this increased to three or four times a year. His rather special conditions of power over Islanders may be appreciated by reference to the creation of social history or birth-to-death cards in 1947. These record cards were begun in the context of Islanders' eligibility for child endowment and as beneficiaries of deceased estates, which were not available to them prior to the Second World War. The form of bureaucratic processing used by the department cut across the tenets of democratic practice, that is, the records from one area were not separated from those of others by strictly enforced rules of privacy. In this regime in the Torres Strait Islands, all spheres of a person's life were accessible to the Protector. As Killoran explained in his examination-in-chief, these cards contained information from Islanders themselves and their parents, from child endowment records, church records, hospital records. Thus, he explained without apparent embarrassment, or the hesitation which might accompany a reservation on the contravention of liberal-democratic practice, any application for child endowment had a ready cross-check. If matters were unclear, a note was sent to the government teacher at Mer to check with the church record on the relevant person (TQ3062).

These 'total information' records were complemented by a style of supervision in which Killoran developed and maintained an active personal association with virtually every Islander family. His was a paternalist presence; on jovial terms, he maintained 'fair weather' through personal, solicitous attention rather than visible demonstration of the considerable power endowed on him by the Torres Strait Islanders Act. After his move to Brisbane he is said to have supervised the whole Torres Strait Islands personally by telephone.[15] In court he projected an affable, egalitarian image as a rugby player, family man and good mixer; he and his wife had encouraged 'an easy movement of people at all levels' in Thursday Island (TQ3038). Their two sons were adopted to a leading family in Torres Strait affairs, and his children's Islander 'brothers' visited his family when they were in Brisbane. Paternalist benevolence with a high profile of personal presence created in those on the other side of the power relation feelings of worthlessness, except insofar as they were acknowledged and rewarded by his beneficence. 'He knows me' was a statement often made to me by Torres Strait Islanders about Killoran, the poignant cry of those bereft of independent status.[16]

In August 1982, it had been contended by the state of Queensland, in response to the plaintiffs' claim to continuity in the Meriam people's occupation and inheritance of land, that 'the former modes of life of the Murray Islanders' had been fundamentally and irrevocably modified by outsiders.

Patrick Killoran presented evidence consistent with his affidavit lodged in 1982: that outsiders had changed the way of life and customs of the Murray Islanders fundamentally.[17] He handled questions on the continuity of a traditional land tenure system by expression of a lack of competence, or of ignorance of whether decisions 'were made in the light of traditional rules and practice', claiming that island councillors saw 'the total area' as 'a reserve' (TQ3084). He professed ignorance of a practice instituted by the Murray Island Council in the 1970s, at a time when he was already director of the Department of Aboriginal and Islanders Advancement, imposing a rental upon Murray Island landowners (TQ3086–87); and although he admitted the existence of customs and practices regarding land inheritance (TQ3092), he claimed that any practices of exclusion from lands exercised by the Meriam at the Murray Islands were just the normal social practices observed throughout Australian society (TQ3093). The witness interpreted the idea of preserving 'many of the finer tribal laws and traditions' of the Torres Strait, which he had advocated in those words in a 1958 report now produced in court by the plaintiffs, as referring to the preservation of the integrity of the area against foreign control, rather than as fostering traditional practices (TQ3099). In other words, his gestures towards Meriam cultural tradition had been more rhetorical than real.

Why did a person of Killoran's experience and personal knowledge of each Islander family remain so self-assured in his ignorance of Meriam culture, one might ask. The answer is that, despite his intimate association with Islanders, he did not cross over the frontier except as part of a power relationship in which personal symbiosis substituted for a relationship of understanding between equals. What the Meriam were thinking, feeling, believing or doing as *a serious and meaningful cultural practice* did not appear to intrude upon his thoughts. They were merely engaging in 'traditional activities': tending their gardens, fishing, feasting on their 'native foods' and 'performing their native dances'.

His professed ignorance was substantially an actual ignorance: the 'absence' of the Meriam was the condition for the retention and nourishment of beliefs and assumptions necessary for the sustenance of power. A perceptual blindness on all meaningful matters Meriam was well nigh complete. Thus, on land and gardening he agreed with the plaintiffs' counsel that 'the Department left the use of the land to the people', that it supported gardening practices held under traditional inheritance patterns (TQ3080). Asked whether the customs and practices they used were traditional, he said he did not know (TQ3082).

In the period in which Killoran worked in the Torres Strait Islands, the island councils, sitting as 'Native or Island Courts', were bound by the statutory provisions of the Torres Strait Islanders Act to make decisions concerning land tenure and inheritance according to traditional practices. Section 18(1) of the Act delegated to the elected council 'the good rule and government of the reserve in accordance with island customs and practices'. This provision was a direct and significant outcome of the inter-island maritime strike against Protection and 'the Department' in 1936, in which the Meriam had been at the forefront. The Islanders had forced the Queensland government's hand in their demand for the right to follow their own customs and practices.[18] In cross-examination on the character of the customs they followed, Patrick Killoran said, 'customs and practices that were in train operated and were put into effect, but just what constituted tradition, I don't honestly know' (TQ3091).

If Killoran's lack of awareness of Meriam culture and cultural practice is as great as he indicated in court, this may help to explain his equation of the reference, in his 1958 report, of preserving 'the dignity and traditions . . . of the finer tribal laws and traditions' through their incorporation into the by-laws of self-government (TQ3099) with the observance of 'St Patty Day' or 'piping in the haggis' within Australian society.

Those Meriam practices he witnessed over the years in the local court, in boundary and inheritance disputes, in matters of trespass, did not seem to suggest an active culture: many of them appeared to him simply as the customs and practices of his own society. Meriam practices of exclusion were equated with those 'observed in our own society' (TQ3093). It does not seem to have occurred to him that two common senses — the Meriam and the European Australian — may have converged at times. So, for example, when he stood at the mid-point of an allotment and stretched out his arms to indicate its division between two landowners, he was following principles of equal division; in Meriam custom he was making things 'fair and square' according to their principles of balance and symmetry. A concurrence of appearances led him to attribute what the Meriam perceived as following 'island customs and practices' to using 'good common sense' (TQ3090).

Yet beneath the surface visible to his eyes, the Meriam were silently following their law and custom. In the very month when Patrick Killoran was beginning his long supervisory term in 1947, Marou Mimi was entering in his diary the way to plant a particular yam before sunrise: this was and is secret family information, to be passed down at times to a friend or *tebud* as a gift.[19]

Killoran was a man of his times and social class; times in which the frontier represented a challenge to the 'civilisers'. His role was to train Islanders 'to accept the responsibilities of all other citizens of the state' (TQ3043), and the 'idea was to give them as much local government as . . . they felt comfortable in handling and were able to do so' (TQ3085). He remained ignorant of just how 'comfortable' they felt in handling their own affairs: when asked about a rental imposed autonomously by the elected Murray Island Council on Meriam landowners for land owned under traditional rules, he replied: 'rates never came up to my knowledge at all, even in discussion' (TQ3089). Thus he remained secure in the certitudes of his own variant of *terra nullius* with regard to the Meriam people. Their birth to death cards were marked 'breed, Torres Strait Islander'. The language of 'blood' and 'race' intrinsic to the dominant conceptual system of the era which formed Patrick Killoran were used by him in court: thus policies of the 1920s to the 1940s were concerned with how Islanders as 'a pure-blooded race, would become extinct' (TQ3075); in 1965 Queensland 'accepted that they were a separate racial group' (TQ3077).

A CONTINUING LAND TENURE SYSTEM

Dr Jeremy Beckett, an anthropologist who had first begun work in the Torres Strait in 1958, was called as an expert witness for the Murray Islanders.[20] He is a scholar well versed in land tenure matters. In the period of his major field work in the Murray Islands, between 1958 and 1961, he set himself the task of inquiring into the character and geographical extent of the group-owned territories around the sandbeaches at Mer Island. This took him to virtually all parts of the main island, where he became acquainted with boundaries and measured garden plots in association with Meriam landowners. He argued for the 'strong continuity' and persistence of the system in 'its essential form' (TQ2237)[21] and the absence of any 'radical restructuring of the land tenure system' (TQ2227).

Noting that 'the entire area of the three islands including the foreshore is subject to ownership', either by groups of close patronage or kin, Beckett emphasised that the notion of lands with no owner was 'inconceivable in Meriam terms' (TQ2291). All the land is owned by groups or individuals. Descent is patrilineal (TQ2214); the principles or rules of inheritance concern the rights of brothers over sisters and older brothers over younger brothers (TQ2300). His particular interest had been in patrilineal territorial groups around the foreshore and their relation to the ownership of interior, mainly garden land (TQ2214). The way in which land should be occupied legitimately was organised by kinship; kinship, he concluded, 'seems to provide the only criteria by which land is claimed'. The kinship system also determined who was allowed on the land temporarily. In other words, with respect to land inheritance and land use there was 'a kinship reason for doing almost everything' (TQ2220). Beckett's perception of land as the genealogical expression of identity 'matches' well with that of James Rice: 'land is of value in itself', it concerns who you are and how you relate to other people. Its relation to the past is forever present, for in walking through the gardens you are walking past a kind of genealogy (TQ2235).

The general principle of ownership and inheritance, recorded by Anthony Wilkin of the Cambridge anthropological expedition in 1898, has been sustained Beckett emphasised during his examination-in-chief, in cross-examination and again on re-examination. Even though 'the transmission of land' may have been 'erratic' (TQ2235), there have been no substantial changes since 1898 (TQ2298, 2373). Given the history of Murray Island as a nonplantation economy, it was land tenure that 'changed least' of the institutions and customs under discussion (TQ2300); 'the principles at the heart of the land tenure system' are referred to and resorted to now, as in 1958–61 when Beckett carried out his field work, and in 1989 when he gave his evidence (TQ2300).

In this regard, Beckett confirmed Wilkin's observation in 1898 that 'no common land' existed on Mer.[22] 'I would regard public land as a new concept' among the Meriam, he said (TQ2292). Moreover, the small plots of land that had been acquired by outsiders, are 'transmitted to heirs in the same way as other land' (TQ2292).

He summarised well the meaning of 'essential continuity' in the land tenure system: first, 'there is private property in Murray Island land'; second, 'the proper way to acquire this is through inheritance from one's parents, or one's adoptive parents or close relatives' (TQ2252). Modifications brought about through European intrusion, he continued, 'are of a kind' which did not 'radically alter the indigenous system' (TQ2254). The intrusion could be seen as giving the system greater flexibility: women have been able to take more land in some cases. The existence of written court records of land disputes and transactions are also a new form of reaffirmation of the traditional system. Describing these records as 'a unique and remarkable written record of the traditional system', the plaintiffs had drawn attention to them as 'a most unusual example of a contemporaneous written account of a traditional land system based on oral foundations, in its day to day operation'.[23] Far from having been extinguished, the system had 'expanded' to accommodate new demands: land continued to be inherited according to oral tradition, but disputes concerning ownership were required by various Queensland Acts to be recorded in writing.

A new context was given to land tenure by 'the introduction of European-supported authorities' Beckett contended (TQ2300). Within these new conditions the same principles were applied: 'these central authorities' did not disrupt 'in any serious way the way in which the ownership of land and the allocation of land was conducted' (TQ2300). This most important statement runs counter to Queensland's argument that the 'native court system', presided over by the government schoolteacher, was an institution totally discontinuous with pre-colonial Murray Islands.

Practically speaking, Beckett found that in the Meriam 'clearly defined system of property . . . people came by land in a fairly predictable and orderly fashion' (TQ2218). The rules on 'who was entitled to inherit or use land' continued to be applied in a majority of cases and these were not contested; a minority which were contested on boundaries or the wishes of deceased persons came to the court (TQ2218-19). Moreover, government representative Jack Bruce, who was resident at Mer for some 30 years, followed a procedure 'in sympathy with Meriam land tenure' (TQ2216).

Beckett had proposed the useful idea of the 'Meriam domain', a social space in which the Meriam conducted their affairs according to the 'canons of custom', running 'church and council as though these were community bodies rather than instruments of external control'.[24] His insight in this respect suggests a framework in which to explore the area of Meriam custom and practices as social facts, that is, as integral wholes operating within their own terms, as unique in themselves.[25] Through this approach one might hope to appreciate the integrity of Meriam people's common sense, to recognise its active presence, to understand it within its own terms and so recognise where it coincided with or diverged from that of European Australian culture.

He sensed the strength of Meriam culture, whether it be manifest in the Meriam people's written request in 1885 to expel the South Sea Islanders who had taken up residence there (TQ2373-74), or even in the 'extraordinary' efforts of émigré Meriam 'to keep up their culture', their 'very lively interest in land' and their capacity to 'go into total recall' about places and custom (TQ2301). He was aware that certain principles of behaviour have become 'natural' to the Meriam. In the final stage of re-examination, senior counsel sought to identify whether in Beckett's view the Meriam were just responding 'to particular social situations' or whether he could identify 'a system for dealing with land tenure' (TQ2372). He did not handle these questions in his customary unequivocal and forthright style, or with the precision he brought to land tenure questions. 'There is a tendency to resort to sets of rules about how things should be properly conducted', he replied; they bend the rules when they can, but 'at any given moment people seem to think they know what the rules are'. In sum, there is an interplay between various rules 'as though it were an orderly system even when it's not to a full degree' (TQ2372).

From his practical experience, he was highly aware that the Meriam feel duty-bound to follow rules against trespass (TQ2235); but he did not make the connection between that sense of obligation and the religiously based, authoritative law identified by Meriam witnesses as Malo's Law, concerning the spiritual and the material dimensions of their attachment to land. They own, use and bequeath the land in Malo's name and in the name of their ancestors they identify the eldest son as the carrier of that right.

During his field work he had occasionally heard Meriam people repeating Malo's Law, which 'asserts the sanctity ... of private property', of not taking the crops of others, and of conserving food by not picking unripe fruit (TQ2232). During this time, however, he saw no 'very significant connection' between the Malo cult and the land tenure system (TQ2232). He saw Malo's Law as 'a general precept' or framework of general principles, not 'a statement of law in our sense of the term' (TQ2232). This comparative insight did not lead him to explore the possibility and its implications that Malo's Law may be 'a statement of law' in the Meriam 'sense of the term'. He cited evidence provided by a Mr Hunt, an early missionary referred to by A C Haddon, that leaders of the Malo-Bomai cult made decisions in land disputes (TQ2232). He limited himself to the undisputed observation that the cult kept the peace primarily by keeping people to their own paths, and thus avoided confrontation with one another (TQ2233). The Malo cult, he finished a little lamely, 'was meant to be a mystery ... and to a considerable degree it remains a mystery' (TQ2233).

Jeremy Beckett's emphasis on the essential continuity of the land tenure system but on highly radical changes in religion and the economy (TQ2299) led to an asymmetry in his exposition of the tenets of contemporary Meriam culture. Unfortunately, a lack of understanding of the inseparability of the Meriam relationship to land from its religious grounding diminished the possibility of explaining *why* the Meriam feel duty-bound to follow the principles to which he referred. The duties associated with the rights of *lu kem le*, the eldest brothers, to provide land to younger brothers and unmarried sisters, are themselves grounded in and derive their meaning from Meriam religion. A C Haddon believed that the Malo institution had dissolved the *lubabat* or totems of the Meriam;[26] Beckett seemed to assume that Christianity 'washed away' the whole Meriam religious endowment which had culminated in the Malo-Bomai sacred order in the pre-Christian era.[27]

PRIDE IN LAND

When she first visited Mer to collect oral accounts of myths and legends, Margaret Lawrie gradually became aware of Meriam people's pride in their ownership of land. Henry Kabere, a landowner, took her up to his banana plantation: 'This is my land', he said with pride. Initially she did not know it was *his*; she believed it was a place he knew well or belonged to (TQ2607). Soon she learnt there was 'one Golden Rule': respect other people's property (TQ2608). She noted how the children never strayed beyond their village boundaries, how the Meriam 'knew absolutely' where the boundaries were, and how as a guest she fell in with the custom of 'not trespassing' on what was obviously private property (TQ2606). In cross-examination she affirmed how the golden rule of private property continues on in the Murray Islands today (TQ2610). The continuity of territorial divisions, or clan territories, is an unbroken thread reaching back to forebears (TQ2683).[28]

It was the wish to understand these Meriam expressions of pride in the ownership of clan territories (she used the Meriam expression *taum akadar*, 'pride speech'), which drew her back to Mer in 1973. Pride speech gives expression to a unity with the land, a unity of I and Thou, a living spiritual unity. It is an expression of the certainties of religious awareness, an awareness which bears the hallmark of Meriam religion.

The witness explained how she could grasp readily the golden rule against trespass: 'Trespass is abhorred at this island', she had written.[29] As a person who comes 'from quite a long line of people who have lived on the land' (TQ2686–87), private property was something she herself had 'particular regard for' (TQ2608).

Margaret Lawrie was a collector, not an interpreter of myths and legends.[30] She was modest in her self-appraisal, and at the same time, realistic. Jeremy Beckett's anthropological evidence on land tenure and inheritance in the main confirmed her own 'conclusions about ownership'. 'Nearly everything [he said] confirmed that what I had learnt and remembered was on track', she told the court with a note of deference (TQ2611). Whatever her lack of expertise in ethnographic method or knowledge of kinship systems, her attempt to explore the meaning of Meriam cultural pride deepened her insights into the inseparability of land from the person and from the range of meanings connected with the idea that land is embedded in genealogy. Lawrie also showed an awareness of how the golden rule of not trespassing pervaded every moment of daily living among the Meriam. Her meticulous approach to her craft carried with it the perception of an acute observer: one does not 'trespass inside another man's knowledge of what he owned' (TQ2665). Myths are owned, and nobody 'stepped out of turn' and intruded on another man's ownership in this sphere either.

Perhaps her understanding of how the range of trespass extended to every aspect of life and meaning systems — to land, to stars, to stories — was easy for her because of her farm background. In this respect at least, awareness of aspects of her own culture helped her to understand aspects of Meriam culture.³¹

Lawrie's understanding goes outside the one dimension of positivist knowledge. In comparing herself with Beckett, she mentioned how she was very interested in the religious side of ownership, and in particular in Malo (TQ2611). This statement was treated by the court as a 'side line', yet, although she nowhere made a link between the Malo myth and Malo's Law or the religious legitimation or spiritual aspect of ownership, she sensed in 'pride speech', and in the unstated charter which seems to be guiding and permeating social life and being, how the Meriam's pride is a form of offering to place. So when Henry Kabere showed her his banana garden with pride, or when people talked of their portion of a clan territory, they were talking about themselves, who they are.

She sensed, but did not articulate, a two-way relationship with the land, both spiritual and material. The gardener is giving back to the land in growing produce, while the land in turn is in the process of renewing the life of himself and his family. The Meriam hold a fellowship with their land, which is in the nature of a dialogue, offering and harvesting (in which the land is giving back). For land is alive and spirited, not a thing, object-like to be manipulated, exploited and mastered.³²

Lawrie returned again and again to the Meriam's 'unbroken links with the past' and the way in which children learned by a process of osmosis, within the daily round of social life, to respect the property of others. The practice of repetition of the repertoire of myth and narrative in the oral tradition remained strong (TQ2629–29A). No important story collected by Haddon has been forgotten by the Meriam, Lawrie had noted in 1970.³³ In cross-examination she confirmed her beliefs about their indissoluble links with their surroundings: 'born to it, yes', she said, using a phrase akin to what the Meriam say themselves (TQ2629A).³⁴

She made plain the difficulty she encountered repeatedly with the way the Meriam hold together the present and the past as a continuum (TQ2683). Because of the golden rule against trespass, when Meriam people make pride speech statements they are also making affirmations about their group ownership. And, like Meriam witnesses and Beckett, Lawrie also understood that their lands within these clan territories are their bloodlines, where, as Beckett explained, ownership is transmitted through the patriline (TQ2214). So the élan with which they express their pride is expressive of the distinctive features of the culture. She found their sense of being this or that clan to be 'of the very essence of people' (TQ2682); its significance was the people's own recognition 'that they belonged' (TQ2622).

Lawrie sensed the importance of myth as the knowledge store of an oral tradition. She did not seem to understand, however, that myth is not historical record, but cultural statement of fundamental, unerring and irreducible truths, which are at one and the same time religious and economic, guides to the resolution of life's contradictions, as well as to day-to-day behaviour. In court she referred to a myth of Meidu, where birds known as *dibadiba* (the source of the name of the sacred necklace worn by the initiates in the Malo rites) flock at sunrise. She was aware that its message to the Meriam, 'though your people eat from sunrise till sunset, they cannot eat all the food you provide'[35], is metaphorical. The island is being praised for its wealth, no one goes hungry. And this, Lawrie perceived, is 'the collective pride of the Miriam' (TQ2620); it is their identity.

Yet its meaning goes far beyond wealth, the medium through which Meriam identity is defined. It is a religious message given in 'economic' form, where the two are aspects of the one cultural statement given in mythopoeic form. Malo *wali aritarit*, Sam Passi's intonation conveys reverence. Wherever there is room enough to plant, the god Malo says, do it. The pride which drew her back again to Mer *is* the identity of the Meriam. 'These were my people', she said with pride in return, conveying a sense of a deeply aesthetic experience. For their gift to her of their pride in themselves — 'This is my land' — displayed the fruits of their labours (a garden not a wilderness) and the 'fruits' of their bloodline (clan land beside the sandbeach). They presented the former in 'economic-material terms', yet each is the expression of 'imperishable bonds' between the ancestors and the living.

Meriam law is more than a law in its narrow, formal sense: the obligation to follow certain rules is expressive of a process of interchanging with the cosmos. In planting and growing and harvesting and offering, the possibilities of interchange with the cosmos are being fulfilled. This accords with Deborah Rose's view of the concern of 'Aboriginal morality' to maintain 'the cosmos as a life enhancing system'. Each part is acting and responding; each depends upon the symmetry of power.[36] She identifies the conditions of what I have termed a reciprocal relationship between the parts of the living cosmic system.[37] Her depiction of Yarralin Aboriginal people's responsiveness runs in parallel. In their cosmological scheme, 'Each part of the cosmos is . . . seen as a moral agent and in behaving morally each part reproduces the relationships through which the whole system continues to enhance life'.[38]

Rose is pointing to a form of social being where 'living as a human being is in itself a religious act',[39] where men and women are kept in touch with ultimate values and the mysteries of creation through ritual experience, *and where the I and Thou of reciprocal giving and returning, between all parts of the cosmos, is an ongoing everyday religious experience.*[40]

Lawrie did not make a link between myth and religion: she did not see the religious basis of pride speech, and she did not suggest explicitly that Malo *wali aritarit*, planting everywhere, or *teter mek*, walking on tip-toe silent and careful along one's proper path, or *eburlem es maolem*, return what is not used back into the land, were religious as well as 'secular' acts.[41] However, both in her published collection of myths and legends and again in court, Lawrie describes the way ownership pertains not only to land or even to knowledge, but to all parts of the cosmos (although she does not herself make this generalisation). In her written statement, she repeated what she says in her book: 'I found that stars, winds, tracts of sea, land and personal names were owned by patriclans, subdivisions of patriclans (patriclans or patrilineages), or individuals'.[42]

Margaret Lawrie's statement on the Meriam's 'ownership' of lands and winds 'alike' was no doubt supportive of the argument that their relation to land did not constitute 'real' ownership, yet much of her evidence in court was welcome to the plaintiffs. She showed herself to be intuitive as well as respectful of other people's customs: her 'good manners' were manifest in a wish not to pry or trespass on another person's customs. Paradoxically, that reticence or circumspection was perhaps a factor in preventing her from asking certain questions which might reveal some of the deeper meanings of Meriam cultural life. What was the connection between Malo ra Gelar as a moral charter, and a set of principles ordering the relations between the parts of the Meriam universe: stars follow their own course across the sky. Continue to sow, keep to your own path, follow in the footsteps, conserve the earth's produce . . . and the myth of Malo?

REFLECTIONS UPON MERIAM LAW AND CULTURE

In the course of the hearing, Justice Moynihan himself frequently sought to clarify issues and so facilitate communication on a range of questions. Nowhere was the argument more muddied than on the character of pre-invasion Meriam society. An assumption which appeared to direct the judge's questions and statements was that, lacking a corporate head, Meriam society had rules that were closer to precepts than laws: 'club justice' 'ruled' and the 'best brawler' won.

Jeremy Beckett had expressed the view that matters 'labelled as Malo's laws' were most likely 'precepts of quite general application not necessarily applicable to any specific place or circumstance' (TQ2234–35).[43] His evidence suggested to Justice Moynihan that the function of 'the enforcers' 'may have been nothing more than the protection of the cult itself', rather than 'the enforcement of laws in respect of the social system outside their cult' (TQ2234).[44]

In the hearing of witnesses at Mer in May and in the examination of Reverend Dave Passi in Brisbane, which began on 15 June — immediately preceding the court appearance of Jeremy Beckett on 26 June — Justice Moynihan had come face to face with the difficulty of how Malo's Law, as claimed by the plaintiffs and many witnesses, may have been applied before Europeans came, in a society without a corporate head or chief. Some witnesses said they did not know. James Rice had said trespassers had their 'jaws taken off to Malo' (TQ1646). He also indicated many times that generally speaking, trespass was something that did not happen (TQ1601, 1615).

Justice Moynihan's developing view of Meriam society and the meaning of Malo's Law not as law, and the authority of Malo and the priests or *Zogo le* not as a moral authority but exclusively that of 'heavies', pressed its way into the proceedings. The following interchange interpolated into the examination of witness Henry Kabere illustrates this point sharply.

Henry Kabere was being questioned on his memories of an island court hearing in a case of a man trespassing on another man's land, which was recorded in the Court Book now produced in court. He had just said Malo's Law was applied to that decision and the man was fined $20, when Justice Moynihan introduced what, to the witness, may have seemed a tangential line of thought on what would have happened in such a situation before Europeans came.

His Honour:	There would have been a brawl and whoever was the best brawler won.
Mr Keon-Cohen:	We have heard, perhaps at some repetition, particular laws which might be said to relate to the notion of trespass.
His Honour:	We have heard rules of expressions of modes of conduct to which the label 'Malo Law' has been

> attached but I suspect we are in the area of
> whether or not that begs the question. It sounds —
> there are people more cynical than I who would say
> it sounds more like a system of anarchy rather than
> a system of law that disputes are resolved by having
> a brawl or avoiding a brawl [TQ1807–08].

Justice Moynihan's assumptions resemble those of Justice McEachern in the case of *Delgamuukw v British Columbia* (1991) (Canada), who saw the actions of the plaintiffs' ancestors exclusively as expressions of 'survival instincts' in a life not 'in the least bit idyllic'.[45]

Justice Moynihan soon returned to the subject again; his concern was whether words 'which say "Don't put your hands on another man's land" ' are necessarily rules of law or simply 'rules of conduct' or 'desirable maxims'. They may simply mean ' "For God's sake don't start an all in brawl between us and the next village" ' (TQ1811).

This particular train of thought crystallised during the hearing of Dr Beckett's evidence, and was carried into Justice Moynihan's findings. Beckett stated that he had not seen 'any very significant connection' between the cult of Malo-Bomai and land tenure arrangements, although Murray Islanders occasionally repeated to him 'what they called "Malo's Law" ' (TQ2232).

Extrapolating from non-Meriam Melanesian societies, Beckett suggested that 'mediation' not 'adjudication' was the order of the day and that the Malo-Bomai cult came into existence partly in order to maintain a degree of peace; people were very quiet, keeping to their own paths and avoiding others' land. In this way people were kept 'apart from one another', so that violence did not break out. The *Zogo le* had an 'executive arm', he continued, which acted as a 'kind of vigilante group called *mogor*' (TQ2233).

Continuing to draw his suppositions from several Melanesian sources, Beckett pointed to the way in which group pressure tended to maintain harmony by isolating people who were always quarrelling with their neighbours (TQ2234). He then recalled an occasion in the early days of his field work when he 'stepped from the path' and intruded into someone's garden, 'something no Murray Island person would legitimately do', and he was 'scolded' for this and made to apologise to the owner (TQ2235). In a general sense, Malo 'precepts' were applied.

Revealing his own assumptions, Justice Moynihan asked rhetorically, 'I suppose in those general senses any group of human beings — perhaps animals . . . has a series of precepts which have to be abided' by in order to 'live together as a group' (TQ2235). This is a demonstrably minimalist position, one which approaches that taken by the defence in the *Milirrpum* case that Aboriginal law was too primitive to be recognised as law.[46]

Following his example about the consequences of the way his trespass was seen by his Meriam hosts, Beckett said that this 'was something one did not do. No Murray Islander would behave like that was the gist of the message' (TQ2236). Although Beckett did not draw this conclusion, whether or not his hosts mentioned Malo's Law by name is irrelevant. In pre-missionary times the Meriam had kept to their respective paths in fear of *gabba gabba*, the stone club of Malo; they had also done so because individually and collectively they had internalised Malo's Law over generations, and as we have seen, young children were socialised into it. 'I was brought up with it', said Reverend Dave Passi. 'It is the general knowledge in Murray Island' (TQ1893). 'Everyone knows that', said James Rice referring to Malo's Law (TQ1599).

The cultural nature of Malo's Law, its embedding within the total ensemble of social relations, is a very difficult notion for an outsider to grasp. There are two closely related reasons for this: first, because it is taken for granted, it is in the nature of everyday life, something you do or do not do, and therefore it is not to be questioned; second, because this set of taken-for-granted behaviours is very different in its source, justification and meanings to the behaviours with which Europeans are familiar.

It was very hard for a Meriam person to explain *in a court* those qualitative and deeply cultural truths which arise out of Malo's Law, the charter of social life, which itself arises out of the myth of Malo-Bomai. That myth enjoins the Meriam to live together; it is a myth about land tenure; it joins not only the living — turning enemies into friends through the mediation of Malo — but also the mortal with the immortal, the here and now with the hereafter and with those who came before.[47]

A besetting difficulty is that, like poetry, myth is metaphorical rather than literal. It is not prosaic, or didactic in a direct way; it is totally inimical to the either-or mentality. Its milieu is, rather, the both-and. The rules or laws which emanate from it are in the realm of the sacred, because the myth itself is sacred. This sacredness is captured in the word *zogo*: 'When we talk about Zogo we talk about Malo, Bomai; as the God and whatever they have, is all included in the word Zogo', Dave Passi explained (TQ2059). The village of Las is where the Malo mask is buried, and Las is sacred to *zogo*; here 'we have come to the heart of Murray', he continued, in the course of cross-examination. That site remains sacred today: 'I will not point out where [the] Malo [mask] was buried', Reverend Passi told the court (TQ2027).

In this perspective, the *Zogo le*, Malo's people, were not the 'biggest and toughest', 'the best brawlers' (TQ2009).[48] They were, in Sam Passi's words, not rulers, but 'people of divine power'.[49] Like other Meriam they were themselves governed by the same reciprocities of rights and duties. Reverend Passi explained to the court how the *Zogo le* were governed by the 'system of Malo law'. 'I cannot think of the Zogo le using his authority to claim what is other people's. It would be against himself and against his nature' (TQ2009; typographical errors corrected).

Reverend Passi had said that 'the *gabba gabba*' (Malo's stone club) was the justice, that the *Zogo le* had soldiers to fight for him (TQ2006–08). This was a punishing kind of religious institution; but, like the mediators or intercessors of God of the Old Testament, they practised what they preached. As Sam Passi explained it to me in 1982, the *Zogo le* were exemplars in the manner of Malo: 'Malo doesn't walk . . . Malo doesn't touch . . . Malo walks on tip-toe along the right path'.[50]

Awe and reverence on the one side and fear and dread on the other side are two complementary but inseparable sides of Meriam life. Taken alone, the former tends to idealise the Meriam;[51] of itself the latter serves to debase and even vilify their social life, to reduce them to savages ruled solely by the club, their sociality totally contingent on fear. This is the position which, as we shall see, Justice Moynihan accepted in the first instance. Coupled with this awe of the club were what we call 'good manners', associated with the idea of shame, a deeply cultural matter and a concept so 'unlawlike' that Queensland quickly took hold of it. 'So it's good manners to follow those Malo sayings' (TQ2159), Queensland's counsel sought to force words into the mouth of witness, Gobedar Noah, who had been outlining the responsibility placed upon him as a landowner.

A difficulty was that the authority of Malo-Bomai and in consequence, Malo's Law, did not coincide with Justice Moynihan's own assumptions. He found it difficult to comprehend the absence of a common power which curbs 'competition diffidence and glory', the 'natural dispositions of men' in Meriam society;[52] they were not subject to the command of chief or sovereign. At least implicit in Justice Moynihan's perception of the pre-Christian Meriam is a life barely removed from 'Hobbes' picture of the full state of nature', that is, from the 'solitary, poor, nasty, brutish and short'.[53] The idea of a hereditary religious order with an executive arm uniting the eight clans in a system of reciprocities, the two-sidedness of Malo as exemplar or role model and executioner, and the concept of a sacred centre at Las incorporating the site of the sacred houses (*pelak*), were unfamiliar ones. In Justice Moynihan's perception, Meriam like Eddie Mabo and Reverend Passi 'seized upon' features of Malo in order to fulfil a 'wish to preserve Meriam identity in a way acceptable to the wider community'. Their syntheses were flawed by what he saw as their selection of features acceptable to themselves and the wider community and, in Eddie Mabo's case, a 'curious concoction of fact and fantasy' about the Malo-Bomai institution as 'the "traditional" government of Murray Islands'.[54]

The next chapter pursues further the argument that the judge's rather limited perception of the existential world of the Meriam may have its source in the Hobbesian assumption about a human nature 'peculiarly appropriate to a possessive market society' as the *universal* state of human nature.[55] He ignores the way in which the social processes of history created behaviour and desires lacking any motives other than 'self-interested contractual relations with others';[56] he then projects these social values on to the pre-Christian Meriam. These assumptions prevent him from taking seriously the synthetic ideas of Reverend Dave Passi as other than starry-eyed utopianism, a nostalgia for a romanticised version of the times of his ancestors, 'a propensity for selective', if honestly intentioned, reconstruction of the past.[57]

His perception is a world away from Meriam perspectives which may be summarised thus: the moral order, which the coming of Malo enshrined, carried the possibility of a transcendence of the old barriers of enmity. The major elements are the metaphor of eight clans in one body, which the octopus represented, regulated by a set of rules; and the conversion of enemies to friends, which brought about the end of an isolated existence through the long sea journeys of gift exchange, known as *wauri* voyages.[58] It was these elements, referred to by many witnesses in the court, and by Meriam outside the court, which provided the foundation for the acceptance of Christian teaching: in the Meriam perception, their grandparents and great-grandparents knew enough to recognise the 'true message' when it came.[59]

NO ORDINARY CASE

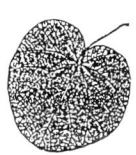

 A TRIAL OF TRUTH: OUTCOMES

THE PLAINTIFFS' CLAIMS TO CHAINS OF TITLE

Justice Moynihan heard evidence from the plaintiffs, Meriam witnesses, expert witnesses for the plaintiffs and the defendants, in the Supreme Court of Queensland, over 67 days in Brisbane in 1986, at Mer and Thursday Island in 1989 and again in Brisbane in 1989. His three-volume Determination of Issues of Fact of 227 pages was delivered on 16 November 1990.[1] It was based upon 3,489 pages of transcript, exhibits, including the witnesses' written proofs of evidence, and the pleadings (statements of claim as amended, affidavits, defences, statement of facts, particulars of land, reefs and seas claimed, and replies), which were appended to the Determination in their final form as annexure A.

Eddie Mabo's 36 claims were rejected by Justice Moynihan; the evidence given in the proceedings did not lead him to conclude that Eddie Mabo 'was adopted as heir by Benny and Maiga Mabo, or that Benny transferred land to him during his lifetime'.[2] On 16 November 1990 in Townsville, I shared with him the news that all his claims had been rejected by the court: the anguish of disbelief was visible in him as he announced to two of his friends, 'I'm out of the case now'. Fourteen months later he died.

Meriam witnesses, who appeared for Queensland, some of whom were his relatives, had contested his right to many of the plots of land he claimed, the position of certain land boundaries, and many of his claims regarding the alleged authority of 'the *Aets*'. A deathbed disinheritance by Benny Mabo was claimed and Eddie Mabo's short stay with his natural father at Thursday Island became a decisive ground for Justice Moynihan's conclusions rejecting the claim to his real adoption by Benny Mabo.[3]

The plaintiffs' witnesses who felt qualified to comment on Eddie Mabo's adoption said they believed he was the adopted son of Benny Mabo, as did defence witness Marwer Depoma, who appeared in court to dispute boundary claims by Eddie Mabo (TQ1216). Reverend Passi's conclusion, given to me after the case was completed, sums up the opinions of most of the plaintiffs' witnesses: that Eddie Mabo was raised and treated like a son and that his last name was taken for granted and went unchallenged by Benny Mabo himself.[4]

Ironically, Eddie Mabo's attempt to put together what he had absorbed through the words and example of Benny and Maigo Mabo ('My text books were my parents')[5] and what he had read in Haddon, Idriess and later writers, seems to have been a significant factor in losing him credibility in the eyes of the judge.[6] Beckett perceives the poignancy of Eddie Mabo's situation: 'It is ironic that while anthropologists become credible expert witnesses by writing, "natives" render themselves inauthentic by reading: tainted with literacy it seems they can't go home again!'.[7]

Reverend Dave Passi's claims to land at Zomared, Mer Island, and Giar Pit, Dauar Island, were taken by Justice Moynihan to be part of 'a general inchoate right as a Passi' to individual land claimed by the Passi family group as presented in three chains of title not subject to dispute (Determination (D) 213, cf 213A–213C). The table setting out claims submitted by Reverend Dave Passi to Passi land at Giar on Dauar Island, through at least five generations, covering a period prior to annexation to the current one, is presented in Figure 2.[8]

Evidence as to claims by James Rice, the third plaintiff, to land at Dauar was considered to be in 'an unsatisfactory state'. In the judge's view, 'the facts are now largely lost' and he was not 'prepared to act on it'; garden lands claimed at Bazmet and Deimi at Mer were not disputed by Justice Moynihan (D221).[9]

AN ENDURING LAND TENURE SYSTEM

After outlining the main features of a system covering the Meriam's relationship with their land, Justice Moynihan drew conclusions from the evidence regarding 'aspects of a continuous "system" operating in Murray Island society' today (D173). Village land, garden land, places of public ritual observance, adjacent reefs and fish traps were considered in turn. The first two were crucial to the Murray Islanders' claim, for they involve the question of the continuity of a system of land ownership. The fourth, relating to sea claims, is considered in Chapter 10.

Beginning with village boundaries, Justice Moynihan noted the continuing divisions into 'single residential lots', each with a single unit dwelling mainly inhabited by married couples and their children (D173). Each site is divided from the one adjoining by a boundary defined by a geographical or artificial feature.

> The rights associated with a site include a right to use it for domestic residence to the exclusion of others and an entitlement to determine the disposition of the land, either during life or as a consequence of death [D174].

Entitlements continue to be predominantly via a blood relative in the male line 'although this is now an extremely flexible concept' (D175). The Determination gives little active role to 'territorial affiliation' (through patriclan membership),

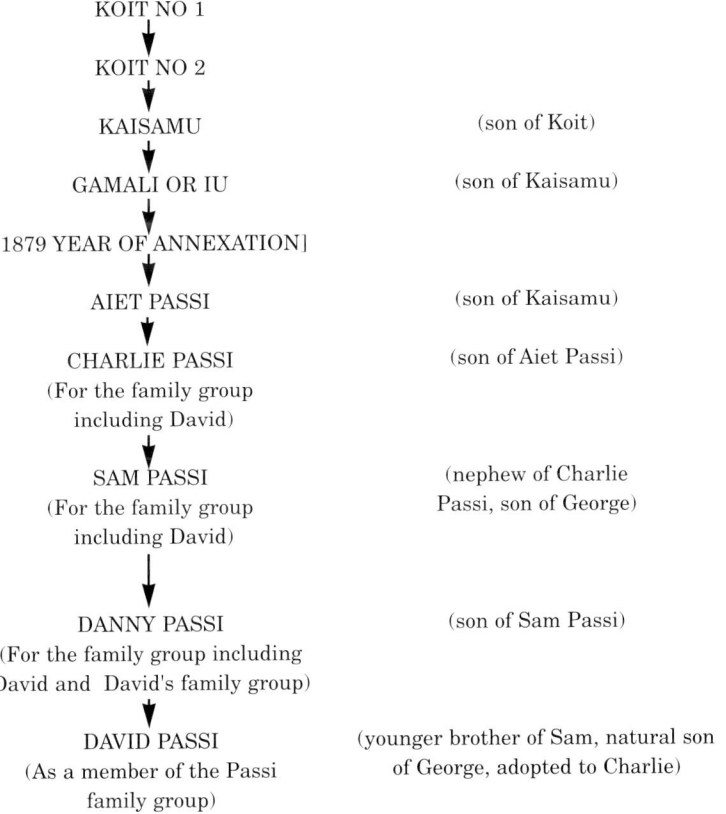

Figure 2 D Passi's claim to Giar, chain of title

in controlling access to village land in contemporary life, despite evidence to the contrary from many Meriam witnesses and from Margaret Lawrie (TQ2609, 2682–83).

The Determination drew three main conclusions about the continuity of a land tenure system in respect to garden land. First, the evidence established that the Meriam 'recognise the continuance of claims to garden plots', disputing or recognising individual claims of entitlement to those plots (D178). Second, traditional rules of inheritance continue for village residential land, and daughters may be given garden land as dowries (D179). Third, the evidence revealed no notion of title by vacant possession, and no notion of relinquishment of title by abandonment (D177).[10]

As the inquiry had been told, garden land plots are small; some measured by Beckett in 1959 were as small as 36 x 25 feet (11 x 7.5 metres), others as large as 485 x 180 feet (148 x 55 metres). Some were under full cultivation at the time of the hearing at Mer, others were not (TQ2205). Justice Moynihan concluded that Murray Islanders continue to make and cultivate gardens, hand down land through their families in accordance with custom, and recognise the rights of other landowners at the Murray Islands.

> I have little difficulty in accepting that the people of the Murray Islands perceive themselves as having an enduring relationship with land on the [Murray] Islands and the seas and reefs surrounding them [D157].

Referring to 'deeply ingrained social and cultural attitudes' of respect for others' land and for land boundaries among Murray Islanders, he reported that these attitudes were part of the personal make-up of Murray Islanders. He went on to explain that these deeply ingrained attitudes, expressing the right and proper way to behave, are like our good manners. He contrasted these 'good manners' with the legal provisions of his own society, which are laid down objectively in written statutory form or regulation and policed by officials of the state. He felt that 'a strong sense of the observation of propriety in respect of land' and 'of the appropriateness of being in your place or locality' rather than in somebody else's place was reflected in such words as 'shame and trespass' (D157).

His conclusion parallels closely those drawn by Beckett and Lawrie, ones which seem to have been favoured by the judge during the proceedings in Brisbane in 1989 (see Chapter 7). There was agreement that unwritten codes of conduct had become part of Meriam character; what they were 'brought up with', as Reverend Passi said. The morality that Haddon wrote about concerning social obligation was, as an everyday practice, 'enforced not by a special judiciary or executive body but by public opinion'.[11] This feeling of social obligation — the obligation to respect others' rights, the mirror image of others respecting one's own rights — was seen as 'a powerful social sanction'. Lawrie had recalled her observation that children never strayed beyond their own village boundaries: this was 'a custom, a practice' they observed, not something forced upon them. 'Force is not a word that occurred to me. It was the way they lived' (TQ2612).

As we have seen, the Murray Islanders' claims were distinctive in important ways. They claimed specific plots of land themselves and on behalf of family groups; they had drawn up for the court the boundaries of their village and garden lands. They claimed usufructuary rights (use and enjoyment of property) to specified lands, and they cited Murray Island law, which many of them identified explicitly as Malo's Law, which instructs them to cultivate and conserve the land and its produce, and to keep their hands and feet off land belonging to other Murray Islanders.

Justice Moynihan saw some of these rights and duties as a reason for differentiating between Murray Islanders and Justice Blackburn's characterisation of the Yolngu people of Yirrkala on the Gove Peninsula: 'I am . . . dealing with a very different society and very different relationships and attitudes towards land' to those of Yirrkala people (D12). He saw the Murray Islands as 'the home of a dynamic society' (D13), in which the Meriam retained and carried forward from pre-contact times 'a strong sense of relationship to their Islands', having 'no doubt that the Murray Islands are theirs' (D155–56). After listening to many Islander witnesses repeat and explain parts of Malo's Law in court, he concluded that Malo's Law 'is a manifestation of social attitudes deeply imbued in the culture of Murray Islanders' (D137).

In enumerating the factors which combined to create and re-create social cohesion, he placed the main emphasis on cultural factors: socialisation through 'a constant pattern of examples of imitation and repetition' was, he concluded, paraphrasing Lawrie, 'part of their environment — the way in which they lived' (D124). And he had absorbed Haddon's conclusion that rules of conduct were defined and largely enforced by public opinion.[12] He drew attention to the feelings of shame the Meriam experienced when their misconduct became the subject of public ridicule as a most potent force in social regulation. 'Words such as shame and trespass . . . reflect deeply ingrained social and cultural attitudes' among Murray Islanders today (D157).

Justice Moynihan mentioned sorcery and *maid* (powerful hostile magic) which, he concluded, like *sab tonar*, the practice of placing a taboo on a garden (D128), may be embedded deeply in the memory of some Murray Islanders; but he concluded that as effective practices they have 'ceased to be part of the fabric of the society' (D128–29).

The Determination follows Beckett's characterisation of 'what has been called Malo's law'; it is 'a manifestation of general precepts of conduct', 'a general framework in which to make decisions not a system of law', rather like 'our . . . concept of good manners' (D137; cf D157). Although not always explicit, Justice Moynihan's rejection of the idea of the existence of a system of Meriam law has much in common with the definition of law as 'a command of the sovereign', the ultimate position taken by the defence in *Milirrpum*.

Justice Moynihan's observations here are similar to those of Chief Justice McEachern in his judgment in *Delgamuukw v British Columbia* (1991). The latter stated that what the Indian 'witnesses describe as law is really a most uncertain and highly flexible set of customs which are frequently not followed by the Indians themselves . . . there always seemed to be an aboriginal exception which made almost any departure from aboriginal rules permissible. In my judgment, these rules are so flexible and uncertain that they cannot be classified as laws.'[13]

In the context of his rejection of the Meriam plaintiffs' claim to the operation of a system of indigenous law, Justice Moynihan did not find any connection between these 'precepts' and Malo beliefs over the period in which the Malo-Bomai religious order was forced to cease its role of social regulation (D137). This, I am arguing, was fatal to the process of understanding Meriam social life, Meriam meaning systems and the character of the Meriam people.

MALO AND THE FULFILMENT OF THE OLD MORAL ORDER

Underlying Malo's Law and giving it a sacred endowment is the myth of Malo and Bomai (Malo's maternal uncle) and the narrative of their long sea journeys across the western and central islands to Mer in the east. The origins of Malo's Law within the sacred charter of the myth were not explained to the court by the expert witnesses. No doubt this contributed to Justice Moynihan's finding that the origins of Malo's Law were 'diffuse and obscure' (D137). Furthermore, the meanings of the narrative sequences of the myth in marking out the named landscape of the Meriam, and the consequent drawing of that sacred track into their social orbit, did not become clear to him. Through the Malo myth, those in the far-away islands and coastal villages of New Guinea, the non-reciprocal 'enemies' of the 'other side', were drawn into a reciprocal relationship of giving and returning through what have become known in Meriam oral tradition as *wauri* voyages. *Wauri* is the Meriam name for the cone shell, which, either unmodified or as armlets, was the most valuable item in Meriam gift exchanges.[14]

Justice Moynihan was aware that the Malo myth 'is a matter of enormous complexity and significance' for 'understanding the culture of the [Meriam] people'. He was sensitive to a quality of 'deep mystery', and there is a note of humility in his admission that 'my understanding of it is inadequate in the extreme' (D132). The 'story', as he repeatedly called the narrative sequences of the myth, inadvertently trivialising a sacred text, was presented to the court from Margaret Lawrie's book, *Myths and Legends of Torres Strait*. That version is a retranslation of the myth as written by Aiet Passi (Sam, Dave and George Passi's grandfather) for the linguist Sidney Ray in 1898.[15] Justice Moynihan did not become conversant with the character of the myth as a sacred charter that provided the foundation of a moral order among the Meriam.

The myth of the two culture heroes Malo-Bomai consists of two complementary narratives. In the first, Bomai, the more sacred of the two heroes, travels from Tuger, in West New Guinea, to Mer, transforming himself into the shapes of different sea creatures as he goes from island to island. He arrives at Teker on the southern side of Mer in the form of an octopus, and is recognised as a *zogo* or supernatural being by a woman who is fishing on the reef. The basket into which she and her husband place Bomai is stolen by her brothers-in-law from the village of Las. Eventually the people become friends and agree that Bomai should remain at Las. In the second narrative, Malo arrives with his four brothers to find his maternal uncle, Bomai. Some of his party spear Malo in the back; they give the Murray Islanders the drums they brought with them and teach them new dances.[16] As a creature which unites eight tentacles in one body, Malo (the name used publicly for the very sacred Bomai) carries a heavy load of symbolic meaning as a religious mediator, bringing together in one body the eight landowning clans or *nosik* of the Murray Islands. Each of these eight 'tribes', as the Meriam call them, has an independent identity defined and reinforced by a separate *lubabat* or totem, a clan territory (in which village land is situated) and an associated wind or season (see Chapter 7), and all the clans had and still retain a marked propensity for feuding. Integral to the law's sanctification in the myth (and, as was revealed in court, the law pre-dates Malo) is the fact that part of the words of Malo ra Gelar (Malo's Law) form one of the five sacred chants or *ikok* sung during Malo triennial religious ceremonies.

Notwithstanding the destruction of the Malo-Bomai sacred order (or 'cult') as an institution, Malo's Law continues to carry the force of a religious commandment. Meriam people who are especially well versed in matters of law and tradition say that Malo's laws are like those of the Christian religion, so in this respect their conversion to Christianity made no fundamental difference. Either religion tells us how to live together: these are the rules we Meriam must follow, said the late Sam Passi. A former chairman of the Murray Island Council, eldest son and therefore the nameholder for Passi land, a man of special knowledge in the tradition of his grandfather, a *Zogo le* or priest of Malo, and an exemplar in the Malo tradition as a champion gardener, he was described by Justice Moynihan as 'an old, influential, impressive traditional Murray Islander' (D192).

Between 1982 and 1984 Sam Passi recorded with me his ideas about Malo and Christianity. In teaching him Malo's Law as a very young man, his grandfather, Aiet Passi, had likened Malo's Law to the Old Testament; it provided fertile ground for the ready acceptance of Christian teaching. In this view Christianity did not mean an abrupt change, but an extension of the old religious–moral order: 'Once you learnt that [Malo's teaching] you can just manage to do something that is written in the New Testament'.[17]

His younger brother, Anglican priest Reverend Dave Passi, had also developed his own interpretation of the two traditions in which he came to 'see Christianity as the fulfilment, the extension of Malo'.[18] He went on to ground his understanding and practice of Malo's Law within the Malo tradition, joining together the meaning of the law as a set of rights and obligations to one another in the here and now with the law as a way of following in the footsteps of his forebears, a statement about land tenure and inheritance.

The state of Queensland had argued that, even if the Malo-Bomai cult had regulated dealings in land in the past, the Meriam had failed to produce 'anything that replaced the [Malo] cult as the regulator of land' (TQ3486). In contrast, the plaintiffs' senior counsel noted the way 'every witness' referred to 'a set of rules of conduct which they felt was obligatory upon them' (TQ3467), contending that it does not matter whether these rules are called Malo's laws or a set of common principles, or whether they are precisely the same as before annexation: 'what matters is that here is a continuity' today with laws that operated in the past (TQ3474). In this context, counsel was correct and prudent in side-stepping consideration of the reasons why witnesses observed a common set of rules of behaviour. The reasons why the Meriam felt themselves bound together in this way were not pursued.

They felt themselves obliged to follow Malo's Law because this formed the core of their humanity as Murray Islanders. Meriam people recall occasions in the 1930s when certain passages of Malo's Law were said while a taboo was being placed on a garden at a time when a particular fruit such as coconut had been depleted. In 1962, Marou Mimi, one of the guardians of tradition, began to foster and promote Malo's instructions that Meriam on the whole island took for granted.

The outward severance between Malo and Malo's Law, which came about through the agency of the missionaries, had had two effects: first, it drove the source of the practice of Malo's Law into silence; second, the cultural revival which swept through the outposts of the former colonial empires in the 1960s and 1970s was given a variety of expressions by the Meriam rather late in the piece. By the middle to late 1970s, a cultural revival found expression among Murray Islanders in ways which sought to bridge the gap between the old and the new.

This was a process of 'selective continuity' which Justice Moynihan rejected as outside the 'real' tradition, which he saw as the sum total of what 'had been'. His findings reveal insight into the way in which Murray Islanders wish to secure 'their and their people's future in a world substantially dominated by others' (D65), a position derived from Beckett. But in their integration of the Malo story with the Christian tradition, Eddie Mabo and Father Passi are seen to ignore 'some of the darker aspects of the [Malo] cult' (D132). This led the judge to see Father Passi's understanding of Christianity as a fulfilment of the ancient promise of Malo simply in terms of his particular temperament or idiosyncrasy (D206), rather than as an expression of a selective continuity in which reciprocal relationships retain the identity embodied in the words brotherhood or sisterhood, in-laws, partners-in-Malo.

Over a period before the court case, Meriam people and other Torres Strait Islanders with special custodial knowledge had begun to articulate their position on Malo and Christianity. As Flo Kennedy put it, Malo's 'teaching' was sufficient for the Meriam of 'those days' to live together according to a moral code; it 'was a good teaching but not the teaching'.[19] She is evoking the same idea as Reverend Passi when he says that Malo gave them the understanding to appreciate and make sense of 'a bigger truth' when it 'arrived'.

Justice Moynihan's deep, though understandable, ignorance of the meaning and significance of Malo as an institution, as a belief system and as moral–legal order, led him to diminish the sense of succession to which each of the plaintiffs gave expression.

THE SPIRITUAL–RELIGIOUS AND THE MATERIAL–ECONOMIC

Justice Moynihan was impressed primarily by what he saw as the cultural difference between the Meriam and the Yolngu Aboriginal people. Reflecting upon the 'considerable debt' he owed to Justice Blackburn's judgment in *Milirrpum* for the light it cast upon his own work, he nevertheless concluded, 'I am however dealing with a very different society and very different relationships with and attitudes towards land to those with which he was contending' (D12). In contrast to the Yolngu, the Meriam's tie to land and sea 'was and is not a religious or spiritual relationship of the kind which emerged, for example, in *Milirrpum v Nabalco*' (D155, cf D170).

In making this contrast, Justice Moynihan focused exclusively upon the way in which competition for scarce resources was socially regulated — an economic preoccupation — at the Murray Islands. Thus he concluded that the maintenance of 'social order', the quest for 'social harmony', not concern for 'the intrinsic value of the land', give definition to the character of the Meriam relationship to their land: the Meriam 'need to control access in the terms of distribution or sharing of life sustaining or socially advantageous resources in a potentially volatile social environment' (D170). This view reflects very closely that of anthropologist Jeremy Beckett. The latter drew attention to the volatile social environment created by a struggle for scarce resources. Malo's Law provided the overall framework manifest in certain precepts which so regulated people's behaviour that they could live relatively peaceably with one another (TQ2232). Justice Moynihan concluded that given the primary focus of Beckett's work, his particular concern was with 'the development of responses and transformations' among the Meriam in the process of contact with the modern world, not so much with pre-contact Meriam society and culture.

Justice Moynihan saw it as useful in 'showing that Murray Island society is resilient and adaptive to change', and 'less useful in founding conclusions' about social life and Meriam ideas about the world before that society was transformed (D44).

Jeremy Beckett was the first anthropologist to follow the Haddon team, undertaking field work at Mer between 1958 and 1961, 60 years after Haddon's visit. In that period the culture had waned. As he reflected a quarter of a century later, the 'centre of gravity' of his study lay in the transitional period when the tide was about to turn on the 'old colonial regime'.[20] Looking back in 1994 on the syntheses made by cultural leaders such as Reverend Dave Passi, Beckett notes that the apparent absence of the idea of Malo as the precursor of Christianity among the Meriam in 1961 does not preclude the possibility 'that its seeds were there, waiting for a more liberal climate such as the 1980s offered'.[21]

In the years between 1978 and 1983, those who took the responsibilities of custodians of Meriam culture were expressing exactly the same principles in relation to the Malo tradition as they did in court. They could have been mistaken for a different people to those whom Beckett had written about in 1963.[22] In the period in which the case began and proceeded, the doldrums of spiritual weariness and lack of confidence had begun to disappear.[23]

Sadly, the perceptions Beckett brought to the court did not discern that such seeds were sown deeply among the Meriam. Perhaps a significant point being missed here is the power of a religious cult (in this case Malo-Bomai) to expand an older totemic culture.[24] The apparent absence of an integrative institution helped create Justice Moynihan's picture of pre-colonial Meriam society as a one-sided 'tribal anarchy' where 'disputes are resolved by having a brawl or avoiding a brawl'.[25] This ignores a two-sidedness in pre-colonial Meriam society and leads to a picture of a rough and ready 'primitive secularism' which, as I have argued in the preceding chapter, has its origins in a generalisation to all humankind, of a Hobbesian essentialist view of human nature.[26]

Justice Moynihan's interpretation of the view that Christianity inaugurated 'a new moral order' (D102, 141)[27] leaves little room for that of the Murray Islander plaintiffs that, some hundreds of years before the missionaries arrived at Mer, the Malo-Bomai myth gave the Meriam a way of living together in widening interrelationships of reciprocity. It put a curb on feuding, widened the possibilities of intermarriage, which itself further reduced enmity while by no means eliminating divisions or 'brawls'. This process gave the Meriam the possibility of 'showing the flag' to those they exchanged and traded with overseas and in this way further consolidated Meriam identity.

Embedded in Justice Moynihan's findings of fact is this legally cogent half-truth about the Meriam. In the context of the Meriam land case, that half may have helped the Meriam to win their case. The other half remained shrouded in 'deep mystery' for Justice Moynihan. Yet, divested of its spiritual–religious core, the depth and richness of Meriam social and cultural life evaporates: for, in the sense that religion places immediate events in ultimate contexts, the Meriam are a people for whom the daily round is a religious experience.[28] There is a certain poignancy in this reduction of the Meriam sense of existence. To blot out their spiritual connection with land is to cut the Meriam off from what Stanner referred to among Aboriginal people as the 'body of patent truth about the universe that no one in his right mind would have thought of bringing to the bar of proof'. This he goes on to describe as the 'inherent and imperishable bonds' between the ancestors and the living through land and totems.[29]

An important complexity in the hearing of the facts arose from the way in which the conversion of the Meriam to Christianity within a generation of the arrival of the missionaries on Mer in 1872 was used by Queensland to drive witnesses into a contradiction between following Malo's Law and worshipping God, not Malo. In his affidavit of 16 August 1982, Patrick Killoran claimed that the conversion of the Meriam to Christianity following the arrival of the missionaries on Mer had destroyed their former way of life and customs.[30] Counsel for the Murray Islanders had argued for an essential continuity in belief, custom and law between the Meriam today and their pre-Christian forebears. In the context of this argument, the defence sought to constrain witnesses to make a choice between Malo and Christianity. For example, in cross-examination by the counsel for the Commonwealth, one witness, Jack Wailu, said he worshipped the traditional Meriam god, Malo-Bomai. In further cross-examination the defence counsel made a rather simplistic effort to drive him into a contradiction between worshipping Malo-Bomai and taking an oath on the Bible:

Q.   Do you agree when you started your evidence you took an oath on the Bible?
A.   Yes, I believe that.

Q.   Do you see the Bible as part of your Christian faith . . . ?
A.   Yes.

Q. Do you believe it is possible to worship Bomai Malo as well as the Christian God?

A. Well ... I go back to worship our God, I meant the way ... they used to practise among my grandfather, the same way I have to practice [sic] to direct me on the right path. That's the way I meant to go back to my traditional God of the land.

Q. So what you said earlier about worshipping Bomai is not right? Is that it [TQ1279]?

The witness, speaking in English, his third language, was not given the opportunity to answer outside an either-or framework, a mode of thinking not essential to Meriam logic.

When it came to Sam Passi's turn for cross-examination, the same tactic was used, but without success; counsel desisted from further questioning along these lines. In reply to questions from the plaintiffs' counsel, Mr Passi had said, 'Yes, certainly I follow them' [Malo's laws] (TQ1101–03), as a Christian I find them 'as good as Christianity' (TQ1103). In cross-examination he went on to make a highly affirmative statement about the uniqueness of Meriam people's identity as 'Malo's Law Christians'.

Q. Is the Bomai Malo religion still a religion for the people on this island, as far as you can say? I use the word 'religion' very carefully, Mr Passi?

A. I don't worship Malo any more, but the rules are there — very good.

Q. That is about land and good behaviour?

A. Good behaviour and we still practice [sic] this. If you want to be a real Murray Islander you follow Malo's law [TQ1115].

Justice Moynihan saw Malo's Law as 'a manifestation of social attitudes deeply imbued in the culture of Murray Islanders', which have the character of a 'general framework' laying down 'general precepts of conduct' (D134). In his perception however, the destruction of the Malo-Bomai cult as an institution had left a vacuum. He saw no religious legitimation or spiritual dimension in Meriam 'interests' in land.

As we have seen, Justice Blackburn perceived the Yolngu's relationship with their land as a spiritual one.[31] Reversing that perception for the

Meriam, Justice Moynihan saw their relationship to the land as an exclusively utilitarian one (D155). Neither depiction is more than half of the truth; the one contributed to the failure of a land case, the other was instrumental in rendering Meriam land tenure (albeit in a distorted form) more accessible to the judge. Both descriptions, I suggest, are part of a culture-bound and specifically social evolutionist perception: the Yolngu, traditionally hunters and gatherers, are 'less like' European societies and perceived as 'most primitive'; the horticultural Meriam, whose interests in small allotments to land appear to be more like those of the English, are seen as more 'advanced'.

Nancy Williams has suggested that, in the *Milirrpum* case, emphasis on the religious dimension of the Yolngu's relationship with their land tended to exclude the social and the economic. She went on to show the connection between the presumed absence of an economic conception of land as 'the substance of proprietary interests' and Justice Blackburn's rejection of the plaintiffs' claim:

> Because it lacked concepts of property that existed in contemporary common law, Yolngu ownership by right of title was found to be a matter of religious belief and not of economic significance. It was therefore not law.[32]

The Meriam's land tenure system has qualities which bear a recognisable resemblance to English property rights. Severed from its source in sacred endowment and religious certitude, their land tenure was perceived by Justice Moynihan as qualitatively different to Aboriginal interests in land which Justice Blackburn had designated as non-proprietary 20 years earlier.

The European concept of property is, as Williams observes, 'fundamentally an economic concept' based upon exclusive individual rights. Its corollary is that the economic conception of property embodied in a system of law is the fully developed system and model against which all other systems of law or practices or custom may be measured.[33] Justice Moynihan made clear his recognition of the difficulty of applying the concepts of one culture in order to judge another. Yet he was unaware that the Meriam relationship to land is both spiritual *and* material. On this culturally specific question of the inseparability of the religious from the economic–material in Meriam existence, his perception appears to have been limited by a framework which operates within the binary, that is, either-or, categories characteristic of Western thought.

Canadian legal scholar Kent McNeil has argued that Aboriginal people's relationship to land 'is generally holistic' and the very distinction between the spiritual and the material may be a European one.[34] Here he is following Justice Blackburn's conceptualisation of the Aboriginal relationship to land as existing within 'one indissoluble whole' in which people and spirit ancestors and their 'universes' are not felt as distinct. While this is true of the Meriam, as we have seen in Chapter 4, the instruction to engage in 'economic activity' — Malo plants everywhere — acts as an outward and visible sign of deeper religious truths. In Sam Passi's thinking it is also a metaphorical statement which says, 'As ye sow, so also shall ye reap'. Malo makes possible that mediation which brings the 'other' into the realm of the 'we' through the reciprocity of sowing and harvesting.

For the modern Meriam person existence is inconceivable without religious mediation. Whether one speaks at a clan or an interclan level, religious mediation remains central through ancestral succession (*lubabat* or clan totems), through Malo symbolised by the octopus, or through Jesus Christ as universal mediator, or all of these mediators. Certainly there are secular agencies such as the elected Murray Island Council which regulate social behaviour; and their meetings always begin with a prayer. Moreover, notwithstanding Justice Moynihan's conclusion that magic and sorcery, along with Malo beliefs and rituals, have no active presence in maintaining social order in Meriam life today, it is a matter of common knowledge among all contemporary Meriam people that hostile magic (*maid* and *puripuri*), and the fear of it, is a continuing and active regulating force in their social life.

As soon as the court had completed its hearings of the facts, the Meriam proceeded to talk about their land within the local idiom. Freed of the constraints placed on witnesses by hearsay rules, by the logic of the either-or categories into which witnesses were required to frame their answers (and hence by the need to be steered away from issues which carried apparent contradiction), by the problem of the translating Meriam concepts into a language accessible to an English-Australian court, by the problem of explaining culturally specific and complex concepts in what for many witnesses is their third language, they spoke about their 'body of patent truth', about themselves, about their land and their ancestors and their totems, and about God and Malo. Sitting on his land, James Rice elaborated on what he had said in a sanitised and truncated form in court: 'These are not any white people's names . . . I say Bazmet — this is my ancestor's name. And this land belongs to my ancestors.'

Reverend Dave Passi explained in a similar vein: 'It's my father's land, it's my grandfather's land, it's my grandmother's land. I'm related to it, which also gives me my identity.' Flo Kennedy went on to explain the meaning behind the naming of lands by ancestors: 'To us they are still alive. Their spirits still live . . . We still have a responsibility to them. Now they told us that the land is ours. And their fathers before them.'[35]

Meriam culture has its own distinctiveness. As Williams's work has revealed in relation to the complexities and authenticity of their land tenure, so too has Yolngu culture. Meriam people's identity is also set within a broad context in which their relationship to the land is founded upon broadly similar general principles to those of the Yolngu. Again, as Williams has noted for the Yolngu, ontology and cosmology (the nature of being and ideas about the universe) 'are embedded in a single matrix',[36] so that the economic and the spiritual are inseparable within 'a system in which economic ends are as explicitly served as religious belief is experienced'. For the Meriam as for the Yolngu the ' "religious", "historic", and "economic" are not mutually exclusive categories; they are complementary and indivisible'.[37]

INTERESTS ONLY PARTLY KNOWN TO ENGLISH LAW

A LITTLE KNOWLEDGE CAN BE A DANGEROUS THING

There are three main areas of danger in the reduction of the Meriam interrelationships with the land to the economic dimension. First, as I have said, it thins out and trivialises European Australians' perceptions of the Meriam's reasons for existence; in so doing it cuts people off from appreciation of the strength the Meriam brought to the case.

Second, the sacred endowment of the Meriam binds together inseparably the 'entities' of ownership and sovereignty that were separated for the purposes of the case. This distinction within English law is not sustainable within the ambit of Meriam law and social life. Given the many-sidedness of Meriam relationships with their land, any attempt to carry this procedural separation into the social relationships of everyday life will create and foster misunderstandings with the Meriam; at some point in time, this misperception will be manifest at least in strained relations, at most in situations of confrontation.[38]

Third, this depiction of the Meriam may help to keep alive the theoretical foundation of social evolutionist assumptions about the superiority of the Meriam as a horticultural people in contrast to Aboriginal people as hunter-gatherers. The findings of fact in the *Milirrpum* and *Mabo (No 2)* cases each characterised the respective people in a partial, incomplete way; the former, consistent with Western evolutionist ideas of a lesser humanity without a system of proprietorship of land. The practical consequences are highly dangerous and potentially explosive: on the one hand it may drive in further a wedge between Aboriginal and Islander people, and on the other it may perpetuate the longstanding discriminatory policies and practices towards the two indigenous peoples.

Unlike the Yolngu plaintiffs, the continuity of certain Meriam chains of title to specified plots of clearly bounded land handed down mainly by patrilineal inheritance, from a time before annexation until today, to owners on behalf of lineage and family groups, was demonstrated to the satisfaction of the court. The Meriam were able to establish the fact of the ongoing regulation of a traditional land tenure system through 'the survival' of rules they had internalised as obligatory. However, if the 'facts' they demonstrated to the court should carry the perception of too great an affinity of their title with that embodied in English law, then 'racial discrimination' in its old form may simply be displaced or supplemented by an inter-cultural distortion which continues to work within social evolutionist categories.

PARADOXES OF CROSS-CULTURAL PERCEPTIONS

Justice Moynihan himself addressed the difficult subject of cultural difference and the intransigent and controversial problem of cross-cultural perceptions. He devoted a whole chapter of his Determination to considerations bearing on the evidence of witnesses and his evaluation of the evidence of important witnesses.

The opening page of the chapter represents the judge's consideration of the problem of understanding cultural difference; in modern anthropology this problem is formulated as the need to understand another culture within its own terms. In his Determination, Justice Moynihan perceived a vast contrast to his own culture in an ownership system where ' "Everything is owned, land, reefs, rocks, stones, stars, winds, tracts of sea" ', he concluded, citing Lawrie

(D57). He was aware that a person's knowledge of his or her own culture may fill the gaps in their knowledge of another culture; he identified the context of legal proceedings in which issues are defined in a particular way by the pleadings, 'by the rules of evidence and the adversarial process'. He saw also the dangers of preconception: 'A different perspective may well have led to different conclusions' (D57). He did not exempt himself thus from the realm of cultural if not legal bias, a discourse which 'encourages apparent precision on factual matters' (D57).

His main point of concentration was not on these foci of bias but on some of the problems of the oral tradition. He gave special emphasis to the selection by Meriam witnesses of positive or presentable features of their culture. He identified their purpose as that of convincing the wider community of the desirability of their pre-contact social life and, within this context, seeking to create a good image of the claimant, so giving recognition or kudos to that person not otherwise achieved (D63). These particular insights have a certain truth. They also miss a point of paramount cultural significance for the Meriam: how certain underlying principles of the culture may form a guide to the creation of a future for their children that retains a fidelity to those principles.

Justice Moynihan gave no examples of what he had in mind on either the bias inherent in legal proceedings or the wider problem of the variable ways in which meaning is constituted in different cultures. It was a gesture towards consideration of cross-cultural translation, not a consideration itself. I would argue that legal proceedings, especially those of an adversarial nature, may highlight the problems of evaluating as well as perceiving difference. Meriam society before European invasion was founded upon face to face reciprocal ties; it was constituted in myth and the thought patterns of the Meriam are constituted in the mythopoeic mode, which is preoccupied with the I and Thou of living systems and processes. From the perspective of the logical constructs of Western legal assumptions and procedure the rules of Meriam society were imprecise and open-ended; the Meriam legal process was a consensual one based upon the imperative of re-creating equivalence, of making things fair and square, as Islanders put it. As we have seen, the oral tradition and the absence of corporate political authority in pre-invasion Meriam society created special, almost insuperable problems of understanding for the court. The former tested the boundaries of the court's rules of evidence; the latter stretched the court's comprehension to its limits.

This latter question exemplifies Justice Moynihan's insight into the process of extrapolating from the knowledge of one's own culture to interpret an unknown one. We abhor not only vacuums, as he observed; we also need to resolve puzzles, and the enigma of a social system without a government or executive in the Western sense had to be resolved in his mind to enable him to give a report on the evidence. The Determination fails to perceive that perceptual biases also contain values. As I have suggested in Chapter 7, the simplicity of his assumptions coloured the summaries and interpretations he interpolated in the course of the hearings; they almost certainly coloured his evaluation of Meriam culture. Their intention was to assist in a process of clarification and often they did this, especially on interpretations of the law. His conclusions about the dangers of cross-cultural bias are accurate; they are also bland and display a lack of insight into the problems as they manifested themselves concretely. His discussion of the distorting effects inherent in the oral tradition in reconstructing the past 'from the perspective of today' (D58) illustrate this point.

As the Determination points out, the Meriam oral tradition began to be modified after 1879 when the first published work appeared in the Meriam language with the gospel according to St Mark. This process modified the language: as the linguist Sidney Ray reported, the 'exuberant grammatical forms' became abbreviated in the transformation from an oral to a written communication,[39] and this 'cut it short' form, to use a Meriam expression, was reflected in the instruction given in the first London Missionary Society school known as the Papuan Institute, which was established at Mer in 1879. Most important for the argument was that, by the time the anthropological expedition arrived at Mer from Cambridge in 1898, many Meriam could read and write.[40] Meriam myths, traditions and customs, many written down by Pasi, the grandfather of Sam and Dave Passi, became part of the first written literature of the Murray Islands in the third volume of the Cambridge expedition. Oral tradition had been transformed into the form and language of a different culture and in the latter form it received a new status.

In the period since the six volumes of the Cambridge expedition were published, some Meriam people had seen the genealogies collected by the anthropologists and a number of witnesses 'appeared to have been exposed to Haddon's work directly or indirectly' (D60). They had also read other written material about themselves not all of which was accurate; for example, many Islanders, including Eddie Mabo, had been influenced by Ion Idriess's *Drums of*

Mer, perhaps the main written source to project an image of the *Zogo le* of Mer as high priests or chiefs who acted as a council, presiding over land disputes.[41]

CHANGE AND 'CHANGELESSNESS'

The Determination gives much weight to the effects of 'selective' reconstruction of the past by some witnesses based on present attitudes and hopes for the future of the Meriam community. Here Justice Moynihan drew not only on Beckett, but more generally on problems of oral history and customary law raised by specialist writers. Specifically, he raised the question of the need to separate what 'was' and 'is' from what 'ought' and 'ought to have been', 'and to be aware that "human memory the fluid memory is a marvellous instrument of elimination and transformation" ' (D62).[42] Justice Moynihan cited Martin Chanock's conclusion that statements about customary law may be less statements about the law as it was in the past, and more 'about what it ought to have been in the past and should be in the present'.[43]

This sorting process necessarily involves a selection; the process of looking back and evaluating the past may show the tenacity and adaptability of culture. Justice Moynihan saw the attempt to select 'contemporaneously attractive aspects' of say the Bomai-Malo cult or the Malo myth and 'integrate them with some aspects of Christianity', as, for example, is done by Reverend Dave Passi, as 'extremely selective and distorting' of the old culture (D64).

This conclusion not only fails to take account of the context in which Chanock raises his questions; it misses his main point. Citing Marc Bloch's important insight into the way customary law underwent changes 'behind a facade of change-lessness', how such law 'remains young, always in the belief that it is old',[44] how 'the "sanction of immemorial time can be given to relatively new rules" ',[45] Chanock concludes that the question one must ask is not so much whether the statements made are true about the period with which they are concerned: 'Evidence about customary law, then, is primarily evidence about the people giving it, about the circumstances and changes with which they are grappling'. Like myth, customary law is timeless: it is a meaningful rather than an 'objective record'. When people refer to customary law as 'old' they are not making a strict statement about its age: 'they are indicating its *high quality*'.[46]

The Determination considers the introduction of the written tradition into Meriam social life and its effect on customary law. It raises a problem of the 'extraneous introduction' by Meriam witnesses of supposed features of past Meriam society, not features which are 'a manifestation of Murray Island society connected with or flowing from the past' (D86).

Two questions were raised by Justice Moynihan on the effects of the transformation of Meriam Mir (and in effect, Meriam literacy in English) into a written language: the first concerns its relevance to the claim to an oral tradition; the second concerns how much 'current tradition' is about Meriam social life as it was, and how much of it is 'a reconstruction of it from the perspective of today' (D58). As I have argued, because he did not perceive the culturally conservationist reasons for the Meriam's preoccupation with the 'past', his exclusive concern was with distortions flowing from reconstruction of the past from today's perspective.

An important point about the introduction of the written tradition is not so much the corrupting effects of extraneous or fanciful or historically inaccurate writings and how these became woven into Meriam world views and perceptions, but the way in which written records, especially the body of Meriam jurisprudence registered in the Court Book, began to render Meriam law immutable.

Chanock considers how only after written forms became established 'did the English courts of the middle ages begin to insist that custom be provable in a real historical sense'. 'Literary forms drove the creativity and contemporaneity of custom out of English law'; 'literacy and the system of precedent' came to do the same in African courts.[47] The demand that claims about customary law be 'historically true' also meant it had to be presented as immutable. This change parallels the way that the social boundaries of cultural groups, once characterised by a fluidity which signified present alliances and gave room for their change, were required to be firm in the manner and following the imperatives of nineteenth-century nation states. As Torres Strait Islander colonial history demonstrates vividly, with the introduction of a single administration, a marine commodity economy and the conversion of Islanders to Christianity, 'Island custom' as it was called became more *explicit*, forming a kind of parallel with the rigidifying of geographical and social boundaries.[48]

In the 1960s, a political situation began to crystallise in which the old, seemingly 'natural' assumptions would either be lost or brought into the centre of awareness. Justice Moynihan concluded that 'Marou seems to have been responsible for the dissemination of what came to be called in the course of the hearing "Malo's Laws" among the community' (D61). My work with the

Meriam, begun late in 1978, which tapped into cultural matters well before the court hearings, points unmistakably to a widespread awareness of Malo's Law. A process of crystallisation of cultural traditions, begun in the late 1930s, found new expression in the 1960s; it made explicit that law which had been followed in everyday life as a sort of 'cultural given' or common sense. The process of the court case itself and the recognition of native title among the Meriam has set going a process of codification of Meriam laws. In making them explicit and in attempting to find *the* one version, they are divested of those qualities which they share with myth where different versions serve as means of verification of truths as well as of mutability.[49] Moreover the realm of secrecy, with its role of regulation, is marginalised: you may still tip-toe, silent and careful . . . you may still follow *teter mek*, footprints of the parents and the forebears, but the old secret ways which convey a sense of mystery and danger in wrongdoing are coming to be supplanted by public by-laws.

A paradox of the trial and the Determination of Issues of Fact is that when the Meriam witnesses continue to do what they have probably always done — to assess the way they want to be now and in the future, to see Malo's Law, as they know it today, as a guide to their social life — they are making a cultural statement which is seen as unintentionally or self-servingly selective. As we have seen, Justice Moynihan seems to have assumed a firm 'then and now' of 'before' and 'today', which is not appropriate to the mythical-customary ways of a predominantly oral culture. The written mode of the Murray Island Court was more comprehensible to him. Yet again, the extraneous and the distorting effects of writing, the very invariability and formalisation given to Malo's Law by its written form, reduces its flexibility in coping with change in a way that might continue the principles of the past.

The court case has contributed towards a strengthening of Meriam culture by making explicit Meriam custom, law and meaning systems. It has also created new paradoxes. In the new circumstances of recognition of native title at the Murray Islands, the laws of Malo, a subject of public reflection and private introspection, are being incorporated into the Mer Island by-laws. As we have seen, Malo's Law exists in various versions, a result of the flexibility of the oral tradition. However the past generations saw it, contemporary Meriam people know this explicitly. The acceptance of one 'standard' version of Malo's Law in written form transforms and reifies Meriam society into bounded categories, inhibiting the creativity and flexibility which are the hallmarks of the oral tradition.

9 TWO CATEGORIES OF LAND LAW: THE HIGH COURT

A CHOICE OF LEGAL PRINCIPLES

Six months before the Full Bench of the High Court resumed in May 1991 for its final deliberations on the Meriam case, the three-volume Determination of Issues of Fact made by Justice Moynihan in the remitter court (the Supreme Court of Queensland) on 16 November 1990 had been delivered to them. The Determination had concluded that claims by Reverend Dave Passi and James Rice to specified allotments of land at Mer, Dauar and Waier were not contested in court by other Meriam. Their claims had been set out as chains of title handed down to the plaintiffs from a time before annexation of the Torres Strait Islands in 1879, when the Meriam had become subject to the sovereignty of the British Crown. In consequence the claims of these two plaintiffs were then made before the High Court. None of Mabo's 36 claims came before the High Court.[1]

As we have seen in Chapter 8, Justice Moynihan referred to a Meriam sense of 'an enduring relationship with land' and deeply ingrained attitudes of respect for the property and the land boundaries of others (D157). He did not, however, find an explicit system of law; precepts were internalised and these were reflected in good manners rather than laws.

His findings were sufficient for six of the seven members of the High Court to declare that a system of rights in land existed and continues to exist at the Murray Islands, although Justice Brennan noted that '[t]he findings show that Meriam society was regulated more by custom than by law' (411). Justice Toohey summarised Queensland's argument that, although the Meriam were present on the Murray Islands before and at the time of annexation, and that 'the Crown in right of Queensland had not attempted since then to dispossess them . . . there was no ordered system of land tenure before annexation' ('an argument of uncertainty'), and that since annexation, land disputes were settled by an 'Island Court which owed little to the pre-contact situation' (487). He then went on to reject the uncertainty argument: its applicability would rest upon evidence of purely capricious rules or practices, applied so inconsistently as to suggest the Meriam presence to be 'coincidental and random', a conclusion inconsistent with Justice Moynihan's findings. Justices

Deane and Gaudron were also unequivocal in their conclusion. Accepting Queensland's argument 'that it is impossible to identify any precise rules of inheritance or any precise method of alienation', and, like Justice Toohey noting the unavoidable 'areas of uncertainty and elements of speculation' in the detailed findings on issues of fact, they nevertheless arrived at a position of certainty:

> Nonetheless, there was undoubtedly a local native system under which the established familial or individual rights of occupation and use were of a kind which far exceed the minimum requirements necessary to form a presumptive common law native title [454].

They argued further that annexation preserved 'the traditional entitlements of the Meriam' and that, notwithstanding the fact that the Crown acquired radical title, the latter's proprietorship was 'reduced, qualified or burdened by the common law native title of the Islanders which was thereafter recognised and protected by the law of Queensland' (474).

Justice Brennan concluded that 'there is abundant evidence that land was traditionally occupied by individuals and groups'. While 'the precision of Meriam laws' may be in doubt and even though Justice Moynihan's findings

> do not permit a confident conclusion that, in 1879, there were parcels of land in the Murray Islands owned allodially by individuals and groups, the absence of such a finding is not critical to the final resolution of this case [431].

In the lead judgment of four separate judgments, three of which were part of the majority decision, Justice Brennan explained why the absence of such general findings on free ownership among the Meriam is not critical to resolution of questions of law.[2] He did so by considering new evidence which showed that the basis of the theory that the indigenous inhabitants 'of a "settled" colony had no proprietary interest in the land . . . is false in fact' (421). It was, of course, this theory which provided the basis of the legal fiction of Australia as *terra nullius*, land of no one. The doctrine which supposes that the Crown may acquire 'absolute beneficial ownership' of uninhabited land was extended within the common law to encompass lands inhabited by peoples whose social organisation and laws were non-existent or 'barbaric'.[3] Thus the inhabitants of the colony of New South Wales were regarded as 'barbarous or unsettled and without a settled law' (420). The key issue here is the notion of an uninhabited country or of a barbarous people, not the term *terra nullius* itself, which a former Chief Justice, Sir Harry Gibbs, has observed, 'seems to have been unknown to the common law'. ' "Barbarous" ', Chief Justice Gibbs went on to say, meant 'not under civilised government'.

> Australia was certainly not unoccupied in 1788 but it is another thing to say that the social organisation of the Aboriginal inhabitants was of a kind which the nations of Europe in the eighteenth and nineteenth centuries recognised as civilised.[4]

As Justice Brennan explained, citing Lord Sumner speaking on behalf of the Privy Council in the case *In re Southern Rhodesia* (1919), that theory rested upon the argument that the gulf between 'the scale of social organisation' of some tribal societies and 'civilised society' is so great that it would be impossible ' "to impute to such people some shadow of the rights known to our law" '.[5]

He also cited the report of the Select Committee to the House of Commons in 1837 on the Aborigines as ' "barbarous" ' and so ' "lacking the rudest form of civil polity" ' that their claims to proprietorship or sovereignty ' "were utterly disregarded" '.[6] Since that time new facts have shown these conclusions to be erroneous. Furthermore, Justice Brennan continued, the assumption of *terra nullius* involved a 'discriminatory denigration' of the social systems of Aboriginal and Islander peoples (421) and thus was 'unjust and discriminatory' (422). Aborigines were fitted unreservedly into this 'barbarous'-without-the-rudiments-of civil polity' category by colonial authorities.

Justice Brennan's judgment combines a summary of recent critical examination of the theory of *terra nullius* internationally, in legal cases and scholarly work, with facts ascertained in relation to Yolngu Aboriginal people, to assist him in selecting the legal principles relevant to reaching a conclusion in this case. The kernel of his argument has two basic components: the rejection of the notion that *terra nullius* could apply to inhabited lands in recent international cases, and the facts as known today contradicting the ' "absence of law" or "barbarian" theory' held by the settlers and embedded in the common law.

Citing the critical examination of the theory of *terra nullius* in an *Advisory Opinion on Western Sahara* (1975) by the International Court of

Justice, Justice Brennan stated that the notion 'that inhabited land may be classified as terra nullius no longer commands general support' (422). The majority judgment in that case stated 'that territories inhabited by tribes or peoples having a social and political organisation were not regarded as terrae nullius' in actual 'State practice'.[7]

Viewed in this light, the idea that even 'some shadow of the rights known to our law' does not exist among indigenous peoples, can hardly be sustained. In former times this 'fiction' of the absence of indigenous rights was justified by the needs embedded within the ' "whole forward movement" ' of white settlement.[8] Such 'an unjust and discriminatory doctrine . . . can no longer be accepted' (422). That policy, which combined the 'necessity' of colonial expansion with the implicit sanctioning of the physical power to back up that process, made very explicit *In re Southern Rhodesia* (1919), 'has no place in the contemporary law of this country' (422).

Justice Brennan noted that when Justice Blackburn sought to apply Lord Watson's assumption that the colony of New South Wales lacked inhabitants with a stable law 'to Aboriginal society in the Northern Territory, the assumption proved false' (421). Justice Blackburn had found 'a subtle and elaborate system . . . which provided a stable order of society', which he recognised as ' "a government of laws, and not of men" '. Justice Brennan went on to observe that, faced with a contradiction between the evidence about the Yolngu and 'the authority of the Privy Council', Justice Blackburn ruled on a question of law that the colony of New South Wales belonged to the category of 'settled' colony (421).

The moral imperative for the law to be properly informed and therefore formulated in a manner which frees it from complicitness in events that compromise the standards of justice here or elsewhere preoccupied Justice Brennan at this point. Since the formation of the expanded theory of *terra nullius* 'is false in fact and unacceptable in our society', he argued, the court can choose one of two legal approaches: 'to inquire whether the Meriam people are higher "in the scale of social organisation" than the Australian Aborigines'; or it could overrule or discard the whole idea of *terra nullius* (421).

In the light of new knowledge and an awareness of the falsity of old assumptions, Justice Brennan took the course of overruling the existing authorities on which *terra nullius* in Australia relied and discarding 'the distinction between inhabited colonies that were *terra nullius* and those which were not' (421).

In 1985, Justice Deane had stated in the case of *Gerhardy v Brown* (1985) that the common law had not yet 'reached the stage of retreat from injustice' attained in Illinois and Virginia in the decision in *Johnson v McIntosh* (1823) (United States of America), when Chief Justice Marshall had accepted the proposition of '"a legal as well as a just claim"' to continued occupancy of their lands by 'the "original inhabitants" '.[9] In citing that judgment with approval, Justice Brennan was also careful to preserve the 'skeletal principle of our legal system' (423).

In like manner, Justices Deane and Gaudron noted the integral connection between the two legal propositions — that the colony of New South Wales 'had been unoccupied for practical purposes' and that consequently 'full legal and beneficial ownership' of all land 'vested in the Crown' — and 'the dispossession and oppression of the Aborigines' (451). They perceived a need for the revision and rejection of the legal foundations of this dispossession on the basis of new knowledge or knowledge that has now come to light. Highly relevant here is the documentation of government recognition of 'traditional entitlements to the occupation of particular lands' by particular Aboriginal tribes and clans. They mentioned examples given by historian Henry Reynolds (450).[10] Justices Deane and Gaudron cited the comment made on 14 March 1841 by James Stephen, head of the Imperial Colonial Office, on a despatch from South Australia:

> It is an important and unexpected fact that these Tribes had proprietary rights in the Soil — that is, in particular sections of it which were clearly defined or well understood before the occupation of their country.[11]

They recorded too how Stephen wrote on 9 June 1843 'of the "dispossession of the original Inhabitants"'.[12]

This then is part of their re-examination of the two propositions which 'compels their rejection' (451). And these are the circumstances which make this case unique: the Meriam case provided the first occasion on which Australia's leading jurists might examine the basis of legal theory in Australia. Justices Deane and Gaudron go on to foreshadow the portents of the decision being made:

> If this were any ordinary case, the Court would not be justified in reopening the validity of fundamental propositions which have been endorsed by long-established authority and which have been accepted as a basis of the real property law of the country for more than 150 years [451].

The case was far from ordinary, they concluded: with the benefit of new findings which showed old 'facts' to be erroneous, the developments of case law in other former British colonies, and the researches of historians and others, long-established authority was being called into question.

RECLAIMING THE INTEGRITY OF THE LAW

The position of the majority of the Full Bench of the High Court was that the integrity of the law may be preserved only if it is freed from a complicity in events which lowered the standards of national justice. In this light, the judgment may be seen as an expression of that kind of concern with law and justice which is essential to the national interest conceived as 'lucid patriotism' or truthfulness.[13]

Like that of Justice Brennan, the joint judgment of Justices Deane and Gaudron is concerned with the effect *on the law* of certain doctrines that underlay and justified ruthless dispossession, in the light of new knowledge acquired in common law countries. These doctrines were based on a misreading of the character of the social organisation and culture of indigenous peoples. To turn one's back on the new knowledge would mean to be party to the practices of disregard and dispossession. This awareness is conveyed in their judgment in a strong sense of disquietude, combined with a restrained recognition of opportunity.

The two legal propositions identified by Justices Deane and Gaudron had been challenged in only one case brought by Aboriginal people, that of *Milirrpum*. Two 'general reasons of principle' formed the basis of Justice Blackburn's rejection of the Yolngu claims to traditional land: that the doctrine of communal native title never formed part of the law of any part of Australia, and that the plaintiffs had failed to establish any pre-existing interest in the land which could be termed 'rights of property' (448). Furthermore, the plaintiffs were unable to show to Justice Blackburn's satisfaction 'that the plaintiffs' predecessors had in 1788 the same links to the same areas of land as those which the plaintiffs now claim'.[14]

Unfortunately for the Yolngu (and hence all other indigenous people in Australia), as Justices Deane and Gaudron explain, Justice Blackburn's statements of overall principle rested upon 'some general statements of great authority' (448) in at least four earlier Australian cases.[15] While Aboriginal entitlement to land 'was not directly involved in any of them', each of these cases drew upon some aspect of the propositions that the colony 'had been occupied for practical purposes' and that Britain acquired unqualified ownership of all the land there. The reasoning in each of the four cases consisted 'of little more than bare assertion' (449). Justices Deane and Gaudron went on to lay a burden of responsibility upon those two propositions as 'a legal basis for and justification of the dispossession' of Aborigines and as part of 'the environment in which Aboriginal people . . . came to be treated as a different and lower form of life' than the settlers and 'whose very existence could be ignored' (451).

In the 1992 judgment they illustrated 'past injustices' of dispossession graphically with respect to one 'flash point' on the lower reaches of the fertile flats of the Hawkesbury River in 1804, an early stage 'of the conflagration of oppression and conflict which was . . . to dispossess, degrade and devastate the Aboriginal peoples and leave a national legacy of unutterable shame' (449). The 'unusually emotive' and 'unrestrained language' used in their depiction of Aboriginal dispossession (456) springs from a realisation of the historical association of widely accepted legal propositions with brutal and self-righteous dispossession. The judgment contains an unmistakable sense of moral outrage at the implications of a shameful history that has a resonance with some of the writings of those associated with the Aboriginal Treaty Committee. Dr H C (Nugget) Coombs, a key figure in that committee, said in 1981, 'The British achieved control of this continent by a series of acts of aggression; sometimes by the most shameful means . . . This must be a source of shame to white Australians'.[16] In the same spirit, Justices Deane and Gaudron concluded in 1992:

> The acts and events by which that dispossession in legal theory was carried into practical effect constitute the darkest aspect of the history of this nation. The nation as a whole must remain diminished unless and until there is an acknowledgment of, and retreat from, those past injustices [451].

NATIVE TITLE AT THE MURRAY ISLANDS

Native title at the Murray Islands was recognised in the declaration of six of the seven judges of the High Court as written in the lead judgment of Justice Brennan:

the Meriam people are entitled as against the whole world to possession, occupation, use and enjoyment of the island of Mer except for that parcel of land leased to the Trustees of the Australian Board of Missions and those parcels of land (if any) which have been validly appropriated for use for administrative purposes the use of which is inconsistent with the continued enjoyment of the rights and privileges of Meriam people under native title [437].

In responding to the claims to specific allotments of land by the two plaintiffs, Reverend Dave Passi and James Rice, Justice Brennan stated that the court was not in a position to declare findings, first, because the facts found by the remitter court were insufficient, and second, because of the way the action was 'constituted' (437). Justice Moynihan found that the Meriam were ruled 'more by custom than by law';[17] and he gave the High Court no basis on which to conclude that 'parcels of lands' existed in free ownership among the Meriam (431). However, Justice Brennan also concluded that 'there is abundant evidence that land was traditionally occupied by individuals or family groups and that contemporary rights and interests are capable of being established with sufficient precision to attract declaratory or other relief' (431).

In the light of the insufficiency of the findings of fact that kind of relief was not sought and the court made declarations on an amended statement of claim in which the two plaintiffs made claims to 'the native communal title of the Meriam people' (437). On the last day of the proceedings in May 1991, the two plaintiffs had abandoned their claims to particular lots of land in their court action and sought a finding and decision by the court of an interest in land by the Meriam people.[18]

Justices Deane and Gaudron concluded further that 'the Crown's ownership of lands in the Murrays after annexation was qualified and reduced by a communal native title of the Murray Islanders' (456). They explained the position of the two plaintiffs' claims to specific areas of land in relation to the state of Queensland and the rest of the Meriam community. Based on their judgment, each may seek 'more general declaratory relief' against the defendant, and they both did that successfully in the latter half of 1992.[19] Each of them has also the right, along with other landowners under 'common law communal native title', to determine their entitlement 'by reference to traditional law or custom' (456).

In ruling against the Yolngu plaintiffs in 1971, Justice Blackburn gave, as one of his three reasons, that 'communal native title' was not recognised in the common law. In discussing native title, Justice Brennan states that the rights and interests of a sub-group or individual 'are, so to speak, carved out of the communal native title', which comes into effect 'for the benefit of the community as a whole and for the sub-groups and individuals within it who have particular rights and interests in the community's lands' (431).[20] Moreover, the resolution of points of contest may be made by a 'community consensus' based upon customary principle, a practice registered in statutory provisions conferred on the Murray Island Court.[21]

THE UNIQUENESS OF NATIVE TITLE

Justice Brennan stated that the term native title 'describes the interests and rights of indigenous inhabitants in land', that these may be 'communal, group or individual' and that its nature and incidents vary from community to community and must be ascertained as matters of fact. He concluded, 'Native title has its origins in and is given its content by the traditional laws acknowledged by and the traditional customs observed by the indigenous inhabitants' (429).[22]

This definition may be placed usefully within the context of the rather simplified and rigid version of Yolngu land tenure put before the Supreme Court of the Northern Territory in 1970. As Williams has noted, a simplified frame became the blueprint for those who drafted the Aboriginal Land Rights (Northern Territory) Act 1976, with the consequence that any variations from one group to another became grounds for rejection of customary ownership claims.[23] In the Murray Islanders' case the actual *content* of the native title recognised by the High Court was a matter to be determined by Meriam law, not Australian law.[24]

This perspective, taken also by Justices Deane and Gaudron, is founded upon the assumption that traditional or native title has its own authentic qualities and should not be forced into the conceptual categories of common law ownership. Citing Justice Dickson in *Guerin v the Queen* (1984),[25] a Canadian case with important precedents for *Mabo*, Justices Deane and Gaudron recognised 'the inappropriateness of forcing the native title to conform to traditional common law concepts and to accept it as sui generis or unique' (443).

Justices Deane and Gaudron did their best to be flexible in relation to those 'novel interests' in land of a kind 'unknown to English law'. They did so within the context of two difficulties. The first is that the findings of fact provided the High Court with very little information on what constituted the unique character of the native title they came to recognise at the Murray Islands. Justice Moynihan did not find among the Meriam anything resembling the 'subtle and elaborate system . . . of law' recognised among the Yolngu in *Milirrpum*. As the previous chapter has demonstrated, in his Determination the Meriam were divested of their spiritual relationship with their land. Moreover, their system of rights and responsibilities to land, which differentiates their relationship from that in which land is a commodity, was not identified. The High Court judges faced this lacuna in their final deliberations. On 28 May 1991, nine years after the case had begun, the question was asked: in the light of Justice Moynihan's findings, were the rights being claimed collective group rights or rights to individual ownership? The High Court ruled eventually on an amended statement of claim that the Meriam people as a group had rights and interests in the islands of Mer, Dauar and Waier.[26] Nevertheless the sad truth is that the long and detailed inquiry into the facts failed to reveal the character of Meriam rights and responsibilities to their land. As Frank Brennan concludes, 'The content of those rights and interests, especially of Meriam people among themselves, awaited further definition and clearer anthropological evidence which could be heard and determined before a Court'.[27]

The second difficulty is that the questions addressed by the High Court related to the historical examples of 'novel interests in land' and to features of native title that were measured against a yardstick of 'full ownership' founded upon legal concepts based on the idea of land as an economic category.

Tracing the history of feudal title in the British Isles, Justice Brennan noted the existence of land held allodially, that is, in free ownership, in the Orkney and Shetland Islands (424). Following the conquest of Ireland, it was held in *The Case of Tanistry* (1608) 'that the Crown was not in actual possession of the land' (425). Moreover, following the conquest of Wales, the inhabitants 'needed no new grant to support their possession' of land 'under the common law' (425).[28] These surviving interests in land were then converted by the courts into forms of tenure 'familiar to the common law'. Nevertheless, as Justice Brennan concluded, citing Viscount Haldane in *Amodu Tijani v Secretary of Southern Nigeria* (1921), 'there is no reason why the common law should not recognise novel interests in land which . . . are different from common law tenures' (425). Speaking on behalf of the Privy Council, Viscount Haldane had concluded:

> There is a tendency, operating at times unconsciously, to render [native] title conceptually in terms which are appropriate only to systems which have grown up under English law. But this tendency has to be held in check closely.[29]

Justice Brennan's historical survey is a reminder about a process in which 'free ownership' rather than feudal tenure existed, for example, in the Orkney and Shetland islands, or of the practice of tanistry, whereby, under Irish and Gaelic law, succession to an estate was conferred by election upon the worthiest male heir. Even in the eighteenth century, these 'surviving interests' were not limited to the colonial world outside Great Britain, but remained matters of adversarial dispute in English courts.

In this historical light, the important step made here by Justice Brennan was that, whatever its variability according to locality, and however 'novel' its interests in land are according to the common law yardstick, native title is not 'extinguished by the acquisition of sovereignty', an insight for which Australian historian Henry Reynolds has rightly received credit.[30] Given this position, Justice Brennan rejected the need to pursue alternative arguments advanced by the Meriam plaintiffs: their rights antecedent or prior to sovereignty 'constitute a burden on the radical title of the Crown' (429). Justice Brennan went on to invoke the argument he followed in *Mabo (No 1)*: that this position 'involves overruling' earlier cases; to do otherwise 'would destroy the equality of all Australian citizens before the law' (429).

Beyond this neither Justice Brennan nor the rest of the High Court went very far on the equality of 'the novel interests' in land of the Meriam or other indigenous peoples whose lands have become enfolded within common law jurisdictions. Thus, in his concluding 'Answers to Questions', Justice Brennan explicitly reserved the term 'ownership' for 'an estate in fee simple or at least an estate of freehold' (437). Meriam title is not common law tenure which, all the judges agreed, is one which overrides native title through legislative or executive action. It may be argued that the very concept of a radical or superseding title is essentially a self-defined superior interest in land.

The unique character of native title and its variability according to local laws and customs may be depicted as consisting of rights far removed from 'real' ownership. Justice Brennan, citing Viscount Haldane in *Amodu Tijani* cited usufructuary right as a very typical or 'usual form of native title' (425). Also citing *Amodu Tijani*, Justices Deane and Gaudron identified this among a range of cases, noting the course taken by the Privy Council in recognising 'a "full native title of usufruct" which qualified and reduced the proprietary estate of the Crown as radical owner'.[31] They went on to list three limitations to common law native title, even where from a practical viewpoint it 'approaches full ownership' (442). These are restrictions on alienation, the right to sell land; a consequent limitation of title to a personal right not a legal or beneficial interest in the actual land; and finally, consequent upon the first two, its susceptibility to extinguishment by Crown grants or an estate in fee which are inconsistent with native title (443).

Justice Toohey alone addressed the question of whether the title claimed by the Meriam could be termed a possessory title, a form of fee simple title. The title presumed by English law to exist among indigenous occupiers of land acquired by settlement, a possessory title termed 'common law Aboriginal title',[32] is clearly an 'ownership' form in contrast to native or traditional title, as Justice Toohey called it. And although the latter may in some contexts be 'equivalent to full ownership', as Justices Deane and Gaudron suggested (442), as we have seen, the matter was not only left vague: the weight of cases cited points typically to notably 'lesser', more minimal rights. Pearson has argued that Justice Toohey's decision not to reach 'a firm conclusion' (497) on whether the plaintiffs were entitled to possessory title precluded any possibility of 'a relatively easy translation of Aboriginal rights to land into the common law'.[33] If Justice Toohey's intimation that 'possessory title may be more robust than native title' in withstanding extinguishment proves to be true,[34] then the radical title acquired by the Crown upon annexation does not automatically extinguish any possessory title held by the Meriam.

Certainly the 'mere usufruct' level of native title, when taken in conjunction with its variable nature, can have the effect of creating a hierarchy of titles on the one hand; on the other, it can lead in practice to the perception of indigenous rights as only 'a shadow of the rights known to our law'. Pearson recognises in this potential ranking process of the interests in land of different groups into more and less like common law title, a step backwards towards that perception which distinguishes the 'higher' from the 'lower' in the scale of social organisation.[35] As we shall see in Chapter 11, this is precisely what happened by the end of the first year following the High Court's recognition of native title.

NOT 'ANY SORT OF CUSTOM': THE MINORITY PERSPECTIVE

Justice Dawson's minority judgment is something of a cameo of all the arguments of the past for *terra nullius* and the proprietary rights which followed the declaration of British sovereignty. It offers, in condensed form, a seemingly empirical statement of self-evident truth: the absence of 'any sort of custom' or 'system of laws, regarding the control and disposition of land' at the Murray Islands (474). Moreover, in Justice Dawson's view, customary rights unrecognised by the Crown are also extinguished by the establishment of sovereignty. Without the presence of 'any sort of custom', the statutory powers of the island council 'to govern the reserve "in accordance with the customs and practices of the islanders" ' (474), or the requirement of by-law no 35, 1980 to the Torres Strait Islanders Act, for transmission of land of a deceased landholder according to local custom, are meaningless: 'these provisions cannot preserve that which has been found not to exist' (475).

Justice Moynihan's one-sided characterisation of Meriam relationships with land and with one another were used by Justice Dawson to dismiss not only the specific claims made by the plaintiffs, but also their participation in any sort of general system as well. Justice Moynihan's findings were read by Justice Dawson as evidence of the absence of a system of land laws in 1879. The most superficial aspects of the findings— 'distribution or sharing life sustaining resources' in a semi-anarchic world—combine with Justice Moynihan's rather ephemeral indicia of behaviour, such as what he called our 'concept of good manners', feelings of 'shame' at trespassing, to create a picture of something far short of a system of land tenure. Thus Justice Dawson observed how Justice Moynihan had 'formed the view' that it would be merely speculative 'to conclude that there was any particular system controlling the use of land on the Murray Islands before European contact' (473).

Consistent with this interpretation of Justice Moynihan's findings are Justice Dawson's conclusions on relevant legislation and executive actions. These centred on the creation of reserve lands 'for the use or benefit of the aboriginal inhabitants' by the application of powers under Crown lands legislation (469); reservation of lands at the Murray Islands or elsewhere in the colony 'was in no way a recognition of any traditional land rights' (472). Here he followed the position taken by Justice Blackburn in the *Milirrpum* case: that the creation of reserves 'implies the negation of communal native title'.[36] This interpretation was disputed by Justices Deane and Gaudron, who argued that 'reservation from sale or lease "for use of the Aboriginal inhabitants of the State" should clearly be construed as intended to protect, rather than extinguish, any existing native rights of occupation and use' (455).[37]

Much of Justice Dawson's dismissal of successive arguments put by the Murray Islanders arose either from the Crown's assertion of its rights to the land to the exclusion of any rights of ownership by the Meriam (475) — the *terra nullius* argument — or the absence of Meriam customary rights, his interpretation of the findings in the Supreme Court of Queensland. So, for example, unlike the situation pertaining to *The Case of Tanistry* (1608), in Ireland where the conquered inhabitants were allowed to remain in possession of their lands, using and enjoying them according to common law principles, the Meriam's continued occupation of the Murray Islands after annexation was merely 'at the pleasure of the Crown' (475).

Even those claims made by the Murray Islanders which bear a strong resemblance to the principles of English land tenure were rejected. Thus in response to Justice Moynihan's finding 'that all land was considered to be in the possession of a particular individual or family group', there being 'no concept of public or general community ownership' in the pre-annexation Murray Islands, Justice Dawson concluded nevertheless, that 'traditional native title . . . does not support the claim of an individual to a particular parcel of land' (472). His reasoning hinges on the reported absence of 'any *particular system* controlling the use of land' before the annexation of the Murray Islands (473, emphasis added). Again, government purchases of lands from Meriam landholders in 1913, the 1960s, and 1973 for specified sums of money (recorded in the Court Book and witnessed in writing by the government representative on the island in the 1913 sale) were discounted. According to Justice Dawson's judgment, given 'the circumstances' (presumably that *all* the land was owned by the Crown), words such as ' "owned" by or "belonging to" the native inhabitants', 'sale' or 'purchase', do not reflect 'the true legal position', being merely 'an imprecision in the language' (473–74).

Given this interpretation of Justice Moynihan's findings, Justice Dawson returned to the argument he followed in *Mabo (No 1)* in 1988 on the Murray Islanders' legal challenge or demurrer to the 1985 Act, which we considered briefly in Chapter 3. If, as he argued, the plaintiffs lack the traditional rights which they claim, then they enjoy the same rights as all other Queenslanders. Any special rights enjoyed by the Meriam under legislation relevant to them are additional to 'those rights which are enjoyed generally' (480). From Justice Dawson's perspective, the conclusions he reached in 1988 — that deprivation of rights not enjoyed by other Queenslanders may *create* equality — are integral with his interpretation of Justice Moynihan's findings. In his view, the facts assumed to exist for the purposes of a ruling on the Murray Islanders' legal challenge in 1988 were not proven in the Supreme Court of Queensland. Consequently, Justice Dawson found again that there is no inconsistency between the 1985 Act and the Racial Discrimination Act 1975.

RESPECTING INDIGENOUS LAND LAW

The High Court decision makes a new departure in its respect for indigenous law. In Noel Pearson's words, it is different because it respects 'an inherent right' arising 'out of Aboriginal law and custom'.[38] The judgment has stirred a new level of questioning, sometimes within unexpected and conservative quarters. Thus, for example, Raimond Gaita points to an irony in the judgment of Justice Blackburn in *Milirrpum*: how the spiritually based obligation to land of the Yolngu, 'of a deeper kind than could be conveyed by the notion of (mere?) ownership', was not taken to be 'a "burden" on the radical title of the Crown'.[39] The writer problematises 'the narrow concept of ownership' which Justice Brennan rejected and which provided 'the source of grave injustice which shamed the common law'. Gaita goes on to note how awareness of a 'racially conditioned blindness' led five other justices to seek resources within the common law through which 'to reclaim its integrity'.[40]

We can recall how Justice Blackburn came to reject Yolngu claims to proprietary interests. Perceiving their relation to land as one of obligation not of ownership, he came 'to say that the clan belongs to the land' rather 'than that the land belongs to the clan'.[41] Given the spiritual origins of their interests in land it appeared to Justice Blackburn that the Yolngu's 'feeling of obligation to the land was "more cogent" than their feeling of ownership'.[42] This one-sided perception of the Yolngu's relationship to land is tied integrally to Justice Blackburn's three criteria of property rights: the right to use and enjoy, the right to exclude others, and the right to alienate. The Yolngu plaintiffs did not demonstrate the existence of the first two to his satisfaction; the third 'right' did not apply, for integral to the Yolngu's relationship to their land is the right, or, more precisely, the ancestral injunction, not to alienate.

I have argued that the Meriam's attachment to land is spiritual as well as economic, and that this dual relationship is part of the unbreakable tie with land which is referred to as inalienability. Whatever may have been their private reflections, the justices of the High Court were bound by concepts connected to and inherent in feudal concepts of property and ownership. That is, they were bound by what legal scholar Kent McNeil referred to in the context of the *Milirrpum* case as narrow European 'indicia of ownership'. Reflecting upon Justice Blackburn's decision on the Yolngu claim in 1971, he concluded:

> It seems, then, that the more an indigenous people's attitude to land was spiritual rather than material, the less likely would they be regarded by English law courts as having proprietary interests.[43]

In Australian law, the Meriam have a native title approaching proprietorship which, to them, is inalienable ownership of land. In a fundamental sense there is no straight line between the two laws; in important respects they are incommensurable. As the final chapter of this book attempts to show, events in 'the native title era' demonstrate that failure to give due regard to that incommensurability creates vexed relationships. In rejecting the assumptions of *terra nullius*, the majority of the High Court justices moved across an abyss; the next chasm is not about a question of law, rather it concerns a deeper understanding of socially embedded 'facts'.

The High Court made a historic decision in recognising native title at the Mer Islands and in overturning the doctrine of *terra nullius*. Yet within that judgment lay two provisos which, with a third, were to become major issues of contest in the 'era of native title'. The High Court's decision did not encompass foreshore or seas at Mer or beyond, and leased areas were excluded from the decision.[44] A third issue concerned the fiduciary or trust relation of the Crown to indigenous inhabitants. Within a year of the decision each of these three was to find expression in major land claims.[45] Since sea property is integral with land ownership among the Meriam and the subject of claims made by the Murray Islanders in this case, rights to the sea and customary marine tenure at the Mer Islands are considered in some detail in the chapter which follows.

V

NATIVE TITLE IN AUSTRALIA

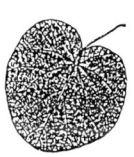

10 THE SEA: WITHIN THE COMPASS OF NATIVE TITLE

THE MERIAM FLAG IN TERRITORIAL WATERS

As a result of the judgment in *Mabo (No 2)* and the issues it raised concerning the recognition of native title in Australian law, the federal government introduced the Native Title Bill into parliament. At the same time as the federal Senate debate on this Bill was concluding on 21 December 1993, the Murray Islanders were pressing their declaration proclaiming a Mer Islands economic zone within Meriam traditional maritime boundaries. Two weeks earlier, the chairman of the Mer Islands Community Council, Ron Day, stated on behalf of the Meriam community, that the push for the declaration of a Meriam economic zone was 'made on the understanding that their [the Murray Islanders'] licences to fish in the area was given to them and their forefathers in "Birth" '.[1]

Ron Day drew public attention to the fact that Meriam people's livelihood and economic prospects lay 'wholly and solely with the marine resources' of the area.[2] The Meriam believed that commercial fishermen had already destroyed certain marine species in other parts of the Torres Strait. Having embarked upon a community-based commercial fishing project, installed a community-owned freezer at Mer, and created a cash flow to Meriam fishermen and women in the later part of 1993, the community council was confident that the project would become commercially viable, provided the Meriam themselves had the power to control the resources of the area. As they see it, other Torres Strait Islanders are welcome to fish in these waters from their dinghies and sell their fish to the Mer Islands freezer, on the same terms as the local fisherman.

In itself, the creation of an economic zone within traditional boundaries where the Meriam build their own economic base, and conserve and manage the marine resources of the region, might seem reasonable, a just and independent solution to longstanding problems of economic dependence. Through their own efforts, the Meriam, secure in their 'native title' to most of their lands, embarked on a project for which they are qualified. In this fishing project, the cash earned flows back into the community and, hopefully, will conserve its natural resources. The project 'is seen as the first step in building an economic base and will conserve and managing the existing marine resources of the region', Mr Day concluded.[3]

At this point, the Meriam were not putting their case for rights to the sea before an Australian court; they were asserting their 'natural inheritance' to areas from which they have traditionally gained their livelihood. According to their 'natural inheritance', ownership of land extends across the foreshore, and Meriam traditional maritime boundaries go beyond the 'home' or fringing reef that extends offshore from about 500 to 1,000 metres and is perpetually covered by shallow waters.

The Meriam 'economic zone' cuts across existing Australian coastal fisheries arrangements in which coastal waters are seen as freely available to all fishermen.[4] They, like all other coastal peoples around Australia, are subject to the common law principle that the sea and the coastal zone should be freely available to everyone. This belief, also pervasive in New Zealand, has been seen as the source of a legacy of official neglect of Maori fishing rights.[5] The experience of sandbeach Aboriginal people in Australia's northern coastal waters confirms this conclusion.[6] And in some parts of coastal Australia Aboriginal people have been prosecuted for engaging in community-based commercial fishing.[7]

The distinction made in European thought between land constructed as a commodity property and the seas as international commons contrasts sharply with relationships to land and sea among the Meriam people, other Torres Strait Islanders and Aboriginal sandbeach cultures. Their patterns of inalienable ownership of land and sea space form one integral whole. A culturally defined unity of land and sea space among saltwater coastal and island peoples is evoked in such terms as 'sea-country', 'cultural coastscapes', 'salt-water country'.[8] Today, global competition in the exploitation of the sea and the seabed is combined with projects for the domestication of sea life. Given this conjunction, the clarification of rights to sea space of indigenous saltwater peoples takes on new urgency.

The High Court had not been asked to consider Meriam claims to any portion of the sea. The findings of fact in the Supreme Court of Queensland were that the foreshore and reef flat rights claimed by the plaintiffs were not sustained by the evidence given in court (D185). The Murray Islanders' claims to cays and reefs lying within the jurisdiction of the Commonwealth were withdrawn and the Commonwealth was struck out as a defendant on 7 June 1989. The overall effect was to limit the recognition of native title at the Mer Islands to land above the high water mark.

In their statement of claim, the Meriam plaintiffs claimed that the three Murray Islands and their 'surrounding seas, seabeds, fringing reefs and adjacent islets' have been 'continuously inhabited and exclusively possessed' by the Meriam people 'since time immemorial' (paragraph 1). The inseparability of sea and land in the customs, traditions and practices in determining questions of social life is reflected in the totality of their claim (paragraph 3). This inseparability of sea property from land was repeatedly drummed into them from an early age. Plaintiff James Rice explained to the court, 'Father said then at Dauar: "This is our boundaries, this is our land, this is our reef." He used to tell the whole story [of our land and sea property], come back and tell the whole story again' (TQ1531). From a Meriam perspective this inseparability was reflected in the inclusion of lands, seas, seabeds and reefs under the general category of 'lands' (paragraph 6).

That integral relationship finds expression in ownership systems and in rules and customs regulating the tenure and use of land and sea. The boundaries demarcating one plot of land from another extend into the sea; the evidence of this most visible to a Western eye is *sai* or stone fish traps, which have been built out from the foreshore. The Meriam identify the builders of the *sai*, which stretch for some 4 kilometres, with the two mythical ancestors, the brothers Kos and Abob. The brothers, who lived at Akub in the clan territory of the Zagareb people, built fish traps at Dauar and Mer.[9] These three-sided stone enclosures are built to trap the fish at low tide.

The spiritual link between customary owners and specified sites in the sea is made through the areas of seashore traversed in the final stages of the journeys of Malo-Bomai. At Begegiz in Peibre clan territory lies the site known as Malo's canoe, a site in the water of sacred significance. Gobedar Noah, a landowner from Magaram clan, narrates that part of the myth which tells of the coming of Malo to Teker in Magaram clan territory:

> Malo moved from place to place and from shape to shape of different sea creatures in the deep water until he comes to that place in the deep water and came to the place at Teker where a woman named Kabur was line fishing on the reef. First when she was fishing it was low tide and when she saw the boat coming along from Dauar and Waier it kept changing until at the last moment when she was fishing at a reef called Taparau Malo (Bomai) changed into an octopus. All of a sudden the water came up to her waist mark; it was still low tide on the other side and when she

> looked down she saw something red. 'It's an octopus. It is *zogo* [sacred] for you, my husband, Dog', she said to him. So she got a spear and stooped down and speared the octopus and the blood flowed out and formed a lagoon. In Meriam language we say, *Karem keusar igomdari*.
>
> That place is sacred to me; it's sacred to anybody. We've got that one and the High Court decision as laid out to us right [only] up to the high water mark. High water. What about the sacred site in the water?[10]

In 1898, Anthony Wilkin of the Cambridge anthropological expedition observed that proprietorship of 'shore property extended over the reef'; 'every property that adjoined the shore was bounded by the edge of the reef'. These 'foreshore rights of landed property extend not only over the adjacent reef but to the water over it'.[11] This shore property, that is 'land' extending to low water mark, was marked by a number of sub-divisions: the largest 'collective' unit was the clan or *nosik*; within these divisions are villages among which plots of land are clearly identified as 'family-owned'.

In the plaintiffs' statement of claim, the rights to the foreshore and reefs were pleaded in the same way as, and as an extension of, those to residential land, that is 'individual family' or lineage rights to particular sand-spits, lagoons and fish traps, reefs and seas. Differences between the size of the group on whose behalf the plaintiffs claimed land below high water were exactly the same as for tenure of dry land. In the claim by Dave Passi it was understood that all Passi lands and sea areas were held by the eldest son on behalf of the Passi family; Eddie Mabo and James Rice held all land and sea areas on behalf of their immediate families.

However, the evidence presented to the court by the plaintiffs and by the expert witnesses was that, in contrast to contemporary practices in relation to both residential and garden land, rules against trespass embodied in Malo's Law are not always followed today. Justice Moynihan then took current use as the criterion of ownership: the plaintiffs had no rights to the 'reef flats areas' because, according to evidence given in court, they were no longer excluding one another from the reef areas claimed.

Justice Moynihan ruled that, whatever the mode of ownership of seas in the past, 'Islanders today seem to regard the reef and sea as accessible to them all with produce available to all',[12] the position pleaded by Queensland.

The Murray Islanders indicated the practice of free use of the natural resources of the seas and seabed, as far as and including the fringing reef adjoining one of the lands claimed, 'and that seems to have been so for some time now' (D215).

SEA CLAIMS IN COURT: USE AND OWNERSHIP

The plaintiffs Reverend Dave Passi and James Rice stated in court that they did not choose to exercise their rights to exclude other members of the Meriam community. Dave Passi had explained at length how he followed Malo's Law, *Tag mauki mauki, Teter mauki mauki,* one might say, religiously, with respect to the land. He claimed a fringing reef at Dauar Island 'perpetually covered at high and low tide' and a lagoon at Waier named Neh, 'an area of water perpetually covered at high and low tide', Ziai Giz, a sand area 1 metre by 3 to 4 metres at Waier, a well-known spot for turtle eggs and turtles (the area is too small for them to turn around and hence they are 'held captive'), and a sandspit at Waier claimed to low water mark.[13] In his evidence in chief Passi said:

Plaintiff:	[I] have the power to stop people going there but do not restrict because it [turtle eggs] is 'a source of food for people' [TQ1997].
His Honour:	You might have the right [to exclude other people] but you choose not to exercise it?
Plaintiff:	Yes [TQ2001].

In a similar way plaintiff James Rice stated that people 'can go fishing there but they know this area belongs to me' (TQ1643). Other witnesses bore them out; as a consequence, the claims to specific sea areas did not 'arrive' at the High Court.

McIntyre has observed that, since the High Court's recognition of native title in the Murray Islands was conceived as an exclusively communal right of the Meriam in relation to the whole world, that declaration could be applied equally to the surrounding seas. Consequently, Justice Moynihan's conclusion that rights had been lost to particular sea areas adjoining lands claimed, and that practices of exclusion according to a system of boundaries as claimed by the Murray Islanders had given way to 'a more pragmatic approach' (D194, 205, 214), 'may be of no significance at all'.[14]

However, there are certain misconceptions embedded in the conclusions of Justice Moynihan on Meriam ownership rights to reefs and seas. Stronger than those to which I have pointed regarding his understanding of the Meriam relationship to land in its limited, European sense (see Chapter 8), they constitute a misrepresentation of the kind of people the Meriam are and the character of their property rights.

There are at least three main lines of misunderstanding here. The first relates to use and enjoyment of sea property as the criteria of ownership. The second concerns cultural difference in the meaning of 'sea property'. Compounding and to some extent influenced by the first two is a third factor (with several causes): the changes in Meriam society in the period of colonisation which find expression in variations in group and community practice with respect to practices of exclusion from foreshore and reef properties.

USAGE AS THE CRITERION OF OWNERSHIP

Justice Moynihan made the assumption that rights must be exercised in order to keep them alive, a position not (necessarily) held by the Meriam. The same issue was embedded and implicit in the hearing of the Yolngu claims in *Milirrpum*.[15] The notion that 'failure to exercise a right is assumed to extinguish it', is as Baxi points out in the context of Justice Blackburn's finding, a matter of considerable variation between legal systems. He makes a distinction of importance to the Meriam case: 'To *have* a right is to nurse a *potential* jural relation; to *exercise* it is to bring forth an *actual* relation'. He goes on to observe how 'most developed legal systems' may display 'a very great tension between simply having a right and *not* exercising it', and this tension may be registered in legal terms by such measures as prescription, laws of limitation. Failure to consider the possibility of analytic separation between having and exercising a right, Baxi concludes, constitutes one of *Milirrpum's* 'principal vulnerabilities'.[16] The same vulnerability, it would seem, is exhibited in this case with respect to the sea rights of the Murray Islanders.

Baxi points to the dangers of 'transference of western legal concepts and social values to the appraisal of an indigenous legal order'. His critical remarks on Justice Blackburn's perspective are apposite to Justice Moynihan's application of 'the "western" standard of use and enjoyment' as the criterion of ownership in a manner which assumes extinction of a right through lack of use:

An intemperate critic might be moved to say . . . that it is not merely blatantly eurocentric but also a manifestation of high-handed juristic imperialism. And such a critic would have a valid point.[17]

In 1969, in the context of the claim by Yolngu clans against Nabalco Pty Ltd and the Commonwealth of Australia, the anthropologist W E H Stanner identified 'the greatest single handicap' faced by the Yolngu as 'the widespread but erroneous idea among Europeans that the day-to-day usage of land was itself the system of ownership and possession'.[18] This warning may usefully have been given to the Meriam plaintiffs in respect of their foreshore and sea rights. They explained how they *allowed* other Meriam to use their foreshore, reef flats and seas, giving reasons for the change; it was unthinkable to them that anyone would take this to mean the relinquishment of those rights. Yet this is precisely what Justice Moynihan thought. Earlier he had concluded 'that there was a system providing for access to the produce of the reef flat areas', 'that boundaries played a role in this', that the system seems 'to have been lost and replaced by a more pragmatic approach', and that he therefore rejected the plaintiffs' claims to areas of reef and reef flats (D185). He completely misread plaintiff Passi's statement about current use (non-exclusion), taking that latter to confer entitlement upon 'any erstwhile intruder', so dismissing the claim to proprietorship as 'a legal fiction' (D185). Moreover, despite the claims to family entitlement, Justice Moynihan saw 'territorial affiliation' (D185) or 'village groupings' (D184) as the basis of access, thus dismissing any claims to more precise bases of ownership.[19]

WHAT IS SEA PROPERTY?

Integral with ownership of reef and seabed among the Meriam is their ownership of 'the waters above the reefs', which, like ownership of stars, winds and myths, was not a concept meaningful to Justice Moynihan. In the following court interchange between Justice Moynihan and Reverend Dave Passi, the judge began by introducing and defining the notion of usufructuary rights, and then concluded from the plaintiff's response that his claim was limited to the 'fruits' of the seas that happened to be there at a particular time.

His Honour:	Mr Passi tell me this: in relation to, for example, the area of the lagoon — whatever it is that you claim, what's the nature of the claim that members of the Passi family are entitled to take from it, whatever's edible or useful and to be able if they want to exclude others from doing the same thing, is that the sort of claim we're talking about, or is it more than that? If you have any difficulty understanding my question by all means say so? . . .
Witness:	I remember my father telling me that I'm to use it — if I can use the word from Giar Pit. I remember my father telling me that any fish, turtle that was caught in those waters had to come to my ancestors and have my ancestors' permission. If my ancestors said 'I'll have all of it', that was it, if he claimed all of it. If he didn't, he would share it.
His Honour:	See I suppose in the end it's a matter of ultimate resolution, but from the dialogue that he and I just had, his claim is not to the waters at all. His claim is to the first right of refusal to whatever's taken from particular waters, and it's not the same thing.
Mr Keon-Cohen:	Yes, I understand that, Your Honour.

At this point Reverend Passi suddenly made it clear to the court that his claim was more than the rights to things 'edible or useful': it was the sea itself that he was claiming.

Witness:	I am sorry Your Honour, the waters and what is taken from the waters.
Mr Keon-Cohen:	Both, so that we're clear.
His Honour:	I'm not sure what a claim to the waters then means.
Mr Keon-Cohen:	Do you understand Mr Passi the distinction between claiming the waters as if you own them like the pieces of rocks and earth that you own on the land, and claiming the fish and the turtles and the eggs that might from time to time be found in the waters? Do you appreciate that distinction? . . .
Witness:	Yes, we claim all, the waters and the fish and turtle, everything found in it [TQ2006–07].

CULTURAL PRIDE: OLD FORMS INTO NEW

In his evidence in court, marine biologist and conservationist Dr Robert Johannes noted two unique features of the Meriam system of marine tenure, comparing it with systems with which he was familiar in the Pacific islands. First is the ingenious practice of building crayfish houses outside the reefs, and second is the practice of subdividing the ownership of *sai* or fish traps: 'individual holes' or 'corners' are 'owned by different people' (TQ2789). Bamboo poles which still retain their leaves serve a double function: as boundary markers on the reefs and as snares for birds. These poles may be quite unique as boundary markers; a novel and imaginative way of protecting property rights. These poles were noted by Matthew Flinders in 1802.[20] Lawrie saw them as a mechanism for making more or less equal numbers of fish stay on either side of the bamboo. Drawing upon his comparative knowledge, Johannes advanced the hypothesis that the leafy bamboo 'spooked off' the fish, preventing them from concentrating on one side (TQ2753) — an imaginative way of creating balance and symmetry in the interests of peace.

According to evidence given by the Meriam to Anthony Wilkin of the Cambridge anthropological expedition in 1898 and repeated in court by their descendants, the sea tenure follows exactly the same principles as land tenure. The *sai*, reef flat areas and 'outside' or further out to sea to certain named fishing grounds, are the property of the clans and lineages who resided within clan territories. As Johannes stated in court, the bequeathing of fish traps and the exercise of the right to exclude continues today (TQ2749). He noted too how statements contradicting claims of others were common (TQ2805). Anger was aroused especially by infringement, destruction or theft relating to crayfish houses (*keiar meta*), which their owners make by piling up coral and in which the crayfish grow and are conserved until the owner needs them.

However, the active expression of ownership rights by clans and lineages or families to sea property waned over a time, partially reawakening since the late 1960s. Anthropologist Jeremy Beckett found no 'active expression' of ownership rights in respect of fish traps, the home reef, or the area in between during his field work at Mer between 1958 and 1961. 'The fish traps were not in use at any of the times that I visited Murray Island', he stated in court, although he recalled his impression that one was revived after his departure in 1961 (TQ2254).

In 1967 Margaret Lawrie saw fish traps being repaired and used (TQ2643).[21] Johannes interpreted the changing attitudes of the Meriam towards sea property as demonstrative of a world on the wane giving way to 'a reawakening cultural pride' comparable with that which he had observed elsewhere in the Pacific islands (TQ2791). Commenting on the undulations in 'the exercise of rights to traditional fish-traps . . . at different periods in Torres Strait' he concluded, the 'custom still prevails' among some owners (TQ2749).

My own observations are that the exercise of rights of exclusion to foreshore and reef flat areas has relaxed in respect to other Meriam. However, exercise of these rights is closely related to whether a landholder actually lives on adjoining land, and neither Reverend Passi nor James Rice resided at Dauar or Waier. In June 1993, landowners who reside on land adjacent to fish traps expressed to me strong attitudes on their right to be asked, 'I always tell my grandchildren that before you go out to another man's lagoon, you have to ask. I think this is the best way, the way I've been taught. That's our custom.' 'If they [my relations] help me [build the fish trap] that's different. They can have some [fish].' 'That crayfish house at . . . is mine. If anybody wants to go and get some cray he'll have to go and ask me . . . if it's a close relation I just tell them to go and get it.'[22]

A recent study of children's food-gathering activities at the Mer Islands found that the children (all under 15 years and from one patriline) made a major contribution to family subsistence. Leaving aside nut collecting and fruit harvesting, all the children's food resources were marine: turtle, turtle eggs, and fish, including varieties of shellfish.

An important finding of this study is the degree to which local knowledge is being preserved: ' "the best place to find clam shell" is on the southern and eastern reef margin'. Children, the study concluded, begin to have adult local food-getting knowledge around five or six years of age: 'nearly all children know what foods are commonly acquired, how to procure these foods, and how they should be processed'.[23]

The study makes a significant statement on the health of the Meriam subsistence economy, and a major statement on the health of the culture as a whole: the children receive local (traditional) knowledge from adults and re-create it. Children are praised for their efforts and, in a series of unstated reciprocities between adult response and children's self-esteem, the culture is reborn and reinvigorated. In this case the children were praised for some of their efforts; they were also scolded by the owners of the land at the village of Werbadu in Magaram clan territory for going there for turtle eggs and were told not to go back. They did not go back.

Preliminary results of a further study by the same researchers on the harvesting of marine life for subsistence needs by adults and children suggest that more than 90 per cent of these activities were conducted on foreshore and reef areas belonging to respective patrilineages/families. Murray Islanders will generally go to reef areas owned by their clan, but avoid collecting fish inside fish traps which are not owned by their particular family.[24]

Customary owners today speak generally of returning to their old maritime boundaries, and over the past 14 or 15 years I have seen them doing so in practice. 'I feel we have to go to the mark we used to have. The traditional boundaries.' 'Because we get our *ged* [land] now we want to go back to our traditional system. So we want to claim all our boundaries.' As Johannes stated in court, the central issue for the Meriam 'is their collective right to the home reef', to the waters and the seabed within Meriam traditional boundaries. Not only the Meriam, but every Torres Strait Islander is adamant about that (TQ2817). He recalled how crayfish divers had been 'chased off' by the Meriam (TQ2817), how since about 1986 they began to challenge outsiders fishing in their waters outside the reefs (one fisherman was fishing between Waier and Dauar), and how another marine biologist working with Johannes was himself confronted by Meriam owners while taking underwater photographs of crayfish houses for research purposes (TQ2806). The system of extended rights to specified and named fishing grounds out to sea, usually directly in line with boundaries of off-shore territories, was said by Johannes to be in 'partial remission' but certainly not 'heading for extinction' (TQ2786).

The Meriam today are agreed that, however relaxed they are on rules relating to sea property, the fact of their ownership continues. The main reason the Meriam themselves give for the relaxation of rules of exclusion among themselves is that they have intermarried and become one people. In relation to their observance of rights to sea property they point to the custom of *kopat*, which means 'everybody together'. Any Meriam person will tell you how this is expressed in everyday life: the first turtle caught for the season is brought to one place and the whole community is invited to share it. It is a festive occasion. The repair of a fish trap is often a community project. The owner of part of a lagoon may approach other members of the community to help him; they are then given fish caught in the lagoon. But the lagoon still belongs to the traditional owner or owners.

Through more than a hundred years of colonisation the Meriam have shared a common fate. The experience of commercial marine activity created new bonds of cooperation and common endeavour. And Christian universalism wrought changes in the consciousness of Meriam people which the Malo-Bomai order had begun. Food for subsistence needs is abundant on Dave Passi's section of foreshore at Dauar and Waier. He feels no need to restrict access. Yet neither he nor James Rice feel the same way about free access to their plots of garden land. Land is a scarce resource on the three islands, and Malo's Law is followed more or less literally with respect to garden land.

There are also some specific reasons for changes in the exercise of rights to clan and lineage-owned sea property: four of these are identified here. The first is the concerted assault on the custom by government schoolteachers, beginning with Jack Bruce, who lived at Mer from 1890 until his death there in 1922. He vigorously exercised a right endowed on him by the Queensland government to place Meriam owners' exclusive rights to fish traps into abeyance. The underlying justification of his action lies in the assumption of English law that the sea and its 'fruits' should be accessible to all. The anthropologist Anthony Wilkin recorded his view of the negative implications for a fishing community of shore property extending over the reef saying it provided fertile ground for dispute over rights to a catch: 'At present things are a little better', he wrote of the success of Bruce's moves to eradicate the custom.[25]

Johannes had been reticent on the subject of land–sea boundaries: in court he stated that he and his colleagues withdrew from situations that involved controversy between landowners. Having heard and read about boundary disputes among the Meriam, he recalled that 'we were sensitive to it so we recoiled very quickly when we saw evidence of it' (TQ2805).[26]

A second reason for changes in the exercise of rights relates to the existence of alternative food supplies: store food, for example, tin corned beef or 'hamper', became a stable part of Meriam diet from the 1920s onwards, and, since the sea was no longer the sole source of food, people could 'afford' to be generous. The third reason is the effect of a compulsory concentration of the population on the north to northwest side of Mer, with a consequent abandonment of some *sai*, and the reduction of fishing activity in the waters surrounding Dauar and Waier. A fourth reason was the development of the trochus industry, which modified the exercise of rights to fishing grounds outside the reef, and which took men on the luggers to fishing grounds not always chosen by themselves. Nevertheless the 'Company boats' owned by the clans, which operated from the 1890s to the beginning of 1936, respected the basic division within Meriam customary sea tenure between the 'Meriam side' and the 'Dauar side' of the isles of Mer.

WITHIN THE COMPASS OF NATIVE TITLE

THE MERIAM AND RIGHTS TO THE SEA

Greg McIntyre has argued that Justice Moynihan's dismissal of ownership rights to the sea claimed by the plaintiffs 'is not a jurisprudential view which would necessarily be universally adopted'.[27] Citing the position taken by Justices Deane and Gaudron that 'traditional law or custom is not . . . frozen as at the moment of establishment of a colony', McIntyre sees an appropriate test of title as one which ascertains the particular rights which are in accordance with the customs of that community in its process of development.[28] In his view, whatever the pattern of ownership of 'particular plots' of sea property, there is no reason why the Meriam could not claim proprietary rights to the sea as against the whole world.

At the level of statute law in Queensland, high water mark is the point at which native title 'ends'; according to the Torres Strait Land Act (Qld) 1991, communities cannot claim customary marine areas unless three conditions are satisfied: the areas claimed must fall within the definition of 'tidal land'; the traditional, historic or economic association must be proven; and the Governor-in-Council must declare that the tidal land is so claimable (1,S2.12). Tidal land is 'land that is ordinarily covered and uncovered by the flow and ebb of the tide at spring tides' (1,S1.04), the largest tides of the monthly cycle. Sea waters and non-tidal seabed are included among 'not available Crown lands' (1,S2.16).[29]

A C Haddon noted what he 'termed a spatial projection of the idea of proprietorship' from land to sea, a uniquely sea people's conception of proprietorship. Just as foreshore rights extend 'to the water' over the reef adjacent to a person's land, 'so the inhabitants of certain areas appear to have a pre-emptial right to certain distant fishing stations which lie off their part of the coast'.[30]

Beckett echoed this view in court. He commented on the way in which residential clan-owned areas around the island formed vantage points for control over and monitoring of the activities of others in closer and distant seas (TQ2254). In the great maritime voyages of the Meriam, the *wauri* (cone shell) voyages, the Komet *le*, a clan 'facing' present-day Papua New Guinea were the traders for the Meriam.[31]

In the course of the case, some Murray Islanders claimed cays or fishing areas outside their part of island territory. For example, Dave Passi claimed Eurr Cay outside Dauar. Claims to sections of the Great Barrier Reef by Eddie Mabo were removed from the statement of claim after the case against the Commonwealth was dropped. These claims involved areas outside the limit of Queensland jurisdiction — which is set at 3 nautical miles from the high water mark at each island — and are subject to Commonwealth jurisdiction.

Eddie Mabo's claim had included a portion of the Great Barrier Reef (Op Nor), to which he claimed exclusive use, together with a sandy cay which was on a radial line northeast of the village of Las. The section of the Great Barrier Reef was an area ten miles from Mer and hence, in Commonwealth terms, part of its jurisdiction. Following a hearing before Justice Toohey in the High Court on 3 May 1989, an agreement was made on 26 June between counsel for the plaintiffs and the second defendant (the Commonwealth) deferring all claims by the plaintiffs against the Commonwealth until the High Court had 'finally disposed of' all claims adverse to the first defendant; that claims to any portion of the Great Barrier Reef be deleted from the statement of claim and references to 'lands', 'seas', 'seabed' and 'reefs' are limited 'to areas within the territorial seas'.[32]

McIntyre records reasons for 'strategic negotiations' between the plaintiffs' counsel and the Commonwealth which led to the deferral by the plaintiffs of any further hearings relating to claims to seas outside the 3-mile limit. 'The Commonwealth . . . was suggesting that its generally benevolent approach to action by the plaintiffs would be less benevolent' were such a claim to be pursued. To avoid 'any seriously antagonistic position' being taken by the Commonwealth at that strategic point, the plaintiffs agreed to concentrate their focus on the main question: to establish the existence of common law title.[33] The hearing before Justice Moynihan in the Supreme Court of Queensland was about to be situated physically at Mer and Thursday Island, a procedure incurring considerable expense. A certain discretion was called for.

In the period following the High Court decision, when the Meriam turned their attention to the issues of ownership of fringing reefs and recognition of traditional maritime boundaries, they were reasserting their identity as a modern maritime people. As we have seen, their perspective has crystallised around a

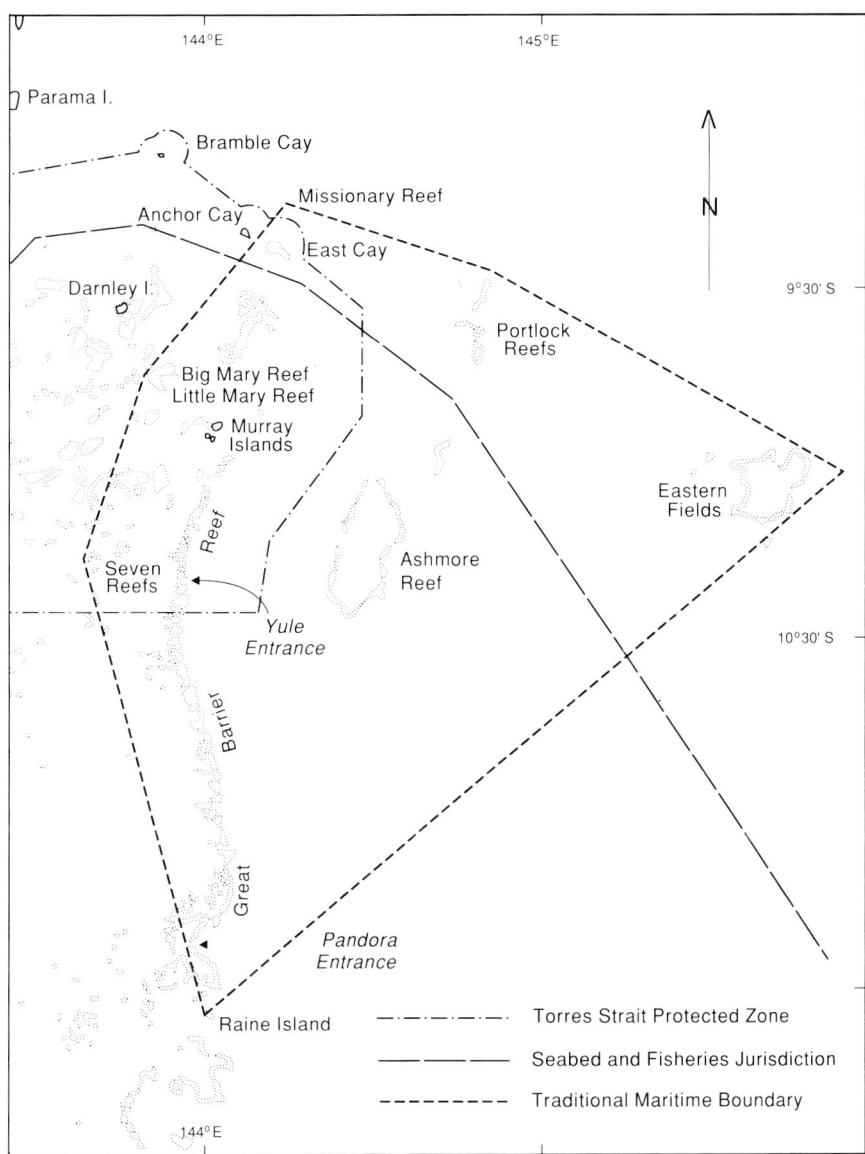

Map 3 The traditional maritime boundaries claimed by the Murray Islanders

program of self-development on cooperative lines for commercial fishing within traditional maritime boundaries. According to information given verbally to the author, these boundaries include the area from Missionary Reef through Big Mary Reef (more than half-way to Darnley Island [Erub]) to Seven Reefs, and

Seven Sandbanks to Raine Island to Eastern Fields, and many named reefs and sandbanks inside those boundaries (Kerget or East Cay, for example [see Map 3, drawn by Andrew Passi for the Mer Islands Community Council in May 1993]).[34] The economic zone declared by the Meriam people on 6 December 1993 goes beyond the 3-mile Queensland territorial sea boundary; they follow these traditional boundaries which coincide in one direction with the boundary of a protected zone for marine resources provided for by the Torres Strait Treaty.[35] The Meriam see themselves as the owners of that area and all its resources.

Whatever the current practices among the Meriam in excluding or not excluding each other from the sandbeaches and water surrounds of the Murray Islands, there is *no doubt* in any of their minds about their right to use and enjoy and to exclude non-Meriam from their traditional waters. Landowner and witness for the Murray Islanders, George Kudub, expressed a view that was general among the Meriam in 1993: 'Because we get our *ged* [land] now we want to go back to our traditional system. So we want to claim our boundaries including the seabed. This is the area we fought for in the past.'[36] The Mer Islands fishing project seeks to 'marry' the so-called traditional (or subsistence) economy with the modern marine economy, in which Murray Islanders participated with their own cutters and luggers from the early 1880s.[37]

CUSTOMARY MARINE TENURE AND NATIVE TITLE TO THE SEA IN AUSTRALIA

From a comparative survey of recognition of native title in the United States, Canada and New Zealand, Bartlett concludes, 'The rationale of native title at common law and its authoritative application dictates that it extends to the sea in accordance with the nature of the traditional connection or use'.[38] Cases in Canada have demonstrated that native title includes areas of waterbed or foreshore lying within traditional territory and this includes off-shore areas in the Arctic, on the Atlantic and Pacific coasts and some regions of the Great Lakes.[39]

Customary marine tenures in coastal Australia have major similarities.[40] The property rights of lineages and clans extend to the sea. As Keen has noted, 'Aborigines generally regard estuaries, bays and waters immediately adjacent to the shore line as being part of their land'.[41] The principles I have outlined with respect to the Meriam are broadly consistent with other Islander and Aboriginal sandbeach peoples.[42] On the basis of comparative knowledge from other coastal states, Cordell concludes that while customary marine tenure 'may not easily be transcribed and translated into western statutory legal frameworks', it embodies 'living customs' and thus provides a basis for commercial marine projects.[43] Highly relevant to customary marine tenure are contrasting notions of boundaries and the limiting effects of state boundaries and statutory fishing zones in northern coastal waters.[44]

In the lead judgment in *Mabo (No 2)*, Justice Brennan stated that under international law the Commonwealth has primary sovereignty over the territorial sea, seabed, airspace, continental shelf, and so on, a sovereignty unchallengeable in municipal courts.[45] Bartlett sums up the current situation: '*Mabo* offers general principles as to the nature of native title but does not prescribe its manner of application to the sea'.[46] Likewise, Sutherland concludes that the judgment does not preclude the application of native title principles to the seabed or recognition of usufructuary and fishing rights.[47]

In contrast to representatives of the Commonwealth government who have suggested that native title may be 'difficult to establish, except perhaps in relation to fishing rights', Bartlett has drawn the optimistic conclusion that '*Mabo* extends to the sea' and that problems of proof 'will be no more onerous than on land'.[48] His starting point is the environment or territory as it exists for seafaring Aboriginal or Islander people: 'To the extent that the environment includes the sea, it is included within the compass of native title'.[49]

Any native title to the sea which accommodates conceptions of the sea and 'sea property' embedded in the principles of customary marine tenure must include foreshore and sea, including waters and seabed. Jackson's definition of title or rights to the sea fits nicely the cultural land–seascape of the Meriam: 'the rights of indigenous people to own, use, exclude others, and manage their maritime estates and all contained within them (permanent or transitory), including the sea-bed'.[50]

Among those who see native title as a danger to Australia there is a tendency also to see rights to the sea as inherent in the High Court's decision. Thus, for example, Howard concluded in 1993 'that land title as envisaged in *Mabo* almost certainly includes sea title (off-shore submerged lands) as well'.[51] Geoffrey Ewing, assistant director of the Mining Council of Australia, reported 'the suggestion that native title could exist to the whole of the coastline around Australia between the high and low water marks'.[52] And the Western Australia Chamber of Mines and Energy has also stated that native title may include foreshore and areas off-shore.[53]

These assertions and predictions about native title to areas of sea are in the process of being tested in the courts and before the National Native Title Tribunal established under the Native Title Act 1993, which includes 'land or waters' in its definition of native title.[54] In Western Australia, claims being made in court by Barunga and Others (the Wororra peoples) and the Yawuru peoples to land in the West Kimberley region, north of Derby and near the township of Broome, include foreshore, reef areas and sea.[55] The Wik Mungkan claim to land on northwestern Cape York Peninsula likewise includes sea territory.[56] Meanwhile commercial fishing projects like that undertaken by the Meriam are in process of elaboration among some Aboriginal coastal communities in Arnhem Land.[57]

11 NATIVE TITLE IN THE RESHAPING OF AUSTRALIAN IDENTITY

A LASTING BREAK IN THE SILENCE?

The 'native title era' in Australia begins with a dialogue of voices across the frontier: stilled voices speak out from *terra nullius*, engaging with those silenced by a belief in the universality of their own law and form of social being. Within a continuing interplay of contrasting standpoints and political engagements, changes in public consciousness have taken place.

Even as sympathetic interpreters of the High Court decision wrote of the 'death of the concept of *terra nullius*',[1] resource-based industry spokespeople and their supporters in parliaments and public life gave strident expression to its absence as a meaningful reality. A softer version of a disbelief in Aboriginal property rights grew out of the need to balance moral ideals with resource developers' moves to reduce title rights to a bare minimum. Both responses rest upon the continuation of the *terra nullius* myth that Aboriginal and Islander societies are primitive and so lack any potential for self-initiated economic development.

Running against this current of opinion are strong statements from those Aboriginal and Islander people who are calling a halt to dispossession and seek a self-determining future on traditionally owned land or on land re-acquired. This final chapter explores the chances and engages with some of the hazards of Aboriginal and non-Aboriginal Australians walking in step into '*terra nullius*'. It argues that cross-cultural cooperation depends ultimately upon a reciprocal understanding of the strong stories which the cultures have to give one another.

ACROSS THE FRONTIER

The breaking of the silence on 3 June 1992 may be of a different order to those breaks which have gone before: gradually everyone had to listen to the voice of the High Court, even though by no means everyone wished to do so. As the news of the decision reverberated across the world, it began to break apart the assumption of an Australian nation essentially without Aborigines and Islanders, a reality that had been consolidated ever since federation in 1901. The Meriam were the carriers of that transformation because they had an especially strong case to argue before an Australian court of continuous possession, occupation and use of their islands. They were also 'chosen' at a particular moment of history when the forces conducive to an outcome favourable to the rejection of *terra nullius* had generated a degree of momentum.

In the first 48 hours following the judgment, emphasis was given in the public arena to the moral rectitude of the High Court's decision. On 4 June, journalist Cameron Forbes wrote in the *Age*, 'Mabo Decision a Victory over White Arrogance'.[2] Other media commentators echoed the High Court in a similar vein: ' "Legacy of Unutterable Shame" Declared in Land Rights Case' (*Australian Financial Review*), 'Ruling a Moral but not a Legal Advance' (*Canberra Times*), 'Historic Win in Fight for Land Rights' (*West Australian*).

In an overnight reversal from silence to shouting, recognition of the injustices associated with the old certitudes became part of everyday life. The rejection of the 'outrageous notion' of *terra nullius* had removed 'the greatest barrier' to the process of reconciliation between European Australians and indigenous peoples, the prime minister told parliament on 4 June.[3] The fundamental issue on which most non-indigenous Australians were totally ignorant became a common public theme: 'few people really know how Aborigines came to lose Australia', the *West Australian* noted without the merest hint of explanation.[4] With the 'moral victory' and 'moral advance' borne by the decision, the removal of 'a solemn blot and insult on the judicial landscape', came the admission that *terra nullius* as an idea was 'always known to be false'.[5] It was as though the shadowed side of the Australian nation had been illuminated by a new light.

Statements emanating from the moral high ground were followed quickly by reassurances from spokespeople for the mining industry and from the premier of Queensland, Wayne Goss, that the decision referred only to 9 square kilometres of land at the Murray Islands.[6] At the other extreme, flamboyant and misleading headlines in certain print media — 'Mabo Recaptures a Lost Continent'[7] — suggested ramifications far exceeding anything that Eddie Mabo had dreamed of. They also provided a context for responsible editors to reassure the majority of its limits: 'Directly or immediately the rights recognised at the Murray islands were not conferred on any other indigenous peoples', the *Age* editorial stated on 5 June; 'Only in the most remote areas is there any land capable of being claimed under the High Court's rule', the *Canberra Times* commented the previous day.

Beneath these reassurances lay 'the cornerstone' on which the decision stood: that the court was 'not free to adopt rules' which 'would fracture the skeleton of principle which gives the body of our law its shape and internal consistency'.[8] Justice Brennan's measured words signalled major limits to the decision. Clearly the clock would not be put back to the days of first settlement and the piece by piece dispossession that followed: the 'radical title' of the Crown prevented any claim to return of lands made freehold by English law; nor could British sovereignty be challenged in an Australian court.

The High Court judgment soon became an international media event. Its historical belatedness contributed to its position as world spectacle in a way that the Supreme Court of Canada's decision in the *Calder* case had not done 20 years earlier. The magnitude of the change may be 'measured' by the failure 'to come to terms with Aboriginal claims "to some portion of their native soil"', as Justice Deane of the High Court had noted in April 1985.[9]

Whatever the subsequent steps taken to divest the High Court's recognition of native title of meaning and to limit the application of the decision, internationally based forces with an imperative comparable with that which proclaimed the end of apartheid in South Africa compelled recognition of native title in Australia. The descendants of the original inhabitants were indeed living 'inside' their various parts of *terra nullius* all along; from now on they must be taken into account.

Tim Rowse has identified a 'moral anxiety' or feelings of disquiet about European colonisation within the conquering culture. He cites Reynolds's argument that the suppression of 'European disquiet' following the 'aggressive questioning' of colonial doctrines and practices in the 1830s, 'was superseded by a triumphal liberalism founded upon a forgetfulness of the human costs of invasion'. The suppression of that moral anxiety, which had been given public expression in the 'first land rights movement' in the 1830s, was incomplete.[10] Rowse notes that 'Reynolds has yet to explain the survival of this moral tradition beneath the surface of twentieth century colonial practice'.[11]

The lands rights movement to which Gurindji people began to give public expression through their leaders Vincent Lingiari and Hobbles Danayarri in 1966 bore a fundamental difference to that of the 1830s: it was a movement that began to join forces across a frontier in relationships of understanding and responsibility. The terms of such a coexistence are made clear in Hobbles Danayarri's 'Saga of Captain Cook', published in 1984: 'a willingness to share Australia's resources with the invaders' on condition that indigenous people's 'original and inalienable ownership of the country is acknowledged'.[12]

In the late 1960s and the 1970s, the modern land rights movement brought to life and stimulated a moral tradition within the conquerors' culture which had been undermined severely with respect to the indigenous victims of colonial expansion: all the upholders of *terra nullius* had was the pitifully false justification that indigenous people merely walked over and roamed the land, little different to the fauna which they hunted.

In the 1970s and 1980s, moral anxiety found expression among some public intellectuals in concern for the forgotten rights of Aboriginal and Torres Strait Islander people: the 'cult of forgetfulness . . . on a national scale'[13] had begun to break. The outcome of the 1967 referendum meant that Aboriginal and Islander people were included in the census. The Aboriginal Treaty Committee, which sprang into life in 1979, is an important expression of a developing sensibility.[14] A silence with respect to colonial peoples in Australia's 'external territories' could no longer be sustained when political independence in Papua New Guinea was declared on 15 September 1975. Within this newly defined social milieu some people were able to listen to the voices of indigenous people — to people like Hobbles Danayarri or to the Meriam plaintiffs. European Australians aware of Australia's terrible backwardness with respect to its indigenous peoples were speaking out with a vigour inspired by the actions of Gurindji, Yolngu and other indigenous people on the savage injustices perpetrated in the name of those born of the conquerors: the land rights conference at which plans for the *Mabo* case were made in 1981 joined forces across the frontier.[15]

This sense of immorality had also been registered among the judiciary. In 1985 Justice Deane of the High Court contrasted Australian with American laws relating to indigenous inhabitants: 'the common law of this land has still not reached the stage of retreat from injustice' attained by American law in 1823, a conclusion described by Henry Reynolds as 'a confession and an indictment of Australian jurisprudence'.[16]

SPEAKING OUT FROM TERRA NULLIUS

'Thou Shalt Not Steal . . .' — Kev Carmody's song rang out over La Perouse, a small space near Sydney with a history of uninterrupted Aboriginal occupation. His words reached out to all quarters of Australia through a vast network of

Aboriginal ABC Radio relays. It was Australia–Invasion Day 1993, the International Year of Indigenous Peoples. People of Aboriginal Australia were refocusing themselves; they were also making fresh contact with those members of the new generation of non-Aboriginal Australians who are responsive to the music, the song, the dance, the graphic art of Aboriginal and Torres Strait Islander peoples.

In commanding Australian Christendom to live by its own principles the Aboriginal singer's words resonated with Reverend Dave Passi's reflection from the pulpit at Mer Island in September 1989, on the Supreme Court of Queensland's recently ended inquiry. In the name of Malo, follow the law which you know comes to you from God: he didn't tell you to take what belongs to other people. The words of each man were an affirmation of rights. They were also appeals to those within the conquering culture to see the point and act accordingly; they were expressions of a belief that, whatever the discrepancy between words and deeds, however long the silence, the fiction of a *terra nullius* had not totally engulfed the soul of non-Aboriginal Australia. And as reactions to the court's decision had already begun to reveal, this belief was right: the conquerors' culture was not a total moral desert, and the judiciary (albeit belatedly) had given expression to a sense of morality and justice that cut deeply into the make-up of non-Aboriginal Australians.

The strength and immediacy of Aboriginal reaction to the High Court's decision had far exceeded the expectations of the Australian public and political leaders. Thus for example, the chairman of the Northern Land Council, Galarrwuy Yunupingu, a Yolngu man from Yirrkala community, had been quick to announce publicly that the government must accept the decision as its cue to land rights legislation and a treaty with indigenous people.[17]

For some years Aboriginal people had been looking for signs of an impending decision by the High Court, compelled to await the outcome of that 'awesome creature the Meriam law suit had become'.[18] Major land claims were quietly in process; unlike the modest and unacknowledged beginnings of the Meriam claim a decade before, a new context created by the recognition of native title made certain that they would have a large press. Within two months of the High Court's decision, three major claims were declared publicly. A claim to over 250,000 square kilometres of land and sea by Kimberley groupings in Western Australia made before the recognition of native title now burst into the public arena.[19] The Yolngu people in East Arnhem Land were preparing to mount a claim to include land leased by Nabalco Proprietary Limited for bauxite mining, the same land about which they had petitioned the Governor-

General in 1968 and fought for in court in the years 1969 to 1970.[20] And a claim to some 35,000 acres (14,000 hectares) by Wik Mungkan people on the north-western side of Cape York Peninsula, including the site of the CRA bauxite mine, was given prominence nation wide.

The factual basis of recent as well as early dispossession began to unfold before the public: many of the claimants could recount the events of their own dispossession. The experience of eviction from the locale known as Mapoon at Port Musgrave was as recent as 1965 and people who grew up at Mapoon still relive the poignant memory of the compulsory move from the area:

> After the War the warning had gone out that they're going to close down the Mission, but the tribal people refused . . . the tribal people said they're going to hang on. But then they got the white police to come in the night . . . the DNA [Department of Native Affairs] Manager had it all planned out where and what time they're gonna come. And some of the people been out hunting. When this white policeman came round he said: 'Pick up your clothes, there's a boat, we're going out. Sleep on the boat on the way.'
>
> Next day they burned the church. They got coconut leaves, put them underneath the church. The police were only notified to shift the people; they didn't want no bloodshed. And once they got the people on the boat the DNA come in and burn down all them homes; the people left early in the morning. When they turned back to see the last bit of Mapoon they saw all these birds flying. And in the air they been fly in the sign of a V. But we don't know whether that victory [was] for the people . . .[21]

Dispossession was well within living memory and its melancholy hung upon the victims. The Wik claim carried a special moral burden: the land from which the people were evicted was reserved for the benefit of Aboriginal people. The practical implications of a breach of trust (or fiduciary relationship in legal terms) were also likely to be far-reaching; the claim being made was not to Crown land but to land leased under the Comalco Act 1957 (Commonwealth), so extending the practical consequences of the High Court decision.[22]

In this early period after the decision on native title, claims to land were clear; the principles which lay behind them were not. Nearly a year later, in April 1993, the issue which gave expression to a suppressed aspiration was crystallised at a meeting of Aboriginal leaders and land councils with the prime minister, described by Mr Keating as 'momentous'. The leaders called for an independent economic base upon which Aboriginal people could provide for their own advancement in their own way.[23] That meeting captured the sentiments being expressed from Cape York to Cape Barren Island, from Mer to Western Australia. This resolve signalled that the break in the silence, which had begun some 30 years earlier, had now become irreversible.

Aboriginal spokespeople quickly took hold of the new opportunities. At the negotiating table in Canberra their steel was tempered and honed in a new bargaining situation in which governments were compelled to listen. Aboriginal public figures were joined by younger leaders like Noel Pearson, executive director of the Cape York Land Council. Etched on the public memory are leaders of substance and determination, articulate in a resolve that Aboriginal and Islander people have a position to defend, principles and traditions they wish to uphold. The outcome of the negotiating process in the passage of the Native Title Act 1993 also partly belonged to them,[24] a situation which carried new possibilities as well as specific dangers associated with the compromises which necessarily accompany the struggle to gain as much ground as possible in political contest. The dangers are associated with the tendency of political bargaining to render invisible fundamentally incommensurable cultural principles, most important of which is the indissoluble tie of Aboriginal and Islander people to their land in contrast to the conception of land as a tradeable item. Amid the confusions created by misrepresentation and simplification, the public became only dimly aware of these contrasting principles. Aboriginal voices can now be heard, but the principles remain embedded within the great Australian silence.

LIVING ONE'S OWN WAY

Despite the well-grounded belief that the Meriam people had an especially good case to put to a court, the findings of fact divested them of the grounding principle of their cultural inheritance: their dual relationship of rights and responsibilities to land was reduced to a non-religious, non-spiritual one. The hearings merely provided the opportunity for their rights to become partly known to English law.

From a Meriam perspective, in recognising the exclusive collective right of the Meriam to the Murray Islands, the High Court was recognising their laws and customs. Justice Brennan stated that native title is a title to land based upon local laws and customs. It is these principles which the Meriam feel bound to follow, as they argued in court. In the period following the decision, plaintiff Reverend Dave Passi explained this to his people and to Father Frank Brennan. Raising his fists he affirmed, 'There are two laws. One is Malo's Law. And it is right . . . The other is the white man's law . . . sometimes it is wrong because it says that might is right.'[25] Reverend Passi went on to call for the respect of others for the Meriam, their law and culture. He was also part of a group of senior Meriam people who incorporated the various principles of Malo's Law into the Mer (Murray) Islands Community Council by-laws during the year following the High Court decision.

The process of a recognition of Meriam law as a substitute for the 'one law' tradition, which was an adjunct of the doctrine and practice of *terra nullius*, is an event of major significance for the Meriam people. In Reverend Passi's opinion, it represents a significant break with the imposition of 'the white man's law' on his people. Yet while most people are aware that the Meriam people won recognition of 'native title' to their land, the principles of that Meriam land tenure have had little airing outside the Murray Islands. A difficulty is that few non-Aboriginal people have had the chance to listen to Meriam voices saying that there are two categories of law, more than one way of relating to land, more than one culture. Their declarations of their local principles are rarely heard because they were hidden, both in court and the Determination of the Issues of Fact, behind narrow definitions of law and ownership. In the public arena they were diffused within the pervasive and taken-for-granted sense of one law and the exigencies of practical politics.

THE RIGHT TO SAY 'HANDS OFF'

This book has sought to show the connection between the Meriam principles of land tenure and their right to say 'hands off'. Land law at the Mer Islands requires that if you, an outsider, even a Meriam not part of that joint ownership, wish to enter or use someone else's land, you must gain the owner's consent. Everyone knows that; that's my right as landowner. I'll tell him to get out! No doubt about it. It's a real property right. 'Hands off', said plaintiff James Rice. 'It's mine. I own it. Not just [the right to] use.' If an outsider wants to dig the soil or the sandbeach, the owner has the right to say no or go ahead. That is intrinsic to being born into the land. It is the law of Malo.

Land title at the Mer Islands has three features. First, land is owned by a lineage or family group where the eldest brother holds the land on behalf of the group. Second, this interrelationship with land confers a system of rights and obligations which makes the land inalienable from its owners. And third, integral with inherited ownership rights to land is the right to decide access to land by non-owners. In Murray Island custom the three are joined together: a sacred right and responsibility is sealed between generations through the you to me of the spoken word. The entrusting process identifies this interrelationship between land and lineage, which cannot be broken.

If the airing of Meriam principles of land ownership has been limited, those relating to the rest of indigenous Australia have been blurred, simplified and misconceived. Because the Meriam have 'proved' the existence of their native title through their action in the High Court, they can continue to follow the principles of inheritance, rules against trespass, instructions to plant and conserve as they did before, but within the transformed context that their title is recognised in Australian common law. The rest of indigenous Australians must prove their native title to land under the Native Title Act 1993.

When Justice Toohey said that, for the purposes of determining indigenous interests in land throughout Australia as a whole, 'the relevant principles are the same', he may have been taking his cue from W E H Stanner, who said that all Aboriginal peoples have a conception of land as property, and that this embodies both a spiritual and a material relation to land, or Nancy Williams's description of the Yolngu clans' being and conception of the world as 'embedded in a single matrix'.[26] I have designated this dual relationship to land as a right (ownership) and an obligation and responsibility to (belonging), where these reciprocal rights and duties refer not only to land, but also to people and families.

The process of translating the High Court's recognition of native title into a national statutory form occurred under conditions unconducive to a process of understanding these contrasting principles. Public debate occurred in a highly confrontational context in which moves were being made to nullify native title. Given the erosion of the potential rights of landowners by resource-based industries and state governments, public consideration of basic principles receded in the struggle by Aboriginal leaders and non-Aboriginal adherents of their rights to land to achieve as much as possible at the bargaining table in Canberra.

The first result was that only limited aspects of the principles of Aboriginal people's relationship to land came to the surface. 'Special attachment to land' and the 'right of consent' became the outward and visible signs of principles which distinguish them as Aboriginal and Islander peoples.

A second outcome was that in the legislation passed by the federal legislature — the Native Title Act (NTA) 1993 — the three features basic to Aboriginal and Islander land tenure inscribed or implied in the Aboriginal Lands Rights (Northern Territory) Act (ALRA) 1976 are either absent or ambiguous. In contrast to that Act, where 'traditional Aboriginal owners . . . means a local descent group' (ALRA, part 1, s3), native title rights are communal, group or *individual* rights (NTA, s223[1]).[27] Secondly, under the Native Title Act 1993, title holders may surrender their native title rights (s21[1]) and 'the grant of a freehold estate in any land or any other interests in relation to land . . . that the native title holders may choose to accept' may be substituted (s21[3]). This leaves the way open for the relinquishing of native title rights to land.[28] Thirdly, the 'right of consent' (that is, the right to prohibit trespass), inscribed in the Aboriginal Land Rights (Northern Territory) Act 1976,[29] is reduced to the 'Right to negotiate' (NTA, part 2, division 3, subdivision B, 17–27): where a government 'proposes . . . to do any permissible future act' (s26[1]) including 'the creation of a right to mine' or 'the compulsory acquisition of native title rights' (s26 [2a and 2d]), native title holders will have the right to make submissions and to 'be appropriately consulted about any access' (NTA, s26[4bii and 4c]).[30]

Between early September 1993, when it seemed that Commonwealth legislation would abrogate rights to equality before the law that were embodied in the Racial Discrimination Act 1975 upheld by the High Court in *Mabo (No 1)* 1988, and the passage of the federal native title Bill on 21 December 1993, Aboriginal leaders clawed back rights to racial equality endangered by the version of the Bill the government had been pressured to propose. This made possible the passage of an Act which simply holds 'in balance the rights of Aborigines over against those of developers'.[31]

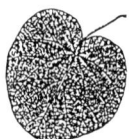

The section which follows, on the outward and visible signs of cultural difference, reveals a general misreading of indigenous cultures in Australia, which, in the post-*Mabo* era, still draws upon the same assumptions as those underlying the concepts of *terra nullius*, in particular, that the 'use and enjoyment' aspect of native title is a simple, stationary, subsistence interest in land, vestigial in contemporary life. As a legal form native title is non-existent; its recognition is a break in a legal system which 'has long since become the natural inheritance of the entire population'.[32] Aboriginal interests in land are seen as mainly or exclusively spiritual: the clan belongs to the land, as Justice Blackburn concluded in *Milirrpum* in 1971. In the modern world this signals 'an economic dead end', because (real) Aboriginal activities are conceived as confined to traditional uses and ceremonies at sacred sites.[33]

CULTURAL DIFFERENCE: THE OUTWARD AND VISIBLE SIGNS

Within a month of the High Court's decision, it was clear that a limited decolonisation process was in train with the 'self-determining principle' to the fore: land claims were being made which included forms of cooperation between customary owners and national park authorities, similar to arrangements which have worked well at Kakadu and Uluru in the Northern Territory.[34] It was soon clear that a very influential section of resource-based industrial interests was going to wage a battle to defeat them.

Interestingly, no objections were made to much more radical proposals for the Torres Strait Islands. Processes well in train in the second half of 1992, to convert the Torres Strait Islands into a kind of Norfolk Island autonomous zone with resource control and political management in local hands, raised not even a ripple of protest. Moves for autonomy, which go back 50 years in the Torres Strait, had been taken up by the Island Coordinating Council in the late 1980s; the High Court decision gave it 'moral force' and the minister's support reflected government approval, it was reported towards the end of December 1992.[35]

On the mainland it was another story entirely. Hugh Morgan's extravagant view that 'the Mabo decision had given substance to the ambitions of communists for a separate Aboriginal State and plunged Australian property law into chaos' rose to public prominence in October 1992.[36] An unqualified lack of preparedness to countenance even the most minor steps towards a measure of self-determination on the mainland, similar in principle to that being negotiated equably in the Torres Strait, took on an almost paranoid character. Two months later the spectre of a black state was projected again by

Hugh Morgan: without a national referendum reaffirming the old *status quo*, such claims, reinterpreted as moves towards sovereignty, would increase 'at the national peril'.[37]

These essentially negative responses had two main expressions, a strident and a softer version: in political-cum-legal moves for its nullification, and in federal government documents foreshadowing a set of attributes of native title arranged in a hierarchy. The two responses share a common ground of 'disbelief' in the strength and dynamic creativity of Aboriginal societies. The 'nullification mentality' rests upon the trivialisation of Aboriginal culture and interest in land and the disbelief in any other kind of interests in land different to those of English law; the 'soft approach' is often lost in the mists of a pure spirituality among Aboriginal people, or the emphasis on Aboriginal bush-tuckering.

In the debate which followed the High Court decision, two interrelated rights were identified by Aboriginal people. The first concerned the inalienable right to own, inherit and bequeath land. The second concerned the right to self-determination, which expressed itself in two forms: the right to an economic base on which to develop according to local principles; and the right to decide whether other people may or may not develop resources associated with one's land. In the unfolding of cultural differences in public debate it was not long before Aboriginal interrelationships with land pointed to an incommensurability of cultural principles, which in turn, underlined the demand for self-determination.

Outward signs of these distinctive cultural principles appeared in public debate, so providing some clarification of the meaning of Aboriginal interests in land. The two high points of that process occurred in an interchange between Aboriginal spokespeople and government officials about a 'special relationship' to land (April to July 1993) and around the 'right of consent', which was given eloquent expression at a national meeting of 400 Aboriginal and Islander delegates at Eva Valley station in Jawoyn country, from 3 to 5 August 1993.

A SPECIAL RELATIONSHIP TO LAND AND ITS MISREADING

On 27 April 1993, Aboriginal land councils and the Aboriginal and Torres Strait Islander Commission (ATSIC) produced an 'Aboriginal Peace Plan', a document which engaged directly with the question of the *content* of native title. It did so from a perspective that joined together a special relationship with land *and* the right to legal recognition of native title. Together they provided the basis for a self-determining development that included both 'economic development' and so-called 'traditional activities'.

Partly in response to the peace plan, on 3 June 1993, the federal government released a discussion paper on the High Court decision and native title. That paper appears to have been the result of a concerted but misguided effort to accommodate indigenous interests in land. Of the 33 principles outlined, one principle (number 14) made reference to Aboriginal and Torres Strait Islander people's 'special attachment' to their land.[38]

Misrecognition of the meaning of the special relationship is revealed in the paper's reduction of the outcomes of the decision to 'a land management problem'.[39] It does so *in the name of* conceiving native title as 'an interest in land in its own right with its own characteristics'.[40] It goes on to assert that while 'native title may involve rights to exclude access and permit or deny activities on the land', 'the legal position is that native title holders would not have an absolute right of consent over [validly extinguishing] actions of the Crown'. This would include actions taken in the national interest.

The fallacy of this interpretation of equality is, once again, the failure to take account of the legitimacy of cultural difference, as Noel Pearson noted a few days later, describing the document as 'slimy'. Aboriginal title has to be treated differently because 'Aboriginal culture is inseparable from the land to which Aboriginal title attaches. The loss or impairment of that title is not simply a loss of real estate, it is a loss of culture.'[41]

In Aboriginal custom, Noel Pearson is saying access by strangers to the surface, what grows there, or what lies beneath it, is a matter for its owners. Governments call that 'consent'. Meriam say it is our identity, this is our land, here are our boundaries; we have a right to say 'hands off because it comes from sacred ancestors', or 'I will show you my land. Come, help yourself.' To sell this attachment is trespassing against sacred law.

At this point considerations of *realpolitik* supplanted consideration of grounding principle: gross distortions of cultural differences, which underpinned attempts by an influential section of resource-based industry and most state premiers to undermine the legislation, dominated the media. 'Special attachments' were taken to refer essentially to sacred sites. An examination of public debate and critical comment on the recognition of native title in the second half of 1993 is instructive; it reveals a close connection between the degree of misrepresentation of Aboriginal societies and the attempts to negate the High Court decision. The moral and political energy stimulated by the High Court's decision created a pressing need among some opponents of the recognition of native title to restate and renovate the *terra nullius* doctrine. This was provided by a cultural version of the old belief about the non-adaptability of Aboriginal societies. The old *terra nullius* doctrine rested upon the assumption of the biological inferiority of 'primitive' peoples; strategies of 'protection' in post-1901 Australia had used skin colour as the criterion of biological inferiority. Contemporary theory rests upon assumptions of *cultural* inferiority. Identifying the central feature of cultural difference — the inalienability of land — anthropologist Ron Brunton asserted that Aboriginal society displays 'non-adaptive culture traits'. '*Mabo* is an economic dead-end' because Aboriginal and Islander land cannot be bought and sold. In a monograph released in April 1993 by the Institute of Public Affairs, Brunton first 'disposed' of Aboriginal societies as stationary. He went on to uphold the rights of Aboriginal people to decide *individually* whether they wish to remain members of small traditional communities (still backwaters in his view) or join other Australians in modern pursuits.[42]

Brunton argued that Aboriginal people are not one special group or even many special groups: therefore they cannot claim any rights unique to their genealogical and social ties with pre-existing indigenous inhabitants; they have no separate claim to land or to special policies different to any other disadvantaged groups in Australia. This latter view was intrinsic to arguments against land rights in the 1970s and 1980s; in the post-*Mabo* context the arguments are extended in formulations such as 'special policies are a form of protection and dependency', other Australians, such as the convicts, were dispossessed, there should be equal recognition of sites of historical and cultural significance for other Australians as well as Aborigines.[43] This position is tantamount to a new assimilationism. It finds expression too in regard to the law and to Australian identity: 'We are one people with one law'; 'the future of Aborigines lies as Australians, not as Aborigines.'[44]

In the sphere of practical politics, since the beginning of 1993 moves were made to reverse native title back to *terra nullius*. The election of a conservative government led by Richard Court in Western Australia in March 1993 gave impetus to the concerted move to 'protect ownership of title threatened by the recent Mabo decision'. Speaking to the Australian Petroleum Exploration Association conference, Court claimed, 'the Mabo decision had raised false hopes among some sections of the Aboriginal community'.[45]

These moves were to culminate in legislation in Western Australia 'offering contempt, not respect, for native title', in the words of Richard Bartlett. Known as the Land (Titles and Traditional Usage) Act 1993, it extinguished native title without compensation, violated the RDA and made grants to Aboriginal persons a matter not of right but of the 'grace and favour' of the minister. Its effect differed little from the Queensland Coast Islands Declaratory Act 1985, by which the Queensland government had sought to put an end to the Murray Islanders' case. On 16 March 1995 the High Court declared the Western Australian Act invalid.[46]

ONE VOICE FROM THE VALLEY: THE RIGHT OF CONSENT

In the weeks that elapsed between the peace plan delivered by Aboriginal leaders on 27 April 1993 and the release of the government discussion paper on proposed native title legislation on 3 June, no real negotiation with Aboriginal people had been initiated. The practical reality of that disregard for Aboriginal opinion lay in the preparedness of the government to ignore a fact inherent in Aboriginal people's so-called special attachment to land: the right to self-determination, referred to by the land councils as the 'right of consent' and by the mining industry as the 'right of veto'.

Responsible sources in the media were calling for just outcomes and the striking of a balance that satisfied everyone.[47] Even as such statements were being made, the government was expressing the irreconcilability of real self-determination and the overriding powers of mining in internally contradictory documents. And on the ground at McArthur River in the Northern Territory its actions were verifying for Aboriginal people that the national interest meant nothing more than the interests of the resource-based industries.[48]

Moreover, in both softer and more strident form, native title was being divested of a coherent and wholistic right to land and re-presented as simply a bundle of rights. By a further sleight of hand, the smallest twig in the bundle was then taken to constitute the whole.

In the weeks following the critical reception of the federal government's discussion paper, a further document was released in which the somewhat 'misty principle' of native title[49] was dissected into a series of attributes. A draft of proposed legislation issued on 9 July listed eight attributes of native title arranged in something resembling 'a menu of descending rights', the first two — exclusive possession and the right to exclude — being two of the three essential attributes usually associated with 'real' property in the English legal tradition.[50] The others were in order: the right to be consulted, the right to conduct ceremonies, descending to rights to traverse or camp, hunt or fish, collect or cultivate food, collect materials for weapons, tools, ceremonial, spiritual, cultural and domestic purposes.[51]

Each attribute would be required to be demonstrated as deriving from traditional practice and supported by current practice. This approach has been compared with the 'techno-minimalist criteria' of rights defined by Chief Justice McEachern in *Delgamuukw v British Columbia* (1991): here the Indian holders of 'aboriginal rights' must demonstrate that they *'use the lands in a manner they say their ancestors used them'*.[52]

The document provided an opening to minimise native title surreptitiously in the name of 'special attachment': the 'menu of descending rights' was not unlike the attributes of native title rights circulated by Mr G Savell, chief executive of the Association of Mining and Exploration Companies, Western Australia, 'a bundle of rights' exercised separately or together.[53] Native title was, he said, a weak title or not a title at all, being 'best described as land use'. Noting the absence of a 'definition of what native title really is', he designated it as 'a bundle of rights' rather than 'a full land title with the force and rights of European land title', rights which 'Aboriginal interests would have us believe'. He projected the same set of attributes as those at the lower end of the government 'menu' of rights as pertaining to pre-1788 Aboriginal rights: 'Aboriginal people lived on the land, took sustenance from it, took living materials from, worshipped and held ceremonies on significant sites and held the land they occupied against their neighbours if they could'.[54] The legislatures and the welfare system have protected those rights since colonisation, he concluded. Three days later, there came a statement from John Hyde, executive director of the Institute of Public Affairs, suggesting a lack of clarity about whether native title confers 'merely the rights necessary for traditional land use', rather than 'a general right of exclusion'.[55] Aboriginal societies were being openly and self-servingly divested of the very right that gave them the power to protect those principles which created and conserved the imperishable bonds composing their 'natural inheritance'.

These were critical events in the consolidation of a national unity among Aboriginal people, which was to have historic expression on 5 August at Eva Valley in the Northern Territory, when some 400 Aboriginal and Islander delegates called together on the initiative of the Council for Aboriginal

Reconcilation and ATSIC, gave nationwide expression to the right to determine access of outsiders to their land.

The broad context of this first national meeting of Aboriginal and Torres Strait Islander people called to formulate a response to the High Court decision was the draft legislation presented to Cabinet by the prime minister on 27 July offering Aboriginal people not the right to exclude, but only the 'right of negotiation'. Tribunals would be empowered to rule on unresolved outcomes subject to federal and state government rights of veto in 'the national interest'.[56]

In rejecting the proposed national legislation on native title, the Eva Valley Statement, as it was called, requested the government to 'only move on this issue with the support of Aboriginal and Torres Strait Islander people'. The meeting demanded the right of informed consent on all development projects — mining, tourist and pastoral.

This position had been foreshadowed on 20 June when 50 Aboriginal leaders meeting in Darwin had written a letter to Mr Keating criticising him for announcing proposed native title legislation without even informing them. They had warned that any native title legislation would fail without Aboriginal support and they nominated two Aboriginal leaders, Mick Dodson, social justice commissioner of the Human Rights and Equal Opportunity Commission, and Noel Pearson, executive director of the Cape York Land Council, to take part in drafting such legislation.[57]

The key principle enunciated was that no grant of interest on native title land 'can be made without the informed consent of all relevant title holders'.[58] Their total opposition to the terms of the legislation, which reduced this key clause to the right to negotiate, moved into high political profile. Mick Dodson said:

> We don't agree with anything they've done. They haven't bothered to talk to us about it. They haven't negotiated with us about it and they don't have our consent to do what they want to do.[59]

RESHAPING AUSTRALIAN IDENTITY

The High Court decision is itself a step in the reshaping of identity, albeit minimal, conservative and qualified: European law is no longer a universal statement of law, but is qualified by interests of a kind partly known to English law. In the long era of *terra nullius*, the powers that be were complicit in a silence created by their incapacity to contemplate that a culturally meaningful social life existed on the other side of the wall they had built for the 'inmates'. Whatever the conclusions of the fact-finding judge about the absence of 'real law' among the Meriam people, the latter have been able to stand up and say, 'There are two laws. Our law gives us the right to say "Hands off. You are trespassing against our law."'

STRIKING A CHORD OF RESPONSIVENESS

The Eva Valley resolve brought into prominence the extent — and the limits — of the understanding of European Australians of the meanings underlying the words: the right of indigenous people to decide and do things in their own way. The following example, drawn from public debate in the Eva Valley context, illustrates a lacuna in public understanding of Aboriginal people's relationship to land as a living, adaptive one, not a static category.

A month before the Eva Valley meeting, Hal Wootten QC, a long-standing advocate of justice for Aboriginal people, sponsored a joint statement of religious leaders and former royal commissioners into Aboriginal deaths in custody that spoke out 'for the principles of recognition of surviving Aboriginal rights to land' and for 'the largest measure of self-determination for Aboriginal people that Australia can accommodate'.[60] Responding to Eva Valley, Wootten went on to address specifically the *content* of the Aboriginal position. Calling for a 'generous rather than a grudging outcome' to the recognition of native title, he noted 'the striking way' in which the one strong voice from Eva Valley revealed 'how deeply concerned Aboriginal people are about the right to control access to their land'. He then went on to show the integral connection between 'our nationhood and sense of national identity' and 'our ability to act generously, honourably and courageously as a nation towards our indigenous people'.[61]

Hal Wootten was giving voice to the silent level of non-Aboriginal Australia which the High Court decision had contacted; his was an expression of the reawakening of a silenced responsiveness. The *Age* stated editorially on the same day how the High Court decision 'went to the essence of our perception of ourselves as a nation'.[62] The Eva Valley unity ('everybody working together') gave Aboriginal people a new 'claim to the political high ground', the *Australian* concluded on the import of the historic meeting.[63] It went on to identify the grounding principle — the issue of consent — but did not explain why it was fundamental: 'For Aborigines in the north', consent provisions had been 'the very heart and soul of land rights'.[64] 'Consent' taps into the association between land and identity: the right to ward off strangers by 'showing the flag'. In modern times it is embodied in the right to self-determination.

The impulse for self-determination has two separable components. One concerns equal rights as against domination by outsiders. Taken alone it may simply end up as 'the right' to oppress one's own people, to mine uranium, or to engage in ecologically destructive forms of development. The second feature is cultural in the sense that it seeks to sustain forms of development that are cooperative, in attempting to combine limited entrepreneurship within the framework of community-owned major plant. Both aspects exist within the right to self-determination and 'economic independence'.[65]

The Jawoyn people have made their concerns, both spiritual and economic, the subject of plain statement. They are owners of the Katherine Gorge (Nitmiluk) and Eva Valley station is in Jawoyn country. In 1993 they won the cultural tourism award for activities they developed with very little government assistance. They are also owners of Coronation Hill, a site sought after by mining industry developers. John Ah-Kit, president of the Jawoyn association, indicates the association's priorities: 'Bula is everything that the Jawoyn say it is, and it is very sacred country. We certainly hope that the plan [to mine there] has run its race and it won't be tackled again.'[66]

European Australians find it hard to show the kind of understanding or respect which appreciates the seriousness of Aboriginal intentions. Cut off themselves from the give and take of reciprocal engagement with Aboriginal or Islander people by their own misconstruction of the indigenous worlds as exclusively spiritual and unmovingly 'traditional', they then experience a sense of loss, a longing for the harmonious and spiritual side of Aboriginal life which they take to be the whole. They seek to fill a social life hollowed out by the domination of the materialistic ethos of commodity cultures. Ian Anderson has referred to the locking of 'colonized people into either of two conceptual prisons' — the traditional or the modern — conceived as radically separate, and their consequent entrapment 'in a time warp' between past and present.[67] In the era of native title legislation, it is this 'anthropological time-warp', to use Slattery's critical comments on the frozen status imposed on First Nations in British Columbia in *Delgamuukw*, which is perhaps the most serious and universal danger today for Aboriginal and Islander peoples, whether it is embodied in legislation nullifying native title or in legislation and legal decision which seemingly embrace it.[68] The other side of this imprisonment is the locking of those born of the colonisers into their own prison of separateness and the silence embodied in the certitude that European law and culture are simply 'natural'.

There is nonetheless a reservoir of public sensibility responsive to issues of social justice which becomes visible at moments of crisis. When so-called land management issues, and the exclusive rights of state governments to protect non-Aboriginal developers' rights to plunder Aboriginal land were projected through public media, people began to speak the language of the 'fair go'. In September 1993, when non-Aboriginal people became aware of the complete turnaround by the federal government and the imminent abandonment of Aboriginal rights under pressure from resource-based industries, an active body of opposition began to form. The move to suspend the Racial Discrimination Act to validate pastoral and mining leases back to 1788 brought forth an immediate flow of opposition from non-Aboriginal Australians.[69]

The reality is an inarticulate but worrisome sense among European Australians that there is something more to be responded to behind the now visible 'cultural pride' given expression by the Meriam or the Jawoyn or the Yolngu or Gurindji or Michael Mansell's people. Ill-equipped to interrelate with Aboriginal or Islander people, they seek refuge, renewal and contact through Aboriginal art and dance, through the songs of Yothu Yindi or Kev Carmody or Koori bands. Meanwhile, a lack of depth of response is engendered by a world where face to face reciprocal relationships of human interchange are turned into the abstract relation of exchange of things; the belief that this represents the height to which Aboriginal people must evolve carries with it a superficiality which inhibits response to the real meaning of 'special relationship' to land. Thus dedicated supporters of Aboriginal rights are themselves only partially aware of the capacities of Aboriginal and Islander societies: Hal Wootten notes with disappointment and lack of comprehension 'an unconscious racism' among European Australians who, he believes, find it hard to take land rights seriously.[70] By themselves, isolated expressions of anti-racism may lead back to the simplicities of formal equality and ultimately to the inequalities that are signified by the failure to appreciate uniqueness and diversity: equality must allow room for the subleties of being Meriam or Yolngu at the same time as being Islander or Aboriginal people, or indigenous rather than European Australians.

IMPULSES TOWARDS COOPERATION

Responsiveness to issues of social justice and racial equality may take on new meaning through a rejection of evolutionary empiricist assumptions about 'them' and 'us'. It might begin with the realisation that a 'special relationship to land' is dynamic not stationary, that it is both spiritual and economic, and in that two-sidedness lies the possibility of self-determination which is not a threat to Australia's economic development. Such self-determined development would necessitate a recasting of development goals and practices, which may have more in common with principles of ecologically sustainable development and less with economic rationalism.

Some Aboriginal spokespeople are addressing the issue of a more complex national identity. Peter Yu, executive director of the Kimberley Land Council, voiced the thoughts of many communities when he predicted and advocated change in the structural relationship between Aboriginal and non-Aboriginal people.[71] In the terms of the argument here, in order to have any real meaning, structural change would have to result in a change in power relations that allowed the principles of reciprocity to land and to people to come into a position of dominance. Commercial projects now beginning to become a practical possibility within Aboriginal and Islander communities would be and are being framed and guided by cultural principles which embody reciprocity-cooperation as a central value. These, as many people have suggested, are under threat both from within (Murray Island is an example) and without. Changes in power relationships, in the name of self-determination and the right to economic independence, in no way guarantee the upholding of those principles which are claimed to typify the Aboriginal or Islander way. Without a regard for underlying cultural principle, change in power relations, in the long run, will merely replicate the forms of social relationship characteristic of non-indigenous Australia. People, for example, at Murray Island, sense this; unless their interests in land and the basic principles that regulate them are brought to the surface, the latter will be undermined.

Today these landed communities continue to give a central place to face-to-face interrelations, but the sweep or range of those reciprocities transcends the old group divisions, finding expression in demands for community autonomy and development. The hope is that these landed communities may show a lead significant to the rest of indigenous and non-indigenous Australia.

It has been argued that Aboriginal people's 'concept of responsibility for the land has much in common with contemporary principles of sustainable development'.[72] Similar conclusions have been drawn on coastal people's attitudes towards the sea.[73] In the process of declaring their own economic maritime zone, the Meriam have registered publicly a similar attitude.[74] Yet as writers on Aboriginal peoples and development in the east Kimberleys have noted, while in the past stewardship of land included active propagation of native plant species, Aboriginal acquisition of pastoral properties already degraded by pastoral activities, the effects of drought and absence of weed control, should not be taken automatically to imply a sustainable relationship with the environment.[75] To be successful, Aboriginal people's activities 'directed at the market . . . require new skills and capacity to use the diverse institutions which form the market'.[76]

The conclusion has also been drawn that communities with 'strong bonds of mutual cooperation' and with potentially viable economic systems are most likely to fulfil their members' needs.[77] Against this there is the view that the 'highly structured' procedure of sharing in traditional Aboriginal societies, where 'unvarying rule' expresses kinship rights and obligations, 'makes Aboriginal society particularly unsuited to operate community cooperatives' where 'each member has the same entitlements and obligations'.[78] While kinship obligations are writ large in Aboriginal societies, so are inter-clan reciprocities, and this view therefore distorts the realities of contemporary Aboriginal and Islander societies. In Meriam society, for example, responsibilities to kin remain a first priority; at the same time new customs of sharing have emerged, signifying the community, not simply the clan or lineage. For example, *kopat* means 'everyone together': the first turtle caught for the season is offered to the whole community, not just to kinfolk. The Meriam depict their overall identities as diversities-in-unity: Malo brought about inter-clan unity — eight clans in one body, symbolised by the arrival of Malo in the shape of an octopus. This made possible a *new cooperation between clans*; Christianity enlarged and deepened this aspect of reciprocity. Today Meriam groups contine to exist as diversities-in-unity, given *both* to rivalry *and* to cooperation. In other words, they are not 'naturally cooperative', but developments have occurred, creating larger unities.[79] Thus during 1993–94, lineages–families cooperated in a community fishing project based on a fleet of personally owned dinghies: men and women fished, sold their catch to the community-owned freezer, and kept up to 90 per cent of the proceeds for their families, the remainder being used for running costs.

Diversities-in-unity are the very essence of an exchange process grounded in the face-to-face medium at the centre of small, landed communities like the Meriam, the Yolngu or Yarralin people. The Yolngu people of east Arnhem Land have a metaphorical image which illustrates such a non-homogenising, non-abstracting form of being in unity. It arises from the experience of the joining of tidal salt water from the sea with fresh water streams in the lagoon: the distinctive pattern of their merging does not totally dissolve their separate identities. Coombs sees this as an image relevant to the reshaping of Australian identity; a unity 'expressing and protecting diversity and autonomy'. 'At various levels the streams continue to exist influencing and changing, but not destroying the diversity in the character of the lagoon'.[80]

DIVERSITIES IN EXCHANGE

The instruction in Meriam law that says Malo plants everywhere is an 'economic' message and a message for mind and spirit too. When Eddie Mabo went south 'in search of something', that 'thing' was to know what the ruling culture had denied him. He identified the best of European Australian culture; he found moral Europeans who would not only share their knowledge, but do so in a way that helped his culture to grow. Their exchange drew its strength and meaning from the principles of reciprocity which lie at the core of Meriam culture, principles often shadowed or beleaguered in the syntheses created through the abstract exchange processes of commodity cultures.

Through a process of comparison and contrast, he came to see Meriam culture and its future. Out of this came strong experiences, and out of their dramatic culmination in pride in self ('I did my dance') came the Black Community School and his vision to 'sow' and 'cultivate' on Meriam soil: a school in the tradition of Malo as reclaimed and interpreted by him, which drew too on the best of European Australian culture.[81] Realisation may have fallen short of that vision, yet it illustrates how 'the cultural way', as the Meriam call it, may grow. There is too the associated hope that a 'strong story' may strike a chord within the other and so create a bond of understanding. Reverend Dave Passi has developed his own syntheses; he sees the way Christian teaching struck the central chord of Meriam people's beliefs. They answered back with the realisation that Christianity completed the thought of the past; in this fulfilment lies the uniqueness of the Meriam people today.

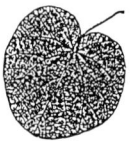

Islander and Aboriginal people's relationships with their land have been abiding ones. Those relationships are also under threat. For the present, the urgent issue for Aboriginal and Islander people is to grasp the 'chance to recover lost rights and traditional lands . . . now, because, as time goes by, the struggle will get harder'.[82] This makes the first priority to halt dispossession. A second threat is longer term. Decolonisation is accompanied by neo-colonial forces, and as the example of Papua New Guinea, the Torres Strait Islanders' nearest neighbour illustrates, powerful forces are working towards the dissolution of indigenous culture. Father Frank Brennan and social justice commissioner Mick Dodson both identify this danger: among the threats to Aboriginal relationships to land are those 'Aboriginal owners who choose or are cajoled, persuaded or simply slip into another way of looking at the world, another way of looking at their land'.[83] This might become manifest, for example, where compensation or royalties are accepted as a 'pay-off' by a land trust 'on behalf of' a particular landholding group, without the group's informed consent. This dissolution is often a subtle process proceeding along seemingly neutral lines. Mick Dodson notes how

> indigenous peoples have quickly recognised that international law, word processors and even human rights rhetoric can hold the lines of power as fiercely as the guns and strychnine of times past. All this might give rise to deep pessimism.[84]

The fight for recognition of their right to their land brought the Murray Islanders closer together. The remarkable outcome of the case offered an opportunity to reflect upon who they are, their potential as a people. It led to and facilitated the public expression of their right to follow customary law, not secretly but as an expression of their cultural inheritance. Customary adoption practice is a highly significant example. They began rethinking the relationship between longstanding and newer authority (the heads of clans and families and the community council elected by the people of Mer Islands). This process holds within it conflicts and paradoxes present within the Murray Island community, both among émigrés to mainland Australia and residents of the Mer Islands before the recognition of native title.

The road the Meriam have had to travel since 3 June 1992 has been far from easy. Many land disputes held in abeyance during the case have moved to the centre of public life. Unresolved problems of political authority and leadership have arisen in the new context of the High Court's recognition of the Meriam people's exclusive entitlement to the Mer Islands. This very exceptional situation has released their often suppressed desire to take command of all their affairs and to face new and confronting questions. In 1993 the Mer Islands Council initiated a community fishing enterprise which sought to encourage personal initiative. It was seen as an economic base for a self-supporting modern life which draws on the vast wealth of Meriam seafaring and fishing knowledge and tradition (see preceding chapter). Of major concern to senior Meriam people is how to nurture institutions which accord with Meriam values and traditions; and how to resist easy money schemes[85] that may, in the longer run, spell the doom of the social practices and cultural values which Meriam men and women defended so eloquently in court.

On 18 September 1995 Edward Koiki Mabo was finally laid to rest at his beloved Las village by his family, in-laws and the Meriam community.

National Reconciliation by Bruce Petty, from the *Age*, 6 June 1992 (courtesy Bruce Petty)

As a national hero he was farewelled by the Australian government and people. His vision went beyond the immediate needs of his own family, island and people; it was, as he said in founding the Black Community School, to bring together the best of two cultures.

In the contemporary world, a global cosmopolitanism mediated by the abstract technologies of the information society threatens to cast us all into the mould of consumers of commodity culture. Exchanging reciprocally our 'strong stories' takes on an urgency for all of us. Fortunately this is the logic of dialogue which some landed Aboriginal and Islander groups take to be natural. In seeking 'not to impose their law upon others but to exchange equitably' they, like Eddie Mabo or Reverend Dave Passi, may find a resonance with the principles which underlie a capacity for moral behaviour by people within the European Australian culture.[86]

A break in the silence has brought new hope to those who seek to marry the best principles of their inherited culture with those of European Australian culture. Those who hold firmly to the principle of the inalienability of land through the ancestral chain may act as exemplars for the dispossessed majority of indigenous Australians who now seek to acquire land which they may also pass onto their children.[87]

NOTES

NOTES TO CHAPTER 1

BEARERS OF CULTURAL CHANGE

1. Hardy 1968, Middleton 1977, Coombs 1981, Williams 1986, 34 n4, Rose 1992, 21–22. While organisations seeking the advancement of Aborigines and Torres Strait Islanders had carried out important work before this time, the Gurindji's action is often seen as marking 'the birth of the modern Land Rights movement' (Swain 1993, 263; see also Coombs 1981, 281 and note 4 below).
2. Lui 1994, 16.
3. 1994, 68.
4. The Gurindji demand 'for land to establish their own cattle station' and 'the action by Aboriginal clans on the Gove Peninsula' against Nabalco and the Commonwealth of Australia 'alleging that their title land had been infringed by the company' had coalesced, heralding the beginning of 'the Aboriginal campaign for rights to land'; this issue became the critical one in the Council for Aboriginal Affairs and came to involve the prime minister, Gough Whitlam, directly (Coombs 1981, 281). Williams cites R M Berndt's opinion that 'explicit and consistent efforts to obtain recognition of rights in land . . . really began with the Yirrkala people in 1963' (personal communication as cited in Williams 1986, 34 n4). See *Milirrpum v Nabalco Pty Ltd and the Commonwealth of Australia* (1971), 17 *Federal Law Reports*, hereafter *Milirrpum*, 141–293.
5. 1969a, 27.
6. *Mabo v the State of Queensland* (1992), 66 *Australian Law Journal Reports* (ALJR) 408 (High Court, Full Bench, 3 June 1992), hereafter *Mabo (No 2),* per Deane and Gaudron JJ.
7. *Mabo (No 2)* 482, per Toohey J.
8. *Mabo (No 2)*, 437, per Brennan J. The area excepted from native title is 'that parcel of land leased to the Trustees of the Australian Board of Missions and those parcels (if any) which have been validly appropriated for administrative purposes'.
9. Proclamation notifying that 'Certain Islands in Torres Strait lying between the Continent of Australia and the Island of New Guinea' are part of the Colony of Queensland, 18 July 1879 (supplement to *Queensland Government Gazette* of 19 July 1879, XXV, 10, 21 July 1879) under provision of the Queensland Coast Islands Act of 1879. For a brief account of a legal challenge in the High Court of Australia to the 1879 annexation (*Wacando, Carlemo Kelly v Commonwealth of Australia and State of Queensland* [1981]) see Sharp 1993a, 228 and 279.
10. See Transcript of Proceedings, Supreme Court of Queensland, 2291–92, hereafter TQ.
11. TQ2228, TQ2272–74.
12. See Chapters 4 and 7 below.
13. R Johannes, TQ2787.
14. See also Peterson on Aboriginal land boundaries in Native Titles Research Unit 1994, 3.
15. TQ148.
16. During 1993, Malo's Laws were being incorporated into the council by-laws by the Meriam at the Mer Islands.
17. Marou Mimi, diary.
18. Ray described Pasi's writing 'as the first unassisted literary effort' by a Papuan person (1907, 228).
19. Thus for example, on bequeathing land, or on traditional Meriam adoption practices, which create heirs to land, 'Government officials say: "We won't believe you;

you must have a written document"', author's notes of conversation with Gobedar Noah, Townsville, 7 December 1993.

20. Eddie Mabo was one of those émigrés; see Chapter 4 below and Book of Islanders 1984, second Miriam man, B134–B139, cf Sharp 1993a, 39–40.

21. Determination pursuant to reference of 27 February 1986, by the High Court of Australia to the Supreme Court of Queensland to hear and determine all issues of fact raised by the pleadings, particulars and further particulars in High Court action B12 of 1982, 16 November 1990, 206; hereafter D.

22. I think the process is very similar to that noted by Deborah Rose, namely how 'most Aboriginal religions are extraordinarily open to accommodating new events and ideas . . . any numbers of permutations, additions, and accommodations are possible as long as the underlying principles are not challenged' (1992, 207).

23. M White, TQ1333.

24. *Taum akadar*, pride in self, is an expression used by the Meriam to refer to the identity associated with clan and family territory. It refers also to cultural pride.

25. See Book of Islanders 1984, Kebi Bala (Dave Passi) B122–B129, B131; Sharp 1993a, 108, 109.

26. See Sharp 1993b, 23–38; 1994b.

27. *Milirrpum*, 293

28. *Milirrpum*, 266 as cited in TQ3467.

29. *Mabo (No 2)*, 411, per Brennan J.

30. See Chapters 7 and 8 below.

31. Williams 1986, xii.

32. Bartlett considers how these assumptions found expression in the Land (Titles and Traditional Usage) Act (1993) in Western Australia (1993b, 7–9).

33. Henderson 1977, 80.

34. Meriam witness, H Kabere, TQ1717.

35. Gobedar Noah, notes of conversation, Townsville, 7 December 1993; cf TQ2119–20.

36. 1969b, 2, 3, 4.

37. Noting how 'some peoples do not appear to regard land as a commodity', McNeil conjures up an alternative conception of land which comes close to that of the Meriam: 'In some cultures land is seen more as a sacred provider, to be used with respect bordering on reverence' (1989, 194).

38. For earlier written work on the *Murray Island Land* case from the standpoint of contrasting cultural perspectives, see Sharp 1990, 1991, 1992, 1993a, 1993b, 1993c, 1994a, 1994b.

39. See Mansell 1993, 57.

40. 1994, 72.

41. Inconsistent grants from the Crown may extinguish native title to the extent of the inconsistency between the grant and the native title. A Crown grant will not always extinguish all native title rights to the land that is the subject of the grant. Debate on issues embedded in the judicial revolution created by the decision include: the relationship between native title and other forms of title, especially the radical title of the Crown; native title and sovereignty; native or traditional title and Aboriginal title; occupation and possession; the meaning of native title as *sui generis* or unique; native title and fee simple title; usufruct; the status of native title in relation to mining and pastoral leases; the fiduciary or trust responsibilities of the Crown on land reserved for Aboriginal and Islander inhabitants; native title and the Racial Discrimination Act 1975; native title and compensation. On the implications of *Mabo* in Australia see Bartlett 1992, 272–99; for Aborigines and Torres Strait Islanders, see Brennan, 1993a, 24–77; for a summary of the main areas listed above see 25–43; the limits of native title, 43–44. Generally, see M A Stephenson and S Ratnapala (eds) 1993, *Mabo: A Judicial Revolution*, a special issue of the *University of Queensland Law Journal*, in which eleven writers examine the impact of the decision on Australian law. For ongoing exposition and critical analysis of the legal implications of the judgment, and especially the legislative and court actions, see the serial, *Aboriginal Law Bulletin*. See also Symposium, *Mabo v the State of Queensland*, *Sydney Law Review* special issue, 15(2), June 1993, reproduced with an additional essay as *Essays on the Mabo Decision*, 1993; Sanders 1994; Goot and Rowse 1994. On the ongoing implications of the decision on native title and the claims before the Native Title Tribunal, *Native Title Newsletter*, AIATSIS 1 – .

42. Rowse 1993b, 8–9.
43. 1993, 22.
44. Gaita 1993b, 46.
45. Gaita 1993a and b.
46. Brennan 1993b, 17. The context of Father Brennan's statement is the reaction of the chief minister of the Northern Territory to the refusal of the Jawoyn people to allow the mining of Coronation Hill, which encouraged the headline 'Chief Minister Blasts "Stone Age" Mining Ban' (cited by Brennan thus).
47. Land Ruling has Little Effect: Goss, *Sydney Morning Herald*, 9 June 1992.
48. Lateral Thinking on Mabo, *Weekend Australian*, 19–20 June 1993.
49. Pearson 1994a, 6.
50. Day 1993; see also Mer Islands Community Council, media releases, 6 and 21 December 1993.
51. Yu 1994, 21–33, and cf Crough and Christophersen 1993; J Ah-Kit, in Native Titles Research Unit 1994, 115–17; The Injinoo Aboriginal Corporation has owned and operated the Pajinka Wilderness Lodge, Cape York, since July 1992. By May 1994 the Injinoo Community had begun to develop the Jardine River Roadhouse and an airline agency; an association representing traditional landowners had taken responsibility for management of the last two hundred kilometres of northern Cape York Peninsula, including a ranger service, erosion control and other land conservation matters (Injinoo Community Council, personal communication, 18 May 1994).
52. 34 *Dominion Law Reports* (DLR) (3d) 145; McConnell 1974, 88–122, places the *Calder* case in historical perspective.
53. 87 DLR (3d) 342. However, not all recent Indian claims have succeeded, see *Delgamuukw v British Columbia* (1991), 79 DLR (4th) 185 (British Columbia Supreme Court), per McEachern CJ.
54. Dodson 1994, 67.
55. Yu 1994, 21.

NOTES TO CHAPTER 2

OF SILENCES AND SECRETS

1. Meriam witness, Gobedar Noah, notes of conversation with author, Townsville, 7 December 1993.
2. Sharp 1993a, Chapter 7.
3. *Mabo and Others v the State of Queensland and the Commonwealth of Australia* 1982, statement of claim, 20 May 1982, hereafter statement of claim 1982, 2.
4. Notes relating to meeting at Tamwoy Town, Thursday Island, around 14 August 1991, as recalled and recorded by Flo Kennedy, Injinoo, October 1992.
5. Olbrei 1982, 163.
6. Olbrei 1982, 143, 144.
7. Olbrei 1982, 164.
8. Olbrei 1982, 147.

9. Sharp 1980, 1.
10. Minutes, in O'Leary to Chief Protector, 7 September 1937, enclosed in letter 37/9577, Queensland State Archives (QSA) A/3941; see also Sharp 1993a, Chapter 7.
11. Olbrei 1982, 78, 80; cf Coombs, Nettheim, 57–60, 82–107.
12. Hocking 1988, xxi.
13. See Sis (Flo Kennedy), in Sharp 1993a, 260.
14. In 1992, Henry Reynolds noted how he had suggested to Eddie Mabo 'that legally the Murray Islanders would have a much stronger case in the courts than Aboriginal people because they used the land for gardening' (1992, 186). Greg McIntyre's paper 'Aboriginal Land Rights — a Definition at Common Law', given at the conference in 1981, reflected work he had done as a solicitor with Aboriginal Legal Aid especially in North Queensland (Olbrei 1982, 222–33). He wrote later: 'Representatives of the plaintiffs at the [1981] conference took up the suggestion [of a test case postulated by Hocking and McIntyre] and later instructed the writer to investigate the institution of proceedings on their behalf' (Hocking 1988, 144–45). The meeting held during the conference was secret; Garth Nettheim, who approached McIntyre and Hocking, probably did not even mention it to them.
15. Barbara Hocking had carried out pioneering work in Australia centred on the theme of whether Aboriginal law now runs in Australia. Over a period of nearly ten years before the conference, she had raised the issue of whether prior titles *did* exist in Australia despite official denial; if so, what was their nature, and were these titles part of the common law? (see 1979, 162–87). On 22 November 1992 the Australian Human Rights Medal was awarded jointly to the five original Meriam plaintiffs and Barbara Hocking. (See Medal Honours Fallen Trio, *Sydney Morning Herald*, 23 November 1992; Ovation and Medal Too Late for Battler, *Age*, 23 October 1992; Mabo Six Win Human Rights Award, *Torres News*, 27 November–3 December 1992.)
16. See statement of claim 1982, para 4.
17. McIntyre 1988, 145.
18. *Mabo and Others v the State of Queensland and the Commonwealth of Australia* 1982, affidavit for first defendant, hereafter affidavit 1982, eighth sheet, 14 (e).
19. Affidavit 1982, exhibit R in attachments, Hon John Douglas to Minister for Lands.
20. 1988, 145–46.
21. Affidavit 1982, fifth sheet, 13.
22. *Queensland Parliamentary Debates* (Legislative Assembly), *Hansard* 1985, 4740.
23. Report, O'Leary to Chief Protector, 9 October 1936, 36/6292, QSA A/3874.
24. This is a useful notion developed by Beckett. He identifies 'the capacity to reserve an essential part of themselves outside the relations of production and consumption, which constituted the dominant order' (1987, 10; cf 10–11, 111–13).
25. Transcript of proceedings in the High Court of Australia, Canberra, 16 March 1988, 174; cf Deane J, 173.
26. Land Holding Act (LHA) 1985, s4(a). Parallel clauses pertaining to Aboriginal councils are contained in relevant clauses of the Act. The lease laws have three specific aspects. Firstly, trust lands are taken to be fee simple lands; a fee simple grant is one form of freehold in common law and is known as the most unconditional estate in land granted by the Crown. Under the Mining Act, the Crown owns all the minerals and can grant permits for miners to enter freehold lands for mining purposes. Secondly, as fee simple grants they are subject to rights to compensation for mining damage. Thirdly, any Crown lease areas released by a council from its Deed of Grant in Trust to a 'qualified person' is not subject to mining compensation rights any longer (LHA 1985, s6[3]; cf McIntyre 1987, 1–13).
27. There are two important differences in the new system. The first is that leases from trust areas are written agreements with a recognised status in the Australian legal

system. A second difference lies in the possibility of removing portions of land from these trust areas and granting them as Crown leases to qualified persons for commercial purposes or as house blocks. Under the Community Services Act 1984 the areas are held in trust as deeds; under the L H A 1985, land in the trust
area may be excised and converted into a Crown lease to an individual member of the community as defined by the island council; a form of tenure with a strong affinity with individually based proprietorship (see s9).

28. During the hearing before Chief Justice Sir Harry Gibbs, counsel for the plaintiffs had argued for remittance to the Federal Court rather than the Supreme Court on two grounds: that it was the more appropriate court, and that as non-Queensland residents, counsel might be ineligible. The Chief Justice dismissed both these arguments: the second, as he predicted, would not apply. On the first ground he saw the Supreme Court of Queensland as the appropriate place in which to hear the case, for as Queenslanders arguing about land which formed part of Queensland, had they not brought their action in the High Court, this court would have become the appropriate one.

29. *Mabo and Others v the State of Queensland and the Commonwealth of Australia* 1982, plaintiffs' affidavit, March 1987, hereafter plaintiffs' affidavit, 3, para 2.

30. Author's notes, Mer Island, 27 January 1986.

31. Reynolds 1992, 185–86.

32. Stanner 1969b, 11.

33. Stanner 1969b, 12.

34. This is my paraphrasing of Ron Day's words, Yarra Bank Films 1990.

35. Author's notes of meeting, 29 January 1982.

36. Stanner 1969b, 11.

37. Sharp 1993a, Chapter 7.

38. Williams 1986, 159.

39. Williams 1986, 159.

40. Notes on resumed hearing, 1987, 4.

41. Before Justice Deane (in chambers), High Court of Australia, Sydney, 13 February 1987, transcript of proceedings (hereafter T) 7–8.

42. Before Justice Deane 1987, T14.

43. Plaintiffs' affidavit, 1987, 12.

44. G McIntyre, personal communication, 13 March 1987.

45. G McIntyre, personal communication, May 1987.

46. Informally it was understood by the parties to the case that the financial issue had become significant, the Solicitor-General having made it clear to them that the department would not fund a remitter court to call 27 Islander witnesses and six experts.

47. Undertaking/agreement between the parties, 3 April 1987.

NOTES TO CHAPTER 3

RIGHTS OF A KIND UNKNOWN TO ENGLISH LAW

1. Section 4 concerns 'disposal of the islands' after annexation and the validity in law of Crown lands legislation passed after the islands were annexed to Queensland. Section 5 specifically disclaims any right to compensation by those dispossessed of alleged interests existing prior to annexation of the islands either by the annexation of the islands in 1879 or by any provision of the 1985 Act.

2. Chief Justice Mason, *Mabo and Another v State of Queensland and Another* (1988), hereafter *Mabo (No 1)*, 166 Commonwealth Law Reports, 196.

3. Justices Brennan, Toohey, Gaudron, *Mabo (No 1)*, 211.

4. I am following McIntyre here, *The Law Report*, ABC Radio, 19 April 1988. Thirteen arguments arranged in the following four categories are summarised in a case note by G McIntyre: Inconsistency, Effectiveness/Insufficiency, Coast Waters, Principles of General Law.
5. 34 DLR (3d) 145 (emphasis added).
6. McIntyre, *The Law Report*, ABC Radio, April 1988.
7. McIntyre, case note 2(c): Effectiveness/Specificity, Continuing System of Law, *The Law Report*, ABC Radio, 19 April 1988 (also typescript with author and McIntyre).
8. Transaction no 83, Murray Island Court Records (see Chapter 2).
9. McIntyre in Hocking 1988, 145.
10. 16 March 1988, T134–35.
11. Sharp 1993a, Chapter 7.
12. Castan, 16 March 1988, T143.
13. *Guerin v the Queen* (1984) 13 DLR (4th), 321.

NOTES TO CHAPTER 4

MY FATHER GAVE ME ALL THE RIGHTS AND EVERY RESPONSIBILITY

1. In court Eddie Mabo stated that he left Mer in 1957, when he would have been 20 or 21 years old (TQ73).
2. Lawrie 1970, 337–38.
3. For Sam Passi's reflections on the way this event was handed down in oral tradition, see Sharp 1993a, 251–52.
4. Sharp 1984, Chapter 5; Book of Islanders 1984, B1–B167, is an expression of this; see also Sharp 1993a.
5. Book of Islanders 1984, B134–39; edited versions of cassette recordings made with the author between 1980 and 1984; Sharp 1993a, 39–40.
6. Mabo used the words *Zogo le* and *Aets* interchangeably, see note 14 below.
A considerable amount of court time was spent on conflicting evidence on the word *Aet* (also *Aiet*). Sam Passi told the court he could use the name *Aiet* because he was the eldest in the family (TQ1136; cf Etta Passi TQ1075). Justice Moynihan concluded it was merely a personal name used by the Passi family and the Modee family (D71). On the *Zogo le* see note 14.
7. Book of Islanders 1984, B139; Sharp 1993a, 93.
8. He mentioned Noel Loos and Henry Reynolds at James Cook University (personal communication, c 1981).
9. Book of Islanders 1984, B137.
10. Supreme Court of Queensland Exhibit 35.
11. Mabo 1982, 144. It was this view which, I believe, he repeated to a journalist with the *Australian* newspaper, that led to an article published on 28 May 1986 claiming that Eddie Mabo saw himself as the coming king of Murray Island. Mabo's claim to be *Aiet* of Murray Island was used by Queensland counsel in cross-examination of Sam Passi (TQ1112–13).
12. Beckett 1994, 20. Beckett recalls his surprise at the range and depth of Eddie Mabo's knowledge, much of which could not have come from books: 'He had, for example, an extensive knowledge of plants, which was not to be found in print. Nor could he have got from books, the vivid, detailed mind picture of the land which he presented to the court. The genealogy he recounted went back further than could be found in the *Cambridge Reports*' (1994, 20).
13. Author's notes on the hearings, 27 October 1986.

14. See Exhibit 35 (Mabo's written statement), 13–16 and TQ137. In 1981, at the conference where plans for the case were made, Eddie Mabo referred to 'the *Aet* system of government' as a hereditary authority; he described the *Aet* as 'the central figure of all the sacred people', the *Zogo le* (Mabo 1982, 144). WHR Rivers wrote that 'government in the olden time was probably by the elders, who followed traditional custom in coming to decisions. Since the position of *zogo le* was passed on from father to son, the Malu fraternity came to be a sort of hereditary government, whose authority no one would question' (in Haddon 1904–35, vol VI, 178). He notes Hunt's conclusion (1899) of a hereditary chieftainship with 'head chiefs' and 'inferior chiefs taking a leading part in the administration of justice' (1904–35, vol VI, 178). Haddon himself refers to a *zogo zogo le* (1904–35, vol VI, 286); in 1933 Ion Idriess wrote *Drums of Mer*, a novel about the Meriam which refers to an 'Au [Big]-Zogo-Zogo-le' (1933, 6). Idriess acknowledges a general debt to the Anglican missionary William MacFarlane. 'Rulers is the wrong word' according to Sam Passi; the *Zogo le* provided the example for others to follow: Malo does this, Malo does that; he does not wander from his path (Book of Islanders 1984; Sharp 1993a, 85).

15. Keon-Cohen notes that the consequences of a ruling making oral testimony inadmissible will never be known; that is, whether the other 20% plus 'the "expert" anthropological evidence' would have been sufficient for Justice Moynihan to have found for the Murray Islanders (1993, 199, n30).

16. D.

17. Shnukal 1983, 1988.

18. Stanner 1979, 278–79; cf Brennan, 1994b, 44.

19. The chairman of the Murray Island Council, Ron Day, stated this in the film *Land Bilong Islanders* (Yarra Bank Films 1990).

20. The late Mr Lui Bon.

21. See George Passi, exhibit 292, 13–14. Sam Passi said the law he applied in 'land disputes' listed in the Court Book had 'Nothing to do with English law' (TQ1109, 1110). He explained how he was tutored by Marou and other old people on how to make decisions according to island law. His grandfather said, 'Stand firm on Malo Law' (TQ1110); cf Book of Islanders 1984, B60–B61; Sharp 1993a, 82–84.

22. This question is considered in Chapter 5.

23. See, for example Gobedar Noah, notes of conversation, Townsville, 7 December 1993; see Chapter 5 below.

24. G Noah, author's notes, 7 December 1993.

25. Author's notes, Mer, 18 December 1993.

26. 1972, 27.

27. Bartlett 1993a, 4, says the claim 'was made upon the basis of *individual* rights to land and sea. This peculiar emphasis on individual rights was sought to be supported by proof of recognized and individual entitlement.'

28. George Kudub; cf Day Day TQ1146, Esaka Ghee TQ1178, Dalton Cowley TQ1324, Henry Kabere TQ1717, Douglas Bon TQ2391, Etta Passi TQ1069, who also recalled a court case in which a man's death-bed statement had left all his land to his younger daughter, not to his eldest son (TQ1071).

29. Meb Salee Jr.

30. Gobedar Noah spoke about this with gravity and emotion both in court and in private conversation. Relating how his mother told him in Meriam language when he was between seven and ten years old how 'Koiki [Eddie] is truly adopted to Benny Mabo' (TQ2114), he explained how the 'traditional way' was to 'keep it secret at all times'. Plaintiffs' counsel asked why, and he responded, 'It is a respect to our traditional ways or culture' (TQ2115). He was asked why yet again by the defence and responded, 'in a way that we are the very, very emotional people and these secrets had to be kept'

(TQ2161). The injunction to secrecy has the mysterious, whispered quality of a sacred rite; it is a commandment that brooks no disputation. In reply to questioning by plaintiffs' counsel on why she was obliged to keep secret the knowledge about Koiki's adoption given to her at the age of ten, Mary Noah told the court, 'I can't [tell]. I recognise the cultural way not to tell' (TQ2176).

31. 1993, 3.
32. 1971, 198.
33. Author's notes, 7 December 1993.
34. Author's notes, 7 December 1993.
35. 1986, 72–74 and n13 on the way the gift of names is a process of valorising land ownership among the Yolngu, and maintaining its continuity over time.
36. Yarra Bank Films 1990.
37. Author's notes, 30 October 1986.
38. See Chief Protector to Minister for Health and Home Affairs, 5 March 1936, QSA 36/5997.
39. See also Exhibit 171, 2.
40. The 'wind circle' of Meriam identities depicted an important component of this complex set of layered identities (see Sharp 1993a, 55).
41. 1904–35, vol VI, 167 n1. This is Haddon's footnote to Anthony Wilkin's chapter, Property and Inheritance.
42. 1904–35, vol VI, 169–71; cf Ray 1907, 58–59.
43. Sharp 1993a, Chapter 2.
44. Cassette 050/KB/T1/1/80; Book of Islanders 1984, B130; Sharp 1993a, 68.

NOTES TO CHAPTER 5

IF YOU WANT TO BE A REAL MURRAY ISLANDER YOU FOLLOW MALO'S LAW

1. Ray 1907, 50, refers to it as 'archaic Kala Lagaw Ya', the language of the western islands of the Torres Strait.
2. Marou Mimi, diary, shown to me at Mer, 20 December 1993.
3. Document 31, 43; TQ1162–63; also Marou Mimi, diary.
4. See also other plaintiffs' witnesses, TQ1229, 1237, 1247, 1249, 1253, 1271–72; TQ1317, 1333; TQ1695–96, 1705–06, 1715, 1717–18, 1807–11, 1783–84; TQ2440–41; TQ2091; TQ2133, 2159, 2166–67.
5. Author's notes, Thursday Island, 1983. Marou wrote of this event in his diary of 'Tuesday 11, 1939 (Easter Tuesday)': '9 am. The feast at Deo stoping the coconut thats mean people not to touch any thing at Peibiri from Gigo to Gegred [*sic*]'.
6. George Passi's statements as cited by senior defence counsel, Mrs M White.
7. Notes of conversation, Townsville, 7 December 1993; Lawrie 1970, 337.
8. Author's notes, 7 December 1993.
9. Olbrei 1982, 164; cf Book of Islanders 1984, Kebi Bala (Dave Passi), B130, recorded in 1980.
10. Book of Islanders 1984, B127.
11. Exhibit 197; TQ1887.
12. Book of Islanders, 1984, Kebi Bala (Dave Passi), B125; cassettes 050/KB/TI/1/80, 079–080/KB/TI/1/80; and Sharp 1993a, 108, 107.
13. Yarra Bank Films 1990.
14. For a more detailed account of the myth of Malo-Bomai, see Chapter 8 below.
15. Williams 1986, 159 and 191, n4.
16. Moore 1984, 38 is referring to the collection of A C Haddon at Cambridge University.

17. 1970, 319.
18. See Kebi Bala in Sharp 1993a, 67.
19. Error in transcript corrected by author (TQ1333 'dis-earn').
20. Author's notes, Mer, 18 December 1993.
21. Radin 1957, 232; Sharp 1993a, 11–12.
22. Cassette 050/KB/T1/1/80; Book of Islanders 1984 B126; see also Sharp 1984, 1993a. This compares with Aboriginal people with whom Rose worked in the Northern Territory (1987, 268).
23. 1814, II, 111.
24. D63.
25. D64.
26. Beckett 1987, 141.

NOTES TO CHAPTER 6

HEARSAY OR TRADITIONAL EVIDENCE?

1. Williams 1986, xii.
2. 1986, 104.
3. 1986, 157.
4. Blackburn 1971, 273–74.
5. Williams 1986, 202; Stanner 1969b, 6.
6. Baxi 1972, 23.
7. 1971, 266.
8. 1972, 24.
9. D 172; cf Beckett TQ2243.
10. Forbes 1986, 5–6.
11. Forbes 1986, 131.
12. E K Mabo's evidence covered nearly 1,000 pages of transcript.
13. See Exhibit 35, 1–65.
14. Exhibit 35, 5, 7, 13.
15. Williams 1986, 232.
16. 1921, 2 Appeals Cases 399.
17. 1973-74, 130 *Commonwealth Law Reports* 353, 374, as cited in Keon-Cohen 1993, 193.
18. 1971, 159.
19. As summarised in plaintiffs' affidavit, March 1987, 7; see also TQ179. This was contested by the defendant (TQ180–81).
20. Plaintiffs' affidavit, 9–10, para 19.
21. Plaintiffs' affidavit, 10, para 19.
22. Plaintiffs' affidavit, 10–11.
23. Plaintiffs' affidavit, 7, para 14.
24. Notes on resumed hearing, 23 February 1987; cf plaintiffs' affidavit, 11–12, para 20.

NOTES TO CHAPTER 7

ASSIMILATION OR BASIC CONTINUITY?

1. The total examinations-in-chief, cross-examinations and re-examinations held over five days from 23 to 27 May 1989 at Mer and Thursday Island covered 339 pages of transcript.

2. D 33.

3. Plaintiffs' submission 1989, Chapter 8, 1–2.

4. On his personal decision to re-enter the case as a plaintiff, Reverend Dave Passi mentions the changed context of prejudice to the plaintiffs raised by the defence's new allegations against Mabo that are discussed below in the text (notes of conversation, Mer, December 1993).

5. The plaintiffs had argued that the use of certain areas of land had been granted by Meriam landholders to the Meriam people as a whole (statement of claim, 20 May 1982, 20 October 1986, paragraph 4 [d]) and that some land had 'been purportedly acquired by the firstnamed defendant and others' from Meriam landholders (paragraph 4[e]). They had scheduled two transactions, one of which recorded the Queensland government's purchase of land from Meriam landholders (see schedule 1: transaction A1913 — jail house, court house and recreation reserve; see facsimile, Murray Island records, Chapter 2 above; transaction B: 1913 — government reserve at Omar). Queensland contended that on 1 June 1882, special lease 160 of two acres of land at Mer was granted to the London Missionary Society for 14 years by the Governor in Council; this lease was renewed in 1906 and in 1912; on 1 August 1944 a 30-year lease of the same two acres was granted to the Anglican diocese of Carpentaria, and this lease was renewed on 1 November 1984 (see annexures marked F, G, I and Q in the affidavit of P J Killoran; further details are listed in *Mabo* 1982, amended defence of the state of Queensland, 24 May 1985, paragraph 4, [a] to [h]).

6. On 6 May 1931, two non-Meriam people were granted a 20-year lease of the whole of the land at Dauar and Waier islands for the purpose of establishing a sardine factory. On 15 June 1938, following requests by the Meriam people for unrestricted entry to the islands of Dauar and Waier, the Chief Protector sought forfeiture of the lease and the sardine factory was closed down. The plaintiffs' claim that the lease was wholly ineffective was not finally determined (see *Mabo [No 2]*, per Brennan J 1992, 435–36; per Deane and Gaudron JJ, 454; per Dawson J, 473; per Toohey J, 490).

7. 'The Murray Islanders will have Murray Island to themselves', the government resident, John Douglas, reported on 6 August 1885 (*Queensland Votes and Proceedings*, 1885) in response to requests from the Murray Islanders for South Sea Islanders and others to leave Mer; see Douglas Pitt to Minister for Lands, 13 May 1882 (annexure S in the affidavit of P J Killoran; Charles Bruce to Col. Sec., 15 May 1882 (annexure T); John Douglas to Minister for Lands, 1 October 1885 (annexure R); Henry Chester to Minister for Lands, 23 September 1882 (annexure U) (the latter is headed 'Douglas Pitt and Joseph Tucker have been in unlawful occupation of Murray Island' and annexures S and T refer to notices to quit Murray Island in 60 days).

8. Plaintiffs' witness, M Kudub; cf TQ2081 and throughout. After a further 621 pages of transcript, Keon-Cohen's tenacity and perseverance were rewarded by Justice Moynihan. In the context of the impending examination of leading defence witness, P J Killoran, whose 'materials are massive' (Keon-Cohen, TQ2694), Justice Moynihan readily granted his request for a short break: 'it is just obvious from where I sit, if Mr Keon-Cohen keeps pushing himself much longer, well — '(TQ2694). In expressing her agreement, senior defence counsel noted that at this stage Keon-Cohen had neither a solicitor familiar with the case nor a second counsel, Greg McIntyre being unavailable at this stage of the proceedings (TQ2694–95). However, senior defence counsel had objected successfully to the request by Ron Castan to relieve Keon-Cohen at an earlier stage (TQ2282).

9. The evidence given by the first two defence witnesses, Patrick J Killoran and Margaret Lawrie, is considered in detail in this chapter. The other four were called on specific matters. They were Dr Ruth Kerr, archivist; Colin G Sheehan, a specialist in genealogy; Robert Piper, RAAF historical officer, called to verify that there was no record of a battle around Murray Island during the Second World War, as claimed by Mabo; Donald J Wormer, director and registrar, Lands Department, Brisbane, testified on special lease files concerned with leases by the London Missionary Society and the Anglican diocese issued under the Land Act.

10. The evidence of marine biologist Dr Robert Johannes, which relates to sea tenure, is considered in Chapter 10. Anthropologist Dr Jeremy R Beckett's evidence is considered here.

11. Mr Sheehan's evidence drew upon the ethnographic notes made by the schoolteacher, Jack Bruce (see Bruce to Haddon 1893–1921, Haddon papers, University of Cambridge, bundle 1010, as cited in TQ2580). These include Bruce's analysis of births, deaths and marriages from 1882 as first resident, district registrar and clerk of court; Bruce's first census, 1891; his ethnographic notes, which include a record of illegitimate births, which Rivers did not incorporate systematically into his Meriam genealogies published in Haddon 1904–35, vol VI, 67–91. Meriam 'cultural' adoptions were not recognised by the registrar-general and therefore were not included in Mr Bruce's register (TQ2586). In the argument in court on the age of one of the Meriam witness's grandmother, it became clear in cross-examination that Bruce's designation of her age at marriage in 1892 was only an estimate (birth records began only in 1917), and therefore she may have been older, as the Meriam witness argued, in which case she may have remembered the first missionaries (see Henry Kabere TQ1815 ff).

12. Notes of a conversation, Brisbane, 1 December 1993. Anthropologist, Dr G Langevaad, who had also contributed to the compilation of the defendant's Crown sources, communicated a similar attitude to the author two weeks before he died (personal communication, c 9 January 1992).

13. Lawrie had written in 1970, 'The highly refined system of ownership which pervaded the Meriam world . . . was reinforced by the practice of erecting signs of *gelar* (taboo), and by verbal injunctions' (1970, 319).

14. Williams 1986, 104. Williams identifies these ideas, their sources and their manifestation in legal argument (see 1986, 109–203).

15. Kehoe-Forutan 1988, 10.

16. See Sharp 1993a, Chapters 5 and 7.

17. Affidavit 1982, eighth sheet, para 14.

18. Sharp 1993a, Chapter 7.

19. Marou Mimi, diary, 1 April 1947, signed Chairman Marou, Murray Island Council.

20. According to Beckett, Queensland had indicated to him the intention to call him also as a witness, but had subsequently decided against it (personal communication, Thursday Island, May 1993).

21. See also affidavit of J R Beckett, exhibit 214.

22. Wilkin in Haddon 1904–35, vol VI, 1908, 167.

23. Plaintiffs' submission 1989.

24. 1987, 141, presented as exhibit 213.

25. Durkheim 1949.

26. Haddon wrote: 'One of the chief interests of the social organisation of the Miriam is the complete disappearance of all traces of a totemic system which it is almost certain must have once existed (1904–35, vol VI, 174; see also 254–56). This conclusion is reflected in Durkheim and Mauss 1903, 28: 'totemism is found only in the western islands and not in those of the east'. Haddon also states that '*lubabat*, is anything which is revered as belonging to an ancestor' (242); see Ray 1907, 151, *lu-babat*, an heirloom. In noting the association of persons and groups with stars and constellations, Haddon concludes that this 'is highly suggestive and may be a survival of a division of natural objects between social groups such as is found among many peoples' (1912, IV 220).

27. Beckett (1963, 1987) makes no reference to the existence of totemism. This contrasts with my own findings (Sharp 1993a, 54–57) and those of Kitaoji (1980, 1–17 and figure 2, 8–10). Margaret Lawrie noted the practice of *la nog*, dying movements imitating those of one's *lubabat* (TQ2691). These 'totemic movements' were reported to

her by Meriam people, who explained how they would watch to see if people close to the point of death performed these movements (TQ2691). Justice Moynihan's conclusions take note of her observations, but he suggests that the significance of 'totemic emblems and movements associated with various groups' 'is very much an open question'; that while the Meriam 'know the grouping to which they belong and have some knowledge of the previous implications of that belonging' they are 'of little significance in terms of social order or access to land' today (D 120). In the context of their
field research at Mer in 1994–95, Douglas and Rebecca Bird noted the contemporary relevance of totemism among the eight clans of the Murray Islands (personal communication, Mer, 27 January 1995.

28. Cf TQ2682, 2610.
29. 1970, xxi.
30. 1970, xx.
31. As Flo Kennedy observes, 'white people that have learnt their custom properly are most able to understand Island custom' (Book of Islanders 1984, Sis, B109).
32. See Sharp 1993a, Chapter 3; cf Rose 1992, 220.
33. 1970, 20.
34. Cf Dave Passi on Malo's Law (TQ1893); Douglas Bon (TQ2398); Ron Day (Yarra Bank Films 1990).
35. 1970, 314–15, n3.
36. 1987, 260.
37. Sharp 1993a, 87.
38. 1987, 261; cf Frankfort et al 1946.
39. Eliade 1973, 62.
40. Rose herself argues that 'there is no basis by which to distinguish between sacred and profane' in Aboriginal life (1987, 267).
41. Cf Rose 1987, 267, on the investment of burning off the grass with symbolic meaning; where 'cosmic forces of fertility and renewal are combined to produce continued life on earth'.
42. See TQ2615; cf 1970, xxi.
43. Justice Moynihan's summary; cf Beckett TQ2232.
44. Justice Moynihan's summary.
45. 79 *DLR* (4th) 441, and 208 respectively as cited in Slattery 1992, 115. The judgment continues, 'The plaintiffs' ancestors had no written language, no horses or wheeled vehicles, slavery and starvation were not uncommon, wars with neighbouring peoples were common, and there is no doubt, to quote philosopher Thomas Hobbes, that aboriginal life in the territory was, at best, "nasty, brutish and short" '.
46. *Milirrpum* judgment, 267. The Middle English and 1513 meanings of precept do capture an important aspect of Meriam law: a general command, usually divine, especially as to moral conduct; an authoritative command to do some particular act (*Oxford English Dictionary*).
47. Kitaoji 1977, 209–12; Sharp 1993a, 69–77.
48. Justice Moynihan TQ2009.
49. Book of Islanders 1984, Au Bala, B142; Sharp 1993a, 85.
50. Book of Islanders 1984, B142; Sharp 1993a, 85.
51. Hocking (1993, 76) ignores the whole aspect of 'club justice'. One of the longstanding, frequent activities of the community has been the pursuit of land disputes, for example, with neighbours over boundaries and relatives over inheritances. 'Since time immemorial the problems have always been resolved by the respected senior members of the community, based on the knowledge orally and visually transmitted to the landowning family members by their ancestors, and given as evidence at dispute resolution hearings.' In projecting an image of a peaceful sea people, Hocking's view takes no account of the confrontational character of boundary disputes. The latter was

illustrated graphically in the court proceedings when one landowner, Marwer Depoma, personally confronted the court team who were inspecting one of the boundaries in dispute between himself and Eddie Mabo (see TQ1209 and Chapter 4). Justice Moynihan found the ' "woop [sic] whooping" of the inspection party' by Mr Depoma suggestive of the socially disruptive effects of a Murray Island boundary dispute 'in full cry' (D 186).

52. Macpherson 1977, 23.
53. Macpherson 1977, 23.
54. D 138.
55. Macpherson 1977, 271–72.
56. These are Macpherson's words, 1977, 272.
57. D 206.
58. Sahlins wrote that it was the gift exchange process which allowed transcendence of a life which was 'brutish and static' (1974, 176).
59. I am paraphrasing Reverend Passi's words here (see Book of Islanders 1984, Kebi Bala [Dave Passi], B124–B125; Sharp 1993a, 107–08). Other Islanders have expressed a similar view (Book of Islanders 1984, Kapin [Harry Captain], B24–B26; Book of Islanders 1984, Au Bala [Sam Passi], B60–B61; Book of Islanders 1984, Sis [Flo Kennedy], B95–B96). See also Sharp 1984, 1993a.

NOTES TO CHAPTER 8

A TRIAL OF TRUTH: OUTCOMES

1. D; some 44 witnesses gave evidence in the proceedings (D42).
2. See D149–52, 196–97, 199 and generally 196–204; Eddie Mabo's claims are set out in tabular form on pages 204A–204J.
3. Counter claims to 19 blocks of land claimed by Mabo were made by Caroline Modee by inheritance through her adoptive father and her mother (see D200–01, TQ2515–21). Although other grounds are mentioned by Justice Moynihan (evidence that E K Mabo was 'brought up' rather than 'adopted' by Benny and Maiga Mabo), the main ground he gives for the rejection of the claim to adoption concerns Mabo's relations with his natural father, Robert Sambo: he lived with him for six months on Thursday Island in 1947–48 and Sambo claimed him as a dependant in his tax return for that year. Other evidence included a letter written in 1966 in which Eddie Mabo called Robert Sambo 'Dad', and the evidence of one Meriam witness that the latter had asked him to approach Benny Mabo to give his son back (D150–52). Eddie Mabo had claimed he called Robert Sambo 'Dad' because Sambo had demanded this and that he stayed with him because Benny Mabo was in gaol on Thursday Island, a claim for which no record was found. Maiga Mabo also wrote letters which acknowledge Eddie Mabo as her only son and Bonita (Neta) Mabo as her daughter-in-law (Noel Loos, personal communication, Townsville, 15 January 1995).
4. Notes of conversation, Mer, 8 June 1993. Not all Meriam witnesses were asked to comment on Eddie Mabo's adoption; some refused to comment on any of the claims (for example, plaintiffs' witness, Day Day [TQ1139] and defence witness, Lui Bon [TQ1371]). Presumably, to do so would be to contravene the fundamental Meriam principle that 'keeping to one's own path' meant not interfering in other people's business. In commenting on Eddie Mabo's adoption, Sam Passi made this customary consideration explicit: he said that Eddie was adopted by the Modee family (TQ1136), that adopted persons inherit lands and that the reason he had nothing more to say about the Modee family was because of 'our rule', the 'Malo rule' that one must not trespass on other people's family business (TQ1137). In cross-examination, James Rice explained how he

saw Eddie Mabo living with Benny and Maiga Mabo at Las (TQ1655–56). The perceptions of other Meriam witnesses, a number of whom are related to Benny or Maiga Mabo, may be summarised as follows. George Kudub, the son of Benny Mabo's sister, explained how he grew up with Eddie Mabo, whom he saw as his uncle's adopted son (TQ1193); Jack Wailu, next door neighbour to the Mabo family at Las, said Benny Mabo left all his lands to Koiki (Eddie) (TQ1224); Emanee Akee, who answered questions about the claims of his kinsman, James Rice, but not about Reverend Dave Passi's lands, stated that Eddie Mabo was Benny Mabo's adopted son, whom he saw at the village of Kiam (TQ1291); Henry Kabere recalled Eddie Mabo 'living at Las with his father Benny Mabo' (TQ1735) and how his mother and grandmother told him Eddie Mabo was adopted by Benny, that Malo's Law 'is still going' (TQ1743), that island adoption is 'a law of Malo' (TQ1736), and that because Paipe (Eddie's natural mother) was Benny Mabo's sister, Eddie is a close relation of the Mabo family anyway (TQ1807); Mrs Gunnear Blanco recalled Benny Mabo saying to her in Meriam language, '*Kara ged kemer kemer*, All my lands belongs to Koiki Mabo' (TQ2425); Meb Salee Jr (whose mother, one of the original five plaintiffs, was caretaker of lands claimed by Eddie Mabo) recalled his childhood memories of Mapa Kudub making three gardens and separating the three parts for himself, Mapa and Eddie; he recalled Benny Mabo saying to him when he was about eight to ten years old 'that everything he had was for Koiki' (TQ2454), and how he was told that Eddie was adopted, but 'we weren't allowed to tell Eddie' (TQ2453). In like manner, both Gobedar and Mary Noah recalled the vivid childhood experience of knowledge of Eddie's adoption passed to them in secret: Gobedar was told this before he went to school (TQ2161 and see Chapter 4); Mary Noah explained how Benny 'and grandma' (her grandfather was Maiga Mabo's cousin) told us that the land and everything is for Eddie [when he comes back home] (TQ2175–77); Benny told her that Eddie was adopted when she was ten years old (TQ2176),
recognising 'that cultural way not to tell [Eddie]', she did not do so (cf TQ2187).
5. Mabo 1982, 143.
6. I concur with Beckett's conclusion here: 'Reading between the lines, I get the impression that Justice Moynihan did not regard Eddie Mabo as a real Meriam, but rather as an urbanised political activist, who seeing the main chance, made up for his lack of roots by reading books. Compared with the oral tradition, such knowledge was inauthentic and the feeding back of printed information into oral tradition was destructive of its original character' (1994, 19).
7. 1994, 22 (brackets removed in citation).
8. Figure 2, with the year of annexation inserted, is a facsimile of D213B.
9. In rejecting James Rice's claim to land at Aepkess (Eip Kes), which he claimed to own jointly with Henry Kabere, Justice Moynihan pointed to a contradiction between the James Rice's statement in court that Aepkess is where his grandfather used to sit and sing songs, tell him Malo's Law and his boundaries (TQ 1593), the place where his 'heart is' (TQ1525) ('I put my heart in there' [TQ1509]), and his and Henry Kabere's assignment of rights to it to the Tapim family about February 1989, after the latter had built a house on it (D215, cf 217–21). James Rice explained to me his perception of the whole matter at Mer on 7 June 1993, which begins with two brothers, Amu Amu and Mere, the former being James Rice's great-grandfather. Their sister, Sibisap, married Wagel, son of Koit, who brought her to Dauar. Amu Amu and Mere went and saw their sister and said, 'You stay on the other side of the boundary [of land at Aepkess]'. Wagel and Sibisap had two sons, one of whom was Tapim and whose sons and daughters carried the name of Tapim. 'So when Tapims built a house on the wrong side [of the boundary], because they were sons of the brothers' sister, we [Henry Kabere and I] said "Okay, you stop there" ' (author's notes of conversation). This detailed statement is consistent with what James Rice told the court in cross-examination (TQ1636–38). It

corresponds too with the evidence given by Henry Kabere in court (TQ1709, TQ1862, TQ1877).

10. The statement of claim, paragraph 4(a) states that 'areas of land, sea, seabeds and reefs . . . are severally owned by particular family groups'; paragraph 4(d) refers to 'some areas of land the use of which has been granted' for the collective use of the Meriam people by Meriam landholders; paragraph 4(e) refers to land 'purportedly acquired by the firstnamed Defendant' in the same way (see statement of claim, 20 May 1982, and amended statement of claim, 20 October 1986). See Chapters 4 and 7 above.

11. 1904–35, vol VI, 250.

12. Only when 'the disapprobation of public opinion was ineffectual' was there recourse to certain 'recognised means by which public opinion maintained its authority'; 'the services of the *maid le* [purveyors of hostile magic], or to physical force put into operation by the old men' (Haddon 1904–35, vol VI, 250).

13. 8 March 1991, as cited in Slattery 1992, 114–15 (typographical error corrected by Slattery).

14. *Wauri* was the Meriam name for the sea voyages they undertook for gift exchange and trade. Haddon (1904–35, vol VI, 186–87) discusses the voyages as trade. See Sharp 1993a, 29–39, 63–67, 265–67, for a discussion of the connection between *wauri* voyages and the sacred order of Malo-Bomai, based upon oral testimony; see especially Kapin (Harry Captain), personal communications 1980–81 (Cassettes 040–042, 081–082) and Book of Islanders 1984, B22–B30. *Wauri*, the cone shell (*Conus litteratis*) was 'worth a man or a canoe' (Haddon 1912, 236); cf Lawrence 1994, 356 and 358.

15. 1907, 133–39; cf Lawrie 1970, 326–36. For Sam Passi's version, recorded in 1984, see Sharp 1993a, 29.

16. Supreme Court of Queensland, exhibit 255; Lawrie 1970, 325–26. For the original by Aiet Passi (Pasi), see Ray 1907, 233–39. The version here is told by Sam Passi; see Au Bala, Cassette 135/AB/TI/3/84; Sharp 1993a, 29. For a discussion of Bomai as Malo's secret and sacred name, see Sharp 1993a, 29–30, 44.

17. Book of Islanders 1984, Au Bala (Sam Passi), B61.

18. Book of Islanders 1984, Kebi Bala (Reverend Dave Passi), B125; Sharp 1993a, 67–69.

19. Book of Islanders 1984, Sis (Flo Kennedy), B96; Sharp 1993a, 254–55.

20. 1987, 21.

21. 1994, 19.

22. See Beckett 1963.

23. Evidence of this revival was already visible in Lawrie's work (see 1970); see Kitaoji 1980.

24. In his seminal study of the Hero Cult of I'wai (crocodile) among the Kuuku Ya'u (Koko Ya'o), a sandbeach people on the northeastern seaboard of Cape York Peninsula, anthropologist Donald Thomson draws attention both to the inclusion of *abstract*, non-material things, such as dances as totems, and the integrative role of the cult 'in establishing a common tribal centre . . . and so providing the basis for tribal, as distinct from clan, solidarity' (1933, 459). These two qualities of I'wai resemble closely those of Malo-Bomai, as does the belief in a life after death (493). Senior Kuuku Ya'u man, the late Michael Sandy, told me at Lockhart River how I'wai made possible long sea voyages and exchange, which were similar to *wauri* (Cassette 128/LRS/LR/7/83).

25. TQ1807–08; 'tribal anarchy' is Beckett's expression (1994, 16).

26. Beckett writes of the Torres Strait Islanders generally, ' The world view was anthropocentric, with man using whatever practical or magical powers he could put his hand to' (1983, 203). The 'this worldly' concern of Meriam religion may have led him to reduce the latter to a technology, a tendency of some anthropological studies of Melanesian religious systems. Writing of the Garia of the South Madang area of Papua

New Guinea, Lawrence concluded that 'Anthropocentrism and materialism were undisguised' in a religion which was 'above all a technology' (1967, 29).
27. Justice Moynihan cites Beckett here (1987, 24; exhibit 213); cf TQ2360.
28. I am paraphrasing Eliade here (1973, 62); cf Sharp 1993b, 87.
29. 1976, 19.
30. Affidavit 1982, eighth sheet, para 14.
31. *Milirrpum*, 272.
32. 1986, 202. Writing several years later from the perspective of Canadian land cases, McNeil also drew an important general conclusion on the negative effects of the 'rather strict European *indicia* of ownership' in that case (1989, 194 n6).
33. 1986, 201.
34. 1989, 291.
35. Yarra Bank Films 1990.
36. 1986, 22.
37. 1986, 18. Cf Baudrillard, who develops the argument, together with its important implications, that the economy is embedded in other social relations in societies based upon reciprocity (1975, 75, 91).
38. For a discussion of moves for sovereignty in the Torres Strait, see Kehoe-Forutan 1988; Sharp 1993a, 227–30.
39. Ray 1907, 226 as cited in D58.
40. Ray 1907, 166.
41. Cf TQ1014, 1015; see Idriess 1933, 16; see also Chapter 4, n 6 above. Haddon concluded that there were three *Zogo le* who were drawn from the most important members of the Malo-Bomai 'fraternity' known as *Beizam boai* or Shark brethren: they were entitled to wear the masks in the Malo rites (1904–35, vol VI, 286).
42. No page is given; presumably the quotation for which I have used double quotation marks is from J Vansina (cited thus 'Vansiana [*sic*] *Oral Traditions: A History*, James Currey, London, 1985').
43. Chanock 1985, 8; no date or page as cited in D62.
44. Bloch 1965 edn, *Feudal Society*, as cited in Chanock 1985, 8.
45. Kern 1939, *Kingship and Law in the Middle Ages*, as cited in Chanock, 1985, 8.
46. Chanock 1985, 8, is following Kern 1939 here (my emphasis).
47. Chanock 1985, 9.
48. On the emergence of 'Island custom' and a Torres Strait Islander identity see Beckett 1987, Sharp 1984, 1993a; on the growth of a pan-Islander language, see Shnukal 1983, 1988.
49. Leach (1969, 9) writes that 'each alternative version of a myth confirms his [the believer's] understanding and reinforces the essential meaning of all the others'.

NOTES TO CHAPTER 9

TWO CATEGORIES OF LAND LAW: THE HIGH COURT

1. Justice Brennan writes that 'No such claim was made before this Court by the plaintiff Eddie Mabo' (1992, 437). Justices Deane and Gaudron note that after 'the completion of the argument, the firstnamed plaintiff, Mr Eddie Mabo, died' (1992, 455).
2. See *Mabo v Queensland* before Mason CJ, Brennan, Dawson, Toohey, Gaudron and McHugh JJ, Canberra 28–31 May 1991, judgment, 3 June 1992. Per Brennan J (Mason CJ and McHugh J agreeing), per Deane and Gaudron JJ, per Dawson J (dissenting), per Toohey J, 66 *ALJR*, 408–99. Butt and Eagleson (1993) provide selections from the High Court decision 'based largely on the actual words of the judges' (6) making their decision accessible to a non-legal audience.

3. Butt 1993, 443.
4. Foreword to M A Stephenson and S Ratnapala (eds) 1993, xiv. An enlightening critique of the ethnocentric bias inherent in the concepts of 'civilised' and 'primitive', is made by Green 1975, 233–49. He writes 'All that one can say of this concept [of civilised] is that general principles of law recognized by civilized nations are nothing but those principles of law which are generally recognized by us and those nations which we consider to be civilized', 233. Other international comparative studies which bear on cross-cultural concepts of law within the context of the 'civilised' versus 'primitive' dichotomy include Smith 1968, 191–225; Henderson 1977, 75–137; Barsh 1982, 7–82; McNeil 1989.
5. *Appeals Cases*, 233–34, as cited by Brennan J (421).
6. Brennan J (421) is citing the report of Select Committee on Aborigines to the House of Commons (1837), as cited by Lindley MF, *The Acquisition and Government of Backward Territory in International Law,* Longmans, London(1926, 41).
7. *Advisory Opinion on Western Sahara* (1975), *International Court of Justice Reports*, 39, as cited by Brennan J 1992, 421.
8. *In re Southern Rhodesia* (1919) *Appeals Cases* 22 at 233–34, as cited by Brennan J 1992, 422. The Privy Council was rejecting the argument 'that the native people "were the owners of the unalienated lands" '; they replied that ' "the maintenance of their rights was fatally inconsistent with white settlement of the country" '.
9. 159 *Commonwealth Law Reports* (CLR) 70, 149 as cited by Brennan J 1992, 422–23. See *Johnson v McIntosh* (1823) 8 Wheaton, 574 (21 US, 253).
10. Reynolds 1992, Chapters III and V.
11. Colonial Office Records, Australian Joint Copying Project, file no 13/16, folio 57, as cited by Deane and Gaudron JJ 1992, 450.
12. File no 18/34, folio 106, as cited by Deane and Gaudron JJ 1992, 450.
13. Gaita 1993a, 39.
14. See *Milirrpum*, 198. A particular difficulty concerned the establishment by the plaintiffs of the succession by one particular clan to the land claimed (*Milirrpum*, 185–80). More generally, the court examined practical usage of land 'as a system of ownership and possession' (Williams 1986, 202).
15. The four cases are *Attorney-General v Brown* (1847) 1 Legge 312, *Cooper v Stuart* (1889) 14 *Appeals Cases* 286, *Williams v Attorney-General for New South Wales* (1913) 16 CLR 404, and *Randwick Corporation v Rutledge* (1959) 102 CLR 54.
16. In Olbrei 1982, 57–58.
17. D, as cited in Brennan J 1992, 411.
18. For a discussion of the High Court proceedings on 28 May 1991 that led to the amended statement of claim, see Brennan 1994b, 34–36.
19. On 8 December 1992, the High Court ordered the first defendant, the state of Queensland, to pay half the legal costs (about $200,000) of plaintiffs Reverend Dave Passi and James Rice (State ordered to pay $200,000 in Mabo Costs, *Australian*, 9 December 1992).
20. Community Services (Torres Strait) Act 1984 (Qld), s41(2)(b), as cited by Brennan J 1992, 431.
21. Justice Brennan cites two cases: *Australian Conservation Foundation v the Commonwealth* (1980) 146 CLR 493 at 530–31, 537–39, 547–48; *Onus v Alcoa of Australia Ltd* (1981) 149 CLR 27 at 35–36, 41–42, 46, 51, 62, 74–75. On the relationship between the rights of landowners and the title of the community as a whole, see Castan TQ141–43, 160–63; and Chapter 6.
22. For exposition and analysis of the concept of native title within the context of Western law, see for instance, Smith 1974, 1–16; Henderson 1977, 75–137; Jackson 1984, 255–87.
23. Williams 1986, 8.

24. Justices Deane and Gaudron state that the issues of fact 'provides, for present purposes, a sound basis for some generalisations in relation to native entitlements' at the Murray Islands 'under local law and custom at the time of their annexation to Queensland' (454). They go on to say that 'the identity of familial or individual title-holders and the content of the rights possessed in relation to particular land fall to be determined by reference to local law or custom' (455); cf their statement on the inappropriateness of the court defining the plaintiffs' rights 'in the absence of other persons who may have competing claims to the relevant areas of land' (455).

25. 1984 13 DLR (4th), 339. Bartlett (1985, 370 ff) suggests that Justice Dickson is taking 'a most unusual approach in apparently suggesting that Indian title consists in the rights the Indians possessed under their own sovereignty prior to "discovery" and it is that which the common law gives effect to'. He goes on to propose reasons for this approach.

26. HCA, Transcript of Proceedings, 28 May 1991, 42, as cited in Brennan 1994b, 35.

27. 1994b, 35.

28. *The Case of Tanistry* (1608) Davis 28 (80 ER 516), 4th edn, Dublin (1762) English translation 78 at 110–11; regarding Wales, Justice Brennan cites *Witrong and Blany* (1674) 4 Keb 401 at 402; and McNeil 1989, 174.

29. (1921) 2 *Appeals Cases*, at 403, as cited by Brennan J 1992, 425.

30. See 1992, especially Chapters III and V. In separating the question of native title from that of sovereignty, the majority ruled that the latter could not be challenged in an Australia court (see Brennan J 1992, 434).

31. (1921) 403, as cited by Deane and Gaudron JJ, 442.

32. McNeil 1989, Chapter 7, especially 207–08. For a general examination of possession as the root of title, see Epstein 1979, 1221–43.

33. 1993, 81. Perhaps it may not be 'easy', given the incommensurability between undetachable and inalienable land and land conceived as a commodity; but see Jenks 1917, 11ff, 'An Inalienable Fee Simple?'.

34. Pearson 1993, 81.

35. 1993, 81.

36. *Milirrpum*, 255, as cited by Dawson J 1992, 472.

37. Cf Brennan J 1992, 435; cf Reynolds 1992, 138–42.

38. 1994b, 181.

39. Gaita 1993b, 44. Gaita is writing in the conservative Australian monthly, *Quadrant*.

40. Gaita 1993b, 45, 46.

41. *Milirrpum*, 270–71.

42. Williams 1986, 199.

43. 1989, 195; cf Williams 1986, 202.

44. On the 20-year lease of the islands of Dauar and Waier and its subsequent relinquishment, see Chapter 7, n6 above.

45. See *Utemorrah and Others v the Commonwealth of Australia and the State of Western Australia; Barunga v Commonwealth,* Supreme Court of Western Australia, no 1282 of 1993; *Wororra Peoples and Yawuru Peoples v State of Western Australia*, High Court of Australia, no M147 of 1993; *Wik People v the State of Queensland, Comalco and Others.*

NOTES TO CHAPTER 10

THE SEA: WITHIN THE COMPASS OF NATIVE TITLE

1. Media release, Economic Fishing Zone Declared, 6 December 1993; cf *Torres News*, 31 December 1993 to 6 January 1994.

NOTES

2. Media release, 6 December 1993; cf Day 1993.
3. Media release, 6 December 1993.
4. Following a meeting of interested parties, the Queensland Commercial Fishermen's Organisation agreed to a moratorium on the use of the area and a committee was asked to report on recommendations to the Protected Zone Joint Authority 'on an arrangement mutually acceptable to both the Meriam people and the fishing industry . . . with the aim of maximising the benefits of the fisheries resource surrounding those islands to the traditional people on a sustainable basis', media release, 22 December 1993, *Torres News*, 31 December 1993 – 6 January 1994.
5. Bennion 1993, 5. The belief in the 'freedom of the seas' runs deeply in European thought. The view expressed by Dutch philosopher Hugo Grotius in his treatise *Mare Liberum*, in 1633, has remained unmodified in principle. On Maori fishing rights, see McHugh 1984, 247–73; on the international law of the sea and its evolution, see Ngantcha 1990.
6. Allen 1992.
7. Blokland and Flynn 1993.
8. Cordell 1991b; Smyth 1993; Allen 1992, 1993.
9. Lawrie 1970, 342–43.
10. Gobedar Noah, Cassette 3, Townsville, 2 March 1993.
11. In Haddon 1904–35, vol VI, 165–66, 167, 167 n1.
12. D205; see also D214.
13. Plaintiffs' submissions, 5, 6.
14. McIntyre 1993, 4.
15. Williams 1986, 201.
16. 1972, 28.
17. 1972, 31.
18. 1969b, 6.
19. See also fish traps and 'intermittent activity' (D184) and non-continuance of rights of those 'who originally put the fish-traps in place' (D184), rather than as a culture striving to reassert itself (see D182–84 on fish traps and Beckett TQ2254).
20. 1814, as cited in TQ2349.
21. Lawrie also assisted in repairing a fish trap in February 1967 (1970, 342).
22. Sharp, notes of conversations with landowners at Mer, May 1993.
23. Bird et al 1995, 2–17.
24. Douglas and Rebecca Bird, Mer Island, personal communication, 27 January 1995.
25. In Haddon 1904–35, vol VI, 167. Given the determined prohibition by government officials on the exercise of rights going with sea property, it is not surprising to find expert witness Jeremy Beckett not as well informed on ownership of sea areas as on land ownership, see TQ2255.
26. Johannes and MacFarlane (1984, 257) report in a similar vein on their field research at Mer Islands: 'Attempts to delineate intra-tribal boundaries were abandoned' in order 'not to aggravate family and clan disputes'.
27. 1993, 4.
28. 1992, as cited in McIntyre 1993, 4.
29. Torres Strait Land Act (Qld) 1991, no 33.
30. 1904–35, vol VI, 167 n1.
31. Wilkin in Haddon 1904–35, vol VI, 167; Sharp 1993a, 64–67.
32. Heads of Agreement, signed 26 June 1989. The hearing before Justice Toohey concerned the argument on whether Justice Moynihan 'in the Supreme Court of Queensland was empowered to make rulings as to the admissibility of evidence, and amendment of pleadings, especially the addition or removal of parties' (Keon-Cohen 1993, 186). Justice Toohey ruled on 3 May that the Supreme Court of Queensland may make orders to add parties or to amend that statement of claim. On Justice Moynihan's

dismissal of the Commonwealth as a party, see TQ2720, 7 July 1989; generally, see proceedings, TQ2698–2722; cf TQ2457–58.

33. 1993, 3.

34. Notes of conversations at Mer, June 1993. These boundaries correspond with Haigh's findings based on his field work in 1992 (Haigh 1993). Johannes and MacFarlane exclude Raine Island and Eastern Field Reef (1991). Senior Meriam people were most emphatic in their inclusion of Raine Island as a site indispensable to their survival; Raine Island is a bird hatchery to which the Murray Islanders went for fertiliser for their food gardens. They cited not only their forbears' oral statements; they also produced names of non-Meriam Torres Strait Islanders to whom they suggested I go for further confirmation. Eses Gisa (Gesah) gives the Meriam name of Raine Island as Subkaur to which the Murray Islanders went in northeast (*naiger*) time for *lipam*, (fertiliser) in pre-colonial and colonial times (personal communication, Townsville, 16 February 1995.

My further inquiries at Thursday Island and Mer in December 1993 and January 1995 and at Injinoo in January 1995, suggest the need for further research on oral tradition with respect to traditional boundaries in relation to pre-colonial and colonial times; and clarification of the claims by the Wuthathi sandbeach people of Cape York Peninsula to Raine Island as a traditional meeting point with Meriam people (see Gordon Pablo, chairman, Wuthathi Aboriginal Community Council, personal communication, Injinoo, 20 January, 1995; senior Murray Islanders, Mer Island, 24–28 January 1995). On sea territories in the Torres Strait generally, see Nietschmann 1989, 60–93; on current marine strategy for Torres Strait, see Mulrennan and Hanssen 1994.

35. *Treaty between Australia and the Independent State of Papua New Guinea Concerning Sovereignty and Maritime Boundaries, in the Area between the Two Countries Including the Area Known as Torres Strait, and Related Matters*, signed at Sydney 18 December 1978, Government Printer, Canberra. As Cordell (1993) notes, the customary marine tenure systems and sea/fishing rights of Torres Strait Islanders and Papua New Guinea coastal peoples are not taken into account in the treaty provisions. Haigh (1993) provides a clear overview of the constraints imposed by legally based domestic and international structures.

36. George Kudub, notes of conversation with the author, Mer Island, 11 June 1993.

37. See *Queensland Votes and Proceedings* 1886, 6.

38. 1993a, 15; cf Sutherland 1992; Allen 1993.

39. Bartlett 1993a, 4, 10; cf Cordell 1991a.

40. Cordell 1993, 1–19.

41. 1984, 423. Cf Woodward 1973; Nietschmann 1989; Johannes and MacFarlane 1991; Allen 1992; Smyth 1993; Jackson 1995.

42. In his *Second Report*, Aboriginal land rights commissioner A E Woodward noted that 'the estuaries and tidal flats of Northern Territory Aboriginal reserves have been generally regarded as . . . out-of-bounds to commercial fishermen'. In rejecting the request of the Northern Land Council for recognition of an area 12 miles out to seas as protected by Aboriginal land rights, he noted traditional claims to most off-shore islands, together with 'estuaries, bays and waters immediately adjacent to the shore line as being part of their land' (para 420–423, 1974, 80). His recommendation that the definition of Aboriginal coastal land include 'off-shore islands and waters within two kilometres of the low tide line' (para 91, 15; see also para 425, 81) was incorporated into the Aboriginal Land Rights (Northern Territory) Act 1976.

43. Cordell 1993, 4, 6.

44. Williams 1993.

45. *Mabo (No 2)*, 433, per Brennan J.

46. 1993a, 4.

47. Sutherland 1992; cf Allen 1993.

48. Commonwealth of Australia 1993a; Bartlett 1993a, 10.
49. 1993a, 17.
50. 1995, 91.
51. 1993, 22. Howard cites *The Seas and Submerged Lands Act* case (1975), 135 CLR, 340.
52. 1992, 9.
53. 1993, para 1.5 as cited in Bartlett 1993a, 16, n69.
54. See Native Title Act 1993, s223(1), s225 (a) and (b), and s223(2) includes fishing rights and interests; 'waters' include (a) sea, a river, a lake, a tidal inlet, a bay, an estuary, a harbour or subterranean waters; or (b) the bed or subsoil under, or airspace over, any waters (including waters mentioned in paragraph (a)); see other definitions, s253, 126.
55. See *Barunga v Commonwealth,* Supreme Court of Western Australia, no 1282 of 1993, amended Supreme Court writ, statement of claim, schedule A; *Wororra Peoples and Yawuru Peoples v State of Western Australia*, High Court of Australia, no M147 of 1993, statement of claim, schedule A and B.
56. *Wik People v the State of Queensland, Comalco and Others.*
57. See, for example, Wessell Islands Sea Management Proposal 1993; see also Yolngu Marine Protection Workshop, Arafura Sea Management Issues, Draft Briefing Paper no 1, Darwin, 11–12 May 1993; Manbuynga ga Rulyapa (Arafura Sea), Call for an Indigenous Marine Protection Strategy for NT Coast, Winnellie, NT, mimeo, November 1994, 1–9; generally, see Altman, Ginn and Smith 1993; Williams 1993.

NOTES TO CHAPTER 11

NATIVE TITLE IN THE RESHAPING OF AUSTRALIAN IDENTITY

1. Cameron Forbes, Key Ruling Boosts Blacks' Land Claims, *Age*, 4 June 1992.
2. Cameron Forbes, *Age*, 4 June 1992.
3. Ruling Aids Accord with Aborigines, says PM, *Sydney Morning Herald*, 5 June 1992.
4. Historic Win in Fight for Land Rights, 4 June 1992.
5. J Waterford, *Canberra Times*, 4 June 1992.
6. G Ewing, as reported in *Australian*, 4 June 1992; Goss contrasts the strength of the Meriam 'system of title' to 'individual lots of land' with the presumed 'nomadic situation which existed on the mainland', *Sydney Morning Herald*, 9 June 1992.
7. *Courier-Mail*, Brisbane, 5 June 1992.
8. *Mabo (No 2)*, 416, per Brennan J.
9. *Gerhardy v Brown* (1985) 59 ALJR April 1985, 346, per Deane J, as cited in Reynolds 1992, 178.
10. Rowse 1993b, 21, is using Reynolds's expression (see 1992, Chapter 4).
11. 1993b, 21.
12. Rowse 1993b, 12, is referring to Deborah Rose's commentary, which she published with Danayarri's 'Saga of Captain Cook' (1984, 24–39).
13. Stanner 1969a, 25.
14. The Aboriginal Treaty Committee, formed in the wake of *Coe v Commonwealth of Australia* (1979), gave expression to this developing sensibility, which had other earlier expressions. On the Aboriginal Treaty Committee, see Harris 1979; Wright 1985.
15. Judith Wright, 'Two Dreamtimes', written for Kath Walker (Oodgeroo Noonuccal) says:

> I am born of the conquerors,
> you of the persecuted.

These two lines form the epigraph of her book *Born of the Conquerors: Selected Essays by Judith Wright*, Aboriginal Studies Press, 1991; see Chapter 2 above and Olbrei 1982.

16. Reynolds 1992, 179, cites 59 ALJR, April 1985, 346, per Deane J.
17. He said 'the Federal government would face a barrage of litigation' if it did not pass national land rights legislation or negotiate a treaty, *West Australian*, 4 June 1992; cf *Sydney Morning Herald*, *Newcastle Herald*, 4 June 1992; 'I don't think that's right', the prime minister, Mr Keating, replied, *Launceston Examiner*, 5 June 1992.
18. These words are attributed to Ron Castan, senior counsel for the Meriam plaintiffs, by Cameron Forbes, *Age*, 4 June 1992.
19. See *Utemorrah and Others v the Commonwealth of Australia and the State of Western Australia*; see also After Mabo: Claiming the Kimberley Coast, *Bulletin*, 4 August 1992, 22–24.
20. Mabo Legal Team Hired, *Torres News*, 13–19 November 1992.
21. Cassette 066/MW/CC/1/80, Utingu (Simpson Bay), Cape York, personal story, 9 December 1980. Mrs Wymarra was recounting the events as told to her by the 'tribal people'; she herself, together with another family, made her own way to Thursday Island before the events she describes. Others went to Burketown, Normanton, Cairns and other places.
22. *Wik People v the State of Queensland, Comalco and Others*.
23. Their proposal was reported in Mine Chief Urges State to Legislate over Mabo, *Age*, 26 April 1993; see also Blacks Seeks Law to Secure Native Title, *Age*, 28 April 1993.
24. Brennan 1994a, 6.
25. Cited in Brennan 1994a, 5.
26. Stanner 1969, 4; Williams 1986, 22.
27. Emphasis added. The inclusion of 'individual rights' may reflect the way *Mabo* was argued. Part 3, section 61(1) defines an applicant as 'A person or persons claiming to hold the native title "either alone or with others" '. However, as of 1 September 1994, virtually all applications under the Native Title Act 1993 have been made by individuals on behalf of a group. The situation is very complex. Williams's argument (1986, 8) that the Aboriginal Land Rights (Northern Territory) Act 1976 may suffer from some of the oversimplifications made in the *Milirrpum* case, is borne out by cases where lineages have been reduced to one individual.
28. Under the Aboriginal Land Rights (Northern Territory) Act 1976, an Aboriginal land trust may surrender land with the informed consent of 'the traditional Aboriginal owners' (part II, s19[5][a]). In this legislation the conditions of surrender are more tightly formulated than in the Native Title Act 1993; it is suggested that this makes the rights of the landholding group more secure. Legislation creating inalienable freehold title was certainly proposed by Justice Woodward in his *Second Report*, April 1974. Both Acts operate within the 'firmly established' rule precluding 'alienation outside the native system otherwise than by surrender to the Crown' (*Mabo (No 2)*, 442, per Deane and Gaudron JJ). For a discussion of this rule, see McNeil 1989, 221ff.
29. See Aboriginal Land Rights Act (Northern Territory) 1976, s23, especially (3), s40 and s48. Section 40(1)(b) qualifies that right in the national interest.
30. Recognition of the right of consent was a noteworthy feature of Justice Woodward's reports of the Commission to Inquire into Land Rights in the Northern Territory (see for instance, *Second Report*, 1974, 18, s108); this inquiry arose out of *Milirrpum v Nabalco*.
31. Brennan 1994a, 6. For a summary analysis of this legislation see Nettheim 1993, 4–5.
32. Howard 1993, 22.
33. Brunton 1993, 45.
34. Coombs 1994, 167–70. On moves for a regional authority among Aboriginal groups in the Kimberley region, see Leon Morris, Forty Thousand Years on the Long Road to Yirra, *Good Weekend*, 26 November 1994, 24, 27–28.

35. Kate Cole-Adams, Independence after Mabo, *Age*, 22 December 1992. The Torres Strait Regional Authority was launched on 1 June 1994 'with responsibility for administering national and regional programs', *Native Title Newsletter* 6, 1994, 4, summarising a report in *Cairns Post*, 29 June 1994; see also *Torres News*, 26 August – 1 September 1994, 1.
36. Deanie Carbon, Cabinet to Debate Mabo Case Fallout, *Weekend Australian*, 17–18 October 1992.
37. NT Aboriginal Mineral Claim Causes Uproar, *Age*, 5 December 1992; 10pc of Land up for Mabo Claims, *Weekend Australian*, 5–6 December 1992; Sovereignty — the right and power to govern — has become a political goal of an articulate section of Aboriginal people (see Mansell 1992, 4–5); *Utemorrah and Others v the Commonwealth and the State of Western Australia* makes a claim to sovereignty; Brennan (1993a, 25–27) considers this claim and political claims to sovereignty.
38. Commonwealth of Australia 1993a, 102.
39. ATSIC and Land Councils, media release, 3 June 1993.
40. Commonwealth of Australia 1993a, Chapter 7, Negotiation and Consent, 60.
41. Law must dig Deeper to Find Land Rights, *Australian*, 8 June 1993.
42. 1993, 62.
43. Justice Woodward (c 1985, 28–29) discusses critically the main arguments advanced by opponents of land rights: 'land rights is apartheid', 'everyone is the same', Aborigines are claiming 'more than equality' with other citizens. These are updated and 'refined' not only by Brunton. In calling for a sense of history not a pseudo-history, Dr Colin Howard, former professor of law, wrote that the former concerns a recognition of the dispossession of the weaker by the stronger as illustrated in the dispossession of the Celts of Europe. The moral right to such action is left unquestioned (1993, 22); Brunton 1993, 63. See also Ron Brunton, Mystery in Black and White, *Age*, 28 May 1993; for a critical analysis, see Ian Anderson, Black Suffering — White Wash, *Arena Magazine* 5, 1993, 23–25. For a critique of the underlying position of Brunton's monograph see Gillian Cowlishaw, Mabo Debate Breeds Sinister New Forms of Racism, *Age*, 31 July 1993.
44. Howard 1993, 22; Geoffrey Blainey, Blacks Hold more Land than Whites: Blainey, *Age*, 13 May 1993. Blainey himself has acknowledged the triumph of Aboriginal cultures in his *Triumph of the Nomads*. There is something almost forlorn in his critique of the majority decision of the High Court. Consider his unelaborated and unillustrated assessment of Justice Dawson's 'lonely, long and courageous statement': 'he alone, a conservative, is affirming a democratic tradition' (High Court Playing Politics?, *Age*, 26 June 1993). Unfortunately his misinformed reading of the potentialities of Aboriginal societies lays the basis of somewhat unexpected alliances. One of the surprises of the ongoing debates is the sad spectacle of noted scholars, who have in the past shown a regard for the authenticity of Aboriginal cultures, sharpening their blades on the same steel as the most myopic of the mining industry spokespeople.
45. Court Urges Defence of Mabo-Style Land Claims, the *Australian*, 1 April 1993, misleadingly titled an article. An important context for these moves was given by the multiplication of Aboriginal land claims. By December 1992, seven or eight claims had been lodged, with another nine or ten in January 1993. These included claims to land in the Kimberleys in Western Australia, at McArthur River and Gove Peninsula in the Northern Territory, and at Weipa, Cape York, covering Comalco's bauxite deposit and CRA's Century deposit in Queensland (J B Were and Son, circular to clients, February 1993, as reported in *Australian*, 5 March 1993). The mining industry secured the services of several social scientists as consultants; the situation demanded confidentiality and secrecy both to avoid signalling land claim targets and encouraging unwanted competitors. For example, geographer Stephen Davis was appointed by Western Mining Corporation as its adviser 'on heritage and Aboriginal

matters' (R Gluyas, The Mabo Factor: Learning from the Past, *Australian*, 5 March 1993).

46. Bartlett 1993b, 7–9. The Victorian government foreshadowed the Western Australian legislation by six months with a Traditional Cultural Rights Act, providing special legally based access to specified land 'for defined purposes' (State Goes it Alone, *Age*, 10 June 1993). Aboriginal people would be 'free' to visit 'sacred sites or other areas of cultural significance', the most minimum of the eight rights listed in the federal government's document several weeks later (Kennett Pushes State Compo Plan, *Age*, 8 June 1993). On 16 March 1995 the High Court rejected a challenge by the state of Western Australia to the Native Title Act (Cwth) 1993, see *Biljabu v State of Western Australia*, unreported decision of the High Court of Australia delivered on 16 March 1995 (HCA FC 95/010) declaring the Land (Titles and Traditional Usage) Act 1993 (WA) invalid or inoperative because of inconsistency with the Racial Discrimination Act 1975 (Cwth).

47. *Age*, 7 June 1993.

48. See Jackson and Cooper 1993, 20–22.

49. The Mabo Challenge, Editorial, *Age*, 7 June 1993.

50. Allen 1993, 4. In *Milirrpum*, Justice Blackburn said 'that property, in its various forms, generally implies the right to use and enjoy, the right to exclude others, and the right to alienate' (1971, 272).

51. Commonwealth of Australia, 1993b, 22.

52. McEachern, CJ, 209, as cited in Slattery 1992, 116 (emphasis added by Slattery). See 79 DLR (4th) 185.

53. *Age*, 17 June 1993.

54. All Talk, No Definitions, of Native Title, *Age*, 17 June 1993.

55. J Hyde, Lateral Thinking on Mabo, *Weekend Australian*, 19–20 June 1993. Aboriginal societies were being openly targeted as inferior. This approach reached its zenith in the public arena with National party leader Tim Fischer's designation of their 'primitivity': they lacked even the wheel (Fischer Opens Split on Mabo, *Australian*, 21 June 1993). *Mabo* may be plunging Australia backward towards 'a culture living on witchetty grubs', said a spokesman for one British investment house (Rob Davies of Lehman Brothers, as reported in PM Rejects Investors' Mabo Fears, *Australian*, 14 June 1993).

56. Aborigines Reject Mabo Bill, *Age*, 6 August 1993; see also the conflicting representations of reactions to the same legislative proposal: Mabo Strategy Looking Better, *Age*; Decision Gets Mixed Reaction, *Australian*, 29 July 1993.

57. Fifty Aboriginal Leaders Rebuke Keating over Mabo, and, Blacks Say They Need Figurehead, *Age*, 21 June 1993.

58. See (c) in list of five principles, Eva Valley Statement, 5 August 1993, as reproduced in *Australian*, 6 August 1993; for the full statement see Coombs 1994, appendix, 231–34; Goot and Rowse 1994, 233–34.

59. Aborigines Reject Mabo Bill, *Age*, 6 August 1993; cf Galarrwuy Yunupingu, Mr Keating has 'backed off' his commitment to Aborigines under 'pressure from the land developers', *Age*, 6 August 1993.

60. Mabo's Message of Justice and Reconciliation, *Age*, 9 July 1993.

61. One Strong Voice from the Valley, *Australian*, 9 August 1993.

62. Understanding Mabo, 9 August 1993.

63. United They Stand, *Weekend Australian*, 7–8 August 1993.

64. *Weekend Australian*, 7–8 August 1993.

65. These complexities are indicated by Galarrwuy Yunupingu's statement on the right of the Koongarra traditional owners to opt for uranium mining on their land: 'I do not want the internal political problems of the ALP to interfere with the Koongarra traditional owners' bid for economic independence' (Black Leader Attacks Three-Mine

Uranium Policy, *Age*, 13 August 1994). This report stated that the call 'for mining to proceed' announced by Mr Yunupingu, chairman of the Northern Land Council (NLC), had the support of the NLC as well as the traditional owners.

66. Native Titles Research Unit 1994, 116, 115, 117.

67. 1993, 24. Anderson is making a critique of Ron Brunton's lack of 'real encounter' with or personal knowledge of the actual lives of Aboriginal people (25).

68. Slattery 1992, 117.

69. The Australian Council for Overseas Aid, representing 22 aid bodies, conservation organisations, leading public intellectuals, church groups, Green and other minority parties, all condemned the bill as racist. 'How could the Government argue that it is providing social justice when it proposes to validate actions of the past that themselves may have been illegal and invalid?', Dr Coombs and several colleagues asked cogently (letter to *Age*, 23 September 1993). The legislation is 'nothing short of racial discrimination itself', the United Church of Australia claimed in a letter to the prime minister (*Age*, 29 September 1993). A 'continuing injustice diminishes all of us', said Veronica Brady, affirming the High Court's sense of justice (as reported in the *Age*, 25 September 1993). For a documentation and analysis of events between 2 September and 21 December 1993, see Whimp 1994, 16–19. These protests were welcomed by Aboriginal leaders. Noel Pearson responded, 'Like my colleagues, I was heartened by the groundswell of public support for not rolling back the Racial Discrimination Act' (1994a, 6).

70. Australians Unconsciously Racist, *Age*, 12 July 1993.

71. 1994, 21. A proposal for the declaration of a large 'native title area' made by Professor Garth Nettheim and Professor M J Dettmold (*Sydney Morning Herald*, 24 June 1993) was received in almost total silence (reported in Rowse 1993a, 17–18).

72. Coombs et al, 1989, 9.

73. Cordell 1993, 1–19.

74. Mer Islands Community Council, press release, 6 December 1993, 3.

75. Rose 1985, East Kimberley Working Paper no 5, as cited in Coombs et al 1989, 94; Coombs et al 1989, 91.

76. Coombs et al 1989, 87.

77. Coombs et al 1989, 57.

78. Hirst 1994, 14.

79. See Samana 1988; Sharp 1988, 50–80.

80. Coombs 1994, 230.

81. Book of Islanders 1984, B136; Sharp 1993a, 40. The school was begun in Townsville.

82. Pearson 1994a, 7. For a summary of land claims placed before the National Native Title Tribunal set up under the Native Title Act 1993, see Native Titles Research Unit 1994, 1–10.

83. Brennan 1993b, 13.

84. Dodson 1994, 74.

85. See 'Oil and Gas Mine for Mer', *Torres News*, 25–31 August 1995.

86. These are Deborah Rose's words about Yarralin people of the Northern Territory. She continues, 'Founded in the belief that the Law is everywhere, people hope that others will recognise the key events and find their own strong stories which, as they implement them in their own lives and places, will answer back in affirmation' (1992, 235).

87. As this whole book exemplifies, the passing on of land from parents to children continues to be a sacred bond in Meriam, in Torres Strait and in land-based Aboriginal societies, see Land Fund and Indigenous Land Corporation (ATSIC Amendment) Act 1995.

GLOSSARIES

COMMON LAW TERMS

Common law As the powerful centralised system of justice of the English kings developed in the twelfth and later centuries, the royal justices increasingly developed and administered general rules common to the whole of England, the common law of England, as distinct from local customs, peculiarities and variations.

Fact, 'the facts' The circumstances, deeds, sayings, and inferences from them as distinct from the legal consequences, rules applicable thereto, and legal conclusions . . . circumstances, acts, and events, which in legal controversy are determined by admission or by evidence, as distinct from matters of law which are determined by authority and argument. Thus what A did is a matter of fact; whether it constituted a particular crime or not is a matter of law. A matter of fact is also distinct from a matter of belief or opinion, which may not be susceptible of proof or disproof.

Fee simple In the English law of real property an estate in land, held heritably (fee), and descending to heirs generally, without restraint to any particular class of heirs (simple), as contrasted with a fee tail, or estate tail, or entailed interest. An estate in fee simple comes as close to absolute ownership as the system of tenure will allow.

Fiduciary A person in a position of trust, or occupying a position of power and confidence with respect to another, such that he or she is obliged by various rules of law to act solely in the interest of the other, whose rights he or she has to protect. He or she may not make any profit or advantage from the relationship without full disclosure.

Occupation In international law . . . a mode of acquiring sovereignty over territory not already under the dominion of a recognised state. It has been recognised that discovery is not enough and that, particularly in habitable areas, occupation must be effective, and must amount to actual settlement and administration and the claim to exclude others.

Domestically, it concerns the fact of presence on the land, which may be lawful or unlawful; it may be exclusive, that is, to the exclusion of others, or it may be concurrent with others.

Possession A person having actual possession is presumed to have the right of property and is accordingly entitled to have his or her possession protected unless anyone can prove a superior title.

Adverse possession In English real property, occupation of real property in manner inconsistent with the right of the true owner . . . Adverse possession entitles the possessor to be protected in his or her possession against anyone who cannot show a better title.

Sovereignty The concept of supremacy or superiority in a state by virtue of which some person or body or group in that political society is supreme and can, in the last resort, impose his, her or its will on all other bodies and persons therein.

Declaratory and other relief An order or declaration of the court that the law affects the obligations of the defendant as against the plaintiff in a certain way; other relief may be in the form of an order for the payment of damages (or compensation).

Usufruct In Roman law, the right of using and enjoying the property of another, usually for life, without right to change the character of the property . . . The right is generally comparable to that of a tenant for life.

(drawn from DM Walker, *The Oxford Companion to Law*, Clarendon Press, Oxford, 1980, 253, 454, 463, 469, 899, 1163, 1268; also G McIntyre, Perth, personal communications.)

GLOSSARIES

MERIAM LANGUAGE WORDS

MALO RA GELAR OR MALO'S LAW (EXCERPTS)

Malo *tag mauki mauki*: Malo keeps his hands to himself.
Malo *teter mauki mauki*: Malo keeps his feet off other people's land.
Malo *wali aritarit sem aritarit*: Malo plants everywhere . . .
Eburlem esmaolem: Let it [unneeded fruit] drop and rot on the ground.

Aet, Aiet: see Zogo le.
agud: god.
aritarit: planting, garden preparation, a Malo word from *arit*, to plant.
Au le: senior man.

beizam: tiger shark.
Beizam *boai*: the dancers in the Malo ceremonies, shark brethren who had charge of the sacred emblems of Malo.
bezar: 'lonely' fish.
Bomai: secret and sacred name of the god of the Meriam (*see also* Malo).

dabor: mackerel.
daip: mound made of shell and vegetable matter forming boundary between allotments.
Dauar: one of the three Murray Islands.
deumer: Torres Strait pigeon.

elikup: boundary marker cut from *ur sekerseker*.

gabba gabba: stone club of Malo.
ged: home-place, homeland, habitable island with water resources, womb.
ged kem le: joint owners of land (lineage or family group).
gedub: garden.
Gelam: mythical culture hero who travelled from Moa, highest hill on Mer shaped like a dugong.
gelar: taboo, prohibition, rule, law, commandment.

giz: root of a tree, origin, spring.
giz ged: place of origin, beginnings.
ikok: five sacred chants of Malo.

keiar meta: crayfish houses.
Keo Deudai: Australian mainland.
kerkar: new season denoting renewal, change in continuity.
kerker: seasonal time.
ketai: wild yam.
koki: northwest wind, with which Komet people are associated.
Kole: Meriam name for white people.
kopat: everybody together.

lamar: reborn spirit of a person, ancestor living in the place of *lamar*, the immortals.
Las: village of Mer to which Bomai was taken.
le: term used by two brothers or two sisters for one another, man, person, human being, *wauri tebud*, mortal.
lipam: fertiliser (from bird droppings).
lubabat: totem.
lu kem le: landholder on behalf of lineage or family group; nameholder for family-owned land.

maid: malevolent magic, the power of the singular or non-reciprocal, the power of death.
Malo: public or 'small name' of the Meriam god.
Malo-Bomai: Meriam culture heroes.
Malo ra Gelar: the law of the Meriam people.
mamgiz: springs of common blood, sacred place of *pelak*.
mamus: head man.
mar: shadow, 'double' of a person, spirit energy, ghost of a departed person not yet reborn, a grass-like scented plant from Op Deudai.
Mer: largest of the three Murray Islands, the three Murray Islands.
meriba ged: our land.
mogor: vigilante group or law enforcers.

naiger: northeast time.
nener: boundary marker.

nerutonar: people with a different custom, 'another kind' of people, the hostile other.
nesur: *lavalava* (Torres Strait Creole), 'calico'.
nosik: clan, 'peoples' of Mer.

Op Deudai: Papua New Guinea, West Irian.
Op Ged: face islands, Eastern Islands.
opole: wearer of the sacred mask of Malo-Bomai.

pelak: sacred house.
puripuri: sorcery.

sab tonar: custom of placing a taboo on a garden.
sager: southeast, southeast wind.
sai: stone fish traps, stage in life cycle of frigate bird.
sau: plantation.
sem: yellow hibiscus.
seuriseuri: sacred star-headed clubs of Malo.

tag: hand.
Tami le: assistants to *Zogo le*.
taum akadar: pride in self.
tebud: friend.
ter: fringing reefs.
teter: foot.
teter mek: footprints, footsteps.

ur sekerseker: variety of ironwood.

Waier: the smallest of the three Murray Islands.
wali: a type of creeping vine.
wauri: cone shell, armlet made from cone shell *Conus millepunctatus*, variety *Conus litteratis*.
wauri tebud: shell friend, partner.

zogo: a natural or artificial object of great magical potency, power to communicate with *lamar*, intentional power like cosmic energy moving in a spiral, sacred, the spirit power of Malo, 'divine wrath', holy.

Zogo le: the three *le* entitled to wear the Malo-Bomai masks, persons with sacred or divine power, person with power to discern the movement of cosmic energy.
zogo mir: magical words or chants.

REFERENCES CITED

PRIMARY SOURCES

WRITTEN SOURCES

Mabo and Others v the State of Queensland and the Commonwealth of Australia, in the High Court of Australia, no 12 of 1982. Pleadings: statement of claim by five Murray Islander plaintiffs, 20 May 1982; affidavit of P J Killoran for the first defendant, 16 August 1982 with accompanying exhibits A–Y. Particulars and further particulars, including amended statement of claim, amended defences of the state of Queensland and the Commonwealth, Murray Island Court Reports (two vols), 1890s–1980s, maps, drawings and diagrams of the particulars of claims to land, reefs and sea areas. Transcripts of proceedings before High Court of Australia, Supreme Court of Queensland 1984–89. Exhibits as cited, Supreme Court of Queensland. Undertaking agreement between parties, 3 April 1987. *Eddie Mabo and Another v State of Queensland and Another* (1988) 166 *Commonwealth Law Reports* 186, High Court, Reasons for judgment on plaintiffs' demurrer (1985), 8 December 1988 (*Mabo [No 1]*). Determination pursuant to reference of 27 February 1986 by High Court to Supreme Court of Queensland to hear and determine all issues of fact raised by the pleadings, particulars and
further particulars in High Court action B12 of 1982, 16 November 1990, 227 pages plus annexures (unreported), *Eddie Mabo v the State of Queensland* (1992) 66 *Australian Law Journal Reports* 408 (High Court, Full Bench, 3 June 1992; *Mabo [No 2]*).

Field notes of conversations at Mer and Townsville, 1992–94 (in possession of the author). Author's notes on hearings in the Supreme Court of Queensland, Brisbane, October–November 1986.

Marou Mimi, diary, in possession of Mrs Boged Marou, Mer Island.

Mer Islands Community Council, media releases, Council Office, Mer Islands.

OTHER SOURCES

ABC Radio Recordings, 'The *Murray Island Land* Case', *The Law Report*, September 1986 and 19 April 1988.

Cassette recordings 1978–94, 001–078 with Meriam people, including plaintiffs and witnesses in *Murray Island Land* case (in possession of the author).

Yarra Bank Films, Trevor Graham (Director), *Land Bilong Islanders*, 50-minute documentary 1990.

BOOKS, ARTICLES, THESES

Allen, D.
    1992 Salt-Water Dreaming. In Jull et al (eds), *Surviving Columbus: Indigenous Peoples, Political Reform and Environmental Management in North Australia*, North Australia Research Unit, Darwin, 39–46.

    1993 Some Shadow of the Rights Known to our Law. In *Turning the Tide: Conference on Indigenous Peoples and Sea Rights*, Northern Territory University Faculty of Law, Darwin.

Altman, J.C., A. Ginn and D.E. Smith
    1993 *Existing and Potential Mechanisms for Indigenous Involvement in Coastal Zone Resource Management,* Centre for Aboriginal Economic Policy Research, Australian National University, Canberra (Coastal Zone Inquiry, Canberra).

Anderson, I.
    1993 Black Suffering White Wash?, *Arena Magazine* 5, 23–25.

Barsh, R.L.
    1982 Indian Land Claims Policy in the United States, *North Dakota Law Review* 58, 7–82.

Bartlett, R.H.
    1983 Aboriginal Land Claims at Common Law, *University of Western Australia Law Review* 15, 293–346.

1985 You Can't Trust the Crown: The Fiduciary Obligation of the Crown to the Indians: *Guerin v the Queen, Saskatchewan Law Review* 49, 367–74.

1992 The Aboriginal Land Which May Be Claimed at Common Law: Implications of *Mabo, Western Australian Law Review* 22.

1993a Aboriginal Sea Rights at Common Law: Mabo and the Sea. In *Turning the Tide: Conference on Indigenous Peoples and Sea Rights*, Northern Territory University Faculty of Law, Darwin, 9–20.

1993b Inequality before the Law in Western Australia: The Land (Titles and Traditional Usage) Act, *Aboriginal Law Bulletin* 3, 65 (December), 7–9.

Baudrillard J.
  1975 *The Mirror of Production*, trans. M. Poster, Telos Press, St Louis (1st French edn 1973).

Baxi, U.
  1972 The Lost Dreamtime: Now Forever Lost; A Critique of the Gove Land Rights Decision, typescript, AIATSIS library, cited with permission of the author.

Beckett, J.R.
  1963 Politics of the Torres Strait Islands, PhD thesis, Australian National University, Canberra.

  1983 Ownership of Land in the Torres Strait Islands. In N. Peterson and M. Langton (eds), *Aborigines, Law and Anthropology*, Australian Institute of Aboriginal Studies, Canberra, 202–10.

  1987 *Torres Strait Islanders: Custom and Colonialism*, Cambridge University Press, Cambridge, UK.

  1994 The Murray Island Land Case and the Problem of Cultural Continuity. In W. Sanders (ed), *Mabo and Native Title: Origins and Institutional Implications*, Centre for Aboriginal Economic Policy Research, Australian National University, Canberra.

Bennion, T.
- 1993 Protecting Fishing Rights — Recent Fisheries Settlements in New Zealand. In *Turning the Tide: Conference on Indigenous Peoples and Sea Rights*, Northern Territory University Faculty of Law, Darwin.

Bird, R.B., D.W. Bird and J.M. Beaton
- 1995 Children and Traditional Subsistence on Mer (Murray Island), Torres Strait, *Australian Aboriginal Studies* 1/95, Aboriginal Studies Press, Canberra.

Blackstone, Sir W.
- 1765–69 *Commentaries on the Laws of England*, 4 vols, Clarendon Press, Oxford, UK (facsimile of the first ed, University of Chicago Press, 1979).

Blokland, J. and M. Flynn
- 1993 Fishing Prosecutions after Mabo. In *Turning the Tide: Conference on Indigenous Peoples and Sea Rights*, Northern Territory University Faculty of Law, Darwin.

Book of Islanders
- 1984 Springs of Originality among the Torres Strait Islanders, PhD thesis, vol II, La Trobe University, Bundoora, Victoria, drawn from cassette recordings made by Nonie Sharp in the Torres Strait Islands and Cape York Peninsula, 1978–84, cassettes 001–138 as listed, B167. (See Sharp 1984.)

Brennan, F.
- 1993a Mabo and Its Implications for Aborigines and Torres Strait Islanders. In M.A. Stephenson and S. Ratnapala (eds), *Mabo: A Judicial Revolution*, University of Queensland Press, St Lucia.

- 1993b *Land Rights, the Religious Factor*, Charles Strong Memorial Trust, Flinders University, South Australia.

- 1994a Mabo and the Future of Aboriginal Reconciliation, *St Mark's Review* 158, 4–12.

1994b *Mabo*: Options for Implementation — Statutory Registration and Claims Processes. In W. Sanders (ed), *Mabo and Native Title: Origins and Institutional Implications*, Centre for Aboriginal Economic Policy Research, Australian National University, Canberra.

Brunton, R.
1993 *Black Suffering, White Guilt?, Aboriginal Disadvantage and the Royal Commission into Deaths in Custody,* Institute of Public Affairs, Melbourne.

Butt, P.
1993 Mabo v Queensland: A Summary, *Conveyancer* 67 (6), 442–44.

Butt, P. and R. Eagleson
1993 *Mabo: What the High Court Said*, Federation Press, Annandale, New South Wales.

Chanock, M.
1985 *Law, Custom and Social Order: The Colonial Experience in Malawi and Zambia*, Cambridge University Press, Cambridge, UK.

Commonwealth of Australia
1993a *Mabo, The High Court Decision on Native Title, Discussion Paper*, Australian Government Publishing Service, Canberra (June).

Commonwealth of Australia
1993b Possible Commonwealth and State/Territory Bill in Relation to Native Title, draft, 9 July (unpublished).

Commonwealth of Australia
1993c Mabo, Outline of Proposed Legislation on Native Title, September (unpublished).

Coombs, H.C.
1981 *Trial Balance*, Macmillan, South Melbourne.

1994 *Aboriginal Autonomy: Issues and Strategies*, D. Smith (ed), Cambridge University Press, Cambridge, UK.

Coombs, H.C., H. McCann, H. Ross and N.M. Williams (eds)
   1989 *Land of Promises, Aborigines and Development in the East Kimberley*, Centre for Research into Environmental Studies, Australian National University and Aboriginal Studies Press, Canberra.

Cordell, J. and J.M. Fitzpatrick
   1987 Torres Strait: Cultural Identity and the Sea, *Cultural Survival Quarterly* 11 (2), 15–17.

1991a Negotiating Sea Rights, *Cultural Survival Quarterly* 15 (2), 5–10.

1991b *Managing Sea Country: Tenure and Sustainability of Aboriginal and Torres Strait Islander Marine Resources*, Ecologically Sustainable Development Working Group on Fisheries, Canberra, unpublished.

   1993 Indigenous Peoples' Coastal–Marine Domains: Some Matters of Cultural Documentation. In *Turning the Tide: Conference on Indigenous Peoples and Sea Rights*, Northern Territory University Faculty of Law, Darwin, 159–74.

Crough, G. and C. Christophersen
   1993 *Aboriginal People in the Economy of the Kimberley Region*, North Australia Research Unit, Casuarina, Northern Territory.

Day, R.
   1993 Sea Rights, Traditional Boundaries and Modern Fishing in Mer Island Waters. In Turning the Tide: Conference on Indigenous Peoples and Sea Rights, Northern Territory University Faculty of Law, Darwin.

Dodson, M.
   1994 Towards the Exercise of Indigenous Rights: Policy, Power and Self-Determination, *Race and Class* 35(4), 65–76.

Durkheim, E.
   1949 *The Division of Labor in Society*, trans G. Simpson, the Free Press, Glencoe, Illinois, USA (1st edn 1933).

Durkheim, E. and M. Mauss
　1903　*Primitive Classification*, trans R. Needham, Cohen and West, London (1st French edn 1903).

Eliade, M.
　1973　*Australian Religions: An Introduction*, Cornell University Press, Ithaca, New York, USA.

Epstein, R.A.
　1979　Possession as the Root of Title, *Georgia Law Review* 13, 1221–43.

Ewing, G.
　1992　The High Court's Land-Rights Judgement, *Mining Review* 16(5), November, 8–12.

Fitzpatrick, J.
　1991　Home Reef Fisheries Development: A Report from Torres Strait, *Cultural Survival Quarterly* 15(2), 18–20.

Flinders, M.
　1814　*A Voyage to Terra Australis; Undertaken . . .in the Years 1801, 1802, and 1803, in His Majesty's Ship the 'Investigator'. . .*, two volumes with atlas, G. and W. Nicol, London.

Forbes, J.R.S.
　1986　*Evidence in Queensland: The Statute Law*, Law Book Co, North Ryde, New South Wales.

　1993　Mabo and the Miners. In M.A. Stephenson and S. Ratnapala (eds), *Mabo: A Judicial Revolution*, University of Queensland Press, St Lucia, Queensland, 206–25.

Frankfort, H., H.A. Frankfort, J.A. Wilson, T. Jacobsen and W.A. Irwin
　1946　*Before Philosophy, The Intellectual Adventure of Ancient Man: An Essay on Speculative Thought in the Ancient Near East*, University of Chicago Press, Chicago, Illinois, USA.

Gaita, R.

  1993a Mabo (Part One), *Quadrant*, September, 36–39.

  1993b Mabo (Part Two), *Quadrant*, October, 44–48.

Goot, M. and T. Rowse (eds)

  1994 *Make a Better Offer: The Politics of Mabo*, Pluto Press, Leichhardt, New South Wales.

Green, L.C.

  1975 'Civilized' Law and 'Primitive' Peoples, *Osgoode Hall Law Journal* 13, 233–49.

Grotius, H.

  1972 *The Freedom of the Seas or the Right Which Belongs to the Dutch to Take Part in the East Indian Trade*, Orno Press, New York, USA (1st Latin edition 1633).

Haddon, A.C. (ed)

  1904–35 *Reports of the Cambridge Anthropological Expedition to Torres Straits*, vol VI, *Sociology, Magic and Religion of the Eastern Islanders*, 1908; vol IV, *Arts and Crafts*, 1912; vol I, *General Ethnography*, 1935; vol III, *Linguistics*, 1907, ed S. Ray; Cambridge University Press, Cambridge, UK.

Haigh, D.

  1993 Torres Strait and Customary Marine Tenure — A Legal Baseline. In *Turning the Tide: Conference on Indigenous Peoples and Sea Rights*, Northern Territory University Faculty of Law, Darwin.

Hardy, F.

  1968 *The Unlucky Australians*, Nelson, Melbourne.

Harris, S.

  1979 *'It's Coming Yet . . .'*, Aboriginal Treaty Committee, Canberra.

Henderson, J. Youngblood

  1977 Unravelling the Riddle of Aboriginal Title, *American Indian Law Review* 12, 167–94.

Hirst, J.
  1994 Five Fallacies of Aboriginal Policy, *Quadrant*, July–August, 11–16.

Hocking, B.
  1979 Does Aboriginal Law Now Run in Australia?, *Federal Law Review* 10, 162–87.

  1982 Is Might Right? An Argument for the Recognition of Traditional Aboriginal Title to Land in the Australian Courts. In E. Olbrei (ed), *Black Australians: The Prospects for Change*, Students Union, James Cook University, Townsville, Queensland.

  1988 (ed) *International Law and Aboriginal Human Rights*, Law Book Company, North Ryde, New South Wales.

  1993 Aboriginal Law Does Now Run in Australia. In *Essays on the Mabo Decision*, Law Book Company, North Ryde, New South Wales, 67–85.

Hookey, J.
  1972 The Gove Land Rights Case: A Judicial Dispensation for the Taking of Aboriginal Lands in Australia?, *Federal Law Review* 5, 85–114.

Howard, C.
  1993 The Consequences of the Mabo Case, *IPA Review* 46(1), 21–23.

Hunt, A.E.
  1899 Ethnographic Notes on the Murray Islands, Torres Strait, *Journal of the Royal Anthropological Institute*, vol XXVIII, 5–18.

Idriess, I.
  1933 *Drums of Mer*, Halstead, Sydney.

Jackson, M.
  1984 The Articulation of Native Rights in Canadian Law, *University of British Columbia Law Review* 18, 255–87.

Jackson, S. and D. Cooper
  1993 Coronation Hill Pay-Back: The Case of McArthur River, *Arena Magazine* 7, 20–22.

Jackson, S.E.
   1995 The Water Is Not Empty: Cross-Cultural Issues in Conceptualising Sea Space, *Australian Geographer* 26(1), 87–96.

Jenks, E.
   1917 An Inalienable Fee Simple?, *Law Quarterly Review*, 11–14.

Johannes, R.E. and J.W. MacFarlane
   1984 Traditional Sea Rights in the Torres Strait Islands, with Emphasis on Murray Island, *Senri Ethnological Studies* 17.

   1991 *Traditional Fishing in the Torres Strait Islands*, Commonwealth Scientific and Industrial Research Organisation, Division of Fisheries, Hobart.

Jull, P.
   1994 Indigenous Progress Abroad: Self-Determination, Sovereignty and Self-Government, *Social Alternatives* 13(1), 25–28.

Jull, P., M. Mulrennan, M. Sullivan, G. Crough and D. Lea
   1994 *Surviving Columbus: Indigenous Peoples, Political Reform and Environmental Management in Northern Australia*, North Australia Research Unit, Darwin.

Keen, I.
   1984 Aboriginal Tenure and Use of the Foreshore and Seas: An Anthropological Evaluation of the Northern Territory Legislation Providing for the Closure of the Seas Adjacent to Aboriginal Land, *Anthropological Forum* 5, 421–39.

Kehoe-Forutan, S.J.
   1988 Torres Strait Independence, a Chronicle of Events, Research Report no 1, Department of Geographical Sciences, University of Queensland, St Lucia, Queensland.

Keon-Cohen, B.A.
   1993 Some Problems of Proof: The Admissibility of Traditional Evidence. In M.A. Stephenson and S. Ratnapala (eds), *Mabo: A Judicial*

Revolution, University of Queensland Press, St Lucia, Queensland, 185–205.

Kitaoji, H.
1977 The Myth of Bomai: Its Structure and Contemporary Significance for the Murray Islanders, Torres Strait, *Min Zoku Gaka Kenkû (Japanese Journal of Ethnology)* 42, 209–12.

1980 Miriam Perceptions of Themselves and Those around Them: Cognitive Ordering after One Hundred Years of Culture Contact, paper presented to Australian Anthropological Society Conference, University of Queensland, St Lucia, Queensland.

Lawrence, D.
1994 Customary Exchange across Torres Strait, *Memoirs of the Queensland Museum* 34(2), 241–446.

Lawrence, P.
1967 *Road Belong Cargo*, Melbourne University Press, Parkville, Victoria.

Lawrie, M.
1970 *Myths and Legends of Torres Strait*, University of Queensland Press, St Lucia, Queensland.

Leach, E.
1969 *Genesis as Myth, and Other Essays*, Cape, London.

Lui, G. Jr
1994 Torres Strait: Towards 2001, *Race and Class* 35(4), 11–20.

McConnell, W.H.
1974 The Calder Case in Historical Perspective, *Saskatchewan Law Review* 38, 88–122.

McHugh, P.G.
1984 The Legal Status of Maori Fishing Rights in Tidal Waters, *Victoria University of Wellington Law Review* 14, 247–73.

McIntyre, G.
- 1987 Deeds of Grant in Trust and Freehold Title — Queensland Style, Cairns, mimeo, 3 March.

- 1988 Murray Island Traditional Land Claim. In B. Hocking (ed), *International Law and Aboriginal Human Rights*, Law Book Company, North Ryde, Sydney.

- 1993 *Mabo* and Sea Rights: Public Rights, Property Rights or Pragmatism? In *Turning the Tide: Conference on Indigenous Peoples and Sea Rights*, Northern Territory University Faculty of Law, Darwin.

McNeil, K.
- 1989 *Common Law Aboriginal Title*, Clarendon Press, Oxford, UK.

Macpherson, C.B.
- 1977 *The Political Theory of Possessive Individualism: Hobbes to Locke*, Oxford University Press, Oxford, UK.

Mabo, E.K.
- 1982 Land Rights in the Torres Strait. In E. Olbrei (ed), *Black Australians: The Prospects for Change*, Students Union, James Cook University, Townsville, Queensland.

Mansell, M.
- 1992 The Court Gives an Inch But Takes Another Mile, *Aboriginal Law Bulletin* 2(57), 4–6.

- 1993 Australians and Aborigines and the Mabo Decision: Just Who Needs Whom the Most?, *Sydney Law Review* 15(2) June, 168–77.

Middleton, H.
- 1977 *But Now We Want the Land Back*, New Age Publishers, Sydney.

Moore, D.
- 1984 *The Torres Strait Collections of A.C. Haddon: A Descriptive Catalogue*, British Museum, London.

Morgan, H.M.
    1992   Mabo Reconsidered, the Joe and Enid Lyons Memorial Lecture,
           Australian National University, 12 October, 1–8.

Mulrennan, M.E. et al
    1993   *Towards a Marine Strategy for Torres Strait*, North Australia
           Research Unit, Darwin and Torres Strait Islander Coordinating
           Council, Thursday Island, Queensland.

Mulrennan, M.E. and N. Hanssen
    1994   *Marine Strategy for Torres Strait, Policy Directions*, North Australia
           Research Unit and Torres Strait Island Coordinating Council,
           Casuarina, Northern Territory.

Native Titles Research Unit, Australian Institute of Aboriginal and Torres
           Strait Islander Studies
    1994   *Proof and Management of Native Title: Summary of Proceedings of a
           Workshop*, Canberra, 31 January to 1 February 1994, AIATSIS,
           Canberra.

Nettheim, G.
    1981   *Victims of the Law: Black Queenslanders Today*, Allen and Unwin,
           Sydney.

    1993   The Commonwealth's Native Title Bill, *Aboriginal Law Bulletin* 3
           (65), December, 4–5.

Ngantcha, F.
    1990   *The Right of Innocent Passage and the Evolution of the International
           Law of the Sea: The Current Regime of 'Free' Navigation in Coastal
           Waters of Third States*, Printer Publishers, London.

Nietschmann, B.
    1989   Traditional Sea Territories, Resources and Rights in Torres Strait. In
           J. Cordell (ed), *A Sea of Small Boats*, Cultural Survival, Cambridge,
           Massachusetts, USA, 60–93.

Olbrei, E. (ed)
  1982 *Black Australians: The Prospects for Change*, Students Union, James Cook University, Townsville, Queensland.

Pearson, N.
  1993 204 Years of Invisible Title. In M.A. Stephenson and S. Ratnapala (eds), *Mabo: A Judicial Revolution*, University of Queensland Press, St Lucia, Queensland, 75–95.

  1994a A Troubling Inheritance, *Race and Class* 35(4), 1–9.

  1994b *From Remnant Title to Social Justice*. In M. Goot and T. Rowse (eds), *Make a Better Offer: The Politics of Mabo*, Pluto Press, Leichhardt, New South Wales, 179–84.

Peterson, N.
  1986 Australian Territorial Organization: A Band Perspective (in association with J.P.M. Long), *Oceania Monograph* 30, Sydney.

Radin, P.
  1957 *Primitive Man as Philosopher*, Dover, New York, USA (1st edn 1927).

Ray, S.H. (ed)
  1907 *Reports of the Cambridge Anthropological Expedition to Torres Straits*, vol III, *Linguistics*, Cambridge University Press, Cambridge, UK.

Reynolds, H.
  1992 *The Law of the Land*, Penguin, Ringwood, Victoria.

Rivers, W.H.R.
  1908 Social Organisation. In A.C. Haddon (ed), *Reports of the Cambridge Anthropological Expedition to Torres Straits*, vol VI, Cambridge University Press, Cambridge, UK, 169–84.

Rose, D.B.
  1984 The Saga of Captain Cook: Morality in Aboriginal and European Law, *Australian Aboriginal Studies* 2, 24–39.

1987   Consciousness and Responsiblility in an Australian Aboriginal Religion. In W.H. Edwards (ed), *Traditional Aboriginal Society*, Macmillan, Melbourne.

1992   *Dingo Makes Us Human: Life and Land in an Aboriginal Australian Culture*, Cambridge University Press, Cambridge, UK.

Rowse, T.
1993a Giving Ground, *Arena Magazine* 7, 16–19.

1993b *After Mabo: Interpreting Indigenous Traditions*, Melbourne University Press, Carlton, Victoria.

Sahlins, M.
1974   *Stone-Age Economics*, Tavistock, London (1st edn 1972).

Samana, U.
1988   *Papua New Guinea: Which Way?*, Arena Publications, North Carlton, Victoria.

Sanders, W. (ed)
1994   *Mabo and Native Title: Origins and Institutional Implications*, Research Monograph 7, Centre for Aboriginal Economic Policy Research, Australian National University, Canberra, 1–82.

Sharp, N.
1980   Torres Strait Islands, The Case for Independence: The Underlying Issues, Mimeograph, Melbourne.

1984   Springs of Originality among the Torres Strait Islanders, 2 vols, PhD thesis, La Trobe University, Bundoora, Victoria (see also Book of Islanders).

1987   Faces of Power in the Torres Strait Islands: The 1980s and the 1930s, paper presented to the 57th ANZAAS Conference, Townsville, Queensland, September.

1988   A Melanesian Journey: New Ways in Co-operation, *Arena* 83, 50–80.

1990 Comparative Cultural Perspectives in the *Murray Island Land* Case, *Law in Context* 8(1), 1–31.

1991 A Landmark in Australia: The *Murray Island* Case, *Arena* 94, 78–93.

1992 Scales from the Eyes of Justice, *Arena* 99/100, 55–61.

1993a *Stars of Tagai: The Torres Strait Islanders*, Aboriginal Studies Press, Canberra.

1993b No Ordinary Case: Reflections Upon Mabo (No 2), in *Essays on the Mabo Decision*, Law Book Company, North Ryde, New South Wales, 23–38.

1993c Native Title: The Post-*Mabo* Landscape, *Arena Magazine* 8, 5–6.

1993d Customary Marine Tenure at Mer Island after *Mabo*, unpublished paper in Island Coordinating Council workshop, Towards a Marine Strategy for Torres Strait, 16–17 June 1993, in possession of author (see also Mulrennan and Hanssen 1994).

1994a A Light in the Eyes of Justice. In N. Loos and T. Osanai (eds), *Indigenous Minorities and Education*, Sanyusha Publishing Co, Tokyo.

1994b *Malo's Law in Court: The Religious Background to the Mabo Case*, Charles Strong Memorial Trust, Adelaide.

Shnukal, A.
 1983 Torres Strait Creole: The Growth of a New Torres Strait Language, *Aboriginal History* 7(2), 173–85.

 1988 *Broken: An Introduction to the Creole Language of Torres Strait*, Pacific Linguistics, Series C107, Australian National University, Canberra.

Slattery, B.
 1992 The Legal Basis of Aboriginal Title. In F. Cassidy (ed), *Aboriginal Title in British Columbia: Delgamuukw v the Queen*, Oolichan Books and Institute for Research on Public Policy, 113–132.

Smith, J.C.
- 1968 The Unique Nature of the Concepts of Western Law, *Canadian Bar Review* 46, 191–225.

- 1974 The Concept of Native Title, *University of Toronto Law Journal* 24, 1–16.

Smyth, D.
- 1993 *A Voice in All Places: Aboriginal and Torres Strait Islander Interests in Australia's Coastal Zone*, consultancy report, Resource Assessment Commission, Coastal Zone Inquiry, Canberra.

Stanner, W.E.H.
- 1969a *After the Dreaming: The 1968 Boyer Lectures*, Australian Broadcasting Commission, Sydney.

- 1969b The Yirrkala Case: Some General Principles of Aboriginal Landholding, mimeograph, 1–12, in possession of author.

- 1976 Some Aspects of Aboriginal Religion, *Colloquium* 9(1), 19–35.

- 1977 The History of Indifference thus Begins, *Aboriginal History* 1(1), 3–26.

- 1979 The Yirrkala Land Case: Dress Rehearsal. In W.E.H. Stanner, *White Man Got No Dreaming: Essays 1938–1973*, Australian National University Press, Canberra.

Stephenson, M.A. and S. Ratnapala (eds)
- 1993 *Mabo: A Judicial Revolution*, University of Queensland Press, St Lucia, Queensland.

Sutherland, J.
- 1992 Rising Sea Claims on the Queensland East Coast, *Aboriginal Law Bulletin* 2(56), 17–19.

Swain, T.
- 1993 *A Place for Strangers: Towards a History of Australian Aboriginal Being*, Cambridge University Press, Cambridge.

Thomson, D.F.
  1933 The Hero Cult, Initiation and Totemism on Cape York, *Journal of the Royal Anthropological Institute of Great Britain and Ireland LXIII*, July–December, 453–537, with plates XXVII–XXXVI.

Whimp, K.
  1994 *Mabo*: The Inside Story, *Arena Magazine* 9, 16–19.

Wilkin, A.
  1908 Property and Inheritance. In A.C. Haddon (ed), *Reports of the Cambridge Anthropological Expedition to Torres Straits*, vol VI, Cambridge University Press, Cambridge, UK, 163–68.

Williams, N.M.
  1986 *The Yolngu and Their Land: A System of Land Tenure and the Fight for Its Recognition*, Australian Institute of Aboriginal Studies, Canberra.

Williams, S.
  1993 Arafura Sea: Ownership, Management and Use Issues. In *Turning the Tide: Conference on Indigenous Peoples and Sea Rights*, Northern Territory University Faculty of Law, Darwin.

Woodward, A.E.
  1973 *Aboriginal Land Rights Commission First Report, Parliamentary Paper No 69*, Government Printer, Canberra.

Woodward, A.E.
  1974 *Aboriginal Land Rights Commission Second Report*, Australian Government Publishing Service, Canberra.

Woodward, A.E.
  c 1985 Land Rights and Land Use: A View from the Sidelines. In *Destinations in Law: Papers from the Twenty-Third Australian Legal Convention*, Law Council of Australia and Law Book Company, Melbourne, 24–33.

Wright, J.

   1973 *Alive*, Angus and Robertson, Sydney.

   1985 *We Call for a Treaty*, Collins/Fontana, Sydney.

Yu, P.

   1994 The Kimberley: From Welfare Colonialism to Self-Determination, *Race and Class* 35(4), 21–33.

GOVERNMENT PUBLICATIONS

QUEENSLAND

Proclamation notifying that 'Certain Islands in Torres Strait lying between the Continent of Australia and the Island of New Guinea' are part of the Colony of Queensland, 18 July 1879 (supplement to *Queensland Government Gazette* of 19 July 1879, XXV, 10, 21 July 1879) under provision of the Queensland Coast Islands Act of 1879.

Aboriginals Protection and Restriction of the Sale of Opium Acts 1897–1939. Aboriginals Preservation and Protection Act of 1939, 3 Geo VI no 6. Torres Strait Islanders Act 1939, 3 Geo VI no 7 (as amended). Torres Strait Islanders Act 1971–79. Community Services (Torres Strait) Act 1984, no 52. Queensland Coast Islands Declaratory Act 1985. Aborigines and Torres Strait Islanders (Land Holding) Act 1985, no 41. Torres Strait Land Act 1991, no 33.

COMMONWEALTH

Racial Discrimination Act 1975.

The Torres Strait Boundary, Report and Appendixes, Joint Committee on Foreign Affairs and Defence, Parliamentary Paper, Canberra, no 416 1976. Treaty between Australia and the Independent State of Papua New Guinea concerning Sovereignty and Maritime Boundaries, in the Area between the Two Countries Including the Area known as Torres Strait, and Related

Matters, signed at Sydney 18 December 1978, Government Printer, Canberra. Aboriginal and Torres Strait Islander Commission Act 1989. Native Title Act 1993, no 110. Land Fund and Indigenous Land Corporation (ATSIC Amendment Act) 1995, no 20 of 1995.

ARCHIVAL SOURCES

Queensland State Archives (QSA). Department of Health and Home Affairs. Correspondence 1936–37; especially O'Leary to Chief Protector, 7 September 1937, enclosed in letter 37/9577 in QSA A/3941.

COURT PROCEEDINGS AND JUDGMENTS

Milirrpum v Nabalco Pty Ltd and Commonwealth of Australia (1971) *Federal Law Reports* 17, 141–253, per Blackburn J.

Wacando, Carlemo Kelly v Commonwealth of Australia and State of Queensland (1981), writ of summons no 153 and statement of claim dated 12 December 1978 in the High Court of Australia. Transcript of proceedings, Sydney, 10 July 1979, 13 February 1980.

Calder v Attorney-General of British Columbia (1973) 8 *Dominion Law Reports* (3d) 61.

Hamlet of Baker Lake v Minister of Indian Affairs and Northern Development (1980) Canada, *Federal Court Reports* 1, Part 4, 518–82.

SERIALS AND NEWSPAPERS

Age, *Arena*, *Arena Magazine*, *Australian*, *Australian Financial Review*, *Australian Law Journal Reports*, *Brisbane Courier-Mail*, *Cairns Post*, *Canberra Times*, *Commonwealth Law Reports*, *Dominion Law Reports*, *Federal Law Reports*, *Launceston Examiner*, *Native Title Newsletter*, *Northern Territory News*, *Sydney Morning Herald*, *Torres News*, *Townsville Daily Bulletin*, *West Australian*.

INDEX

Aborigines
  Land Fund and Indigenous Land Corporation(ATSIC Amendment) Act 1995 (Cwth) 232, 257n87
Aboriginal Land Rights (Northern Territory) Act 1976 (Cwth) 179, 216, 254n28
Aboriginal marine enterprise 253n57
Aborigines and Torres Strait Islanders (Land Holding) Act 1985 (Qld) 34–35, 236n26
Aboriginal people (*see* Gurindji, Jawoyn, Wik Mungkan, Yolngu people, land, native title)
Aboriginal Treaty Committee 23, 25, 210
Adeyinka Oyekan v Musendiku Adele (1957) xxii
Administration of Papua New Guinea v Daera Guba (1973–74) 111
Advisory Opinion on Western Sahara (1975) 173
Amodu Tijani v Secretary of Southern Nigeria (1921) 110, 181, 182
Anderson, Ian 225–26
Australian identity, debt to Meriam xxi, 231

Bartlett, Richard 204, 205
Baxi, Upendra 77, 104, 194
Beckett, Jeremy
  and Eddie Mabo 67, 238n12, 246n6; as expert witness 19; on land tenure and inheritance 132–34, 136, 137; on Malo and Christianity 159; and Malo's Law 134–35, 140–42, 158; on Meriam identity 134; and Meriam sea property 197, 201; on Torres Strait Islander religion 247n26
Blackburn, Justice
  on communal native title 179; definition of property rights 185–86; and *Milirrpum* 25, 79, 93, 113, 176, 217; and *terra nullius* 25; and Yolngu law 25, 103–4, 174
Bon, Douglas 94
Bon, Lui 89
Bruce, Jack 27, 48, 200
Brennan, Frank 180, 214, 230
Brennan, Justice 5, 49–50, 171, 172, 173–75, 177–78, 179, 180–82, 209, 214
Brennan, Toohey, Gaudron, Justices (*see Mabo [No 1]*)
Brunton, Ron 220

Calder v Attorney-General of British Columbia (1973) 17, 47, 52, 58, 209
Cape York Land Council 17, 213, 223
The Case of Tanistry (1608) 180, 184
Castan, Ron 27, 29, 30, 40, 45, 47, 49–50, 52–53, 104, 108–113
Chanock, Martin 168, 169
Coombs, H.C. (Nugget) 25, 177, 229, 233n4
Court Book (*see* Murray Island Court Book)
Cowley, Dalton 96

Danayarri, Hobbles 3, 209, 210
Dawson, Justice 52–53, 56–57,
 183–85
Day, Ron 38, 189–90
Deane, Justice 34, 41, 174, 209, 210
 see also Justices Deane and
 Gaudron
Deane and Gaudron, Justices 5,
 171–72, 175–76, 176–77, 178,
 179–80, 249n24
Deed of Grant in Trust (DOGIT)
 34–35, 236–37n27
Delgamuukw v British Columbia
 (1991) 141, 154, 222, 225, 244n45
Depoma, Marwer 37, 70–71, 72–73
Dodson, Mick 3, 15, 17, 223, 230

Eva Valley meeting
 and one voice 223, 224–25; and
 self-determination 218, 221

fishing project at Murray Islands
 189, 204, 228, 231
 see also sea and foreshore

Gaita, Raimond 185, 250n39n40
Gerhardy v Brown (1985) 174
Gibbs, Chief Justice 31, 34, 35, 173,
 237n28
Guerin v The Queen (1984) 52, 179
Gurindji Aboriginal people 3, 209,
 210, 226

Haddon, AC xx, xxi, 85, 94, 135,
 153, 201
*Hamlet of Baker Lake v Ministry of
 Indian Affairs* (1978) 17
High Court of Australia
 final judgment in *Mabo* case 3–5,

248n2; and integrity of the law
174–77; order to Queensland to pay
half plaintiffs' legal costs 249n19;
recognition of native title at
Murray Islands 177–83; rejection of
doctrine of *terra nullius* xxi, 3–4, 5,
12, 172–74, 186, 207–8
see also Mabo [No 1], Mabo [No 2],
native title
Hocking, Barbara 27, 30, 236n15
Howard, Colin 15, 205

In re Southern Rhodesia (1919) 173,
 174

Jawoyn people 225, 226
Johannes, Robert 197, 198, 199, 200
Johnson v McIntosh (1823) 175

Kabere, Henry
 lands 27, 135; and Malo's Law 13,
 89, 140; oral tradition 76
Kennedy, Flo 22–23, 26, 29–30, 32,
 157–58, 164
Keon-Cohen, Bryan 27, 30, 94–95,
 125, 140–41, 242n8
Kerr, Ruth 126
Killoran, Patrick J.
 affidavit 30–31, 160; Director of
 DAIA 11, 48; evidence 128–31; as
 powerful influence 33, 37
Kimberley Land Council 17, 227
Kudub, George 204
Kudub, Mapa 125

land law
 cultural contrasts xix, 6, 105–114
 see also land, land tenure

land, Meriam
  compared with Aborigines 13–14; contrasted with European 14; as inalienable 14; leases of 233n8, 242n5n6; passed down in words 13–14, 21, 112–14, 215; rights and responsibilities to 14, 77–81, 213, 215, 228; sale of 27–28, 37, 48, 242n5
  see also land tenure, sea and foreshore
land rights movement 3, 233n1n4
  see also Gurindji, Yolngu people
Land (Titles and Traditional Usage) Act 1993 (WA) 221
land tenure, Meriam
  boundaries 7; clan territories 6, 7; comparison with Yolngu 109–10, 164; continuity 8, 120; and English law 214; Meriam and English contrasted 6, 14, 162–64, 180; nameholders 6–7, 78–79, 81; three features 215
  see also land, Meriam people, Malo's Law, sea and foreshore
Lawrie, Margaret
  debt to George Passi and Marou Mimi 90; and fish traps 197, 198; and 'Golden Rule against; trespass' 127; on Meriam concept of ownership 85; and Meriam identity 138; on Meriam pride 135–39
Loos, Noel 238n8, 245n3

McIntyre, Greg 26, 29, 30, 31, 42, 47, 78–79, 193, 201
McNeil, Kent 163, 186, 248n32
Mabo, Bonita (Neta) 4

Mabo case, *Mabo*
  beginnings 22–30, 210, 236n14; claims against Commonwealth dismissed 202, 251n32; defendants 31; High Court judgment 3; original five plaintiffs 21; plaintiffs' demurrer 35, 43, 45, 57; public v private rights 58, 108–11; as test case 21–22; as unique 175–76
  see also High Court, *Mabo [No 1]*, *Mabo [No 2]*, Meriam plaintiffs
Mabo, Eddie
  adoption, witnesses on his 245–46n4; claims contested 72, 149–50, 171, 246n3; death of 4; giving evidence 37, 41, 63–65; joining best of two cultures 232; knowledge from parents 23–24; life history 11, 65–68; as national hero at Las village 231; plaintiff 7; pride in Meriam culture 229
Mabo, Koiki (*see* Eddie Mabo)
Mabo (No 1)
  decision 5, 14; equality before the law, meanings of 53–57, 216
Mabo (No 2)
  legal and general implications of 234–35n41; the minority perspective 183–85; rejection of *terra nullius* 3–5, 12, 172–74, 186, 207–8
  see also High Court, *Mabo* case, native title
Malo-Bomai
  and Christianity 9, 10, 156–58, 159–61; compared with Hero Cult of I'wai 247n24; gods xx; and land tenure 74, 93; myth 7, 87, 93, 154–56, 247n16; priests of 66–67, 239n14; religious order 63–64, 69

Malo's Law
  and Christianity 88–89; custom of secrecy 19, 20, 21, 69; as Meriam Law xx, 7, 9, 36, 63, 156–57, 214–15; metaphor in 9, 96–97, 163, 229; as 'sayings' 73; and spoken word 13, 75–76, 105 story (*see also* Malo-Bomai) xx, 93; trespass 7, 21, 64
  see also land, land tenure, Meriam people
Malo ra Gelar (*see* Malo's Law)
Mansell, Michael 226
Marou, Gaul 94
Marou, Mimi
  and cultural revival 8–9, 157; diary 131, 240n2n5; leader of strike 51; and Malo's Law 8, 19, 87, 89, 90, 93, 98
Mason, Chief Justice 45, 55
Meriam Mir xix
Meriam people
  adoption practices 20, 239–40n30; autonomy, demand for 100; bearers of land rights 4–6; comparison with Aborigines 13; identity 6–11, 99, 144, 228, 234n24; native title 12; and oral tradition 8, 13, 14; post-*Mabo* 231–32; refusal to accept a Deed of Grant in Trust 34; rights to lands 4; and totemism 243n26, 243–44n27; viewed as exception 16; wish to give evidence 36–37; writing skills 8, 233n18
  see also land, Malo's Law, sea and foreshore
Meriam plaintiffs
  amended statement of claim 178, 180; claims to land and sea areas 149–51, 192, 202; names 7, 21, 27, 40; statement of claim 21, 246–47n10
Milirrpum v Nabalco Pty Ltd (1971) xxi, 12, 25, 39, 58, 71, 77, 79, 103, 113, 127, 162, 176, 180
Morgan, Hugh 217–18
Moynihan, Justice
  and 'club justice' 139–44; contrasting Meriam with Yolngu 153, 158, 159, 180; determination of issues of fact 11, 12, 57, 79, 149–54, 164–70; and 'good manners' 143; hearings of evidence xix, 8, 35, 36–37, 38, 40–42, 72, 115–16, 123–39; Malo and Christianity 159–60; Meriam ownership 84–85, 162; and plaintiffs' syntheses of old and new 9, 93–94, 144, 157; and rules of evidence 105–14
  see also sea and foreshore
Murray Island Court Book 27, 48–49, 53
Murray Island Native Court 27, 48, 53
Murray Islanders (*see* Meriam people)
Murray Islands xix
Murray Island Land case
  see also Mabo case xxii;

native title
  and Aboriginal people 3–5, 15; and collective rights of Meriam 12; definition 5, 179, 214; and land–sea claims 186, 250n45, 253n55; limits to 15, 234–35n41; and Meriam law

179, 249–50n24; minimised 208–9, 222–23; and moral equality 16; at Murray Islands 4, 15, 233n8; and national identity xxi, xxii, 15–18; and possessory title 182; separated from sovereignty 181, 209
  see also Mabo case, *Mabo [No 2]*
Native Title Act 1993 (Cwth) 15, 206, 213, 215, 216, 253n54
Noah, Gobedar
  and adoption custom 239–40n30; and court procedure 72; and Malo's canoe 191–92; and Malo's Law 89, 90–91; rights and responsibilities to land 78, 80–81; on sacred right to land 75, 76; and written documents 233–34n19
Noah, Kaba 99
Noah, Mary 20, 240n30

oral and written tradition 167–70
  see also Meriam people; Moynihan, Justice

Passi, Etta 75
Passi, George 27-28, 73, 90
Passi, Reverend Dave
  beginnings of *Mabo* case 22; caring for land 85; claims before High Court 171; and cultural renewal 9; and dialogue 232; evidence begun 123; lands claimed 72; Malo and Christianity 10, 91–92, 100, 156, 157–58, 230; and Malo's Law xx, 19, 24, 91, 95, 140, 142–43, 211, 214; nameholder as centre of group 79; and sacred authority 26, 142–43, 164; sea property 193, 195–96

Passi, Sam
  interpretation of Malo's Law 10–11, 97–98; Malo and Christianity 156; Malo's Law and 'real Meriam' 88, 161, 239n21; and Meriam culture 71, 99
Pearson, Noel 17, 182, 185, 213, 223
Pitt, Robert 70

Queensland Coast Islands Declaratory Act 1985 (Qld) (the 1985 Act)
  declared inconsistent with Racial Discrimination Act 5, 53; passage through parliament 32–34; plaintiffs' argument against 46–53; and plaintiffs' demurrer 35, 43, 45, 57; provisions of 45, 237n1; and related legislation 34–35

Racial Discrimination Act 1975 (Cwth)
  and equality before the law 53–57, 216; and the 1985 Act 5
  see also Mabo [No 1]
reconciliation 207–8, 232

Reynolds, Henry 38, 175, 181, 209, 210
Rice, James
  claims before High Court 171; evidence 81–84; identity, source of 39, 163; lands claimed 72, 246n9; and Malo's Law 20, 74–75, 85, 87, 140; and Meriam culture today 37, 76–77, 79; plaintiff 7; and sea property 191, 193; and test case 69
right of consent (*see* self-determination)

Rose, Deborah B 138–39
Rowse, Tim 209
rules of evidence (*see* Moynihan, Justice)

sea and foreshore, Meriam
changing custom 197–200; Commonwealth jurisdiction 190; cultural contrast 200; deferral of sea claims 202, 251n32; distant fishing grounds 199, 201, 202; findings of fact 192–96; fish traps 6, 7, 191, 198; and land 84, 186, 190, 191; and native title 186, 190, 204–6; plaintiffs' claims to 191, 193, 202; and sea Aborigines 205–6, 252n42; tenure 186, 190, 197, 205; traditional boundaries 189, 203, 204, 251–52n34
self-determination 3, 100, 217–18, 225, 227
Sheehan, Colin 126, 243n11
sovereignty 181, 209
Stanner, W.E.H. 3, 13–14, 71, 103, 160, 195, 215

Tapim, Kakim 75
terra nullius
definition 3, 172; expanded doctrine 5, 207; era of 211, 224; in *Mabo* case 33, 57; post-*Mabo* 16, 207, 220–21; relinquishment xxi, 3–4, 5, 12, 172–74, 186, 207–8
see also High Court, *Mabo [No 2]*
Toohey, Justice 4, 43, 171, 182, 215, 251n32

Torres Strait Islanders Act (Qld)
and indirect rule 50–51, 130; as 'the Act' 8, 38; and written wills 76
Torres Strait Islands
annexation of 5, 233n9; as autonomous zone 217; maritime strike in 20, 33, 51
Torres Strait Land Act 1991 (Qld)
tidal land 201
Torres Strait Treaty (1978) 204, 252n35

Wacando, Carlemo Kelly v Commonwealth of Australia and State of Queensland (1981)
challenge to annexation 233n9
Wailu, Jack 96–97, 160–61
Wik Mungkan people 212
Williams, Nancy xxi, 39, 81, 103, 162, 164, 179, 215
Wilson, Justice 56
Woodward, Edward Sir 252n42, 254n28n30, 255n43
Wootten, Hal 224–25, 226
Wright, Judith 25

Yolngu people 12, 17, 38, 39, 58, 71, 81, 93, 103, 127, 162, 164, 173, 176, 179, 211, 215, 226, 229
Yu, Peter and self-determination 17–18, 227